The Presidents' Last Years

The Presidents' Last Years

*George Washington to
Lyndon B. Johnson*

by
Homer F. Cunningham

McFarland & Company, Inc., Publishers
Jefferson, North Carolina, and London

British Library Cataloguing-in-Publication data available

Library of Congress Cataloguing-in-Publication Data

Cunningham, Homer F.
  The presidents' last years : George Washington to Lyndon B. Johnson / by
Homer F. Cunningham.
    p.   cm.
  Bibliography: p. 317.
  ISBN 0-89950-408-6 (lib. bdg. : 50# alk. paper) ⊗
  1. Presidents—United States—Biography. 2. Presidents—United
States—Retirement. 3. Presidents—United States—Death.
I. Title.
E176.1.C95   1989
973'.09'92—dc19
[B]   88-35089
                                                                  CIP

Printed in the United States of America.

McFarland & Company, Inc., Publishers
  Box 611, Jefferson, North Carolina 28640

To the women in my life:
my wife Grace and daughter Ann

Acknowledgments

I would like to thank my wife Grace for her support and encouragement, and for her editing and word processing skills. My daughter, Dr. Ann Putnam, has given invaluable stylistic suggestions. Alton Juhlin, my cousin and a university research librarian, has assisted with editing, especially in the bibliographical references. The librarians at Whitworth College have enabled me to obtain a wide variety of research materials. Barbara Ritchie and Janis Fogelson have helped with editing and proofreading. And I would like to thank the late Beverley Thompson, Jr., and the Texas Educational Association for the grant I received for the purpose of this project.

Table of Contents

Introduction

The American presidency is a unique institution. No other office in the world combines the glamour of a king, the power of a prime minister, and the authority of a field marshal. Yet the man, and someday woman, who would be president must finally answer to the humblest voting citizen in the nation. The strong tradition of the American political process has allowed both inadequate chief executives to continue in office and brilliant presidents to step down. For better or worse, the man in the White House has always captured the imagination of the American public. Hated and loved, feared and admired, the president holds the spotlight like no other American figure. Every gesture or word is noted and revered — or satirized and reviled. Ironically, most of the men who assumed the presidency, when the time came, found themselves anxious to leave it.

Perhaps it can be said that a man's character is shown more essentially in the private moments of his life than in the public ones. The stories of these men after they left the presidency is as fascinating as the narrative of their years in the White House, yet more often than not the stories are blurred by time. In American politics, the old gives way rapidly to the new.

Lost through the years is the fact that Thomas Jefferson, James Monroe and Ulysses S. Grant all died bankrupt. That Grant, by resolve of will alone, held off death by cancer until he could finish his memoirs. That John Tyler in his last days prepared to fight against the United States during the bitter division of North and South. That Lincoln's assassination could have been prevented. That Woodrow Wilson left the White House a shattered wreck of a man. That the world would discover the corruption in Warren G. Harding's administration only after his strange death. This book has been written to tell the stories rarely heard about the presidents in their last years.

How did these men who managed the country manage their lives when suddenly they were private citizens again? How did they earn a living? So many of the presidents left office to find their financial affairs in disarray, and their most urgent challenge to be that of simply making a living.

How were they able to shift from public to private life without devastating emotional consequences? Their stories, each of them, is dramatic — some quietly so, in the manner of Harry Truman, some tragically so, as with Franklin Pierce. All are poignant. The shift from the grandeur and power of the White House to the banalities of everyday existence is always tension filled, irrevocable and complete. For many, their private lives became a reflection of how they lived their lives as president; for others, their private lives became a heartbreaking contrast.

James K. Polk lived for only a few months after he left office, Herbert Hoover for almost 32 years. These men — 35 of them from George Washington to Lyndon Johnson — lived an average of almost 12 years after they left the White House. Time enough for many to begin new lives, for others to brood upon bitter memories and harbor old regrets. For those eight who died in office, the story is of their last days — or hours. The drama, the unexpected, the tragedy, the pain, and also the joy of the last years of the presidents is what this book is about.

Homer F. Cunningham
Spokane, Washington

The 1st, George Washington

The Virginia Planter, 1797–1799

George Washington (1732–1799), the father of his country, came home from the presidency to Mount Vernon in the spring of 1797. He had become one of the best known figures in the world, and the greatest man in his own country. Many Americans wanted to make him "King of the United States." How could such a man come home and be a simple farmer? Yet that is what Washington wanted. He returned to the one place in all the world he loved best, to the house he had largely designed himself, and to the longtime friends who were close by. He loved the seasons of the year, the sights, sounds, and smells of the farm, as well as the work it brought.

The affairs of state, the wrangling of political matters, and the countless tedious social occasions that his office compelled him to attend depressed him. At heart he was a shy man who much preferred his small circle of warm friends to the glittering social and political life of the presidency.

He had given most of his life to the service of his country. Before the Revolution it had taken six years to expel the French from North America, and he resigned from the army after the task was completed. He spent the next years happily at Mount Vernon in the development of his large plantation. However, tensions developed between England, the mother country, and the American colonies. In 1774 the colonies began making united protests to the British government when they met in the First Continental Congress in Philadelphia. They met again the next year, after the battles of Lexington, Concord, and Bunker Hill, and made plans for an organized resistance to the English. George Washington was chosen to lead the American army.

While he did not express a desire for the position, Washington was the only member of the Congress to wear his military uniform to its sessions. At 43 he was again in command of troops. Though often tempted to resign his commission, he led the American forces to ultimate victory and independence. When the colonies met to draw up the Constitution in 1787,

1

they chose Washington as the presiding officer of the Constitutional Convention. The nation then named him as its first chief executive and he served two four-year terms (1789–1797). He rejected a third term and became a 65-year-old private citizen. He was to have less than three years to enjoy the plantation he loved.

In 1797 relations with France had become very tense, and there seemed to be a chance of war. As a public duty Washington reluctantly agreed to accept the appointment from President John Adams to head the army if the conflict between England and France dragged the United States into war. Most felt more threatened by France than by England, for France was in the throes of her Revolution. Washington naturally wanted to appoint his own subordinates, but some feared that at his age he would not be able to command troops and would have to leave the actual military leadership in battle to others. Sharp criticisms were directed at Washington, and even James Monroe, later President Monroe, made uncomplimentary remarks about him.[1] It was a most stressful time for the aging ex-president, and he lost twenty pounds as a result.[2] Fortunately President Adams was able to prevent what might have been a war with France.

After returning to Mount Vernon and for the rest of his life Washington engaged in an extensive correspondence with such men as John Adams, Thomas Jefferson, Alexander Hamilton, John Marshall, and the Marquis de Lafayette. Washington often felt obliged to apologize for his tardiness in answering letters. His diary constantly mentions how much of his time was taken up in letter writing, though he brought an aide, Tobias Lear, from Philadelphia with him to act as his secretary. Lear was a distant relative by marriage and had served Washington most effectively in the nation's capital.

Disturbed by the condition of the buildings and much of the land he found when he returned to his plantation, Washington had the vigor to begin the repair of the old buildings, erect the needed new ones, and make the fields productive again. No detail was too small for his personal attention. It was his custom to spend three or four hours each day in the saddle giving direction for the work. His diary and correspondence are filled with references to the workaday business of managing a large plantation.

The general had many business interests — buying and selling land, investing in various enterprises, and putting up houses to rent. Most of his reading at this time, judging by the records of the books that he bought, dealt with agriculture, building, and animal husbandry, matters that the progressive planter of that day would find stimulating and profitable.

During his final years at Mount Vernon, Washington's family took much of his attention. He had a strong sense of responsibility toward all his extended family, though he had no children of his own. Martha and her first husband, Colonel Daniel Parke Custis, had four children, two of whom died in infancy. The other two, John Parke Custis (Jacky) and Martha Parke Custis (Patsy), were reared by George and Martha. Patsy, the younger of the two, lived with the Washingtons until her death at age 18. She was always in delicate health, suffering from what were called "fits" (probably epilepsy). Medical attention was of no help and she died in one of these seizures. Jacky never seemed to find himself and, always needing money, was a source of concern and embarrassment to the couple. Late in the Revolutionary War Jacky served as aide to General Washington at Yorktown, but died just before the end of the war with what was called "camp fever." Jacky left four young children, two of whom, George Washington Parke Custis and Eleanor Parke Custis (Nelly), came to reside at Mount Vernon and were adopted by the Washingtons. These two children were loved by George and Martha as if they were their own (they were Martha's grandchildren) and were close to the family in Washington's retirement years. The boy never reached the potential that the grandparents saw in him, but he proved to be a real comfort to the family.

The girl Nelly was a joy to the Washingtons. It was for her that the general bought the harpsichord which can be seen at Mount Vernon today. At best she was an indifferent performer, though as a child she was forced to spend hours practicing her music. A visitor described her as sitting at the instrument "weeping and playing."[3] Even after she married and had a child, Nelly lived at Mount Vernon as a member of the family until the general's death. Nelly married Lawrence Lewis, who was from the Washington side of the family. This once again united the Washington and the Custis families in marriage. The whole household at Mount Vernon was overjoyed when Nelly had a baby daughter, born about three weeks before the general's final illness.

The Washingtons carried on an active social life at Mount Vernon. The concept of Southern hospitality was very real to members of the planter class. Visitors of all kinds were constantly in and out of Mount Vernon. Many of them had not been specifically invited, but had come to pay their respects. On many occasions the entertaining was quite a burden to the Washingtons, and at times became a drain on them financially. Relatives regularly came for extended visits, which increased this burden considerably. Social events sometimes lasted for several days. The Washingtons would often journey to nearby Alexandria or even to Federal City, as the District of Columbia was often called, to be with friends.

Fortunately Washington had good health habits. A full day of work and a good night's sleep were rules of his life. He loved the out-of-doors and spent much of his time in physical activity in the open air, often on horseback. The diet of the Washington household was simple and wholesome, with many vegetables, grains, and fruits. No doubt his outlook on life was conducive to good health. He was not given to extremes of emotion, for Washington's disciplined life and sense of duty reflected his own moral code as well as that of his planter class.

Yet during his life he had many physical difficulties, some of them rather serious in nature. His medical history reveals a number of persistent and dangerous health problems. One of the more annoying was the condition of his teeth. Like most of the people of his time, he was constantly troubled with decaying teeth. At that time no adequate dental care was available. True, he did acquire a set of false teeth, but though he attempted to wear them, they were never satisfactory. The teeth were difficult to keep in his mouth while talking, and of constant trouble in eating.

Washington had the usual maladies that most children and young people of his day suffered. When he was 20 he contracted smallpox while he was in the Barbados. The illness was not life-threatening, but his was regarded as a strong case and left him somewhat pockmarked. However, between a third and a fourth of the total population had the same pockmarks, so the condition was not especially conspicuous.

While he was in the West Indies he contracted malaria. At various periods during the remainder of his life he suffered the chills and fever that malaria brings. When these attacks came he regularly took "the bark," a form of quinine that usually proved helpful, but many times he was uncomfortable and incapacitated.

In 1755, while serving with General Braddock in the French and Indian War, he was struck with what was called the "bloody flux." There is no modern-day medical consensus as to what the bloody flux was, but it was very debilitating to the patient. Just two years later he was stricken with a form of dysentery that continued for months. In 1758 he suffered from a lung disorder. From the symptoms described it might well have been a kind of pleurisy. During the latter part of his life he had various discomforts that were put down as "rheumatic pains." In June of 1789 he had a large carbuncle (a deep abscess) on his thigh, which required surgical intervention. The infection was so severe that the doctors thought him critically ill. He was bedfast for several weeks and recovery was slow. In May of 1790 Washington was so ill with pneumonia that his very life was threatened. Some of the doctors did not expect him to recover. In 1791 he developed another carbuncle that confined him to bed, but it was not as severe as the earlier one.

During the late 18th century such a medical history was not particularly unusual. Life expectancy was only about 35 years, depending upon how the figures are interpreted and which authority is believed. If one reached anything like "three score and ten," one probably would have had to overcome a variety of physical problems unthought-of today. Medical treatment then was not very effective; illnesses were largely overcome by the patient's own physical strength and vitality.

The last weeks of Washington's life had gone very well for him. The general's health had been the best in some time. Nelly had delivered a fine baby daughter and was herself in excellent health. A number of especially close friends had visited Mount Vernon.

The Washingtons invited their neighbors, the Fairfaxes, to dine with them at Mount Vernon on December 2, 1788. On Saturday the 7th, the Washingtons returned the visit and dined at Mount Eagle with Lord Fairfax and his family, true to the traditions of hospitality in colonial Virginia among people of means.

The last few days of the general's life were not different from those he habitually spent at Mount Vernon. As befitted the approach of winter, there were fewer guests than usual to be entertained, for the weather was getting disagreeable, making travel more difficult.

On Monday, December 9, Washington had stood on the steps near the driveway of Mount Vernon to bid goodbye to Lawrence Lewis, Nelly's husband, and Washington Custis, a grandson, as they set off for New Kent. He also said his goodbyes to the Howell Lewises and to Lawrence's brother and his wife, who had been visiting at Mount Vernon for the last ten days. The brothers had remarked that Washington had taken his usual ride, "...and the clear healthy flush on his cheeks and his sprightly manner brought the remark for both of us that we had never seen the general look so well ... [or] so handsome."[4]

The next day the general found himself too busy to attend the meeting of the Potomac Company in Alexandria, so he sent James Keith with his proxy to vote and act for him. On Wednesday, December 11, the Fairfaxes, Mrs. Warner Washington, her son Thomas, and John Herbert came to dine at Mount Vernon. They dined in the afternoon as was the custom of the time. No one imagined that it would be the last social occasion of which the general would ever be a part. Sometime after nightfall Washington went outside and noticed that there was a large circle around the moon, usually an indication of approaching inclement weather.

Also on that day, Washington had put the final touches on his plans for cropping and managing the farms on his estate for the coming year. On the following day he would begin taking these plans to the managers of the various farms of his plantation.

Thursday dawned cold, with threatening clouds and some wind. The general began the day at his desk writing a long letter to Alexander Hamilton, who was trying to promote a national military academy and desired to obtain the support of Washington in the project. By now the general was trying to involve himself in as few causes as possible, so his letter to Hamilton, while one of friendship and interest, was reserved. Washington favored the creation of a national military academy, but he declined to get personally involved.

By ten o'clock he was in the saddle inspecting his lands. He took the plans for the new year's cropping with him. A copy would be delivered to overseer Dowal at the River Farm. Washington also wanted to inspect the cow pens which he had heard were not in proper condition. The weather had turned cold. First it had snowed, then hailed, and then came a steady, cold rain. He had been out for five hours when he returned home. Lear, his secretary, noted there was snow on his hair and that his neck appeared wet. The family had kept dinner warm and were waiting for his return. He insisted that his greatcoat had kept him dry, so he did not bother to change clothes before eating. To the family he appeared to be well.

The next day, Friday, December 13, brought snow and cold weather. The general had a slight sore throat and decided not to ride. He wrote a note to his overseer about the cow pens, and stayed inside, spending most of the time with his papers. As the day wore on, he developed hoarseness. By four o'clock in the afternoon the weather had cleared, so Washington went out briefly and marked several trees between the house and the river for removal to improve the view.

After the evening meal, the general, his wife, and Lear retired to the sitting room. A packet of newspapers had come, so he and Lear busied themselves reading. After a little while Martha excused herself to go be with Nelly, who was still fatigued after the birth of her baby. Later the general asked Lear to read aloud the account of the debates in the Virginia General Assembly. When Washington said goodnight to his secretary, Lear suggested that he take something for his cold. Washington replied, "Let it go as it came."[5]

The entry in the general's diary for the 13th was, "Morning snowing and about three inches deep. Wind at northeast, and mercury at 30. Continuing snowing till one o'clock, and about four it became perfectly clear. Wind in the same place but not hard. Mercury 28 at night."[6] It was the last thing the general would ever write.

When the general retired that Friday night in late 1799, there was no thought of approaching death or even of illness. He had a slight cold and some hoarseness, that was all. But sometime between two and three o'clock in the morning, Washington awakened Martha and told her that he was ill. He was having chills and fever. Martha wanted to call the servants and get a fire built, or build it herself, but he refused to let her do that, knowing how susceptible she was to colds herself. So they waited until the servants, in the normal routine of the day, came and started a fire in the master bedroom. By then the general was experiencing some difficulty in breathing.

Martha summoned Tobias Lear, and he was soon by the general's bedside. Lear called for a Mr. Rawlins, one of the plantation's overseers, who understood the art of bleeding. Lear also sent a rider on the fastest available horse to notify Dr. James Craik, the general's personal physician, and Dr. Gustavus Brown in nearby Port Tobacco.

Rawlins was soon at the general's side, ready with his lance, but seemed a bit nervous and his hand shook. Washington, sensing the overseer's apprehension, said, "Don't be afraid." As the blood began to run, Martha, fearing they were taking too much, begged them to stop, but the patient cried, "More, more." Rawlins had drawn a pint.[7]

Around eight in the morning, the patient wanted to sit up. His body servant dressed him and he sat by the fire. Some home remedies were applied as they waited for the doctor. A flannel dipped in sal volatile was put around his neck, and his feet were placed in hot water. He was unable to swallow the mixture of molasses, vinegar, and butter that they offered him.

Dr. Craik arrived about nine o'clock, but the remedies administered were not effective. A "blister" was raised on the general's throat; he inhaled the steam from hot water, vinegar, and sage tea; he was bled again. At about ten o'clock the patient was put to bed. Dr. Craik thought the general was suffering from inflammatory quinsy. An hour later Craik sent for another physician, Dr. Elisha Dick of Alexandria, a younger man who had excellent medical training. The patient was bled again. But Craik recognized that Washington was gravely ill. Sometime between three and four o'clock in the afternoon, both Dr. Brown and Dr. Dick arrived. The patient was bled a fourth time.

The general felt from the beginning that his death was imminent. He said to Lear, "I find I am going, my breath cannot continue long."[8] When Dr. Craik was ministering to him, the patient said, "Doctor, I die hard, but I am not afraid to go."[9] In the late afternoon he asked for Martha and directed that she go to his desk and bring the two wills he had prepared. When she brought them to him, he examined them briefly. Then he instructed her to burn the one and keep the other. She burned the first will in the fireplace in their bedroom where the general could see it and took the other one to her closet.

In the early evening the patient was helped from his bed to sit in his chair in front of the fireplace. Half an hour later he was put to bed for the last time. Blisters were raised on his legs and feet, and a soft poultice placed around his neck. His breathing became a little easier. There seemed to be some disagreement among the doctors as to what measures would be taken in a final effort to save him.

Drs. Craik and Brown diagnosed the illness as a form of quinsy. Dr. Dick felt that it was a "violent inflammation of the membranes of the throat" and that if the condition were not immediately helped it would result in the death of the patient.[10] Dr. Dick urged an operation that would open the trachea below the infection so that the patient could breathe.[11]

The other two doctors disagreed, feeling it was too late to try this relatively new procedure.

At least Dr. Dick persuaded the other attending physicians not to resort to another bleeding. He felt that bleeding was at times beneficial, but that it should be used sparingly on elderly patients, especially those in a weakened condition. The writer has discussed "the Washington case" with a number of qualified physicians. They tended to feel that the general was bled too much, but on little else was there agreement. The whole question of the doctors' responsibility for the immediate death of Washington is still being debated. The prevailing opinion seems to be that the medicine of that day had small chance of saving the patient's life.

The dying man wanted Lear to "arrange and record all my late military letters and papers . . . arrange my accounts and settle my books . . . and let Mr. Rawlins finish recording my other letters which he has begun."[12]

Washington motioned for Lear, who came to the bedside. It took a few minutes, but the general was finally able to speak. "I am just going. Have me decently buried, and do not let my body be put into the vault in less than two days after I am dead."[13] Lear was too overcome to immediately answer, so he just nodded his head. The general then said, "Do you understand me?" Lear answered, "Yes, sir." Washington replied, "'Tis well." The patient felt of his own pulse. Gradually the hand fell from his wrist and his last breath was taken. There was no struggle nor any sound. Martha asked, "Is he gone?" Lear nodded, and Martha replied, "'Tis well," echoing her husband.[14]

There were those who wanted to have the general buried in Alexandria or in the Capitol which soon was to be completed in the District of Columbia, but Dr. Craik ordered that the body be buried near Mount Vernon because of his fear that the infection which had killed Washington might spread.[15]

Lord Fairfax led the small funeral procession down the little hill to the vault which recently had been enlarged and repaired. The general's riderless horse followed the black casket as it was carried from the house. Dr. Davis, rector of Christ's Church in Alexandria where Washington was a vestryman, led the short Episcopal burial service, concluding with the oft-used phrase, "Dust to dust, and ashes to ashes," as the casket was placed in the simple vault.

To a hushed Congress, meeting in Philadelphia, Henry ("Light-Horse Harry") Lee[15] made the famous statement, "First in war, first in peace, first in the hearts of his countrymen."[17]

The 2nd, John Adams

Days of Disappointment, 1801–1826

The result of the election of 1800 was a bitter disappointment to John Adams (1735–1826). He had served only one term as president (1797–1801), and felt that he deserved another. An able chief executive and an honest man, Adams was an aristocratic conservative who belonged to the Federalist party. The opposition party, the Republicans (the party known in modern times as the Democrats), was led by Thomas Jefferson, the master political organizer of his day, and the leading exponent of democracy of his time. When the votes were counted, Jefferson had clearly defeated Adams.

Not only had Adams faced the Republicans, but there was a sharp division in his own Federalist party. One faction was led by Adams, the other by Alexander Hamilton. Though he became secretary of the treasury, Hamilton was not eligible to become president since he was not born in this country. But he wanted to control the party and select its presidential candidate. Real antagonism arose between Adams and Hamilton. It is said that Adams had referred to Hamilton as the "bastard brat of a Scotch peddler."[1] (Hamilton's parents were never married.) In turn, Hamilton's faction had publicly made fun of Adams' portly figure by suggesting that he should be referred to as "His Rotundity." Hamilton had attempted an underhanded political maneuver that very nearly cost Adams the presidency in 1796 when Adams was clearly the choice of the voters. Adams never forgave Hamilton or his followers for the deception. This bitterness colored the 25 years of Adams' retirement.

The split factions of the Federalists were no match for Jefferson's new democracy in the 1800 election, so Adams was turned out of office. Since he did not trust Jefferson's political philosophy, fearing mob rule would result, Adams did not even wait to greet the new president when he came to occupy the "Executive Mansion," as the White House was called then.

After leaving the White House in March of 1801, Adams returned to Quincy, Massachusetts, where he lived until he died on July 4, 1826. The

9

man who had helped to prepare the Declaration of Independence, and who was one of the original signers, died fifty years to the day after the Declaration was announced to the world.

Though his loss of the presidency to Thomas Jefferson had been a bitter disappointment to Adams, his life at Quincy was enhanced by the fact that he was well liked and respected by his own community, and by the presence of his wife of 37 years, Abigail Adams. She was intelligent and capable, outgoing and sympathetic, and personally charming. Her direction of the large household at the Mansion, as their home in Quincy was called, made the declining years of the former president much more pleasant. There is little doubt that Adams was the head of the house, but Abigail, who had always been his confidante, was the one around whom the household revolved.

The Mansion always seemed to be full. The Adamses had five children, four of whom reached maturity and had large families of their own. There were times when five of the grandchildren lived at the Mansion for long periods and were under Abigail's supervision and care. At times there were as many as 13 grandchildren living there at once. In their letters, both John and Abigail often mentioned their large family with delight. So welcome were family and friends that several who were terminally ill came to the Adams' home to spend their last days under Abigail's capable and loving care.

Adams' life at Quincy took on something of a pattern. He was an active farmer with several estates to manage. Early in the day he was likely to be found on horseback looking over his fields and directing the work of several hired men. If the work was near home, he would walk to the fields being cultivated. Many days he would walk more than five or six miles. If the farm work did not require his personal attention, he would walk five miles or more along the country roads for exercise. While he was not a man of wealth, he had considerable land holdings and needed the income from his land to sustain the life of his large family.

Although the fields occupied his attention in the mornings, whenever possible he spent the afternoons in his study either reading or writing. He was a prodigious letter writer—to family and friends as well as to newspapers. What happened in his study shows the mind and heart of the man. His reading was cosmopolitan and omnivorous, extending from the Greek and Roman classics to the most recent authors. His special interests seemed to lie in the classics, history, and philosophy. As he read he would often make notes in the margins of the books. These comments ranged from acceptance to utter ridicule. However, the disagreements are much more numerous than the approbations.

"I understand nothing of this gallimauphry," he wrote. Or "a barbarous theory" or "I am very weary of these deep, profound, studious, elaborate vagaries." Or, "...D'Argens, Voltaire, Johnson, ye are all models of ardent, restless, discontented minds! unsubdued by philosophy or religion."[2] Adams rejected the Puritan belief in predestination, and accepted the concept of freedom of the will. Yet he could never embrace the ideas of the Enlightenment, of the perfectability of man, or that progress was inevitable,[3] issues which were often discussed with Jefferson in their correspondence.

Adams' religious beliefs seemingly came more from his philosophy and reason than from Scripture. As a result, he rejected the concept of the Trinity, yet he felt that the Bible gave all the instructions a man would ever need in order to lead a moral life. While he "was a church-going animal, Adams had very early liberated himself from all the dogmas and teachings of revealed religion."[4] However, "the mystery of life and death had always exerted on him an irresistible fascination."[5] While Adams seldom discussed religion in social conversation, he endeavored, without much success, to get Jefferson into an exchange of letters on the subject of religious beliefs. Yet it is interesting to note that Jefferson gave Adams a copy of his Bible which he accepted very gladly. (Jefferson's Bible was a loose-leaf notebook of clippings from the Scriptures that he particularly liked.) Adams had a profound belief in and respect for God, and never questioned the concept of a future life.

Adams wrote to a large number of friends on a regular basis. Dr. Benjamin Rush, the famed Philadelphia physician, was an intimate friend and fellow signer of the Declaration of Independence, with whom Adams shared his innermost thoughts and feelings. Except to his own family, Adams probably never shared his personal life and thoughts quite as intimately as with Rush. It was Rush who finally got Adams and Jefferson to end their political feud and become personal friends again. Rush had gotten word that Adams' hurt feelings had softened, so he wrote obliquely to both Adams and Jefferson hinting that a reconciliation was in order. The two statesmen then renewed their long correspondence. The resulting exchange of letters is one of the most interesting in American history. Unfortunately, the two elder statesmen never saw each other in person again.

In the early days of the Revolution, Adams and Jefferson worked closely together and were warm personal friends. By action of the Continental Congress, the two were selected along with Benjamin Franklin to frame the Declaration of Independence. When the committee met, Adams insisted that Jefferson do the actual writing of the Declaration itself.[6] Later, both Adams and Jefferson became a part of George Washington's administration. However, widely divergent political views brought a separation between these old friends, and in the partisan politics of the day they became political enemies. When Adams ran for reelection and was defeated by Jefferson, Adams felt that Jefferson had insulted him. Several other matters caused distrust and antagonism between them, although much of this feeling was due to misunderstanding rather than overt, unfriendly acts. When friends of Jefferson visited Adams in Quincy in 1811, they heard Adams' side of the misunderstandings. These visitors tried to explain how Jefferson felt, and Adams was considerably mollified.[7] Adams went so far as to say that he had "always loved Jefferson and still loved him."[8]

It is to Adams' credit that he made the first move toward the renewal of their friendship. Adams sent Jefferson two pieces of homespun cloth with a friendly note. Jefferson responded with warmth saying, "A letter from you calls up recollections very dear to my mind. It carries me back to the times when, beset with difficulties and dangers, we were fellow laborers in the same cause, struggling for what is the most valuable to man, his right of self-government."[9] Adams responded with a long, friendly letter bragging about his grandchildren and affirming their friendship saying, "I cordially reciprocate your Professions of Esteem and Respect. Madam joins and sends her kind Regards to your Daughter and your Grand Children as well as to yourself."[10] After the deaths of Adams' beloved daughter Abigail, known as "Nabby," and Abigail, his wife of some 54 years, he was most anxious that Jefferson be informed. Jefferson responded quickly with genuine grief and understanding.

As time passed, Adams wanted to discuss religion and life after death, but Jefferson was reluctant to debate these topics. However, he agreed with Adams on the probability of a future life, but never would engage in any lengthy discussion on purely theological issues. As they looked at life, Jefferson felt he would like to live it over. Adams, on the other hand, felt that once was enough, that he would rather go on to the future life.[11] Reading their letters is like looking into the very souls of these two extraordinary men, whose lives became the richer for the renewal of their broken friendship.

A considerable amount of Adams' correspondence with others was devoted to a defense of his past political positions. Often when he was criticized or questioned, he would answer the criticism by sending long, involved letters to the newspapers. Some of the exchanges were rather protracted and bitter in nature. One of these was the response of Adams to a book published by Mercy Otis Warren in 1805 entitled *History of the American Revolution,* in which Adams' administration was criticized.[12] He virtually exploded in letters to the press, associates, and of course to Mrs. Warren herself. (Most writers feel that Adams did not deserve such an attack.) Adams seldom came out second best in these exchanges. His sarcasm was biting and aimed at the most sensitive areas of his antagonist. Later the dispute ended in a reconciliation.

For a while Adams considered writing his autobiography. He attempted to get his papers together and began the task, but he was too busy with his farms, his reading and correspondence, to devote the needed time to the lengthy preparation an autobiography required. His son, John Quincy Adams, had intended to arrange and publish his father's papers, but he returned to Washington as a congressman from Massachusetts after he was defeated in his attempt at reelection to the presidency, and became so absorbed in the slave issue that he did little with his father's papers. However, John Quincy's son, Charles Francis Adams, grandson of John Adams, did a creditable job of collecting, organizing and publishing his grandfather's papers.

John Adams never became a recluse on his Quincy farm after he left the city of Washington. He liked conversation and fellowship too well for that. Good food and a few glasses of wine always appealed to him and he frequently dined with friends and neighbors. His own home was always a favorite place for guests, and it can be said that no one was ever turned away who wanted to meet Mr. Adams. Likewise, Adams remained involved in public affairs, serving as president of the American Academy of Arts and Sciences, as president of the Massachusetts Society for Promoting Agriculture, as a member of the Board of Visitors for the professorship of natural sciences at Harvard, and as an elected member of the 1820 Massachusetts Constitutional Convention.

Amidst all the activity about the Mansion, there was also sickness and death. John and Abigail's daughter Nabby had developed breast cancer. On the advice of Dr. Rush, she had submitted to radical surgery, without anesthetic, to remove the breast. The operation seemed to be successful and probably lengthened her life for more than a year. However, the cancer spread and she became ill again. She traveled from upstate New York to Quincy by horse-drawn vehicles to be cared for by Abigail, who made her last days as comfortable as possible. Nabby had an unusually attractive personality, and the Adamses were devastated by her death. At the same time, the widow of their son Charles, who had died several years before, lay in the next room terminally ill with consumption (tuberculosis) and was cared for by Abigail and the others of the household. Abigail's sister, Mary Cranch, and her husband Richard came to the Mansion to be cared for in their final illnesses.

In 1815, Abigail's other sister Elizabeth, also died. The three Smith sisters, Abigail, Mary, and Elizabeth, were very close, and the loss of her two sisters hurt Abigail deeply. She also nursed her servant Phoebe in her last illness. Phoebe was a black woman who had made her home with the Adamses almost all of her life. It is not surprising that Abigail sent John Quincy's three boys to relatives in New Hampshire for several months so she could regain her strength.

Abigail did recover her vigor and enjoyed excellent health again, and was surrounded by grandchildren and great-grandchildren the last several years of her life. Their son, John Quincy, was named secretary of state by President James Monroe, and returned from England, where he had been United States minister, to take up his new position in Monroe's cabinet. However, he did go to the Mansion for a long visit with his parents before going on to Washington. For a while it looked as though his arduous duties in Washington in 1818 would prevent him from taking his usual summer vacation in Quincy. But at the last moment he was able to travel to his home for a month-long visit. This vacation would be the last time he would see his mother.

Scarcely a month had gone by before Abigail was taken ill with typhoid fever. She was apparently recovering when she suffered a massive stroke. For days she lingered, unable to speak or move. Everything that could be done in that day was tried, but she died on October 28, 1818.

In a letter to Jefferson, on the day of her death, Adams wrote, "The dear Partner of my Life for fifty-four years as a Wife and for many years more as a Lover, now lyes in extremis, forbidden to speak or be spoken to."[13] Adams then went on to express his belief in immortality, and said he would wait for "the instructions of the Great Teacher."[14] Jefferson quickly replied, "I know well, and feel what you have lost, what you have suffered, are suffering, and have yet to endure . . . I will not therefore, by useless condolences, open afresh the sluices of your grief nor, altho' mingling sincerely my tears with yours, will I say a word more. . ." He goes on to affirm his belief in another world and to "an ecstatic meeting with friends we have loved, lost, and whom we shall still love and never lose again."[15]

The lonely Adams kept himself occupied by supervising farm work, writing letters, reading, taking long walks, looking after the grandchildren, but life for him and the folk in the Mansion would never be the same. John and Abigail had lived together in harmony for more than fifty years. In many ways their marriage was unusual. They were on equal terms intellectually, and Abigail was not overpowered by his dominating personality. Her understanding of events and people was perhaps greater than that of her husband.

But soon the large house was full again. Louise Smith, a niece who had been in the home for many years, was of great help, along with the cook, two maids, and three children of John Quincy. Adams' son, Thomas Boylston Adams, with his wife and six children moved in from New York. Also, Susanne Boylston Adams, a granddaughter who had had an unfortunate marriage, moved to the Mansion with her infant child. Apparently the large household got along well, for Adams would not tolerate any bickering or show of temper.

At about this time, Adams saw John Trumbull's famous painting of the signing of the Declaration of Independence for the first time. In this picture, the three most famous signers, Adams, Jefferson, and Franklin, were the major figures. The picture was displayed in several cities before it was permanently hung in the nation's Capitol. When it was displayed in Boston, all of Boston celebrated Adams' visit to see the painting.

As always, Adams followed national affairs with interest. The passage of the Missouri Compromise in 1820 was a source of real concern. He recognized the national tension over the institution of slavery and intuitively felt that it would soon threaten the very survival of the Union. John and Abigail had always been foes of slavery, though he could see no way for the survival of the Union unless the South could keep its slaves. However, his confidence in the integrity and devotion of the next generation to carry on was immense.

After staying quietly in Quincy for two years following the death of Abigail, John Adams went to Boston to visit with David Hyslop. It was a gala event. He began to leave the Mansion to visit friends in other places after that. He made his last public address in 1821 when some West Point cadets visited him and he made a short speech of welcome to them at Quincy. The cadets were warm and outgoing and the elder statesman responded in kind. In 1824 General Lafayette of France visited the United States. He naturally wished to see Adams—he had already visited with Jefferson. It is interesting to note that both were somewhat disappointed at the meeting. Adams remarked that this was not the Lafayette he knew, while Lafayette said that this was not the Adams he knew.[16] The next year the famous American painter Gilbert Stuart came to Quincy to paint Adams' last portrait. It was a good picture and caught the vivacious, indomitable spirit that still lived in the aging man.

The most joyful event in all Adams' last years was the election of his son, John Quincy Adams, to the presidency in 1824. However, during the campaign, the opposition party—Jacksonian Democrats—tried to discredit John Quincy by harking back to some of the things they disapproved of in his father's administration. These tactics probably did not hurt John Quincy's support, but they did anger and upset his father who was now 89. The outright lies told about John Quincy during the campaign were outrageous. But John Adams felt that the election of his son exonerated him and his own administration.

Adams was feeling his advancing years in many ways. He could no longer write easily and had to depend on others to record his messages. At times he had trouble reading, and others took turns reading to him. He could not mount his favorite horse to supervise the work of the hired hands, and the long walks in the country had to be abandoned. Only occasionally did he attend church or community affairs. There were times when he had difficulty getting around the house. As he neared his ninety-first birthday he spent most of his time in bed or in the easy chair in his study. However, his appetite was good and his mind was still clear and functioning well.

As the Fourth of July of 1826 approached, the city of Boston was planning a major celebration of the fiftieth anniversary of the signing of the Declaration of Independence. They wanted John Adams, the oldest living signer, to take part in the celebration and he was urged to attend. With sadness Adams had to send his regrets. He was not well enough to journey to Boston or indeed to sit through such an occasion. Josiah Quincy, Sr., gave the principal address and paid special attention to the contribution of John Adams, "that patriarch of American independence."[17]

But Adams would never know the extent of the honor his fellow New Englanders were bestowing upon him, for he lapsed into a coma during the morning of July the fourth. About noon he awoke briefly and with considerable effort said, "Thomas Jefferson survives,"[18] and fell back into unconsciousness. His grandson, George Adams, who had attended the celebration in Boston, entered the bedroom and spoke to the dying second president, who tried to respond but could make no sound. At six o'clock that evening he died. Strangely enough, Thomas Jefferson, the third president, had preceded his friend from Quincy in death by a few hours. The last two statesmen who had helped frame the Declaration of Independence had both died fifty years to the day after the event. President John Quincy Adams in Washington heard of the passing of Thomas Jefferson in nearby Monticello, but it was not until the 6th of July that the president learned that his father was gravely ill and not expected to live. He started for home immediately. As the carriage neared Baltimore the president learned of his father's death, and the party proceeded to Quincy with all speed. John Adams was buried by the side of Abigail in the churchyard of the Unitarian Church in Quincy, Massachusetts, before his son could reach the Mansion.

The 3rd, Thomas Jefferson

Sage of Monticello,* 1809–1826

Thomas Jefferson (1743–1826), who served as president from 1801 to 1809, was committed more passionately than any other individual of his time to the principles of American democracy. He loved and trusted the people, and felt akin to the small farmer, the one-family shop owner, and the day-worker. In them, he believed, lay the true spirit of America, and it was upon these assumptions that he built his political philosophy. The major blind spot in his thinking was the uneasy truce he made with the institution of slavery and with his own slaves in particular. In retirement he lived in a multifaceted world — the world of the intellectual surrounded by his books, the world of the cultured Southerner, the world of the leader of the democratic forces of the nation, and the economically fragile world of the planter desperately trying to support his lifestyle.

Yet of all the early presidents, Thomas Jefferson was the most urbane and sophisticated. He liked the charm of the good life — elaborate table service, polished floors, good wine, classical music, and proper etiquette. His inquiring mind knew no bounds, for he possessed one of the finest intellects in early America — unmatched by any except Jonathan Edwards and Benjamin Franklin. Perhaps he was most content when he was in his study surrounded by his books and drawing boards. No wonder he wrote a friend shortly after returning to his home, "I am retired to Monticello, where in the bosom of my family and surrounded by my books, I enjoy a repose to which I have long been a stranger."[1]

Jefferson was also the most versatile of all American chief executives. He was a philosopher, an architect and builder, an inventor, an author and collector of books, a scientist and expert mechanic, a biologist and agricultural experimenter, a geographer, an educator (he wrote an essay on Anglo-Saxon grammar that was used by students at the University of Virginia), a diplomat, as well as a statesman and political scientist. His

*From the title of the 1981 book on Jefferson by Dumas Malone.

large plantation gave him the opportunity to experiment in the breeding of animals and developing new types of plants, as well as to plan and erect all the buildings at Monticello, including his famous home. Jefferson took great pleasure in designing the attractive winding walks and the gardens of his estate. His well-equipped workshops on the plantation enabled him to construct a variety of machines and produce a number of inventions.

From 1809, when he rode out of Washington, D.C., never to return, to the day he died (July 4, 1826, the fiftieth anniversary of the signing of the Declaration of Independence), this extraordinary yet enigmatic man attempted to lead the quiet life of a plantation owner.

The former president reached Monticello on March 17. The fact that he was succeeded as chief executive by his political disciple and good friend James Madison made it much easier to leave the capital and feel the government was in good hands. It did not take him long to settle into something of a routine that combined his intellectual, cultural, and social interests with the managing of his plantation. His days of retirement were full and productive. He had 17 years yet to live and work on the estate he so dearly loved. Only failing health caused any lessening of his creative activity.

In some ways Jefferson's daily routine was like that of George Washington, as well as many of the planters of his day. He arose as soon as he could see the hands of the clock. As meteorology was one of his scientific interests, he regularly checked and recorded the weather conditions such as temperature, wind velocity and direction, the clouds, and the precipitation. Until breakfast was served at about nine o'clock, he worked on his correspondence, which was worldwide and often dealt with scientific and philosophical issues. At one time he served as president of the American Philosophical Society.

If the weather was not inclement he would ride over his estate on horseback, usually covering from seven to fourteen miles, noting carefully the condition of the fields and crops, the animals, fences, and drainage. When not out in the fields he would spend the time in his study until dinner, which was served at four in the afternoon. After dinner he usually returned to his study until six o'clock, when he would come back to the drawing room where coffee, wine, and desserts were served. It was his habit to remain in the drawing room with friends and family conversing or playing games until he retired for the night.

In his later years the very large debt that he owed plagued Jefferson. By the time of his death there was a real danger that he would actually lose Monticello. As it was, a few years after his death the family did lose their lands and home. Jefferson's daughter Martha, who took care of him during his last few years and was dependent upon her father, was forced to move from the beloved family home.

It may logically be asked how Jefferson's personal finances came to be in such a sorry state. Before he left Washington he had to borrow $8,000 to pay outstanding debts. While he was president he of necessity had to rely upon hired managers and overseers for his estate. However, no hired personnel could possibly give the attention so large a plantation demanded. Jefferson, like Washington before him, returned home from the presidency to find much of the plantation in a state of neglect and disrepair.

The severe depression of 1819 caught much of Virginia in its grasp, Jefferson along with many others. Land went down to less than a third of its former value. Debtors had to pay back dollars that were worth more than those they had borrowed, for the whole Southern economy was very depressed. The large Northern banks of New York and Philadelphia did not find it advantageous to lend money to a region so dependent upon a slow, agricultural economy.

Part of Jefferson's financial difficulty was the result of trying to help a friend. Thomas Jefferson Randolph, Jefferson's favorite grandson, had married the daughter of Wilson Cary Nicholas, governor of Virginia. At Nicholas' request, Jefferson cosigned a loan the governor had made at the bank for $20,000. It was a cavalier endorsement, such as one Virginian would make for a friend among the planter class. But Nicholas defaulted on the loan and died soon thereafter, leaving Jefferson with this additional debt.

Jefferson tried a number of ancillary projects to make his plantation more profitable. He built a grist mill and constructed a large earth dam to provide water for the mill, but a flood destroyed the dam and ruined the project. It is estimated that he lost nearly $20,000 in that effort. He also built a small nail factory at Monticello, but it did not prosper, and again he lost money. He always expected that the next crop would be the one which would bring good prices and solve his financial problems, but it never came.

Jefferson also spent a considerable sum of money on his family. Thomas Mann Randolph, husband of his daughter Martha, became a constant drain on Jefferson's resources. At one time there were 12 children in the Randolph family, and for long periods they all lived at Monticello, completely dependent upon Jefferson. In all probability the son-in-law was at times psychotic, for he could not care for his family or manage his own affairs. Several nephews also were dependent upon the master of Monticello for their keep and education.

The large number of guests, sometimes as many as fifty at one time who came and stayed for extended periods, were a great expense and occupied much of Jefferson's time. On occasion it took 37 house servants to care for these guests. "In Mr. Jefferson's circumstances . . . the immense influx of visitors could not fail to be attended with much inconvenience."[2] It seems that many Americans felt it their right to visit the former president.

A grandson said, "I have known a New England judge to bring a letter of introduction and stay three weeks."[3] Southern hospitality demanded that these casual guests be shown every consideration. In an effort to escape the many visitors who were constantly at Monticello, Jefferson built Poplar Forest, a small retreat house on his Bedford County farm, where he could find some peace and quiet. He constructed it in an octagon shape, unusual in American architecture at that time. It had a portico, a large hallway, and three bedrooms. He usually took a grandchild or two with him when he went to Poplar Forest.

Shortly before his death, Jefferson had to sell his large library to the Congress of the United States in order to keep his estate. These books became the nucleus of the Library of Congress. Jefferson received $23,950 for this library for which he himself had paid more than $50,000.

Just months before he died, the author of the Declaration of Independence devised a plan to sell most of his land through a lottery. Jefferson was embarrassed to be forced to attempt such a measure, but had it gone well, he could have saved his home and the land adjoining Monticello. The state of Virginia granted his request for permission to stage a lottery. Jefferson was confident that the scheme would work, and he died with the feeling that he had saved the home for his family. Unfortunately the lottery did not go well and the family eventually lost not only the estate, but the famous house as well.

When the nation realized what desperate financial straits Jefferson and his family were in, money began to come in from a variety of places. New York City raised and sent $8,500, Philadelphia $5,000, and Baltimore $3,000. Jefferson was most gratified for this help, but it was too little too late to save him financially. There is little doubt that Jefferson spent the latter part of his life in an agonizing search for ways to rescue himself from financial ruin.

When Jefferson retired to Monticello in 1809, one of his slaves was Sally Hemings. Considerable controversy has arisen concerning Sally's relationship with Thomas Jefferson. (Sally was a half-sister of his late wife, Martha, who died in 1782. When Martha's mother died, her father, John Wayles, took as his concubine one of his slave women, Betty Hemings, whose parents were Captain Hemings, a sea captain, and a slave woman in Virginia. When Wayles died, his daughter, Martha Jefferson, received the young girl as part of her inheritance, and Sally Hemings came to Monticello as a slave.)

Two years after his wife's death, Jefferson went to Paris as America's minister to France. He remained there for five years. He took his daughter Martha with him, as well as a few personal and household servants to help create a sense of home. His younger daughter Mary was left with her aunt, but as time went by Jefferson sent for Mary to be with him in Paris. In 1787, when Abigail Adams, the wife of John Adams, who was American minister to England, met Mary's ship in London and sent her on to Paris, she was more than surprised to find Mary had been accompanied, not by a mature woman for a traveling companion, but by ". . . an adolescent girl of considerable beauty."[4] It was alleged that this beautiful slave girl, sometime within the next eighteen months, became Jefferson's concubine and subsequently bore him several children during their life together. It is also alleged that the two maintained this relationship until the time of his death.

In 1802, James Callender, a Virginia newspaper editor, angry with President Jefferson, printed a story charging that Jefferson had maintained a relationship with his slave girl, Sally. In all probability Callender tried to get an appointment as a postmaster out of his allegations. Jefferson stood aloof from the accusations, refusing to comment upon them. Most biographers of Jefferson did not accept the story as true, feeling that it was on a par with charges Callender had made against Washington, Adams, and Hamilton. Since the story was retold by Federalists, Jefferson's political opponents, it was regarded as a political attack. The major biographers of Jefferson—Dumas Malone, Merrill Peterson, Henry S. Randall, Julian Boyd, James Truslow Adams, and Thomas Fleming—give little or no credence to the charge.

But when Fawn M. Brodie published her book, *Thomas Jefferson: An Intimate History,* in 1974, historians began to take another look at the allegations made concerning Jefferson and the slave girl. The book is well written and intriguing, but historians have been far from unanimous in accepting her theory. Brodie, a professor at the University of California–Los Angeles, is not a specialist in the Jefferson era, and her other writings have little relation to Jefferson. However, a reputable historian like Page Smith, in his work *Jefferson: A Revealing Biography* published in 1976, accepted Brodie's conclusions. Smith describes Sally as "full of spirit and fire, undoubtedly ardent—a rewarding companion in bed."[6] How does he know that? Very little record of Sally can be found, and Smith gives no documentation. Smith does accurately note that Brodie disproves a number of the theories advanced by those who say that Jefferson could not have had such a relationship with Sally.[6] It is also possible that John Adams believed the Sally Hemings story.[7]

Brodie as well as Smith rely considerably on an account written in 1873 by Sally's son, Madison Hemings, when he was an old man. The account was published in the *Pike County (Ohio) Republican.*[8] Several comments about this account should be noted. Madison Hemings was scarcely able to read or write, yet the account is written in excellent English. Hemings also says that Jefferson was little interested in agriculture, and that until "three weeks of his death he was hale and hearty."[9] Those who have studied Jefferson know that neither of these statements is true. Jefferson's own records showed how much attention he gave his crops, constantly trying to improve them. The records of Jefferson's personal physicians show how ill he was the last several years of his life. Despite these and other errors, Madison Hemings' account seems to reflect a knowledgeable person with whom there was no doubt that Thomas Jefferson was his father.

Virginius Dabney of Virginia, who received a Pulitzer Prize in journalism, became interested in the allegations against Jefferson and, after considerable research as an investigative reporter, published *The Jefferson Scandals: A Rebuttal* in 1981. He concludes that the story of the slave girl who became the concubine of Jefferson is not substantiated and is full of errors of fact as well as in methods of research. Dabney's conclusion is that "the charge is unproved and unprovable."[10]

There are a few hard facts that can be noted. No mention of Sally is made in any of Jefferson's letters or records, except in the *Farm Book,* which lists all of the plantation slaves. This record lists Sally along with the other slaves, with no particular attention given to her. Those who visited Jefferson in retirement, some for months at a time, do not mention Sally. None of those who saw Jefferson in his final illness noted her presence.

Many slave owners and male members of their families did use slave women for their pleasure, and this could have been true of Jefferson, though no proof has ever been documented. In his book *The Jefferson Image,* Merrill Peterson says of Sally, "While there is not much evidence tending to prove the legend, neither was there positive disproof."[11] Jefferson's relationship with Sally Hemings probably will never be known.

However, the question still remains: how could Thomas Jefferson reconcile his ideological antithesis toward the institution of slavery and the fact that he owned many slaves? At the end of his life it was only an academic question, for his slaves were so heavily mortgaged that he could not have freed them had he tried. In principle Jefferson nearly always opposed slavery. In the first draft of the Declaration of Independence Jefferson wrote a strong antislavery section. However, Benjamin Franklin, a fellow committee member, struck that section from the Declaration. Although he opposed slavery, Franklin realized that the South would never agree to a document that denounced slavery, and that the united effort of the colonies for independence would be lost if such a statement were included.

Jefferson led the effort in Virginia to stop the importation of slaves into his state, feeling it would "in some measure stop the increase of this great political and moral evil."[12] He feared violent confrontations between whites and blacks if the issue was not settled by emancipation,[13] commenting that the "master was almost as much a victim as the slave."[14] While the abolition movement was not very strong during his years of retirement, Jefferson did lend his name and support to the concept of colonization (moving blacks to some other country where they would be freed).

Jefferson also put himself in an incongruous position when he defended two of his deepest beliefs — democracy and states rights. If he spoke as a democrat, believing in natural rights, he would have to eliminate slavery. If, on the other hand, he defended states rights, he would of necessity hold that the states themselves were the only authority that could bring emancipation. Never did he reconcile these points of view or feel comfortable in owning his own slaves. He seemed virtually powerless to take substantive steps to solve this ambiguity or yet see the absurdity of his position.

He had been out of office little more than three years when the War of 1812 began. Many blamed the war upon Jefferson's policies toward England and France. Madison, Jefferson's successor, certainly did not know how to avoid the conflict. Jefferson was in frequent contact with President Madison as the war approached, and also during the actual fighting. The sage of Monticello gave his unqualified and unreserved support to the war effort. His son-in-law, grandson, and grandson-in-law all entered the military service. So many of the men were gone to war that Jefferson noted that only the "silver-grays" were left.[15] The British burned Washington, and many feared that Richmond would be the next British target. Had Richmond been captured, Monticello would have been in real peril. When the Americans defeated the British at Ft. McHenry near Baltimore, Monticello was saved.

Jefferson's great compelling interest during the last few years of his life was the University of Virginia. The closer the time came for the opening of the university, the more absorbed he became in the project. In the minds of many, Jefferson had the clearest idea of democracy of all the founding fathers, and saw that without an educated electorate, the republic could not long endure. He believed that every citizen in the nation must understand the issues in order to be able to vote, and was one of the first of the nation's leaders to see that education for the upper class alone would not satisfy the needs of the country. Thus by 1820 he openly championed the cause of free public schools at the base of a triangle, and the state university at the apex.

In the spring of 1818, Jefferson was appointed to the commission charged with choosing the site and developing the plans for a state university. Although some wished to locate it at Williamsburg, the site of William and Mary College for well over one hundred years, Jefferson was among those who wished to build the university at Charlottesville near the center of the state, and close to his home. Jefferson prevailed, and the university was chartered in 1819. Along with James Madison, Jefferson was elected to the board of visitors, the controlling body of the university, and made its rector.

Jefferson's unorthodox religious views began to attract attention when he was selecting the faculty of the university. Though some charged Jefferson with being an infidel, this certainly was not true. He, along with most of the Deists, believed God to be the first cause, that creation spoke of a Creator. However, Jefferson had some difficulty in accepting Christ as divine. The Presbyterian church in Virginia attacked Jefferson directly over this point of doctrine, not wanting him to select faculty members who shared his views. Further dissention arose when Jefferson sought to make the school completely free from sectarian religious issues. He did not criticize private religious practices and worship, but maintained that issues of church and state should be clearly separated.

He was so involved with the progress of the university that he placed his large telescope in such a position on the mountain of his plantation that he could watch the construction of the buildings on the campus. The University of Virginia was Jefferson's personal creation as much as were the Declaration of Independence, the philosophy of the Republican (what is now called the Democratic) party, and his magnificent home at Monticello.

At times Jefferson felt that the legislature of the state of Virginia was the chief obstacle to establishing an outstanding university, for at first it voted only $50,000 for books and equipment, a sum Jefferson justly felt as much too small. Perhaps the legislature would have been more ready to appropriate the necessary funds had the people of the state shown a more vital interest in the proposed university. Many did not understand what a university was or what it did. Jefferson wrote innumerable letters and used every device he knew to promote his cause, but found it a difficult undertaking.

One of the most challenging as well as interesting efforts connected with the university was finding the right faculty. Jefferson knew most of the outstanding intellects of the Western world, and it was his idea to draw the best minds to staff the school. He had some anxious moments when three faculty members from England were several weeks late in arriving. Naturally he feared that they might have been lost at sea. But his fears were unfounded, as they landed safely in February 1825, just weeks before the scheduled opening of school.

The school opened two months late in April of 1825 to about fifty young men who Jefferson feared were inadequately prepared for university scholarship. The school year was only weeks old when there was a student uprising. Some of the students disliked a number of the faculty, felt that the rules were too strict, and the food unsavory. Jefferson, at 82 years of age, rode on horseback from Monticello to Charlottesville to settle the unrest. He had felt that the example set by the older students would be enough to keep the student body in line. He discovered that good example alone would not provide an acceptable atmosphere, but that firm leadership at the university was required.

Nonetheless, Jefferson saw his dream of a secular university in Virginia established in his lifetime. "The little of the powers of life which remain to me I consecrate to our University,"[16] Jefferson wrote less than a year before his death. He expressed the wish to have his tombstone engraved with the statement that he was the father of the University of Virginia.

Until his illness in 1816, Jefferson enjoyed remarkably good health. But in that year he had a rather prolonged illness, a lung condition the most obvious difficulty, and though he recovered, he was never quite as well. Jefferson had a rugged body of considerable strength and looked younger than his years. He was deliberately temperate in his habits, eating and drinking moderately. His diet consisted mainly of vegetables, cereals, fruits, and meats in small amounts. Jefferson was active physically, riding almost daily until the last few weeks of his life. In fact, he took his final ride on his favorite horse, Old Eagle, just three weeks before his death. Even when he could not mount his horse by himself, he insisted on taking his rides alone, once almost losing his life when the horse was frightened by a deer and threw its famous rider.

The former president had several accidents that were a source of discomfort. In a fall he broke his left arm, which was never quite normal again. Then in another fall he broke his right wrist, which was not set properly. Ever afterward it was very difficult for him to write. He also suffered from rheumatism the last few years of his life.

In his last years an artist persuaded Jefferson and his family to let him make a cast of Jefferson's head. In his desire to get a good cast, the artist let the plaster harden too much. Too weak to get the cast off himself, Jefferson almost smothered before they could chip the mask away. "I nearly suffocated," Jefferson said.[17]

One of the poignant events in Jefferson's late years was his meeting with the Marquis de Lafayette, who had so vitally aided the cause of the American Revolution, and was given citizenship in the United States. His admiration for the Marquis became even stronger during the years he was the United States' minister to France. In 1824, the Congress had invited the famous Frenchman to visit the United States. Though once a member of a very wealthy family, by 1824 the Marquis was in rather poor circumstances as a result of the French Revolution. It was Jefferson who reminded President Monroe of Lafayette's financial problems and suggested that the government aid him financially in addition to inviting him to be a guest of the nation. This the Congress did by voting him a gift of $200,000 and a township of public land in Louisiana territory.

Lafayette landed in New York on August 15, 1824, and remained in the United States for more than a year. His tour became more like a triumphant procession than a visit, for everywhere he went honors were bestowed upon him. However, it was Jefferson that the Marquis most wanted to visit.

Jefferson was 82 and quite feeble when on November 4, 1824, Lafayette arrived at Monticello. He was accompanied by a long procession which included seven carriages, forty or fifty men on horseback, and a group of cavalrymen. As the procession neared Monticello, Jefferson hobbled toward the driveway. Lafayette left his carriage and both men stopped to look at each other. Lafayette had gained so much weight that Jefferson would not have recognized him, and Lafayette found Jefferson "much aged."[18] Then, as they embraced, tears streaming down their faces, a hush settled over the crowd.

Lafayette attended the banquet prepared in his honor at the unfinished rotunda of the new University of Virginia. Two former presidents, Jefferson and Madison, as well as President Monroe, were among the guests as well as nearly 400 others. The banquet began at 3 p.m. and lasted almost three hours, at the conclusion of which Lafayette went on a conducted tour of the university with Jefferson. It was well after nightfall when they reached Monticello, where Lafayette stayed with Jefferson for ten days before resuming his tour of the country.

As the year 1826 approached, Jefferson began to feel the effects of a variety of physical problems. He had suffered intestinal difficulties for many months for which no cure could be found. A chronic and serious urinary infection also came to plague him. By February of 1826, it was evident to Jefferson that he had little time left to live, and in March his grandson was surprised when something Jefferson said indicated that he did not expect to live beyond the summer. In his own hand he drew up his will, leaving almost all of his assets to the family. The will also directed that certain slaves were to be freed. It is interesting that Sally Hemings was not among these. His daughter Martha later did give Sally her freedom, and she went to live with one of her sons. Many of Jefferson's close friends received remembrances such as a walking stick or a picture.

A large celebration was planned in Washington, D.C., for July 4, 1826, the fiftieth anniversary of the signing of the Declaration of Independence. Both Jefferson and John Adams were invited as special guests of the occasion. Adams, who was well past 90, could not travel from New England, but it was hoped that Jefferson, living so near to Washington, could attend. He declined the invitation, however, in one of the last letters he ever wrote.

Dr. Roblen Dunglison, a faculty member at the University of Virginia, was Jefferson's close friend and personal physician. Early in June the doctor journeyed to Monticello to treat the former president. The patient improved slightly, but on June 24 Jefferson sent a note asking Dunglison to come to see him. Sensing that Jefferson had become seriously ill, the doctor immediately went to Monticello and remained there until Jefferson's death.[19] Everyone sensed that death was imminent. Even so, Jefferson expressed concern for the welfare of the university. He worried that his daughter was not getting enough rest, and insisted that she not care for him at night, for his personal servant Burwell was able to do most of the night care. His grandson spent many nights by his dying grandfather. He compared Jefferson's condition to that of "an old watch, with a pinion worn out here, and a wheel there, until it can go on no longer."[20] Jefferson himself told his physician, "A few more hours, Doctor, and it will be all over."[21]

On July 2, Jefferson lapsed into unconsciousness. There were lucid moments still, but in the main he was sinking into a coma. On the third of July he slept until evening, but wanted to know if it was the fourth of July yet. He and John Adams had made a resolution between them that they would live to see the fiftieth anniversary of the signing of the Declaration of Independence. The patient was roused at nine that night for his medication, but he refused it. The family anxiously watched the clock hoping that he would live until the fourth. One of the family members told the patient that it was the fourth before the new day had actually arrived.

On Independence Day at four o'clock in the morning, Jefferson roused briefly and spoke a few words, then drifted back into sleep. At ten o'clock he awoke again and looked at his grandson as if he wanted to speak, but he could not. Burwell seemed to know what Jefferson wanted and adjusted his pillow. The patient became unconscious again. In an hour or so he roused and wanted a wet sponge placed to his lips. A few minutes before eleven o'clock, his breathing stopped. "I closed his eyes with my own hands,"[22] his grandson recalled, noting the great serenity and calmness of spirit with which the dying man awaited the end.

Did the pact that Thomas Jefferson and John Adams made to live until the fiftieth anniversary of the signing of the Declaration of Independence cause the spark of life to linger a few days longer? Or was it, as Page Smith suggests, ". . . an act of that God about whom they had expressed varying degrees of skepticism?"[23] John Adams' grandson caught the emotion of the time when he wrote in his diary, "There is nothing more to be said: with all the volumes of Eulogies that have been published on these men, and the remarks that have been studied upon this coincidence, nothing more has been produced so eloquent as the simple fact."[24] Now the only living signer of the Declaration of Independence was the little known Charles Carroll.

Jefferson had directed that his burial should be private, without a formal procession. In order to comply with his wishes, the time of the burial was kept a secret to all but the family. Yet many neighbors and friends gathered in the rain and waited by the family burial plot for the body which was borne to its final rest by Jefferson's family and servants.

The three statements which Jefferson had requested were written on his tombstone: "Father of the University of Virginia," "Author of the Declaration of Independence, and of the Statute of Virginia for Religious Freedom."

Strangely, his request included no mention of the time he spent as president of the country he loved and nurtured. Did he consider those eight years merely an interlude in a long and productive life?

The 4th, James Madison

Montpelier's Elder Statesman, 1817–1836

A number of presidents have had eminent careers before reaching the White House only to have less than outstanding terms as chief executive. Such a man was James Madison (1751–1836), often called the "Father of the Constitution" for his brilliant role in the Constitutional Convention. He was also the most influential member of the first several Congresses, and had been Jefferson's chief cabinet officer — secretary of state — before his own election as president. But his administration (1809–1817) was beset with serious problems — the War of 1812 the most distressing.

Madison was just 12 days less than 66 years of age when he retired from the presidency. It was a festive time in the capital. Jefferson's Republicans were firmly in control of the government, times were good, the trouble with England was largely settled, and there was new life and vitality in the young republic. James and Dolley Madison were in the full swing of social life in the capital, and remained in Washington for several weeks to attend farewell parties.

James Madison was a small man physically (the smallest president) and quite shy around women. His good friend Thomas Jefferson actually found a wife for him. Madison, at the time of his wedding, was 43 and his wife, the vivacious, charming young widow, Dolley Todd, was 26. Married in 1794, Dolley seemed to be just the wife Madison needed. He was somewhat withdrawn, not given to much socializing. Dolley was attractive and witty, the perfect hostess or guest. There were occasions during a White House party when the president, weary of small talk and pointless conversation, would quietly slip upstairs to bed leaving Dolley the center of the gaiety downstairs. Few seemed to miss "Little Jamie," as he was sometimes called, for "Queen Dolley" was in charge.

On March 4, 1817, shortly after welcoming his friend James Monroe to the White House, the Madisons' possessions were packed, placed on wagons, and sent in a long procession to Orange, Virginia. The trip took several weeks, partly by river steamer, as the roads were so poor. Two

29

weeks later the Madisons left Washington for Montpelier, their plantation home.

The Madisons had made their home in Washington ever since it had become the nation's capital. Now, in 1817, he was leaving the city for the last time, for Madison never returned to Washington during the more than 19 years that remained to him. But when he died, Dolley returned to Washington and once again became one of the prominent socialites of the capital where she was still "Queen Dolley." She remained there until her death on July 12, 1849, when she was 81.

In his retirement, Madison was very careful not to interfere with the new administration. As might be expected, friends, acquaintances, and former officials tried to get the ex-president to influence policies of the new administration, or help them or their relatives to secure jobs in government. If he were asked in person for such a favor, the response was a polite but firm "no." If the same favor were sought by letter, Madison would send the petitioner a printed form letter stating that he would not attempt to influence the president or endorse any office-seekers. He also resisted strong efforts to make him a presidential elector. Never again was he involved in partisan politics, but his vibrant interest in national issues continued.

Before and after his political career, Madison was a Southern planter with all that meant in the early nineteenth century. His ancestral home was Montpelier, in Orange County, Virginia. Like Washington and Jefferson before him, Madison maintained a beautiful home—a four-columned spacious Southern mansion. Remodeled in 1800 and again in 1809, one-story wings were added to each side, giving the home a total of 22 rooms. A vestibule which had a semicircular window of 13 panels, one for each of the original 13 states, opened from the portico. Adjacent to the vestibule was the large drawing room which contained a number of paintings, several by Gilbert Stuart, busts of Washington, Franklin, John Adams, Jefferson, Lafayette, and a mantel of French marble, a gift from Thomas Jefferson.

To the left of the formal drawing room was a large family parlor with a fireplace, and French windows looking toward the Blue Ridge mountains. The furniture was less formal than that found in the drawing room. Here was where the family and guests gathered for informal times together. When Madison became too feeble to make the trip up the stairs to his own bedroom, the family parlor became his room. Just back of the parlor was the dining room which held portraits of Napoleon, Louis XIV, and Confucius. A wide oak stairway led to the second floor which contained the bedrooms, Madison's library of over 4,000 volumes, and store rooms. The long halls were highly polished.

To the right of the drawing room, Madison's aged mother (who died in 1829 at 98) maintained her own separate quarters. She had her own staff of servants as well as her own kitchen and dining room. She and her son were on good terms, but understandably she wanted a life of her own.

The grounds were in keeping with the elegance of the home. Boxwood, cedar and oak trees lined the gravel road that ran from the gate to the front portico; a smaller portico at the back of the house overlooked the gardens. There were formal gardens with beautiful flower beds as well as the usual kitchen garden to supply fresh vegetables for the table in season. Nearby was the columned ice-house where ice cut from the pond in winter could be stored for summer use. Like most Virginians, Madison was fond of good horses. He kept the long wooden fences in excellent repair, and maintained the pastures for both horses and cattle within easy sight of the house.

A plantation the size of Madison's needed many workers. There were nearly a hundred slaves at Montpelier, a situation which placed Madison in a severe dilemma. He was convinced of the immorality of slavery, that it was inconsistent with the founding principles of the nation, yet he felt that the whole Southern way of life would collapse if slavery were suddenly abandoned. Madison worked hard for the idea of compensated emancipation, and for resettlement of the freed slaves in either the Western lands in the United States or in the Western area of Africa. But he was not willing to free his own slaves without compensation, for that would mean his financial ruin. The ex-president lived with this gnawing dilemma the whole of his adult life. "His failure in the seventeen-eighties to free himself from dependence on slave labor, and to secure a law for gradual abolition in Virginia doomed him, it seemed, to live within a system he abhorred."[1] The older he became, the greater this problem bore down on him. He never resolved it in his own mind any more than did the nation as a whole.

Madison hoped that the national Western lands could be sold to American settlers for $600 million, and the money used to pay the owners for their slaves and resettle the freed slaves elsewhere. He saw that with the coming of the cotton gin, slavery was gaining such a hold on the South, that if something were not done quickly the problem could never be peacefully settled. To his dying day he was a part of the American Colonization Society in its effort to free the slaves and resettle them. Ironically, in his last days he was forced to sell 16 of his own slaves to avoid financial catastrophe.

Madison was a good planter, a progressive farmer. He accepted and followed new methods of agriculture, but only in retirement did he find time to try innovations. He turned to the production of wheat before most of Virginia saw the advantages of growing grains. The dangers of over-cultivation were obvious to him, and he began to rebuild the soil in various ways including the use of chemical fertilizer. He practiced contour plowing as well as irrigation and he was far ahead of his time in his efforts at reforestation.

In the depression that followed the War of 1812, Madison, along with the other planters, had a difficult time remaining financially solvent. But he refused to traffic in slaves as a cash crop, and was one of the first to see that slavery was immoral as well as economically unfeasible and would eventually prove too costly to continue. Yet even in hard times Madison was innovative. He began successfully to breed horses as well as mules. From the Merino sheep he obtained good wool which he wove into cloth. Among the other goods he produced for sale were pork, beef, and hides, but tobacco remained his chief cash crop.

As time went by, Madison was forced to sell some of his land. At first he owned 5,000 acres around his Montpelier estate, 10,000 in Kentucky, property in Washington, and some securities. Also, Madison lost a large sum of money when a brother-in-law, Richard Cutts, unwisely handled a real estate deal for the ex-president.[2] Added to all these problems were the large amounts that Dolley's son, Payne Todd, lost in his compulsive gambling escapades. Many times the Madisons paid to keep him out of prison because of his gambling debts.

The details of the trouble Payne Todd was to Madison is a long and sordid story. Payne was a small child when Dolley married Madison, and Madison tried to be a good father to him. But the boy developed a penchant for gambling that he never overcame. Excessive drinking as well as the gaming tables became a way of life for him. No one knows how often his parents saved him from utter ruin, but it has been conservatively estimated that Madison paid at least $40,000 of Payne's gambling debts,[3] for that day an enormous sum, certainly enough to have made Madison's last years free of financial worry.

After Madison's death, Payne took hundreds of his step-father's letters and sold them to pay gambling debts. Fortunately, most of these letters found their way into the hands of scholars. Dolley's last years were saved from poverty by an act of Congress which enabled the government to purchase Madison's papers for $25,000. She also received a substantial settlement from publishers who marketed Madison's own writings. Through these papers and writings historians have learned more about the Constitutional Convention than from any other source.

The constant stream of visitors to Montpelier was a drain on the energy and financial reserves of the Madisons. Custom demanded that even casual visitors, many of whom were not known by the family, must be graciously entertained. With the 22 rooms in the house there was plenty of space, but the Madisons' hospitality became an enormous liability. Relatives, family and friends came often and stayed long.

Yet even in the midst of his financial problems, Madison found time and energy to turn his attention to Virginia, his native state, and to the nation. Shortly after he left the White House, Thomas Jefferson involved

Madison in the founding of the University of Virginia at Charlottesville. On February 16, 1819, the board of visitors (trustees) — of which both Jefferson and Madison were members — converted the yet unopened Central College into the University of Virginia. Jefferson was elected rector (president). Madison's primary area of concern was in the selection of faculty.

When Jefferson died in 1826, Madison was elected rector of the university, a position he held for eight years. He lavished love and attention on the school. When Madison retired as rector, the school had 218 students, four times the original number. In his will he gave his own large library to the university, but unfortunately it was lost in the fire of 1895 at the university.[4]

Madison also served his native state as a delegate to the Virginia Constitutional Convention of 1829–1830, but declined the chairmanship because of his age. Instead, he placed James Monroe, the ex-president, in nomination and he was elected. Madison's major effort in the convention was to work out a compromise between the eastern and western parts of the state on the issue of representation, but the sort of compromise that might have brought lasting harmony was not achieved. Madison was not happy with the way the Virginia constitution was ultimately written, but he had done his best. Certainly the state as a whole appreciated his labor and the convention honored him at its conclusion. Dolley, who accompanied her husband to the convention, participated actively in the social life of Richmond while she was there. This was the first time in 12 years that the Madisons had left their home community.

Perhaps Madison's contribution in the framing of the United States Constitution was his greatest effort, but his defense of the fundamental document was almost its equal. It was in the attacks of the state of South Carolina against the tariff (1828–1833) and her assertion of a state's right to nullify an act of Congress that Madison's response showed him to be an extraordinary statesman. The nullifiers tried to tie both Jefferson and Madison to their cause. But Madison could not tolerate this and answered the nullifiers in a series of brilliant letters that were given wide distribution by the press. The "Father of the Constitution" became its most eloquent defender.

In the famous 1830 Webster-Hayne debates before the Senate on nullification, both Senator Daniel Webster and Senator Robert Hayne claimed the support of Madison. He had to make his position known and he spoke with clarity and brilliance. He wrote, "Nullification has the effect of putting powder under the Constitution and Union and a match in the hand of every party to blow them [up] at pleasure. . . ."[5] His effort helped keep Virginia from joining South Carolina in her attempt at nullification. If Virginia had followed South Carolina in this matter, other Southern states might well have taken the same position, and the Civil War could have started years earlier, a time when the nation might have been even less prepared to preserve the Union than it was in 1860.

In examining the literature regarding the lives of the presidents, it is interesting to note that often one of the last issues discussed, if it is discussed at all, is the subject of religion. Is it that religion is thought to be of particular interest only at the time when death is obviously near? One wonders. Madison was a religious person all his life. However, he seldom engaged in purely theoretical talk about religion, and he was rather private as to his own beliefs. He believed in a "God all Powerful wise and good."[6] This belief, plus a concept of an orderly universe, were perhaps the basis of all his other religious views. He was inclined to go from nature to nature's God in his thought process. While he accepted Scripture, he was likely to arrive at his own concepts philosophically rather than by Biblical authority. Perhaps it should be pointed out that Madison felt both time and space were infinite, a fascinating point of view in light of present-day speculation. Finally, Madison had no fear of death or of the hereafter, a belief in line with his acceptance of the theology of his own Episcopal denomination.

Madison left the White House at age 66 and died at 85. The first ten years of his retirement found him in reasonably good health. The last nine years often witnessed a struggle with various ailments. When he returned to his plantation in 1817 he was vigorous and active. Although he had competent overseers, most days found him in the saddle going from field to field, supervising the activities of the workers.

During the summer of 1827 he began to experience health problems, and in the late fall of that year he had a bout with influenza. It took him many weeks to recover, and seemed to be something of a turning point in his life. Never again would he be the vigorous man he had been before. During the next summer he suffered from what was called "bilious indisposition." The writer is at a loss to translate that ailment into today's language, but probably it was some sort of gastric disturbance that persisted over a period of time. At one time the illness was so severe that he could not attend the meeting of the board of visitors at the university, the first he had ever missed.

In 1830 he was somewhat improved, so he journeyed to Richmond for three months to participate in the Virginia Constitutional Convention. But the next year witnessed the onset of painful rheumatism in his hands (probably some form of arthritis). By the following year the disease was so advanced that he could write but little and what he did attempt was almost illegible. By the midsummer of 1831 the stiffness had become quite general. During this time there were periods when his wife Dolley scarcely left him. He described his own condition by saying, "My malady, my debility, and my age [are] in triple alliance against me."[7] In the summer of 1832 both

Andrew Jackson and Henry Clay visited him as a part of their campaigns for the presidency. Madison took no stand, feeling he should not engage in partisan politics. Even his diary gives no hint of his preference.

For the next three years he was a semi-invalid, staying close to Montpelier. A few times there were brief remissions in his condition, and on one occasion he was able to ride for three or four miles at a time, but these remissions were few and brief. However, when he could he still visited nearby friends, sometimes traveling thirty miles to a dinner party. Occasionally he gave his failing strength to the task of sorting and arranging his papers. The scholarly community is still indebted to him for this effort.

In 1834, illness forced him to resign his position as rector of the University of Virginia, something he did very reluctantly. In April of 1835 he drew up his will. He remembered a number of charitable institutions, a few nieces and nephews, but most of the estate went to his wife Dolley. From mid-1835 to June of 1836 he spent almost all of his time either in bed or his chair. As a rule, each day by nine in the morning he was helped out of bed to his chair, was shaved and dressed in a robe, wool gloves, and a wool cap. At ten in the evening he was put to bed for the night. At times he could barely talk, but his mind and memory remained clear.

On June 27 he dictated some commentary about a book he had read. He then signed it in an illegible signature, the last time he would put a pen on paper. On the morning of June 28, Jennings, his devoted valet, got him up, dressed and shaved him as usual. Another servant, Sukey, who had been with him seventy years, brought him breakfast. His niece Nelly Willis chatted with him and urged him to eat. She noticed that he was having difficulty swallowing and asked what was the matter. He responded a bit facetiously, "Nothing but a change of mind, my dear."[8] She turned away for only a moment, and when she turned back, he had died.

One of the country's most respected statesmen, the "Father of the Constitution," was gone. The next day neighbors carried the casket to the family cemetery plot at Montpelier where a simple stone marks the site.

James Madison was the last member of that little group of brilliant and dedicated statesmen who gave birth to the nation. His contribution was unique and invaluable. Had he lived another year, he would have died in the fiftieth year after the framing of the Constitution.

The 5th, James Monroe

A Retiring President Faces Bankruptcy, 1825–1831

When James Monroe (1758–1831) left the highest office of the land on March 4, 1825, after eight years of service, he was faced with the specter of bankruptcy. He had been so busy serving the government in diplomatic posts, as senator, as secretary of state and president, that he had not had an opportunity to establish a profitable plantation of his own. Though he owned considerable property, huge debts were charged against him. He was "beset with financial difficulties, embroiled in the personal wrangling of presidential aspirants, and forced to defend his conduct [while president] against base calumnies."[1]

The Monroes began the journey from Washington to their plantation home, Oak Hill, in Loudoun County, Virginia, on March 23, 1835. Their earlier home, Albemarle, was close to Jefferson's home, Monticello. Albemarle was a fine home, but it did not have the grandeur of a Mount Vernon, a Monticello, or a Montpelier. Monroe, as a United States president, preferred something more elaborate than Albemarle, so before completing his second term in office, he built an exceptionally fine home at Oak Hill. Jefferson helped Monroe and his wife design the new home. The bricks were fired on the property and much of the lumber was cut from timber on the land. In size it was approximately 90 feet by 50 feet, with nine 30-foot Doric columns around the front portico.

The mansion was elegantly furnished and beautifully decorated. Jefferson selected the marble from Italy for the mantels in the drawing room and the dining room. Both of the Monroes loved Oak Hill. There they hoped to find the quiet and peace of a country home. The former president wanted to manage his plantation and spend time with his family and friends, as well as study in his library of over three thousand volumes.

The Monroes had two daughters who reached maturity, Eliza (Mrs. George Hay) and Maria (Mrs. Samuel L. Gouverneur). Both of the daughters brought their families to Oak Hill and stayed for long periods of time. The house was often full of guests, some distinguished, and others, simple folk who were friends. Monroe rode almost every day. If a guest wished to accompany him, the ex-president provided a horse and they rode together. If no guest or family member wished to ride, Monroe would ride alone over the fields. He had one bad fall in which he broke his wrist and lay on the ground in the field for some time before he was found and taken to the house. He was several weeks recovering, and his wrist never did heal properly.

The Monroes lived less than six years at Oak Hill after leaving the White House. Mrs. Monroe died on September 23, 1830, at age 62, and the former president, because of financial adversity, was forced to leave Oak Hill in the fall of 1830 to live with a daughter in New York.

As a diplomat in the services of his nation Monroe had spent much of his own money. On several occasions Congress did not pay for his transportation to diplomatic posts nor his expenses while on these special missions to which the government had sent him. When Monroe left office he documented these expenses and sent them to Congress asking that a special committee be appointed to investigate the claims and then remunerate him. Congress did nothing to help him until he was a penniless, dying, old man living on the gratuity of his daughter and son-in-law in New York.

Few seriously doubted the validity of Monroe's claim, but the former president was caught in a violent partisan fight in Congress between the Jacksonians and their opponents, with Andrew Jackson at the center of the controversy. Monroe had been president during the "Era of Good Feeling," and even though he was reelected in 1820 by the largest majority of electoral votes since George Washington's unanimous elections (1788 and 1792), in no way could he be considered a great president.

There was no heir-apparent to Monroe, but there were several strong candidates. No one received a majority of electoral votes, and the election was thrown into the House of Representatives, which chose John Quincy Adams as president. Since Jackson had received more popular votes and also more electoral votes than Adams, the followers of Jackson were outraged. This controversy was at its height when Monroe presented his claim for compensation for the money he was owed. There is little wonder that the Congress was too caught up in purely partisan struggles to examine Monroe's claim carefully. However, there is adequate evidence that Jackson, for whatever reason, blocked the effort of Monroe to receive his just compensation.[2]

Monroe tried to keep himself solvent by selling his land. He did have large land holdings, but they brought little or no income. While he was overseas, 950 acres of his land near Charlottesville were sold to satisfy local obligations. Eventually he sold all his land except the plantation at Oak Hill. Shortly before his death in 1831 he had to put Oak Hill up for sale.

Several years ago the writer was in Leesburg, Virginia, on a research project and stopped at the courthouse to check some records. When the county clerk was asked about Monroe, his answer was blunt and direct. "Monroe was a deadbeat." he replied. "People were always trying to collect what he owed them." The clerk may not have realized that had the Congress fulfilled its obligation, Monroe's reputation might have been salvaged.

In 1828 Lafayette offered to give Monroe half of the large tract of land Congress had given to him when he visited the United States in 1825. However, Monroe did not feel it proper to accept, so he refused the generous offer. There had always been a strong attachment between Monroe and Lafayette. When the French Revolution was in full swing and Lafayette's life was in danger, Monroe, as an American diplomat, helped save him from the guillotine.[3] In like fashion, Mrs. Monroe helped to secure the release of Lafayette's wife from a revolutionary prison cell in Paris.

Finally Congress acted on a part of Monroe's claim and did vote him partial payment in the sum of $30,000. But the money came just weeks before his death, after he had abandoned Oak Hill and was dependent upon his daughter and son-in-law. This money plus the sale of his lands probably paid his outstanding debts, but the final settlement of his will and debts took years.

Another onerous situation which made his last years difficult was the continuing dispute concerning who was ultimately responsible for General Andrew Jackson's military action in the so-called Seminole War of 1817–1818.[4] The Seminole Indians, together with a number of escaped slaves, were raiding the American towns along the border between Spanish Florida and the United States. Spain could not or would not control them. General Jackson, who was sent to the southeast border to protect American citizens, crossed over into Spanish territory in pursuit and soon had the Indians on the run. In the process he found two rather disreputable British subjects who were helping the Indians, so Jackson had them hanged without proper authorization from the federal government. Jackson was accused of insubordination and exceeding his orders. However, he claimed he had received a letter permitting him to do whatever was necessary. (No such letter was ever found.)

John Calhoun was Monroe's secretary of war when the incident occurred. In a cabinet meeting, Calhoun pointedly criticized Jackson, while Secretary of State John Quincy Adams defended him. Monroe found himself in the center of the personal dispute between these presidential aspirants. He had been ill at the time of the incident and had not sent or seen the orders which Jackson claimed to have received, but both sides accused Monroe of duplicity. These claims and counter-claims developed into one of the bitter disputes of the 1820s and continued on into the next decade.

The quarrel was still going on during Monroe's last years of life. Just 16 days before his death he was again involved by those trying to use him to their own ends. Monroe's last document was a letter outlining his final effort to tell the American people what had happened in the Seminole War. At the time he was dying and could hardly speak, but he managed to sign his name to the document. John Quincy Adams, who knew the statement had been taken in extremis, said of the incident, "There is a depth of depravity in this transaction at which the heart sickens."[5]

Monroe steadfastly refused to participate in partisan issues. For example, the John Quincy Adams followers tried to get Monroe to run on the ticket in 1828 as vice-presidential candidate. He quickly and firmly refused.[6] However, he did preside over the Virginia Constitutional Convention at the time when their new constitution was written. He served on the University of Virginia Board of Visitors (trustees), along with Jefferson and Madison, for he strongly supported education. As Madison had done before him, Monroe became a local justice of the peace for several years in his home county. He even had the opportunity once again to become the governor of Virginia after he left the White House. This he also refused. Shortly after he moved to New York, his last public role was to serve as the presiding officer of an all-city celebration marking the adoption of a more democratic government in France after Charles X was driven from the throne.

When he left the presidency, Monroe was physically exhausted. He appeared older than his 67 years, for the high office had taken its toll. There was nothing obviously wrong with his health as he returned to Oak Hill. He felt that he was simply tired and run down. The next several years seemed to bear out this assumption, for he was lacking in vitality and energy, and complained many times of not feeling well. The Virginia Constitutional Convention (October 1829 to January 1830) in Richmond proved to be a drain on his energy. Weakness forced him to quit his post before the convention had finished its work. When it was over he was so tired and ill that he took the slower steamboat back to Washington rather than endure the rigors of stagecoach travel of that day. John Quincy Adams, who saw him there, thought he looked emaciated and ill. Monroe then journeyed on to Oak Hill where his health seemed to improve.

His wife, Elizabeth Kortright Monroe, had been in delicate health for several years. She was 10 years younger than her husband, marrying him when she was only 17. She had accompanied him on his diplomatic missions, taking all the rigors and inconveniences of travel that faced everyone in that day. She crossed the Atlantic a number of times and endured the inhospitable inns and rooming houses of Europe and the United States. Being more socially gifted than her husband, she was a great asset to his career and became a popular first lady.

Quite unexpectedly Elizabeth Monroe died on September 23, 1830. The ex-president was inconsolable and for a time his friends worried about him, wondering if he would ever recover. Although it was then the custom to bury the deceased on the next day, she was not buried for several days. The fact that Monroe was so distraught, together with the delay in burial, gave rise to the story that he could not bring himself to accept the fact that she was really dead. This is not true, for at the time of her death the family burial vault was in the process of being built. Work on the vault was hastened to completion, and Mrs. Monroe was buried in the family plot under the large pine tree in front of the house at Oak Hill.

Monroe's family felt he should not live in the house alone, so he went to live with his daughter Maria Gouverneur in New York City. There is little doubt that the state of his finances helped make the decision to move him to New York. The Gouverneurs lived in a modest Dutch-style home on the corner of Prince and Marion streets, near the Bowery. The city of New York took notice of Monroe's presence there, and he received much attention. He became a familiar figure in his neighborhood as he traveled about dressed in his black knee breeches and wide-buckle shoes. However, he socialized very little.

During the winter of 1830–1831 the former president did not have good health. He was troubled with fatigue and a failing appetite, but his chief complaint was a constant racking cough night and day. No one can be sure what an accurate diagnosis would have revealed, but nothing seemed to bring relief, including the horehound syrup that he constantly took and trusted so much. One physician felt that a long rest at Saratoga Springs with its warm baths might help, but he was too weak to go. He said of himself, "I am free from pain, but my cough annoys me much, both night and day."[7] Some have speculated that he may have had tuberculosis. When John Quincy Adams stopped to see him in the spring of 1831, he was shocked at Monroe's emaciated appearance. As time went by the former president spent more time in bed and gradually grew weaker. For several weeks before he died he found it difficult to hold a very long conversation. He got no better when summer came, but steadily declined. The family was aware that death must come soon. For several days the end seemed imminent, and at half past three o'clock on the afternoon of July 4, 1831, James Monroe died. He was the third president of the first five in office to die on the fourth of July. (The other two, Thomas Jefferson and John Adams, died on the same day, July 4, 1826.)

Although he had been in the town slightly less than a year, the city of New York gave Monroe the largest funeral that had ever been given there to anyone up to that time. He was buried on July 7. Official announcements were printed, the newspapers gave pages to the event, and thousands of people came out to honor the former president. There was a long funeral procession, guns were fired in salute, bells were tolled, and a great ceremony was held at city hall where President Duer of Columbia College gave the eulogy. Most of the city's business establishments closed during the funeral. The body was then taken to St. Paul's Episcopal Church where the religious service was conducted. The body was buried in the Gouverneurs' family vault in the Marble Cemetery on Second Street. As the nation mourned Monroe's death, flags on land and sea were at half-mast, crape was worn by officials, and gun salutes were fired.

The body remained in New York until July of 1858. On the centenary of his birth in April 1758, the Virginia legislature stated that all deceased Virginians who had been president of the United States should rest on Virginia soil. Steps were taken to bring Monroe's body back from New York to Virginia. All the living relatives of Monroe were contacted, and they favored the new burial site. Much secrecy surrounded the exhumation, for officials feared that many people might gather and cause confusion. Virginia representatives met with those of New York City at the cemetery for the removal of the body, which was taken to New York city hall where it lay in state for several days. The steamship *Jamestown* then bore the body to Richmond, Virginia, where it was buried at Hollywood Cemetery in a tomb befitting a chief executive. Another Virginian, John Tyler, who became president of the United States in 1841, was later given his final resting place just a few yards from Monroe's tomb. Mrs. Monroe's body was exhumed at Oak Hill in 1903 and buried beside her husband in Richmond.[8] Also, the body of the Monroe's daughter Maria, which had been buried at Oak Hill in 1850, was later placed beside those of her parents.

James Monroe was the last of what has been called the "Virginia dynasty" — four of the first five presidents were from Virginia. All four of these Virginians were plantation owners. Two of the four, Jefferson and Monroe, died bankrupt. This should say something of the economic vulnerability of the plantation system as well as the failure of the institution of slavery. Certainly Monroe's experience points to the fact that the federal government, until recent years, cared but little as to the financial plight of its ex-presidents.

The 6th, John Quincy Adams

"Old Man Eloquent," 1829–1848

Few presidents have significantly influenced the course of history after they left office. John Quincy Adams (1767–1848) is the most notable of those few. It is difficult to fully appreciate the magnitude of his lifetime of achievements. After a brilliant career in the diplomatic service, climaxed by an outstanding eight-year term as secretary of state, he reached the pinnacle of political success when he became president of the United States (1825–1829), only to have the rewards of the nation's highest office turn to ashes in his hands when his term in the White House was labeled a failure. He returned to his home in Quincy, Massachusetts, to brood and to become as inconspicuous as possible. Little did anyone dream that his most useful and productive days lay ahead of him when at 65 he became a freshman Congressman from a barren New England district.

This old man, a political "has-been," soon became the most influential member of the House of Representatives and the recognized leader of the antislavery forces in the nation's capital. He was also a most eloquent defender of a strong federal government, as opposed to states' rights, which was the refuge of the slaveholder. At an age when any sensible retired president should have been content with a comfortable rocking chair before the fireplace, John Quincy Adams was at the center of the abolitionist maelstrom that swirled about Washington.

Somehow it seems fitting that this Nestor of the Congress should have been stricken while on the floor of the House, rising in an apparent effort to address the chair. He died a few hours later in the Speaker's chambers.

John Quincy Adams was the son of John Adams, the second president of the United States, the only instance in which a father and son both became the chief executive of the nation. Before John Quincy Adams reached the presidency, he held a number of very important diplomatic positions. He headed the peace commission that drew up the Treaty of Ghent in 1814, ending the War of 1812 with England. For five years he was a member of the United States Senate. Much of his career was spent serving

42

as minister (or ambassador) from the United States to foreign capitals, including the Netherlands, Portugal, Russia, and England. His diplomatic career was concluded by a most brilliant term as the nation's secretary of state (1817–1825).

Adams did not enjoy his tenure as president. On November 7, 1828, just after he had been defeated in his bid for a second term, his diary records, "No one knows, and few conceive the agony of mind that I have suffered from the time that I was made by circumstances, and not by my volition, a candidate for the Presidency till I was dismissed from that station by the failure of my re-election."[1] He left office depressed and dejected, ready to separate himself completely from public affairs. At a farewell dinner given him by Henry Clay in Washington, D.C., Adams said, "It is my intention to bury myself in complete retirement as much as a nun taking the veil."[2]

Few today realize how vicious the press often became during the time of the Adams presidency. Many charges were made against him. He was blatantly accused of "pimping" for the Czar of Russia, of gaining the White House by corrupt means, and of using public funds for his own private purposes. These allegations were spurious and libelous. Adams, a moral and sincerely religious man, felt a deep anger and hurt that he never quite forgot.

After putting his personal affairs in Washington in order, he returned to his ancestral home in Quincy, Massachusetts. (The Adams house was commonly referred to as "the Mansion," although it was not ostentatious nor elaborately furnished.) After reaching his Quincy home, Adams' primary interests centered in his books and his writing. He owned the largest private library in the country. A scholar in his own right, he was well educated at Harvard and in Europe. He had a lively interest in the classics, especially in the great Roman authors whom he read in the original Latin. He had long been familiar with Milton and Shakespeare. He read the prominent European writers of his time and had met most of them overseas. European visitors were surprised to find that he spoke French like a native and was at home in German and Italian. He considered himself something of a poet, but sadly his talent did not equal his interest or his effort. One of his ambitions was to edit and publish his father's papers, which were in his possession. While he did begin the task, his election to the House cut short this literary effort. It was left to his son, Charles Francis Adams, to edit and eventually publish them.

His other great interest was in his orchards and gardens. In season he spent hours each day among his trees and plants. His ambition was to develop better fruit trees and garden plants for New England. Visitors were always somewhat amused to find his study filled with all sorts of tree cuttings and plants, which were to be found under papers and books, on bookshelves and chairs, or on the mantel over the fireplace. Yet despite all his interest and efforts, none of his experiments produced a noticeable improvement in either the trees or the garden plants of the region.

During this time in Quincy he did not see many people. He had never been much of a socializer or party-goer. Certainly he is not to be thought of as a misanthrope, but he did not seem to need the constant association of friends. He did have a small circle of friends with whom he spoke freely, and occasionally intimately, but more often than not he kept his own counsel. Some have described him as "frosty," probably an accurate term. By nature he was cold and distant, and remained the stiff Puritan aristocratic intellectual to the end of his life.

It should be noted that he did make new friends even late in life. Theodore Weld, the outstanding antislavery theoretician, is a good example. However, Adams never let friendship dictate his policies or attitudes, and this often added to his rather lonely existence. In reading his diary it is evident that he enjoyed having friends to his home as guests to dine or to have a drink, usually wine. The Adamses did go to the homes of friends to dine on occasion, but on a limited scale.

Throughout his life Adams rigidly scheduled his time and always set specific goals for himself, allowing less than two hours a day for leisure or rest. His custom was to retire by nine or nine-thirty and arise at four in the morning to begin the day. From four until nine he stayed in his study writing letters, keeping his diary, preparing speeches, working on legislation, or doing research on issues before Congress. He made the comment that the morning was half wasted if he waited until six to arise. He maintained this schedule until he was almost 80.

Exercise was as much a part of his life as his Bible reading. He was in his mid-seventies before he gave up horseback riding. When Congress was in session he usually walked the more than a mile from his home to the Capitol and returned on foot at the end of the day. Until the end of his life it was his custom to take long walks in Washington as well as in Quincy.

All of his life Adams took great delight in swimming. In season he would seek the good swimming spots in the lakes, ponds and rivers of New England for a vigorous swim. In middle age he could easily swim a mile, but by age 63 his usual swim was half that distance. In Washington he would seek one of his favorite spots and take his swim "au naturel." On several occasions all of his ingenuity was required to preserve his dignity and modesty while swimming. One hot afternoon while he was president, he retired to his favorite swimming hole along the Potomac, divested himself of his presidential attire, and was having his usual good time in the water when a tramp came along and stole his clothes. What could a president do in such a situation? Adams saw a boy walking along the river and prevailed upon him to go to the White House and obtain a change of clothing from the first lady, enabling the agitated chief executive to return home. The fact is that he had several similar close calls while swimming.

The last swim that John Quincy Adams took was in the Potomac near the place where the Tiber Creek flowed into the river. Congress was meeting well into the summer because of the war with Mexico. Adams, nearly 80, had a sudden "irresistible impulse"[3] to go swimming just as the dawn was breaking in mid-July, 1846. After putting his clothes on a rock, he entered the water and swam for about half an hour. The next two mornings found him in the water at dawn in the same place.

Yet a cursory reading of his diary shows that Adams was afflicted with a variety of physical ailments during the last couple of decades of his life. At times he felt that he was not physically up to the task. Often he spoke of his "declining faculties."[4] His eyes constantly gave him trouble. They were watery, or "rheumy," as described in that day. Glasses might have helped him, but he steadfastly refused to even consider them. Perhaps the most distressing physical symptom was a constant cough which at times became quite severe. In 1836 he had a serious leg infection. During the last years of his life he was bothered by a rather pronounced palsy.

Adams was a small man, only five feet seven inches tall, bald-headed with a crown of white hair around his head. He did not wear a beard, but had very long, bushy sideburns. Someone observed that his face was as "wrinkled as a dried persimmon."[5] Though not fat, he had something of a paunch. He did not appear to be particularly vigorous, but he did an amazing amount of work. Never careful about his dress, the former chief executive continued to wear knee breeches many years after they had gone out of style. He was the last member of Congress to wear them.

Upon his return to Massachusetts after his presidency, Adams paid no particular attention to public issues, nor did he in any way attempt to influence the course of events. But this situation was to dramatically change. Without his knowledge, the *Boston Courier* in September 1830 made the comment that Ex-President John Quincy Adams should be considered as a desirable candidate for Congress in the November elections. The real question was would he accept the position. When asked, "What do you say about going to Congress?" Mr. Adams answered, "I have nothing to say to it."[6] When asked if it would be degrading for a former president to become a member of the national legislature, Adams replied, "No person could be degraded by serving the people as a representative in Congress. Nor, in my opinion, would a former President of the United States be degraded by serving as a selectman of his town, if elected by the people." Adams then added, "I have not the slightest desire to be elected to Congress."[7] His son, Charles Francis, urged him not to consider accepting the position, as did many of his friends.

But since Adams had not flatly said, "I will not accept the position if elected," his friends placed his name on the ballot for Congress from his district. Adams did not solicit any support nor ask one individual to vote for him, but the people elected him by an overwhelming majority. Adams received 1,817 votes, his nearest rival only 373.

How did the former president feel about being elected to Congress? His diary gives the answer: "I am a member of the Twenty-second Congress ... I received nearly three votes in four throughout the district." He even confided to his diary something of his deepest personal emotions. "My election as President of the United States was not half as gratifying to my inmost soul. No election or appointment conferred upon me ever gave me so much pleasure."[8]

Although the Congress to which he had been elected in November 1830 would not formally meet until December of the next year (1831), Adams left for Washington in early December of 1830. His wife followed later. While it is true that he had some personal business interests in the city, the national government was his major concern. Adams felt that President Andrew Jackson was not to be trusted, and wanted to observe what was afoot in Washington. The former president knew most of the nation's important people, and many of them frequently sought his advice. He was a national figure and had known all the presidents (and presidents-to-be) personally from Washington through the time of the Civil War with the exception of Zachary Taylor. His understanding of the problems of the nation was profound. He had witnessed the Revolutionary War, the framing of the Constitution, the War of 1812, and the phenomenal growth of the United States, and now saw his beloved country preparing to enter the devastating Civil War. The prospect filled him with dread and foreboding.

Travel was most difficult in those days, especially in winter. After leaving Quincy for Washington in 1830, Adams traveled by coach, river boat and coastal vessel. His route took him through Hartford, New York, Philadelphia and Baltimore. The trip from Baltimore to Washington was one of the worst stretches of road on the whole trip. He arrived at his Washington home on Sixteenth Street in time to prepare for open house on New Year's Day of 1831. It was the custom of the city for government officials and the "gentry" to hold open house on the first day of the new year. Three hundred guests came to the Adams home.

In April Adams and his wife Louisa traveled back to Quincy to spend the summer in New England. He felt a need for his orchards and gardens, and the familiar haunts that he loved so well. For the rest of his life he followed the same pattern. Most of his summers were spent in New England, and he would return to the city of Washington in the fall. The coming of the railroad made the trip much easier, but it must have been an onerous journey for an old man to make under those primitive conditions.

On October 27, 1831, John Quincy and Louisa Adams left Quincy yet again for Washington. After a busy time in preparation, the former president took his place in the Twenty-second Congress on December 5, 1831. Adams was given a seat on the semicircle just in front of the Speaker's desk. A former president could hardly be treated as just another freshman Congressman. Only once, due to illness, was he absent from his duties for any length of time.

The Twenty-second Congress had some notable figures as members. Future president James K. Polk was there; two other future presidents, Millard Fillmore and Franklin Pierce would soon be colleagues of Adams. Edward Everett, the great orator who joined President Lincoln at Gettysburg for the dedication of the battlefield, was also a member of that House. The Senate contained a number of giants among its membership: John C. Calhoun (later vice-president); Daniel Webster, probably the greatest orator ever to address a Congress; Henry Clay, the "Great Compromiser"; and Thomas Hart Benton, the outstanding spokesman for the West. In all probability there has never been such a prestigious gathering in the history of an American Congress.

The issue that brought Adams to the attention of the nation as a Congressman was his opposition to slavery, and it did not take long for him to become the leader of the antislavery group in the House. The fight became the passion of his life, making him the most venerated as well as the most hated member of the Congress.

A point often missed is that although Adams hated the institution of slavery as an offense to God and humanity, he made no attempt to take the slaves from the states which already had them, especially if the force of arms was advocated. He felt that the Constitution gave each state the right to decide for itself whether it would have slaves or not, and that the federal government did not have the power to make even one state give up its slaves against its will. The Abolitionists, on the other hand, thought the nation as a whole could force the Southern states to free their slaves. Like most reformers, the Abolitionists demanded complete agreement with their position. As a result, they opposed Adams on occasion despite his open and effective fight against slavery. There were times when they did not support his campaigns for reelection to Congress.

Adams presented many petitions to Congress which came to him from various organizations and citizens throughout the nation concerning the slave question. Adams felt that Congress was obligated to consider any such petition sent to it by a citizen. This stance angered the South and caused many heated debates and outbursts in Congress. As a result, members of the House thought it best not to allow such discussions, and the so-called "gag rule" was put into effect. This rule, passed in 1836, would not allow any petition relating to slavery to be received in the House—the petition would be laid on the table without action. For eight years, in debates which often became very vicious and bitter, Adams led the fight against the gag rule. Finally, when the House was organizing in December 1844, the gag rule was defeated by a vote of 108 to 80. Overjoyed, Adams wrote in his diary, "Blessed, forever blessed, be the name of God."[9]

During the long and bitter fight against the gag rule, Adams was a master parliamentarian, holding the floor of the House for days at a time. The bitterness expressed by the South knew no bounds. Before the House, Henry Wise of Virginia said of Adams, "Words cannot express the personal loathing, dread and contempt I feel for this man."[10] At times Adams was called the "Madman of Massachusetts," a mischievous old man, a scoundrel, Harlequin, old reprobate, curmudgeon, miscreant, scalawag, and knave. Feelings ran so high that on a number of occasions members of the House armed themselves with Bowie knives or pistols before taking their places in that deliberative body. Because Adams was the leader and the primary spokesman for the antislavery forces, he naturally became the chief target of the proslavery group.

In the spring of 1842, there was a serious attack on Adams personally—an attempt to get him censured by the House itself, if not expelled. At first it looked bad for the old man, but he roused himself for the struggle and the antislavery forces came rushing to his defense. Henry Wise led the assault on the ex-president. Adams very skillfully defended himself, taking days to present his case. After all the attempts by the proslavery element to discredit him, Adams emerged exonerated. His greatest fear had been that his own temper might get out of control in the debate. In the fall of 1842 he was easily reelected to Congress without any personal campaigning on his part, and became the most powerful member of that body.

On one occasion, when James K. Polk, later president, was the Speaker of the House and had ruled against Adams as the presiding officer, Adams had responded, "I am aware there is a slaveholder in the chair."[11] On another occasion, Adams referred to Jefferson's "inventive memory." He spoke of Calhoun as "darkened by his . . . icy-hearted dereliction of all the decencies of social intercourse."[12] His son Charles Francis Adams commented that his father "made his points by attacking."[13] Those who did not have a strong case or could not effectively engage in debate were afraid to tangle with this irascible elder.

However, it must be noted that many good things were also said of Adams. The most touching term used in praise and honor of Adams is a phrase taken from Milton, when Adams was called "Old Man Eloquent." Some feel that Benjamin Lundy was the one who first used the term in reference to Adams, but no one knows for sure.

The summer of 1843 brought a number of prestigious invitations to speak in New England and the state of New York. Accompanied by his family, the speaking trip proved to be something of a triumphant procession. Everywhere he went he was greeted by large, enthusiastic crowds. Gala receptions were held in his honor at every turn. The press gave him acclaim and a great deal of attention. John Quincy Adams, who had been a very unpopular president, was now perhaps the most revered man in the country.

He was invited to deliver the major address at the laying of the cornerstone of the newly formed Cincinnati Astronomical Society. Adams had always been interested in science, especially astronomy, so he accepted the invitation. The trip involved winter travel by carriage, stage, and railroad in very sparsely settled country. Travel in cold weather could be very disagreeable and on occasion rather dangerous. Many times trains were derailed, leaving the passengers without food or heat. But Adams was determined to make the journey, though it involved a great deal of discomfort and some hazard. His participation in the celebration in Cincinnati brought him considerable acclaim.

In November of 1845, Dr. George Parkman, an old friend, dropped by the home of Charles Francis Adams where the ex-president, now 78, was visiting with his son, to take John Quincy Adams to see the new facilities of the medical school of Harvard. As they were walking toward the college, the congressman collapsed and had to be taken back to his son's home. Dr. John Bigelow, the family doctor, was called and diagnosed a slight stroke. In a few days Adams was much better, and early in January he returned to his accustomed seat in the House of Representatives. When he came in for the first time after his illness, he was given a standing ovation by the members of the House. While to all appearances he seemed to have made a full recovery, he never did have quite the energy he had before the illness. He made fewer speeches, traveled less, and engaged in fewer debates. He was reelected to the House in November 1846 with only token opposition.

In the spring of 1848, several of Adams' friends noted a renewed vigor and interest in life on the part of the elder statesman. On Thursday, February 17, 1848, Adams attended a reception for the mayor of the city of Washington, D.C. The next day he conducted a meeting at the Library of Congress. On Saturday, the Adams family had open house, which was attended by hundreds. The next day, Sunday, February 20, Adams attended church twice as was his custom. The next morning, seemingly in good health, he was driven to the Capitol. A motion came before the House to honor eight generals of the Mexican War. Adams had been against the war because he felt that slavery would be extended into the newly acquired territory, and did not want to honor its generals. Observers noted that his face turned red and that he grasped the edge of his desk as if he wanted to rise and address the chair, when suddenly he slumped back. Friends gathered around the fallen "Old Nestor." Washington Hunt of the state of New York shouted, "Mr. Adams is dying."[14]

A sofa was brought in and Adams was carried to the rotunda of the Capitol. Since the rotunda was drafty, the patriarch was then moved to the Speaker's chambers. Several members of the House who were physicians did what they could for the stricken statesman. His wife was called, but he did not recognize her when she arrived. His last words were, "This is the last of earth: I am content."[15] He lingered in a coma until the evening of Wednesday, February 23, when he peacefully died.

The nation mourned his passing. The outpouring of grief was spontaneous and deep. A congressional delegation, including Abraham Lincoln, accompanied the body back to Massachusetts, where Adams was interred in the Unitarian Church in Quincy beside his father. Isaac Holmes, a member of the proslavery bloc, put it well when he said, "When a great man falls, the nation mourns; when a patriarch is removed, the people weep."[16]

The 7th, Andrew Jackson

Old Hickory, 1837–1845

The general was obviously dying. It was June 8, 1845. Andrew Jackson (born 1767) slipped into unconsciousness, but a little brandy revived him. He bid goodbye to each family member and his friends. "My dear children, and friends, and servants, I hope and trust to meet you all in Heaven, both white and black — both white and black."[1] These were his last words. Someone present suggested that Hannah, "a black servant in whose arms Rachel Jackson had died, leave the room. 'I was born on this place and my place is here,' the beloved Hannah firmly replied."[2] She remained beside the general to the end. It was as he wished. At six o'clock the famed statesman quietly stopped breathing. Sam Houston had come from Texas in an effort to see his chieftain before the general died. Unfortunately, Houston arrived just minutes after death came to the Hermitage. Houston entered the room, stood by the bed, dropped to his knees and sobbed. He then turned to the small son he had brought with him and said, "My son, try to remember that you looked on the face of Andrew Jackson."[3]

A very popular general in the War of 1812, Andrew Jackson was swept into office in the election of 1828 (serving until 1837) by his appeal to the so-called "common man." His vigorous administration gave new meaning to the power of the presidency. He was the leader, the designer of policy, the mover in government. Often he was referred to as King Andrew I, the Chieftain, or the Dictator. To his friends he was known as Old Hickory, a name he acquired as a general. In his own eyes he felt that he knew what was best, and anyone who opposed him was stupid, a cad, or a traitor. Yet the people loved his style, and a whole era of American history bears Jackson's stamp as well as his name.

Jackson's take-charge attitude was well illustrated in an incident recorded by Gerald W. Johnson. Just after the inauguration of his successor, Martin Van Buren, Jackson and a group of his men were talking together. They began enumerating the many accomplishments of his administration, concluding that all they really wanted to achieve under his leadership had been completed. "It was then that Jackson confessed to two things he had left undone—he had not had the opportunity to shoot Henry Clay or to hang John C. Calhoun."[4] (Clay and Calhoun, members of the United States Senate, and generally regarded as statesmen by historians, often vigorously opposed Jackson.)

So often did Jackson disdain his political enemies that he frequently denigrated them, such as when he referred to John Quincy Adams as a "lying scamp."[5] Yet historians regard Adams as a man of the highest rectitude, perhaps the most scrupulously honest man ever to occupy the White House. It should be noted that Adams was the man who defeated Jackson for the presidency in 1824, and then the general, in turn, defeated Adams in 1828 to gain the White House for himself.

Perhaps the most interesting and unusual aspect of Jackson's post-presidential years was his overt attempt to influence the course of national government and his own Democratic party. No other ex-president so openly gave advice to presidents and other officials in government, no other former chief executive so obviously sought to direct his own party in its policies and strategies. Other ex-presidents may have at times worked behind the scenes, but Jackson never had the gift of intrigue. The only method he knew was to speak out, to attack. In a letter to President Van Buren, the man he had personally chosen to succeed him in the White House, he wrote "My course have [has] been to put my enemies at defience [sic] and pursue my own course."[6]

Often Jackson's advice was rejected out of hand. But as famed writer William Graham Sumner observed, "It was still worthwhile to court him and to get his name in favor of a man or a measure."[7] Jackson wrote countless letters expressing his views, and many of these found their way into the press. That visitors by the hundreds came to the Hermitage, Jackson's home near Nashville, Tennessee, shows something of the impact he made on the public.

After seeing the inauguration of his successor, Andrew Jackson left Washington and started for his home. He was so ill that the new president urged him to remain as a guest in the White House until he felt better and the winter weather was more suitable for travel. But Jackson was so anxious to go home that he insisted on beginning the trip with only a few days' delay. "The journey to the Hermitage renewed Jackson's faith in his own rectitude. 'I have been everywhere cheered by my numerous democratic republican friends' . . . even some 'repentant Whigs' joined in giving him a hearty welcome."[8] When his carriage neared the Hermitage, a large group of neighbors stopped the ex-president, and read messages of welcome and veneration. Old Hickory was moved to tears by this show of affection.

By this time Jackson's life-style had dramatically changed. Gone were the days of cockfighting, hard drinking, and dueling.[9] Part of this change can be attributed to the gradual passing of the frontier and its vigorous, lusty ways. But a part of it must be credited to Old Hickory's firm resolve to be more of a gentleman. When he wished, his manners and social conduct could match those of any of the Eastern aristocrats. "When it suited his purpose he could outshine a French Marquis as an exhibit of graceful manners,"[10] much to the surprise of such rugged westerners as Missouri's Senator Thomas Hart Benton. As he grew older the general's church attendance was regular and his interest in and support of charitable causes increased. Certainly a transformation had taken place in the military hero who had been a brawling frontier soldier. It was the new Jackson who came home to the Hermitage in retirement.

The general had hardly unpacked before he wrote a long letter to the new president. "My dear sir, the Treasury order is popular everywhere I have passed. But all the speculators, and those largely indebted, want more paper, the more it depreciates the easier they can pay their debts. . . . Check the paper mania and the republic is safe and your administration must end in triumph."[11] The interesting thing is that Jackson's own financial policies, which were largely continued by Van Buren, are regarded by many as a major cause of the Panic of 1837. This panic hurt Jackson's personal finances as it did much of the Western world.

As time went by, unsolicited advice still came from the Hermitage. He again wrote Van Buren, "You may rest assured that nineteen-twentieths of the whole people approve of it [the Specie Circular] — all except the speculators and their secret associates and partners."[12] When the new House of Representatives could not maintain a quorum, Jackson angrily sent word to have the sergeant-at-arms bring members of Congress to the chambers by force. "It is no time for the Democratic party to use delicacy or unusual comity to those who have combined to destroy our Government."[13] When President Van Buren decided to make a trip to the western states for political reasons in 1839, the general wrote to the White House, "If my health permits I will meet you at Memphis, if that should be your rout [sic], and escort you to the Hermitage, stopping at such intermediate points as may be convenient."[14]

Long before the election of 1840, Jackson warned his party that if the Whigs nominated General William Henry Harrison, the famed frontier Indian fighter, the campaign would be a hard one. The Whigs did nominate Harrison. As the election of 1840 approached, Jackson recommended to Van Buren that he drop Richard M. Johnson as the Democratic candidate for vice president, even though he had served as vice president during Van Buren's first term. The Democratic convention did not nominate anyone for the vice presidency, leaving that issue up to the states. This was the only time in American history that such a ploy was used.[15] These were a few of the instances where the crafty old ex-president exerted considerable influence over national policy. Not only did he give advice, but Jackson took the stump himself and campaigned vigorously for Van Buren in 1840.

Naturally the old general was quite disappointed when Harrison defeated Van Buren. But just a month after his inauguration, Harrison died suddenly, leaving John Tyler the first to succeed to the presidency upon the death of an incumbent. Tyler was at heart a states-rights Democrat, but he did not like Jackson, so he left the Democratic party and became a Whig. Although Jackson and Tyler heartily disliked each other, both realized that at times they needed the other. Jackson sought to influence Tyler, and Tyler in turn looked to Jackson for help.

Tyler sought Jackson's help in bringing about the annexation of Texas. On several occasions Texas had asked to be annexed by the United States, but the growing strength of the antislavery forces in the North had always managed to prevent it. Finally, when it looked as if Tyler had worked out a solution to the dilemma, Sam Houston, the recognized leader of Texas, did not cooperate as Tyler had expected. So Tyler, through his confidant, Senator Robert J. Walker of Mississippi, asked Jackson to help get Houston in line.[16] Immediately Jackson sent an urgent letter to Houston, who had been a political protege of Jackson, imploring him to accept the terms of annexation. Houston replied in a very warm, cooperative spirit, and soon Texas was annexed. Altogether Jackson played a large part in the annexation of Texas. He had long feared that England would become a major influence in the Americas if allowed to gain a foothold in Texas.

Jackson helped use the Texas situation to get James K. Polk elected president in 1844. Jackson had strongly backed Van Buren for the Democratic nomination in 1844. However, both Van Buren the Democrat and Clay the Whig nominee tried to avoid committing themselves on the Texas issue during the campaign. This angered the whole South, which wanted Texas to become a slave state. In the Democratic convention the South refused to back Van Buren's nomination. Jackson urged Van Buren to alter his stance on Texas. But Van Buren did not follow his mentor's advice, so in the very end Jackson reluctantly backed Polk, who was nominated after days of haggling. Polk went on to win a very close election over Henry Clay. Jackson again had correctly assessed the situation. In a letter to Francis Blair on May 7, 1844, he wrote "Clay [is] a dead political Duck."[17]

The struggle to elect Polk and annex Texas were the last political efforts of Jackson's life. He was 78 and very ill. As the election returns came to the Hermitage, the dying general kept a careful tabulation of the vote as it reached him. It proved to be a close election, with New York the pivotal state. Whichever way New York went the election would go. Former President Van Buren strongly supported the ticket and made a major contribution to the Democratic victory in 1844. Jackson's influence had helped keep Van Buren and New York loyal to the Democratic party.

Jackson's correspondence records many letters written between the time Polk was elected president in November of 1844 and Jackson's death in June of 1845. Most of them are filled with advice about political matters. Eleven letters were to Polk, each telling the newly-elected chief executive what he should do. The last two letters Jackson ever wrote were to Polk. On May 26 the general wrote, "It would be a fortunate thing for your administration and the country could Mr. Van Buren be got to go to England [as ambassador]."[18] On June 6, just hours before he died, Jackson wrote in his own hand, "I wish you to recollect the caution I gave you about the Treasury Department. Here you are to be assailed, and without great vigilance and energy in yourself your administration wounded deeply."[19]

In the twilight of life, old and ill as he was, Jackson continued to exert considerable influence. The political leaders feared his wrath and curried his favor. Dozens of the important men of the day came to the Hermitage to consult him. James says, "A stream of visitors came to pledge allegiance, Whigs to confess their sins and beg absolution."[20] Those who came away with a hickory cane from the Hermitage felt they had truly been to Mecca. Just how he inspired such devotion is something of a mystery. During Jackson's last year of life Clay observed, "All who approach that man are fascinated."[21] Johnson describes Jackson's impact as "aura of the fantastic."[22]

Few former presidents have had an easy time in retirement. Jackson was no exception. One of his major problems was his finances, largely caused by his adopted son's lack of responsibility. He loved this son deeply and many times came to his rescue, often at considerable cost to himself. Another problem was his declining health. There were a number of occasions when his very life seemed threatened. In examining his correspondence written after returning to the Hermitage, the majority of the letters mention his financial situation or poor health.

Unfortunately Jackson used most of his savings while he was in the White House. He still had his plantation at the Hermitage as well as land in western Tennessee and Mississippi, and he had no major debts. When he left Washington in March 1837, he took $5,000 with him. When he reached the Hermitage he had exactly $90 in his pocket. He did not squander his money, but when he met people he knew and liked he spent money on them.

When Jackson arrived at the Hermitage it was necessary for him to undertake a major rebuilding of his home. A fire in 1836 had done considerable damage, and upon his return the general made the rebuilding his top priority. It was too late in the year to do much about the plantation. Most of the crops had already been put in by his overseer. However, Jackson did give the farm work his personal attention and soon the estate began to show this care. He was able to send 74 bales of cotton to New

Orleans that fall, which was a good yield. Consequently he began the year 1838 debt free, with good prospects for the coming year, though the Panic of 1837 had made things harder for him.

But unexpected troubles soon came. Things had gone so well that the general helped his adopted son, Andrew, Jr., buy a plantation of 1,100 acres along the Mississippi River in Coahoma County, Mississippi, called Halcyon Plantation. The transaction did not require Jackson to borrow against his own property to make the down payment. Beginning in March 1839, they were to make four equal payments of $23,000 each. At the time it seemed quite a manageable arrangement. They met the first payment even though times were hard.

By the winter of 1839–40 the general was short of funds. He discussed these problems with Andrew J. Donelson in a letter dated December 10, 1839.[23] His son's financial plight had taken all his ready cash. Andrew, Jr., had foolishly borrowed money he did not really need and the father had rescued him from his creditors. At times the general's son was simply dishonest, but the father still trusted him and felt that he would settle down and be a credit to the Jackson name. When Albert Ward's financial empire in Nashville crumbled, it was discovered that young Andy, among several others, had gone surety for Ward. Creditors turned to those who had endorsed Albert Ward's loans and began legal means to recover their losses, which were large. This action brought to light other liabilities of Andrew, Jr., obligations that the father knew nothing about.

Meanwhile, Jackson had promised to attend the twenty-fifth observance of the battle of New Orleans. The general was out of funds again. He wrote to H.M. Cryer, "I am out of funds, and I cannot bear to borrow ... or travel as a pauper."[24] At the same time he was being pressed for other debts which his son had incurred. However, the general did make the trip to New Orleans by drawing in advance on his cotton crop. On his return he promised to try to "stimulate him [his son] to use every exertion to meet it [the note]."[25] The father borrowed $3,000 which he placed to Andy's credit at the bank.[26] This story was repeated over and over again. Neither father nor son changed their ways, so it became harder for the father to keep securing the money to save his son from bankruptcy.

Jackson's financial situation became worse. On New Year's Day, 1841, he learned that the slaves at Halcyon Plantation were hungry. Even the Hermitage began to look neglected and run down, and the best horses on the plantation had been sold to pay debts. The general was not legally responsible for most of his son's debts, but as a matter of honor the repayment of these debts was as binding to the ex-president as a legal obligation. In a letter to W.B. Lewis in March 1842, the general pointedly tells how he felt about his son. The boy "had been adopted and raised by my dear wife and myself, was the only representative to perpetuate my name ... I could not withstand stepping forward to extricate him."[27] Frank Blair and James C. Pickett raised a purse that greatly helped Old Hickory. A few months later other friends lent the general more money. Jackson tried to help his situation by sending his cotton to England to get a better price, but the scheme backfired and he suffered losses as a result.

The general took his obligations seriously and constantly sought to pay his debts. He was a good farmer and managed his plantation well. As time went by he was able to make progress toward reducing his obligations. As a result, by the time he died he had managed to pay all his major debts but two. One was a $15,000 loan from Frank Blair of Washington, one of his best friends, and the other a much smaller amount due General Panchin of New Orleans. At the time of his death his estate was worth more than $150,000,[28] most of it in the Hermitage with its fine mansion and 1,200 acres. Regrettably, Andrew Jackson, Jr., squandered the whole estate in ten years.[29]

In spite of his difficulties, Old Hickory constantly gave political matters his personal attention. When the Democrats won in 1844, electing James Polk to the White House, Jackson was elated. But very quickly the situation became onerous. The public knew that Jackson was very close to Polk, so hundreds of office seekers descended on Jackson begging him to influence the new president to give them government jobs. The general saw as many as he could, but obviously could not make binding promises. The elder statesman did not need this kind of pressure. Jackson commented, "I'm dying as fast as I can, and they know it, but they will keep swarming upon me in crowds seeking office."[30]

For most of the time after he left office, Jackson was in poor health, at times desperately ill. Only a heroic soul like Jackson could have managed to stay active in the face of such a series of illnesses. Johnson comments, "Pain was never absent for a day, and for the last two years hardly for an hour."[31]

It is evident that Jackson was suffering from tuberculosis, which was very common in those days. Johnson says that "one lung was consumed, and hemorrhages grew more frequent, more serious, more exhausting."[32] His hearing was impaired, he saw little out of the right eye, and his "memory was uncertain."[33] Many times his letters tell how difficult it was to write.

Yet there is a record of almost 90 letters that he wrote in 1844 and about 60 in just over five months in 1845. The letters at times ramble a bit, but they show a thoughtful, observant man with a clear mind. He did not feel sorry for himself, though his health was in progressive decline. He was very ill in 1841, but managed to recover. In 1844, those around him despaired of his life. He himself did not expect to see Polk inaugurated as president, but he lived three months beyond that date.

Again in August of 1844 he was very ill, and although he recovered, he never was able to ride a horse again. Up until that time he was often on horseback inspecting his fields and directing the work of the plantation. He developed what were called dropsical symptoms (retention of body fluids). He needed help to make his daily visits to his wife's grave, only a few yards from his dwelling. Now he suffered from dizziness as well as from frequent lung hemorrhages. In March of 1845 he complained of being short of breath. It was just a question of time until he would be on his deathbed.

Jackson's wife Rachel, who died in 1828 shortly before he took the office of president, had always been a much more religious person than her husband. She often was called to visit the sick and the dying when a frontier minister was not available. She would gather the children of the community for Bible stories. Before Rachel died, Jackson had promised her that he would join the church (Rachel was a Presbyterian). He made good that promise shortly after he left office. One reason he waited until he left the White House was that he did not want the public to think that he made this decision for political reasons. The minister who counseled him as to church membership was concerned about his vindictive feelings against his enemies. Even when he joined the church he only forgave them as a group, not as specific persons. And he forgave only his own enemies. He did not include those who had slandered his wife, for he felt that this slander had shortened her life.

Andrew and Rachel had married after Rachel thought she was legally divorced from her first husband, Lewis Roberts. The legislature of Virginia had granted Roberts the right to sue for a divorce, but unfortunately Roberts left part of the legal process undone. Rachel assumed that the proper legal steps had been taken and married Jackson. When it was discovered that a technicality still left her legally married to Roberts, the couple found themselves in legal difficulties. Even though they did remarry, tongues wagged, and all sorts of innuendos and accusations were cast at them. He fought four duels over this matter, killing several people. Even when Jackson was running for the presidency almost forty years later, the general's political enemies talked about the adulterous couple who were going to pollute the White House. This slander angered Jackson, but it deeply hurt the religious and sensitive Rachel. A feeling of guilt followed her to the grave. "The hardest thing for Old Hickory to say was that he had forgiven his enemies. . . . Those who had slandered her remained for God to deal with."[34]

It is somewhat surprising to find so many of Jackson's letters during his last years expressing his acceptance of the will of God and a resignation for God to take him when He chose. He concluded a letter to Francis Blair on March 18, 1845, with the words, "I am always ready to say the Lord's will be done."[35] About the same time he wrote to Andrew Donelson, "I await with resignation the call of my god."[36] He often expressed his hope of heaven as he did in a letter to Amos Kendall when he wrote, "Here my friend, I must close, tendering you with my prayers for your health, long life and prosperity, and that we may at last meet in a blissful immortality."[37]

Shortly before his death Jackson was offered the casket which had held the body of a Roman emperor, but he immediately refused it saying that he wanted a simple burial such as his wife had had.[38] Toward the end he could not lie down and had to sleep propped up in bed or in a specially designed easy chair. When Sunday, June 1, 1845, came, Jackson felt that it would be his last Sunday. He was wrong by one week. The doctor gave him opiates to help relieve the pain. During the last week many visitors came to pay their respects. He received most of them and conversed in a clear, lucid manner. Thirty people came to see him in one day alone. On Thursday, June 5, three days before his death, he ordered supplies for his son's Mississippi plantation. On the same day, his daughter-in-law Sarah caught snatches of the words of an old hymn that he was repeating:

When through the deep waters I call thee to go,
The rivers of woe shall not thee overflow.

Then two days before his death, he wrote a legible letter to President Polk.[39]

As the Presbyterian minister conducted a short religious service, the body of the former president was laid to rest beside the grave of his wife Rachel. Memorial services were held all over the land. Some of his bitter political enemies refused to attend, just as Jackson himself had earlier refused to attend a memorial service for Chief Justice John Marshall. But to the people as a whole the late president was a national hero, a great and honored American statesman, and for his passing they expressed their great respect and their grief.

The 8th, Martin Van Buren

The Magician Loses His Touch, 1841–1862

When Martin Van Buren (1782–1862; in office 1837–1841) was defeated for a second term as president in the election of 1840, he had 21 years yet to live. His most compelling desire of those years was to recapture the presidency. Ironically, Martin Van Buren can be remembered as the only ex-president to see eight successors in the White House.

Andrew Jackson, who preceded him, had been a popular two-term president and was strong enough to pick his successor. Van Buren of New York had been Jackson's secretary of state and vice president, and was a natural choice as his successor. Jackson was a war hero who became an effective president, but he did not have the capacity to build a strong political organization. This responsibility was left to Van Buren, who in effect became Jackson's alter ego as well as his political manipulator, and who was so successful that he was often referred to as the "Little Magician," the "Fox," or "Little Van." Thus Martin Van Buren, an independently wealthy widower, became the eighth president. He had a difficult administration, for the nation was having serious financial and social problems.

When Van Buren ran for reelection in 1840, he was defeated by the Whigs, who conducted a new type of political campaign. They had a popular military hero, General William Henry Harrison, as their candidate. Van Buren didn't have a chance. The Whigs rode to victory on a sudden burst of enthusiasm generated by a campaign filled with slogans, torchlight parades, political songs and banners, as the populace crowded around the party emblem of a log cabin. Nearby the people filled their cups from a barrel of hard cider, while they were regaled by strong-lunged political orators. "Tippecanoe and Tyler Too" was their slogan. It was a natural one, for in 1811, as governor of Indiana Territory, General Harrison had won a great victory at Tippecanoe over the Indian chief Tecumseh when the British, as part of their preparation for the War of 1812, had incited the Indians to attack the Western frontier. John Tyler was the vice presidential nominee. The Whigs won a major victory and introduced an entirely new concept into presidential campaigns. At 58, Van Buren's national leadership had come to an end. With some justification he called the election a "victory of buffoonery." The 1840s and 50s was a period of violently partisan conflicts and extremes. Name-calling was perhaps at its worst. "Bucktails," "Hunkers," "Barnburners," "Loco Focos," and "Doughfaces" were a few of the names used.

As is common with those who have been defeated in a race for the presidency, Van Buren could not understand his loss, feeling that the people would soon come to their senses and return him to office. He remained in Washington for a week after seeing Harrison inaugurated, then returned to his hometown, Kinderhook, New York. To his fellow New Yorkers he was still their hero, and was welcomed home by a brass band and a large turnout of friends and neighbors. During the following four years he gave his attention to the next election (1844). He also realized a dream of many years by building a grand mansion on a large estate in his community.

A number of American presidents had large estates with names which became significant in the minds of the public. There was Washington at Mount Vernon, Jefferson at Monticello, Madison at Montpelier, Monroe at Oak Hill, and Jackson at the Hermitage. Van Buren felt such a residence would endear him to the people and assure perpetuation of his public image. So he built Lindenwald, a magnificent estate near Kinderhook, New York. Set in the beauty of upstate New York, it was a large and ornately furnished mansion. From Lindenwald, Van Buren expected to entertain important people and direct political movements. Many prominent people did come, and many large social affairs were hosted there, but it never developed into the seat of power and influence that he had expected. Van Buren did not recognize that there was no Washington, Jefferson, or Jackson to welcome visitors to his estate. His solitude and loneliness developed into bitterness, an emotion from which he never completely recovered.

Though he personally opposed slavery, Van Buren had hoped to keep the issue out of the 1844 election, seeing that his chance of success would be enhanced if he did not have to deal with this thorny question. The Whigs, who had defeated him in 1840, made so many blunders and had so much bad luck that he felt he would recapture the White House. The new Whig president, William Henry Harrison, died one month after taking office, and John Tyler, who succeeded Harrison, was so embroiled with the Whig leaders that they read him out of the party. What an opportunity for Van Buren! But the moral question of slavery became the chief issue, and the "Little Magician" was caught unprepared to effectively address it. He could not satisfy both the North and the South as he once had. The major question was, should Texas, a slave-holding, independent republic, be admitted to the Union as it had requested? Van Buren was not ready to admit Texas as a new state immediately and unconditionally. He therefore gave a qualified answer to the Texas question. When Van Buren did not call for the immediate admittance of Texas, the Southern Democrats became disenchanted with him and withdrew their support for his candidacy.

The Democrats met in their 1844 convention in Baltimore and gave Van Buren a majority of the votes for the nomination, but he could not get the necessary two-thirds vote that the Democratic party demanded. As the convention dragged on, neither Van Buren nor his nearest challenger, Lewis Cass, could gain the two-thirds vote. It was then that the Democrats turned to "dark horse" James K. Polk on the ninth ballot as their compromise presidential candidate. Polk had been an outstanding Speaker of the House and had many friends among the Democrats.

The Democratic convention added a last insult to Van Buren. It tried to bury him, or at least put him into a dignified, silent retirement. Just before the convention ended it passed a resolution that read, "We hereby tender to him [Van Buren] in his honorable retirement the assurance of the deep-seated confidence, affection and respect of the American Democracy."[1] In spite of all that had happened to Van Buren, he was able to carry his own state of New York for Polk. Had Polk not carried New York he would not have been elected to the White House.

Polk, with his idea of pushing the American frontier to the Rio Grande and then the Pacific Ocean, had won a close election, and talked to Van Buren as though he wanted the former president to help him in his administration. But when "Little Van" tried to exert leadership, he was summarily rejected by Polk. The "Little Magician" had lost his last chance at the political miracle he so assiduously sought.

After his loss in 1844, Van Buren tried to maintain control of New York's politics and thus keep his chances alive. But Polk and the leaders of the Democratic party in Washington would not cooperate with him. When 1848 came, the Free Soil party (a basically abolitionist movement) was trying to gain national recognition. The Free Soilers persuaded Van Buren to run for president on their ticket. He was nominated at Buffalo by a screaming, frenzied convention. To the surprise of everyone, he agreed to accept the nomination. The big question was, why did he agree to run on a third-party ticket?

One view is that Van Buren accepted the nomination as a political ploy to further his own ends, "a none-too-noble attempt to harness an otherwise sacred cause to his own promotion."[2] Others feel that Van Buren ran on the Free Soil ticket as a matter of principle and conscience. "Ambition to reenter the White House could indeed have had but the slightest influence with him when he accepted the Free Soil nomination."[3] Both points of view have cogent arguments. The writer tends to feel that Van Buren's open stand against letting slavery into any new territory, and thus limiting its spread, was the basic reason for his willingness to associate himself with the Free Soilers.

Some felt that Ohio and New York were so upset at both the Democrats and the Whigs that they might vote for Van Buren. If so, the election would have been thrown into the House of Representatives, as no candidate would have gained a majority of the electoral votes. Then, if either of the major parties decided it would prefer Van Buren to the other political candidates, Van Buren could have been elected president. However remote, such a possibility is always the hope of a third-party candidate. In any case, Van Buren lost out and was now without a political base of power.

From this point on, Van Buren's efforts were only familiar gestures so often repeated that they seemed rather pathetic. He did support the Democratic candidates in the next three presidential elections — Franklin Pierce, James Buchanan, and Stephen A. Douglas — but exerted little influence. Until he was well into his seventies, "Little Van" kept hoping that political lightning would strike.

In his late sixties Van Buren fell in love and wished to marry again. His first wife, Hannah Hoes of Kinderhook, had died in 1819 after 12 years of marriage. They had four sons: Abraham, John, Martin II, and Smith Thompson. Van Buren had lived for almost 30 years as a widower, and at 68 he proposed marriage to a 40-year-old spinster named Margaret Silvester, the daughter of good friends.[4] She was a frequent guest at Lindenwald, and he was often in the Silvester home. Her mother approved of the marriage, but the daughter said she could never marry him. They continued to be friends, but Van Buren remained unmarried. He had hoped that she would accompany him on his European trip.

In 1853 Van Buren went to Europe and stayed for more than two years. It was something new for a former American president to travel abroad, and the proper protocol was in doubt. Should he be received as an American official or as a private citizen? Van Buren solved the dilemma by saying that he was a private citizen and should be received as such. However, foreign governments did offer him differential treatment, which he seemed to enjoy. In London he ordered full court regalia from a fashionable tailor. He stayed in the finest hotels, and as had been his custom, he dressed in fashionable and expensive clothes. He visited Cavour, the builder of unified Italy as a nation, as well as the royal families of Holland, England, and the German states, and seemed always to be received as an honored guest. Since his family was Dutch, he persuaded the ruler of Holland to provide him with a family coat-of-arms, which he prized. Leaving his ill son, Martin Van Buren II, in London for medical treatment, he rented a villa by the sea in Sorento, Italy, and began to work seriously on his autobiography. Van Buren had little formal education, and the work progressed rather slowly. The first draft was never quite completed. However, the parts of it that have survived do prove interesting, for most of the writing is politically oriented.

The son he left in London did not improve, so he was moved to Paris, where his father rented excellent accommodations and personally nursed him. But Martin II died in Paris in the summer of 1855 after a lingering illness that the best physicians in Europe could not cure. The saddened father returned to Kinderhook with the body of his son. He never returned to Europe.

Several observers have felt that the role of a farmer and the rural setting at Lindenwald which Van Buren chose for himself did not quite fit his life-style. His habit of wearing the finest clothes of the latest design, the expensive, ornate, well-kept carriages and groomed horses, the elegant furniture that adorned Lindenwald, as well as the great social events staged there, somehow seemed out of place in the country atmosphere. Even some of his important guests were nonplussed at how to use the finger bowls at formal Lindenwald dinners.[5] Gradually Van Buren seemed to grow to like the soil and actually took an interest in the farm work, riding his horse about the estate at a much faster pace than the family felt he should.

Van Buren's churchgoing tells something of his eccentricity. Being of Dutch descent it was natural that he attend the Dutch Reformed Church of his community. Weather permitting, he arrived in his fine English coach. When snow covered the ground, he used his sleigh drawn by a steed that had loudly jangling brass bells attached to the harness. As buffalo robes were in vogue at the time, he used one to protect himself from the elements. If the weather was very cold, he would bring a little foot stove into the church to keep out the chill. By this time in his life, his famous head of blond hair was becoming only a memory, so he would place one of his large bearskin gloves on his head to further guard against the cold. Even into advancing age his voice could be heard above the others when the congregation sang hymns.

As the slave question dominated all other issues, and South Carolina led the Southern states into secession, Van Buren was most concerned about the survival of the nation. However, he did nothing to try to influence the course of events. He did not support Lincoln in the election of 1860. But as Lincoln began to deal with the nation's problems, Van Buren took courage, feeling that a strong leader was at the helm. As the Union began to break up, there were five living ex-presidents: Van Buren, Tyler, Fillmore, Pierce, and Buchanan. (At no other time before or since have there been as many.) Pierce wrote to Van Buren suggesting that he, as the senior former president, should call the five of them together to see if anything could be done to save the Union.[6] Certainly such a meeting was unlikely to bring positive results. Tyler was a Southern states-rights man who soon became a part of the Confederate government. Fillmore was indecisive, and Buchanan doubted the legality of any effort to keep the South from seceding. Van Buren, no doubt the most able of these five living ex-presidents, saw such an effort as utterly futile, for he summarily turned down the suggestion, although he loved the Union and hated slavery.

Aside from a few attacks of asthma, Van Buren did not have any chronic debilitating physical problem with which to contend. As a result, he did not have a long, lingering illness leading to his death. One author says his asthma developed into "a malignant catarrh" (whatever that might be). He did travel to New York City for medical treatment in the early spring of 1862, but his life did not seem threatened. During this time in New York he often visited with friends.[7] He returned home and resumed his extensive correspondence. However, in June he was for the most part confined to his bedroom, sitting much of the time in an easy chair covered by a blanket. He gradually became weaker, and in the middle of July his son, Smith Thompson, wrote to the other two sons saying that they should return to Lindenwald to see their father. Shortly after they arrived he lapsed into unconsciousness and died on Thursday morning, July 24, 1862, at the age of 79.

His body lay in state for three days in the large banquet hall at Lindenwald, then fellow townsmen placed the coffin on their shoulders and carried it to the hearse. Many notables were in the 81-carriage procession which drove to the little church where he had worshiped for so long. Martin Van Buren was buried in the town cemetery at Kinderhook.

The nation was in the midst of the Civil War, so not much public attention was given his passing. Some of the large city newspapers did not even carry a notice of his death. Though in many ways he was an able administrator, he never captured the imagination of the people. Too often he was regarded as the political manipulator, as the nicknames "Little Magician" and the "Fox" might suggest.

To this day he is not well remembered. In four states there are counties that bear his name, as well as a few small towns throughout the country. Occasionally the name of a street recalls the former president. Even in his home state, New York, Governor Charles Evans Hughes in 1910 vetoed a bill to build a monument to his memory. In 1934, when some presidential signatures were placed for auction, his brought $2.25, $1.75 less than Polk's.[8]

The 9th, William Henry Harrison

President for a Month, 1841

When President William Henry Harrison (1773–1841) died one month after his inauguration, and Vice President John Tyler took office, the United States had its third president within a month—the only time in history that so rapid a turnover occurred.[1]

Harrison was nominated as the Whig presidential candidate in 1840. At the time he was living at North Bend, Ohio (near Cincinnati), in a simple but large western-type frame house, and serving as the county clerk in the local courthouse. The Whigs turned a well-to-do old general in his dotage into a viable presidential candidate by ignoring the fact that he had come from a wealthy old-line plantation family of the tidewater region of Virginia, and portraying him as a simple, western frontiersman, with little culture, sitting in front of his cabin drinking hard cider.

In contrast, Democratic incumbent Martin Van Buren was represented as a smug, snobbish aristocrat, eating off gold-trimmed plates and drinking champagne. By these methods, the inventive and energetic Whigs won an election that normally they would have lost. "An agreeable and un-distinguished man (certainly no great shakes as a general) and a political nonentity"[2] was elected president of the United States. The election was a landslide for Harrison in the electoral college—234 to 60. But the popular vote was close—1,275,016 to 1,129,102.

Two outstanding Whigs, Henry Clay and Daniel Webster, were available as presidential candidates in 1840, but "it was clear that stolid, innocuous old Harrison was the preferred candidate of the party faithful."[3] At almost 67 he certainly was not unknown. In his life he had been a famed "Indian fighter" (raised to the rank of general), territorial governor of Indiana, a member of the House of Representatives, and a successful farmer and frontier land developer.

Perhaps the most interesting aspect of Harrison's presidency, besides the brevity of his term, was the type of campaign that put him in the White House for a month. In the previous chapter the campaign which took

Martin Van Buren out of office was briefly discussed, but merits further comment. This was an entirely new kind of campaigning. The strategies which put Harrison in the White House and made John Tyler of Virginia vice president can be found in many political activities of modern times.

The new type of campaigning used by the Whigs reached the masses and involved a large segment of the population in the election, virtually turning politics into an entertainment, a game which everybody could play.[4] One of the distinctive features of this campaign was the use by the Whigs of the slogan, "Tippecanoe and Tyler Too." (Harrison had won a battle called Tippecanoe against the Indians, and John Tyler was their vice presidential nominee.) The slogan was so natural, so euphonious, and probably the most effective slogan ever used in an election.

Songs with political words were sung, such as,

> Make way for old Tip, turn out, turn out!
> Make way for old Tip, turn out, turn out!
> 'Tis the people's decree,
> Their choice he shall be,
> So Martin Van Buren turn out, turn out!
> So Martin Van Buren turn out, turn out![5]

Bands often played as the people sang, and glee clubs were organized to perform the songs at the Whig rallies.

The Democrats made fun of Harrison, saying he belonged in a log cabin. The Whigs seized the idea by using the log cabin as their emblem, and held rallies in some very large log cabins built for the occasion. At times thousands of people marched in parades and processions, and at night carried lighted torches. Loyal supporters displayed banners and created floats — often a log cabin on wheels — for the processions. Hard cider was the popular drink at the Whig rallies. The party faithful gleefully chanted, "Van, Van is a used up man."

Two current slang expressions were said to have originated in this campaign. A large paper ball ten feet in diameter with slogans printed on it was rolled down the street. The expression "keep the ball rolling" was used to exhort the faithful to a renewed effort in the campaign.[6] Also, among the many theories about the derivation of "O.K." is one that said its origin was in this election. "Van Buren was called 'Old Kinderhook' after the place he lived, and often by just the first letters of these two words."[7]

On January 26, 1841, Harrison started for Washington from his home in North Bend, to assume the presidency. He traveled by river boat to Pittsburgh, then south down the Monongahela River to Brownsville. From there he went by carriage to Baltimore, where he arrived on February 9, his sixty-eighth birthday. He traveled by train to Washington, the first president-elect to enter the capital by train. All along the trip he was met by large, enthusiastic crowds. Every town wanted to hold a reception for him. He deported himself as a down-to-earth man of the people, for no doubt it was the way he felt.

Harrison made a prophetic statement as he left Cincinnati: "Gentlemen and fellow citizens . . . perhaps this may be the last time I may have the pleasure of speaking to you on earth or seeing you. I will bid you farewell, if forever, fare thee well."[8] Mrs. Harrison, who had been married to the general for 45 years, and had been described by one Whig writer during the campaign as "one of the handsomest old women I've ever seen,"[9] was too ill at the time to go with her husband to Washington. She hoped to join him when the weather moderated. She never saw him again.

From the moment of his election he had no peace, for immediately he was hounded by office-seekers who dogged his steps and crowded upon him at every opportunity. Each mail brought letters from prominent people making pressing suggestions as to whom he should select for his cabinet. Finally he named Daniel Webster as his chief cabinet officer, secretary of state. Henry Clay—he and Webster were the most notable leaders of the Whigs—was very upset by this appointment and returned to his home in Kentucky shortly after the inauguration, mistakenly feeling his days of party leadership were over.

Great crowds came to the capital for the inauguration. Many of these visitors had no place to stay. Philip Hone, a wealthy New Yorker and a staunch Whig, left a most interesting diary of these times. He noted, "Every hole and corner is filled."[10] Fifty thousand crowded around the White House for the inaugural ceremony. The *Niles Register* of Baltimore commented about the inauguration, "The ladies, too, (God bless them) the ladies have shared fully in the excitement of the hour: their eyes glancing, their cheeks glowing, and their tongues (for ladies have such things) were in rapid and harmonious motion."[11]

Harrison had written an excessively long, flowery, and somewhat bombastic speech for the occasion. With reluctance he showed it to Webster, who shortened it and cut out much of the reference to Roman history. Webster commented, "I have killed seventeen Roman proconsuls as dead as smelts, every one of the them."[12] As it was, the speech, which very few could hear, took an hour and forty minutes. Harrison delivered it on a very cold day without wearing a coat or hat. He rode his own horse in the parade, still with no coat, during the three hours of the ceremonies and parade. Many feel that this ultimately led to his death, which came one month to the day after he was inaugurated. Another of his problems was more private. He complained that he had not had time to perform "the necessary functions of nature."[13] Some have suggested that this problem contributed to his fatal illness.

After the parade the president felt ill and rested for awhile, then got up to greet the guests at the White House. So sore was his hand and arm from shaking hands with the hundreds of people he greeted, that he soon merely nodded and said hello. That evening he attended three of the large inaugural balls held in his honor. When he retired for the night he felt considerable physical distress, but was up early and began the task of giving or refusing government jobs to the vast number of petitioners.

During the month that he was in office the president was very busy, but he did not seem unduly pressed or under a strain. Though his wife was not with him, there were several other family members at the White House. His widowed daughter-in-law, Mrs. William Henry Harrison, Jr., acted as the hostess of the executive mansion.

Harrison's lifetime habit of church attendance continued in Washington at St. John's Episcopal Church on H Street at 16th, where he occupied pew number 45. He had intended to become a communicant member of St. John's.

He began each day with an early morning walk which he usually took alone. If he met someone he knew he would frequently bring them home to have breakfast with him. Often in the morning he would go to the local markets and buy food needed at the White House.

While he was out on one of his walks, a rain shower overtook him and he became chilled. Thinking it amounted to little, he delayed getting into dry clothing. He developed a headache, then chills and a fever. On Saturday, March 27, a physician was called. At first the illness seemed like just another bad cold, but Harrison did not respond to treatment. In that day and time, bleeding was often used in such cases, but because of his age it was not prescribed. Cupping (applying a heated cup to areas of the body to "draw out the poisons") was used along with other old-time treatments. The fever increased, symptoms of pneumonia began to appear, and there was intestinal distress. The disease was diagnosed as "bilious pleurisy."

On Saturday morning, April 3, he asked to have the Bible read to him and a prayer offered. At that time he expressed the opinion that he was sicker than the physician admitted. Four other consulting physicians were called in to assist the attending doctor, Theodore May. By late afternoon the doctors told the family that there was little hope for the president's recovery. A minister came to give him spiritual comfort. By ten o'clock that evening he had lapsed into unconsciousness. The last statement he made was recorded by one of the attending physicians, Dr. N.W. Worthington, "Sir, I wish you to understand the true principles of the government. I wish them carried out. I ask nothing more."[14] Some thought this message was meant for Vice President John Tyler, but there was nothing specifically said to indicate what the dying president meant by these words. At eleven o'clock Harrison roused, coughed, then sank into unconsciousness again. He died at 12:30 Sunday morning, April 4, 1841.

Since Vice President Tyler was out of the city, Daniel Webster, as the ranking member of the cabinet, made the announcement of Harrison's death. "An all-wise Providence having suddenly removed from this life William Henry Harrison, late president of the United States, we have thought ... to make this announcement."[15] Harrison's daughter-in-law Jane Findlay, Irwin Harrison, several nieces and nephews, a grand-nephew, and a grandson were with him when he died. Diarist Philip Hone noted that the president "expired, exhausted by the enthusiasm of his ad-mirers, with a 'violent diarrehoea' ... related to the fact that his time was so much taken ... that he could not get to the bathroom regularly."[16]

Signs of mourning appeared all over the city of Washington. Newspapers had wide black columns on the front pages, and during the funeral most of the city's businesses closed. The body lay in state at the White House for the public to view. The funeral was conducted on April 7. Military companies paraded and cannons boomed. The president's horse walked in the procession, saddled but riderless. The elite of Washington gathered for the simple Episcopalian service for the dead. Approximately 40 clergymen were in attendance, as well as 24 pallbearers wearing white sashes. The new president, John Tyler, the cabinet, the Supreme Court, and leaders of Con-gress were present. The final resting place was in his home community, North Bend, Ohio, at what today is called Memorial State Park.

There was some doubt about what title John Tyler, the vice president, should take. He solved the problem by proclaiming himself president. (The Constitution does not specifically say what a vice president, becoming the chief executive upon the death of a president, shall be called.)

After Harrison died, the Congress voted to give his wife Anna $25,000, the amount of the president's salary for one year. Harrison had large land holdings in the West, but like the majority of these landowners, his cash flow was limited. The money from Congress was of considerable help to the president's widow. She survived him by almost 23 years and lived to be more than 88. She is buried beside him at North Bend.

Harrison's will was probably the crudest of all those written by a presi-dent. Today such a will would have no standing in court, but because it was written by a president, and the bequests were so predictable, it was pro-bated. The will was not witnessed and lacked any date. Except for the first line, there was no signature, and there was no residuary clause. Not all his property was included in the will, only specific pieces of real estate. In fact, the will showed a great lack of knowledge of what he owned, and much of the real estate was not well described. But most of his assets went to his widow as he had designated.[17]

The president who had been elected in the most spectacular political campaign to date, died in office with little to show that he had ever been there.

The 10th, John Tyler

Patriot or Traitor? 1845–1862

How could an ex-president actively wage war against the United States? As the Southern states began to secede from the Union in 1860, John Tyler (1790–1862) became a leader in the secessionist movement in Virginia. Fifteen years after he had left the presidency, he was considered a traitor by the Union, but an outstanding patriot by the Confederacy. He served in the Provisional Congress of the Confederate States, and was then elected to the Congress of the Confederacy from the state of Virginia, one of the last to leave the Union.

When President William Henry Harrison died just one month after taking office, Tyler became president (1841–1845), the first vice president to assume the presidency upon the death of an incumbent. From the beginning he disagreed in important policy matters with the leaders of his own party, the Whigs. Their differences became so fundamental and their rhetoric so vituperative that he was read out of the Whig party while he was still president. At heart Tyler was a states-rights Democrat, but he joined the Whig party because of his extreme dislike for Andrew Jackson, the founder of the modern Democratic party. As a result, Tyler had no viable opportunity for election to the presidency in his own right.

The most important personal incidents in Tyler's administration were the death of his first wife, Letitia Christian, on September 10, 1842, and his subsequent marriage to Julia Gardiner on June 26, 1844. Letitia had been an invalid during the days she lived in the White House. Tyler's daughter Elizabeth, and his daughter-in-law Priscilla Tyler, wife of his son Robert, acted as hostesses for the White House. Mrs. Tyler had never recovered from a stroke she suffered just before her husband became president. After her death her body was taken to Cedar Grove, Virginia, for burial.

During the winter of 1843–44, the president began courting Julia Gardiner, a young woman from New York, who was the daughter of the Honorable David Gardiner of Staten Island. The president proposed marriage, but she was reluctant to give her assent. For whatever reason, she was

71

more favorably disposed to marrying the president after the death of her father. Some say that she transferred her affection from her father to her older suitor. They were married in New York in a quiet ceremony performed by the Right Reverend Bishop Onderdonk.[1] At the time of their marriage Tyler was 54 and Julia, 24. She came from a family of considerable wealth and possessed much personal charm, beauty, and poise. The only objection that Julia's mother raised to the marriage was to question whether the president could give Julia the fine life-style to which she had become accustomed. The couple took a month-long honeymoon in his summer cottage at Hampton, near Port Comfort, Virginia. During the rest of the Tylers' stay in the White House, she served very commendably as the first lady.

The Tylers, so far as anyone can gather, were very happy together. She usually referred to her husband as "the president," even when writing to her family. They had their first child during the summer after leaving the White House, a boy named for her father, David Gardiner. Six other children were born to the Tylers, the last in the summer of 1860. Altogether Tyler had 15 children.[2] (Lyon Tyler, son of John and Julia, became president of William and Mary College and at age 72 married a woman of 32. They had two sons, one born in 1925, the other in 1928.[3]) Many of John Tyler's letters have been preserved,[4] and show his great love and concern for his large family.

The Tylers left Washington on March 5, 1845, for their new plantation home in Charles City County, Virginia, first traveling on a river steamboat which took them to Richmond. After a short stay, another river steamer took them to their home where they went ashore in a small rowboat. Tyler chose Sherwood Forest as the name for his estate because it was located in a beautiful wooded area near the James River. (Westover, Berkley, and Shirley were famous plantations near Sherwood Forest.)

For the next 15 years the Tylers lived the lives of Virginia planters. Because he resided in a strong Whig community, it took him a few years to make peace with some of his neighbors who were still angry at him over his break with the Whigs while he was president. They attempted to humiliate him by electing him "Overseer of the Roads." He turned the tables by forcing them to give a portion of their time to do road work themselves, as the law required. He would call them at the most inconvenient times and require a full day's work. Soon they asked him to resign his elected position. He refused. After a few years he won their respect and admiration and soon was welcomed into their social life.

Tyler was a progressive planter, not relying solely on cotton as so many in Virginia did, but growing wheat and corn as well. There were 70 slaves on the plantation. Often he engaged in experiments seeking to increase the yield of the crops. These experiments ranged from using fertilizer to trying new plowing techniques. He did not become wealthy, but made an adequate living. In examining his correspondence it is soon clear that though there were some years when his cash flow was rather low, he still lived the comfortable life of a Southern planter. Western lands were an attractive area for speculation in his day, and Tyler invested in them to good advantage. After his death these investments were very helpful to Julia and their children.

In general, Tyler remained healthy, but there were times when he was ill, as his correspondence shows. On occasion he suffered from digestive discomfort and from colds that often forced him to bed. Four of the eight children born to his first wife died before he did. But all of the children born to Julia outlived him.

Tyler was frequently called upon to comment on matters of government and politics. State and national political leaders often visited him. He was frequently in demand as a speaker. Much of his time was devoted to the affairs of William and Mary College in Williamsburg, Virginia, where he held official positions in the administration of the college. Today he would be recognized as one of its regents.

The family led a very active social life. It was the custom of the planter class to visit back and forth frequently. Julia made an excellent hostess, and people seemed always anxious to meet the former president. The family made many trips to Julia's home on Staten Island. Juliana Gardiner, Julia's mother, came south to Sherwood Forest almost every year. Julia's sister, Margaret, was frequently in the Tyler home. The Tylers' summer home near Hampton was named Villa Margaret in her honor. The family spent more than $10,000 on this summer home, making it one of the better summer places of the area. Julia's activities were many and varied. One of her more visible efforts attracted considerable local attention when she wrote an answer to the charges made against slavery by Harriet Beecher Stowe in *Uncle Tom's Cabin*.

Tyler's political activity in his last years is a story of disillusionment, frustration, and lost hopes. Until 1856, his participation in political affairs after leaving the White House was minimal, limited to personal observations and a few speeches. Meanwhile he had left the Whig party and had become a states-rights Democrat. But when the election of 1856 came, he was so incensed at what he considered the encroachment upon the states by the federal government, that he became very much involved in the political affairs of Virginia. His efforts were not so much in running for office as in defending his own state in its struggle to preserve what were considered Virginia's constitutional rights.

All too often the student of American history gives scant attention to the constitutional and philosophical issues that preceded the secession of the Southern states in 1860 and 1861. One need not say that the states were correct; nothing so invalidates a political theory as its failure in practice. Furthermore, slavery was an example of the grossest type of inhumanity. Even so, such political theoreticians as John C. Calhoun of South Carolina and Henry W. Wise of Virginia too often have been written off as inconsequential and frivolous. Their arguments and theory on the rights of states are, to the contrary, cogent and powerful once the basic assumption that the federal union was a compact of states is accepted. To understand the mind of the South, these arguments must be considered.

Most scholars are familiar with Calhoun's *Exposition and Protest,* but few have read Henry A. Wise's *Seven Decades of the Union* (which included a memoir of John Tyler), published in 1881. Wise was a congressman from Virginia, and governor of that state. (He often fought bitterly with John Quincy Adams in the House of Representatives.) The argument of his book, and of itself, is rather compelling. Its logic and development express the very point of view that John Tyler gave his life to defend. Yet it would appear to be nearly a forgotten work.

When John C. Fremont, the nominee of the new Republican party in 1856, stated his views in opposition to slavery, Tyler became very concerned, for he maintained that the federal government was the agent of the states, and that the states had a right to nullify their act of joining the Union if and when they chose. He declared that 50,000 Virginians would be under arms if Fremont were elected.[5] In August of 1856, Tyler spoke openly of the breakup of the Union.[6] The issue of states' rights, as expressed in the slave question, continued to be the most discussed issue of the day. The election of Abraham Lincoln as president in 1860 was the final disillusionment to John Tyler. He was ready to lead Virginia out of the Union if no satisfactory understanding could be reached with the federal government.

However, even in secession, Tyler desperately wanted to keep peace. As a result, Virginia called what they termed a Peace Convention to meet in Washington in February 1861. Their objective was to work out a solution that would preserve the rights of the South and still avoid war. Tyler talked personally with President Buchanan and President-elect Abraham Lincoln. No common ground was found. Even as they spoke, Tyler did not believe that Lincoln realized how close the South was to secession. Tyler had hoped that a way could be found to save the Union and preserve Virginia's rights as a sovereign state.

Early in 1861 Virginia called a state convention to consider secession from the Union. On March 17, 1861, the convention drew up the Declaration of Secession, with Tyler as one of its leading advocates.[7] He was the Nestor of the group, an ex-president of the United States who now led his native state in action. He felt that Virginia was driven out of the Union. The Declaration of Secession was ratified by the people on May 23, 1861. The sovereign state of Virginia was no longer a part of the United States.

It was now time for the citizens of Virginia to consider how to defend themselves. They joined the Confederate States of America, which had been organized in February 1861. Tyler was chosen to be a member of the Provisional Congress of the Confederacy. When the state came to elect its representatives to the permanent congress, Tyler ran for the Confederate Congress. He had two opponents for the office, but was elected by an overwhelming majority. However, he did not live to join that body.

These were most difficult times for the whole Tyler family. As the war clouds gathered, Julia's mother was most anxious for Julia and the children to come to Staten Island to be with her where she felt they would be safe if war came. In the end, several of the children did go to live with their grandmother, but they had to run the federal blockade and then go to New York by way of the West Indies. John Tyler, Jr., who was living and working in Philadelphia when the war broke out, was set upon by a mob and was most fortunate to escape with his life.

The story of John Tyler's last hours is recalled by his wife in an account written shortly after his death, and is included in the printed record of his letters.[8] Her husband had gone to Richmond to attend to his duties in the new government. Julia had intended to go to Richmond sometime in mid-January, 1861. However, she had a dream on January 9 in which she saw her husband suddenly taken ill just as he was getting up for the day. The dream so disturbed her that she immediately left Sherwood Forest to be with her husband. She arrived in Richmond with their new baby and nurse Fanny only to find that he was in the best of health. He was glad to see her but did not take her fears too seriously. The next day, Julia recalls, their rooms in the Exchange Hotel were filled with visitors and government officials. Several remarked how well Tyler looked. In the night, Julia suffered from a headache. Tyler got some medicine for her and she soon felt better.

In the morning, Sunday, January 12, when Julia awoke she found her husband dressed and standing by the fireplace. When he saw she was awake, he told her he was having a chill. He wanted some hot tea, so he went down to the dining room. As he started to get his tea he stumbled and fell. In a few moments he was unconscious. After being placed on a couch for a few minutes, he regained consciousness and was helped up to their rooms. He then made a strange comment, "Her dream is a true one, and I leave my wife and my children to God and my country."[9]

A doctor was called and gave a diagnosis of a bilious attack with bronchitis. The doctor thought he would soon recover. Tyler still received a few visitors. On Thursday his condition did not improve and he was ordered to take a complete bed rest. He passed a fairly comfortable day on Friday. However, after he had slept about an hour that evening, he awoke with a feeling of suffocation, so Dr. Brown, who was in the hotel, was called. He prescribed mustard plasters and brandy. Dr. Peachy, who had treated him earlier, came into the room. Tyler said, "Doctor, I am going." The doctor replied, "I hope not, sir." The former president added, "Perhaps it is best."[10] Those were his last words. He died a little past midnight on Saturday morning, January 18, 1861.

In her written account Julia said, "The bedstead on which he died was exactly like the one I saw him upon in my dream, and unlike any of my own."[11] On hearing the news of his death, the Confederate Congress adjourned for the day and devoted their session on Monday to eulogies of Tyler.

The body lay in state in Richmond over the weekend. The Virginia House of Delegates paid him high tributes. On Tuesday the funeral service was conducted at St. Paul's church. The great and near-great of the city accompanied the body as it was laid to rest in Hollywood Cemetery, not far from the grave of President James Monroe.*

It is difficult to classify John Tyler as a traitor even though he did help Virginia, his own state, in its preparation to fight on the side of the Confederacy against the Union. Tyler believed, as many did, that the United States was a compact of sovereign states, none of which could be forced to act against its will. He honestly believed that the Union was violating the rights of his sovereign state of Virginia, and therefore must be opposed, by force if necessary.

The writer sees in Tyler an honorable man of deep religious faith whose life's decisions were made with the feeling that he would be judged by a just God, but a man misguided in the cause he chose to support in the closing days of his life. He loved his country, but he loved his native state more.

*Monroe's body had been moved from its first burial place in New York City to Richmond two years earlier. The two memorials, standing close together, make an impressive sight.

The 11th, James K. Polk

Exhumed for Posterity, 1849

The way in which the eleventh president (1845–1849) of the United States died and came to be buried in Nashville, Tennessee, is an intriguing story. At 49 years of age, James Polk (1795–1849) was the youngest man thus far to be elected to the nation's highest office. When he died, barely three months after leaving the White House, he was buried according to the instructions in his will. However, the extraordinary wording of this document set in motion a series of events that ultimately resulted in the exhumation of the body and burial on the grounds of the state capitol.[1]

A few months before the Polks left Washington they purchased for their retirement a grand home in Nashville built by Felix Grundy in the 1820s. The dwelling needed some remodeling to meet their needs, so the builders began their work, promising to have the job finished before the Polks returned to Nashville in March of 1849. Actually the work was not completed until mid-May of that year. The couple enjoyed their new home only a few days before the former president became gravely ill. When he died on June 15, 1849, he was 53 and his wife, 46. At first Polk's body was buried in the city cemetery, but was soon moved to a vault that had been built on their property on Vine Street, where it lay for almost 50 years.

Fortunately her husband left Mrs. Polk with enough financial resources to live comfortably until her death in 1891 at 87. At the time of her death she was still living in the same house on Vine Street in Nashville. The couple had no children.

According to the will of the former president, the house was to be given to the state of Tennessee and to be maintained by the state for the use of the nearest blood relative of the Polk family. In many respects it is one of the strangest wills of any drawn up by a president. For example, in several places he used the word "forever" in describing how long the house should be in the Polk family.[2] In this case, forever was less than three years after the death of his wife.

After the death of Mrs. Polk in 1891, much litigation was necessary to finally dispose of the property. As a group, the heirs (there was no direct heir) asked the state of Tennessee to pay them $22,500 for the house so it could be used as a memorial.[3] The state refused to pay the $22,500 or commit itself for the long-term upkeep. Eventually the courts decided that the house and its furnishings should be sold at auction and the inheritance divided among 40 Polk relatives. A man from Philadelphia bought the property, immediately razed the mansion and built apartments on the site, calling them Polk Flats. This left the graves of both the Polks located on the grounds of the Vine Street house on a very small plot of land in the midst of encroaching housing. As a result, the state legislature of Tennessee declared the bodies of the Polks wards of the state. In 1893 the bodies of the Polks were exhumed and, in a long solemn ceremony, were moved and reburied on the grounds of the capitol, making Polk the only president to be buried on the grounds of a state capitol, and the only one to have three burial sites.

Polk's last days tell the story of the physical and emotional toll the presidency often takes on the man who occupies that office. They tell of an interminable voyage home only to find the house unfinished. Well over a year before he left the White House his declining state of health was clearly seen by those close to him and was no doubt a major factor in his decision not to seek a second term in 1848.

Few presidents have had so many major problems to face or have had such an array of villainous charges brought against them personally and politically as Polk did. His administration witnessed a major foreign war, and an increase in the size of the nation by nearly 50 percent with all the attending problems that such a sudden territorial growth entails. Each time the question of slavery was raised, the whole nation came face-to-face with the morality of slavery in a way it had never experienced before. The South tried to defend slavery as a justifiable economic necessity, while the North saw it in all its ugliness. This question would be the paramount issue until it was finally resolved by the Civil War. When the usual economic, social, and political considerations that always accompany a period of rapid growth in a dynamic and divergent society are added to the slavery question, it is easy to see why the period of this administration was immensely complicated.

During the last year of his term of office, Polk's physical appearance began to show the troubles that plagued his administration. "Portraits painted of him during his last year in office showed a shocking change in his physical appearance . . . his face was thin, deeply crossed with lines of worry, and his eyes tired . . . he had aged markedly and almost suddenly."[4]

An examination of Polk's diary shows that he felt extraordinarily weary in the last months of his stay in the White House. Toward the end of his term it was the most often mentioned item in his journal. At the last grand levee held during his administration, he did his best to greet the many guests who came to bid him farewell. At times he actually leaned against the furniture in order to continue standing. "Remained on my feet continuously for several hours and was exceedingly fatigued,"[5] Polk recorded in his diary. On Saturday, March 3, 1849, he wrote, "I was exceedingly fatigued and exhausted."[6] These comments came from a man only 53 years old, at a time when almost all the politicians of any age took such duties and hours as a matter of course.

In the last summer of his term in office he did take a short vacation at Bedford Springs, Pennsylvania. It was hoped that the warm mineral waters and the clear, cool mountain air would improve his health. Besides William Day, his own valet, a naval doctor accompanied him to Bedford Springs. This trip was the first time in over a year that the president had been more than three miles from the White House and its pressing duties.

Fortunately he did get some rest and relaxation. He greatly enjoyed escaping the heat and humidity of a Washington summer and found the weather cool enough to sleep under a blanket. He enjoyed the morning hikes in the mountain air and commented that the "rest, mountain air and water has invigorated and improved me."[7] But when he got back to Washington he found so many matters requiring his attention that he was soon fatigued again.

President Polk had worked hard to effect a solution to the slave problem, but he did not realize that at its base slavery was a moral issue and could not be solved by compromise or political action. Certainly he saw the gravity of the ideological controversy and realized that the approaching conflict could in fact threaten the nation itself. The disquiet of mind and the constant turmoil over slavery gave him troubled days and sleepless nights. When he saw that General Zachary Taylor was to succeed him, he was more apprehensive than ever, at times wondering how the republic could survive the discord he saw approaching. He confided to his diary that "General Taylor is, I have no doubt, a well-meaning old man. He is, however, uneducated and exceedingly ignorant of public affairs, and, I should judge, of very ordinary capacity."[8] He regarded Taylor's inaugural address as rather poor and said, "He read it in a very low voice and very badly as to his pronunciation and manner."[9]

President-elect Taylor arrived in Washington somewhat before his inaugural day but had made no effort to contact President Polk. Some of the president's cabinet felt that Polk should call on Taylor, but the president made it clear that he would under no circumstance call on Taylor before the General had made a courtesy call on him. In all probability Taylor did not realize that protocol required him to make a visit to the White House. Taylor's son-in-law, Senator Jefferson Davis of Mississippi, arranged for him to call at the White House, and accompanied Taylor as he visited President Polk. The meeting was cordial, and the president invited the president-elect to a White House state dinner as the guest of honor. The leading members of both parties, as well as much of official Washington, were present at the affair.

March the fourth was the customary day for the new president to take the oath of office, but since the fourth came on Sunday in 1849, the Polks moved out of the White House on Saturday, the third. The president then rented private rooms until he left Washington to begin his journey home to Nashville. However, Polk stayed in the Capitol during the night of the third so that he could act upon any legislation that Congress might pass at the last moment. Several pieces of important legislation were pending at the time. He remained at the Capitol until four in the morning when he went to Willard's Hotel and retired, for he was "exceedingly fatigued and exhausted."[10] But at six in the morning, two bills passed by Congress were brought to him and he signed them. The Congress then adjourned. Although he had very little sleep, he and his family attended the First Presbyterian Church on Sunday morning and were warmly greeted by a multitude of well-wishers. His diary recorded the familiar words, "I was much fatigued by the very severe duties of the past weeks."[11] However, he did express his joy at being out of office. He records, "I feel exceedingly relieved that I am now free from all public cares."[12]

The next day Polk went with General Taylor to the Capitol and witnessed the General's inauguration. After the ceremony the new president and the ex-president rode together from the Capitol to Polk's quarters, where he took his leave of the newly inaugurated president. During the afternoon hundreds of people came to bid Polk farewell. He continued to receive them until ten o'clock that night when he and his family boarded the boat that took them from Washington. He was never to see the city again. The Polk family's journey home to Nashville was a circuitous and seemingly endless route through the South made by coastal steamer, trains, and river steamboats.

The next morning Polk's journey, now by rail, took him to Richmond, Virginia. He had not intended to stop there, but the city had arranged an elaborate reception and turned out in mass to see him. Because the state legislature officially invited him to visit them in their chambers, there was no way he could refuse to accept their hospitality. However, he resumed his journey the same day (Tuesday, March 6, 1849), reaching nearby Petersburg at dusk. By then he was "much fatigued and suffering from a severe cold,"[13] but he felt obligated to attend an elaborate dinner and make a talk. The journey was continued that same evening, but the party did not reach Weldon, North Carolina, until well into the night. Again, a reception was given the out-going president. At about ten the next morning,

March 7, his train arrived at Wilmington, North Carolina, where he spent the day greeting people and attending a variety of receptions.

Early on the morning of Friday, March 9, his steamboat reached Charleston, South Carolina, and the whole exhausting schedule was repeated. Here he found the weather hot and oppressively humid, in sharp contrast to the snow he had just left four days earlier in Washington. By night he had "great fatigue."[14] Much the same sort of schedule was continued as he stopped at Savannah and Macon in Georgia, and at Montgomery, Alabama. On Friday, March 16, his diary recorded, "I retired at a late hour, greatly fatigued and quite unwell."[15] Though ill, he continued his journey on a river steamer to Mobile, arriving at ten the next morning. He called his reception at Mobile "most imposing and magnificent."[16] His party continued the journey and reached New Orleans on Wednesday, March 21. Reluctantly he stayed in the city because of a rumor which had spread concerning an outbreak of cholera. In his diary Polk tells of the elaborate preparations for his reception, of the long, hot, exhausting rides about the countryside, and of his illness.[17] Polk tried to leave New Orleans the night of Wednesday, March 21, but the city fathers prevailed on him to stay although he told them he was not feeling well.

He left New Orleans on Friday, March 23, as he continued on the way to Baton Rouge. On this trip a man on board the steamship died of cholera. The boat put the body ashore and it was immediately buried. The boat next stopped briefly at Vicksburg. On Tuesday morning, March 27, the former president arrived at Memphis, Tennessee. Two of his nephews met him. He tried to avoid another reception, pleading ill health, but he was pressured into staying for a dinner. The next day he was very ill and stayed in his stateroom all day. There was no physician on board so he was given no medical attention. That evening when the boat stopped at Paducah, Kentucky, a physician attended the former president. The doctor said that Polk did not have cholera and treated his illness with a variety of medicines.

On Thursday Polk went to a comfortable hotel in Smithland, Kentucky, and was attended by two doctors. On Monday, April 2, he felt better and continued his journey. The boat soon docked at Nashville, where the former president was greeted by an immense crowd. Although obviously ill, he spoke a few words to the people that had gathered to honor him. He noted, "When I had done I was exceedingly feeble and exhausted,"[18] but also that "The meeting of my old friends had produced an excitement which contributed to sustain me during the day and to enable me to bear the fatigue."[19]

Because the work on their home was not quite completed, the Polks went to nearby Columbia, Tennessee, to visit his mother. There he was given a hero's welcome. He responded with a short speech and then went to his mother's home. He had not seen her in more than four years. During that time she had aged considerably, so much so that the former president was shocked. But she, although 73 years old, was in much better health than her famous son. The next day he stayed in bed and by Sunday was able to attend church with his mother, but that afternoon a doctor was called.

The next two weeks were spent trying to recuperate. Slowly he did begin to improve. He then returned to Nashville, but the house was not ready so he and his wife Sarah made a short visit to her mother in Murfreesboro. A week later they returned to Nashville to their as-yet-unfinished home. At this point they determined to move into the house even though it was still not ready for them. They occupied just a few rooms. Most of the house contained carpenters and painters who were trying to avoid the boxes of books and personal effects that were scattered about. Polk set about supervising the unpacking and placing of their goods, and directing the carpenters as they finished their work. He even directed the gardeners in getting the grounds in shape, although he could do little himself.

Some of the legal matters involved with acquiring the property had to be attended to, and he purchased a needed pair of horses for their carriages. The confusion about the house upset him, and the little he attempted to do taxed his waning strength. However, he did see a few old friends briefly.

On Saturday, June 2, he and Sarah took a drive together. It was then they decided to leave the city since some fatal cases of cholera were being reported. They planned to leave Nashville for his mother's home in Columbia on Monday. On Sunday Sarah dressed for church, but the former president told his wife he was too ill to go and did not want her to leave him. Dr. Robertson was summoned, and he suggested a consultation of doctors. Sarah was informed that her husband was gravely ill. Polk himself suspected that he would not recover. Against Sarah's protests, he reviewed the financial arrangements he had made for his wife's security. At Polk's request, Dr. Hays, a brother-in-law, was summoned, but neither he nor any of the several other physicians attending the dying former president could offer any help.

To a Presbyterian minister who visited he made the comment that "I am about to die and have not made preparation."[20] His mother brought her minister, a Methodist, to see Polk, for he insisted that he wished to be baptized a Methodist. He requested that the Rev. John McFerrin, who had made a profound impression on him at a camp meeting in 1833, baptize him. McFerrin came and baptized the former president, who made a public confession of faith for the first time, although he had been a faithful attendant at church all his life.

His condition grew steadily worse until very quietly, with no struggle, his breathing stopped at four-forty on the afternoon of June 15, 1849. Some are of the opinion that he had indeed died of cholera, but no such diagnosis was made at the time.

James Polk's body lay in state in the home where he had hoped to live in retirement. The coffin bore a simple silver plaque which was engraved with his name and the date of his birth and death. The Rev. McFerrin preached the funeral sermon quoting the same Scripture he had used at the service that years earlier had so impressed the future president. Throughout the nation many memorial services were held in the memory of James K. Polk, president of the United States.

Polk is but another in the long list of those who have reached the pinnacle of political success but have paid for their achievement with broken bodies or even death.

The 12th, Zachary Taylor

The Civil War Postponed? 1850

When President Zachary Taylor (born 1784) died in the White House on July 9, 1850, just 16 months after taking office, the country was perhaps in the most critical situation it had known since the adoption of the Constitution, for there was real and imminent danger that the problem of slavery would dissolve the Union and destroy the nation.

The abolitionists of the North were demanding an end to slavery, dramatically calling for freedom at the risk of splitting the Union. Slave owners and their sympathizers in the South were determined, no matter what the cost, to defend the plantation system. There was no question in their minds that secession was preferable to seeing the abolitionists prevail. It was in this explosive situation that Taylor became the nation's chief executive.

He was elected largely because of his reputation as a general, an Indian fighter, a rugged frontier soldier, and the hero of the Battle of Buena Vista in the Mexican War. The nickname, "Old Rough and Ready," seemed to fit him quite well. Of the five elected presidents from 1828 to 1848, three were army generals (Andrew Jackson, William Henry Harrison, and Zachary Taylor). The electorate was looking at personalities, not issues. Unfortunately, of the three generals elected during this period, Jackson alone proved to be a capable executive.

"Old Rough and Ready" was honest, intelligent, strong-willed to the point of obstinacy, impulsive, and determined to do his duty as president as he saw it. However, he was politically inexperienced and naive, with few marks of culture or sophistication. He was laughed at by much of official Washington "for his rough ways and combative temperament."[1] Squat and thickset, with bow legs, he looked far better on horseback than before a group or behind a desk. One visitor described his personal encounter with the president in his office like this: "Taylor sat at his desk. He wore a shirt that was formerly white. . . . It was spotted and spattered with tobacco juice. I was in mortal terror, but I soon saw there was no danger. With as unerring an aim as the famous spitter in Dickens' *American Notes,* he never missed the cuspidor, or put my person in jeopardy."[2]

Margaret Smith Taylor was in poor health during her husband's term of office. This may have been the reason why the White House was known around Washington as the "dirty house."[3] The first lady spent much of her time sitting in a room that gave her a view of the city. As she sat she usually used snuff (a form of tobacco kept in the mouth) and at times would expectorate on the fiber rug on which her chair was placed. When the Taylors left the White House, a shovel was used to scrape the floor in an attempt to clean the room for the incoming Fillmore family.

In the summer of 1850, the slave issue threatened to explode. Congress was ready to seek a compromise, but Taylor was determined to face the problem in his own fashion. Although a slave owner (he owned 300 slaves at one time[4]), he was not in favor of extending slavery beyond its present limits. He wanted California admitted as a free state, and New Mexico and Utah to join the Union without reference to slavery. This position brought him in direct conflict with Congress, as well as the rabid slave element of the South and the abolitionists of the North. He was sitting on a powder keg and was not inclined to move.

The California gold rush was at its height when Taylor came to office. It was sheer madness — people arrived by the thousands in an effort to get rich. A stable government was imperative. The Californians met in their own constitutional convention and drew up a document which prohibited slavery. The South was outraged, the abolitionists overjoyed; the nation was forced to face the slave issue as never before.

Robert Toombs, congressman from Georgia speaking for the South, thundered in the House that California, New Mexico and Utah should not be closed to slavery, for this territory was "purchased by the common blood and treasury of the whole people." If the South was to be degraded, he continued, "I am for disunion."[5] In other words, if the president had his way, Toombs was for secession. The situation had become desperate.

It was possible that secession could have become a fact had Taylor remained in office, for he was determined to have his way, and the South began weighing its options. Taylor was "hated and dishonored in the South . . . because he put the interests of the Union above all others."[6] The fact that the Southerners were determined to preserve their rights any way they could, and Taylor was ready to engage in direct and immediate action if necessary, could have started a war in 1850. If ever a situation demanded a Solomon it was then, but a recalcitrant and obdurate old general was in the White House. Taylor felt he could handle the situation even if the South tried to secede, and he was prepared to act if the need arose.[7]

Henry Clay of Kentucky, now 73 years old, came out of retirement and returned to the Senate. He felt he could effect a compromise and save the

Union. Two others, John C. Calhoun and Daniel Webster (perhaps, along with Clay, the greatest trio ever to occupy the Senate together), were also there. Calhoun from South Carolina felt the South was being swallowed up by the North, and doubted the Union could continue. Webster spoke for the North in his determination to preserve the Union. It was the last great effort of all three. Clay was old and ill, Calhoun was dying, and Webster had only two years to live. (These three had dominated the Congress for thirty years, yet none reached the presidency, a prize all assiduously sought.)

Clay presented a series of compromises, proposals which historians have called the Compromise of 1850. Among its provisions, California was admitted as a free state (a *fait accompli*). It also provided for handling of the vexing territorial problems of the Southwest. Further, it proposed the Fugitive Slave Act, which theoretically allowed the Southern plantation owners to recover their slaves who had run away or had been spirited away by the Underground Railroad; also, slave trade was prohibited in the District of Columbia. Both sides gained something and at the same time each gave up something in return. Clay and Webster felt the compromise might well save the Union. Calhoun was sure it could not and vigorously opposed it. Taylor ignored the drama taking place in the Senate.

Although only a month from the grave (he had "consumption"), Calhoun insisted on presenting the case for the South. The speech defended the right of the South to take its slaves into any of the territories as property. The South's rights were being trampled upon, he insisted. Calhoun was too ill to deliver his well-worked-out speech. It was read by a colleague, Senator Mason, as Calhoun lay on a litter in the front of the Senate chamber. The only parts of him that seemed alive were his piercing black eyes as they flashed defiance at his enemies. The next day Webster gave the North's answer in what many feel was the greatest speech ever given in the United States Senate. He spoke as an American and pleaded for the preservation of the Union. During the first moments of Webster's speech, Calhoun was helped to a chair at the rear of the chamber so that he might show the courtesy of hearing Webster's reply to his own speech. Few realized that Calhoun was there, certainly not Webster. As the eloquence flowed on, Webster mentioned how he regretted that Calhoun was not there to hear him. The slumped figure attempted to rise, but could not and fell back into his chair. Again Webster commented how he regretted that illness prevented Calhoun from being in attendance. Calhoun, unable to bear it any longer, declared in a hollow voice that could be heard all through the chamber, "The Senator from South Carolina is in his seat."[8] When Webster realized that his colleague from South Carolina had risked death itself to pay him this courtesy, he stopped abruptly and momentarily lost his trend of thought. He bowed to Calhoun and soon Webster's unrivaled oratory was resumed.

Still, the general who occupied the White House was determined to veto the bill and push ahead with his own plans. But death intervened, and Millard Fillmore of New York succeeded to the presidency. He signed the compromise and it became law. The most radical secessionist activity abated in the South, and the North sincerely hoped that a solution to the question of slavery had been found.

On July 4, 1850, President Taylor went to a celebration at the Washington Monument. He sat in the direct sun without a hat, and dressed too warmly for the day. The heat was overpowering. After the ceremony at the monument he spent some time in walking along the Potomac. When he finally returned to the White House he was very hot and hungry. He ate quantities of raw fruit and consumed a considerable amount of cold drinks, mostly ice water and milk. A physician, Dr. Alexander S. Wotherspoon, was at the president's residence for dinner that evening and admonished him not to overindulge in eating cherries and drinking too much cold fluid. Sometime after dinner the president developed cramps and mild nausea. Simple home remedies were tried, though Taylor resisted taking any medication. Nothing of a serious nature was suspected. He often had relatively mild digestive upsets. However, the president spent a restless and uncomfortable night.

Taylor was a man of 65 who had had a serious illness that nearly took his life just a year before, and whose health was regarded as tenuous. He had sat for two hours in a very hot sun and had eaten a large quantity of cherries and consumed a number of cold drinks. Is there any wonder that he felt badly during the night? It certainly is understandable that those around him were not alarmed at his indisposition.

On Friday, July 5, the general did not feel well, but he continued his presidential duties. Among other things, he signed the final Clayton-Buliver papers, the last act of any importance that he would perform. He was rather uncomfortable Friday night. So the next day, Saturday, July 6, Dr. Wotherspoon was called to the White House to see the ailing chief executive. The physician administered opium, and calomel, a strong purgative. The patient felt better by evening and the doctor left the White House. On Sunday, Dr. Wotherspoon became concerned because his patient had not recovered and called other physicians for a consultation.

Dr. James Hall, a civilian physician in Washington, and Dr. Richard H. Coolidge, a military doctor, were summoned to the presidential mansion. On Monday they were joined by Dr. Robert C. Wood of Baltimore, the president's son-in-law. These four doctors were in attendance until the president died.

Even though the president seemed worse on Sunday morning, no one expressed fear of his demise. A fever developed and the digestive symptoms continued. The patient was restless and uncomfortable. He was thirsty and ate cracked ice continually. However, there was no loss of mental faculties. "In two days I shall be a dead man,"[9] he proclaimed. By evening of that day there was real anxiety as to his condition.

On Monday the president's condition gave little cause for optimism to those in attendance. The diarrhea was checked, but the vomiting continued. By Monday evening it was openly admitted that his condition was desperate. Only Dr. Wood was the least bit hopeful. He felt it was "very like Taylor's attack at Erie."[10] Bulletins informed the public of the president's condition. By midnight it became evident that the president was critically ill.[11]

All sorts of contradictory messages reached the people, and rumors spread rapidly. There was one report that the president had died several hours before death actually came. Others said he was improving. On Tuesday morning Senator Webster told Congress that the president was dying. Vice President Millard Fillmore was sitting in the presiding officer's chair at the time. The Congress immediately adjourned. At five o'clock in the afternoon the gates to the White House were closed. The public was now aware that Taylor was dying.

At seven o'clock the Rev. Dr. Smith Pyne, Episcopal rector of the church Taylor attended, arrived at the White House to give spiritual comfort to the dying president. As yet the doctors had not been able to provide any relief. His pulse rate decreased. The physicians gave the patient forty grains of quinine and more calomel. He was bled and blistered. Nothing helped. One wonders how a seriously ill man could survive all the doctors did to him. At ten o'clock it was announced that the president was not expected to live.

Shortly before he died the president asked how long he had to live. Dr. Wotherspoon replied, "I hope for many years, but ... I fear not many hours." The president answered, "I know it." He continued, "I have endeavored to discharge all my official duties faithfully. I regret nothing, but I am sorry that I am about to leave my friends."[12] Death came a little after ten-thirty the night of Tuesday, July 9.

The Congress continued its feud with the president even while he was on his deathbed. On Saturday, July 6, the House, as an amendment to another bill, had voted to censure the president for nothing more than politically vindictive reasons. The Southern cabal had won a temporary victory. In Monday's final vote, one day before the president died, the censure was overwhelmingly defeated. But the nation still faced a real crisis. Fortunately, the Compromise of 1850 was accepted, and the questions of secession and slavery were delayed for another ten years. The Civil War permanently settled both of these issues.

When Fillmore was informed of the passing of his chief, he responded, "I have no language to express the emotions of my heart ... I am overcome with grief."[13] It is said that the new president "did not sleep a wink" the night of July 9.

The press generally gave glowing reports of the character and accomplishments of Zachary Taylor. However, behind the scenes some very unflattering things were said about him. One person offered the opinion that Taylor's death made Henry Clay very happy. On the other hand, the city of Washington was almost as quiet as a Sunday on the day after the death of Taylor. Memorial services were held all over the country. Bells tolled, guns were fired in salute, people gathered in little groups, and signs of mourning appeared in many homes and businesses. Black-columned newspapers were published in scores of cities across the land. Many Canadians openly expressed their sadness. Horace Greely's *Tribune,* which opposed slavery and thus appreciated Taylor's effort to stop the expansion of slavery, praised the departed president in superlative terms. Some newspapers wondered openly if the Union would survive.

Mrs. Taylor would not allow the body of her husband to be embalmed, so it had to be packed in ice until the funeral, which was not held until Saturday. Three times before the funeral she had the ice taken from the body by the undertaker so that she might view the late president again. The family looked on the face of their husband and father Friday evening for the last time. Mrs. Taylor was so overcome that she could not stand or walk without help. In fact, some of the family were concerned that she might also succumb.

The casket was moved to the East Room of the White House, and the public was admitted to view the body. But the crowd became so unruly that the undertaker had to threaten to call the police to restore order as the public shoved and pushed to get close to the coffin.

At noon on Saturday, July 13, official Washington gathered in the East Room for Taylor's funeral service. Friend and avowed foe alike came to the White House. The new president, Millard Fillmore, and the cabinet were near the bier. Clay and Webster, of course, were present. The Rev. Pyne conducted the service, assisted by a choir and the chaplain of the Senate. Dr. Pyne's discourse dwelt upon Taylor's integrity and conscientiousness.

The Marine honor guard carried the coffin from the East Room to the catafalque, and the funeral procession began its journey toward the Congressional Burying Ground. There was considerable pomp and circumstance for the occasion. The catafalque was drawn by four white horses. The president's favorite horse, "Old Whitey," was led in the procession, his master's boots pointing backwards in the saddle. The Army in dress uniform made up a large part of the procession. General Scott with his yellow feathers in a tall plume was the most spectacular figure. Altogether there were more than 100 carriages, plus those on foot, in a procession which stretched for almost two miles. More than 100,000 people viewed the grand spectacle as it passed. Taylor's branch of the service, the Army, fired the military salute as the body was placed in the vault.

Mrs. Taylor left the White House the evening of the funeral and never returned. She stayed with friends for a few days, then left Washington on July 18 to stay for several months with her daughter Margaret in Baltimore, after which she left for New Orleans, where members of the family cared for her in her home at East Pascagoula until her death.

The family felt that the final resting place for the Taylors should be in Kentucky, for both had considered themselves Kentuckians. Years before, the president had erected a stone wall around the little family cemetery near Louisville where several family members had been buried. In early November of 1850 an immense crowd gathered in Louisville to see the general's body put in its final resting place in the family burial plot. And two years later the body of the late president's wife was placed by that of her husband.

The 13th, Millard Fillmore

The Indefatigable Ex-President, 1853–1874

It is hard to imagine the White House with no bathtub, or no cooking stove in the kitchen. The first bathtub and the first kitchen stove were installed in the executive mansion during Millard Fillmore's administration (1850–1853). These innovations did not attract much attention at the time, but they say something about Fillmore the man (1800–1874), who was progressive in his outlook and committed to raising the quality of life in America. His efforts to recapture the presidency in the election of 1856 as the candidate of a third party, his post–Civil War activities in the city of Buffalo, New York, as well as his new career in the practice of law, show the energy and ambition of the man who occupied the White House for less than three years.

As vice president, Fillmore had succeeded to the presidency upon the death of Zachary Taylor on July 9, 1850. Fillmore was an able chief executive who helped the country through the crisis of 1850, but he is not remembered as one of the giants of American politics. His chance of being elected president in his own right in 1852 was slim at best. His own party, the Whigs, rejected him and nominated the flamboyant General Winfield Scott, a hero of the Mexican War. The Democratic candidate, Franklin Pierce, defeated Scott in the November election.

Fillmore's days in office were filled with tension. The question of national power versus states' rights became the dominant political issue as slavery cast its ominous shadow over the nation. Daniel Webster, Henry Clay, and John C. Calhoun, the great triumvirate, were about to retire from politics, leaving a distressing lack of leadership in government. Fillmore should be given considerable credit for the manner in which he maintained his poise and presidential dignity while he endured political abuse and the embarrassment of defeat in the fall of 1852.

Tragedy followed Fillmore as he left the White House. He and his wife, Abigail Powers Fillmore, attended the inauguration of Franklin Pierce that early March day. The weather was bitterly cold in Washington, and Mrs. Fillmore was not properly protected against the winter chill. Washington Irving, the famed American writer and longtime family friend, accompanied Mrs. Fillmore to the inauguration. He noted how cold it was, and that Mrs. Fillmore was shivering during the ceremony.

The Fillmores returned to the rooms they had taken at the Willard Hotel. Mrs. Fillmore had not been well for some time, but no one considered her condition alarming. She seemed very tired and somewhat dispirited, and retired early that evening. By morning she had a high temperature, and soon developed pneumonia. All the help that medicine of that day could give was hers, but she gradually lost her fight for life. The president and the couple's two children, Millard Powers and Mary Abigail, were constantly beside her, but despite a few periods of slight improvement, it became evident that she could not recover. On the morning of March 30, 1853, she died in their hotel apartment.

The next day the family left for their home in Buffalo, New York, with the body of their wife and mother. The day after their arrival in Buffalo, the body was buried in the family plot of the local cemetery. For a brief moment the nation shared the grief of the ex-president, but soon returned to the press of other matters. The widowed former president had a most difficult time adjusting to the life of an ordinary citizen living in a modest Buffalo home with limited resources and no immediate means of earning a living.

Tragedy again struck Fillmore. His only daughter, Mary Abigail, died suddenly in July of the next year. She had gone to nearby East Aurora, New York, for a few days to visit her much-loved paternal grandfather, Nathaniel Fillmore. She seemed to be in perfect health. Her grandfather, Old Nate, like the whole family, was very fond of this vivacious, attractive, and warm-hearted girl of 22 — and suddenly she died, apparently from cholera, which was epidemic that summer. Her father and brother arrived at the home of Old Nate just a few hours before her death. There is a question as to whether she realized that they had come to be with her.

Fillmore was shattered by her death. She had on occasion acted as hostess at the White House during her father's administration. In Buffalo she ran the family home on Franklin Street. For months it seemed to the former president that the joy of life had disappeared. He wrote to longtime family friend, Dorothea Dix, "I feel life has little left for me. My good son only of all my little family remains."[1]

Dix, an inveterate reformer who championed women's rights and opposed slavery, carried on an extensive correspondence with Millard Fillmore over a period of years. The letters, found many years after their deaths, give a new dimension to understanding a long-neglected American president. Dix first met Vice President and Mrs. Fillmore when she was seeking aid for her projects. When Fillmore became president, she was often a guest at the White House. Some feel that the recently found letters of Dorothea Dix indicate that she hoped, or even expected, that Fillmore would marry her after his first wife died. While there is some indication that this may have been true, there is no proof. Certainly there is little or no evidence that Fillmore ever considered such a relationship.

Fillmore was reluctant to practice law in Buffalo again. He feared that it might not be appropriate for a former president to face little-known opposing lawyers in purely private and local matters. He had little experience which might qualify him for a career in business, and his personal financial resources were too limited to enable him to establish a business of his own. He would have been able to live quietly in his modest Buffalo home, but this would not make it possible for him to take his place among the country's prominent citizens. He felt, with some bitterness, that the nation did not adequately care for its former presidents. His financial condition and his personal loneliness probably led him to become involved in politics again.

Fillmore's reentry into the political arena came at a time when America was suffering from many instances of intolerance. Though never a racist or ecclesiastical bigot himself, he joined forces with the leaders of the anti–Catholic, anti-immigrant, and antislavery movements in order to obtain a political base to run for office again in 1856. Many Americans disliked the Roman Catholic church. No doubt most of this feeling was due to the fact that this was a church which knew no national boundaries and had its headquarters in the city of Rome. The prejudice was augmented when so many Catholic immigrants came to the United States from European countries, attended Catholic churches, and caused the church membership to increase rapidly.

Pope Pius IX tried to ease the situation after disturbances took place in several American cities by sending his personal representative, Gaetano Cardinal Bedini, to America. However, the cardinal did not understand America and made several seemingly insensitive remarks. Public reaction against the cardinal was extreme in several cities, and at times he was actually in personal danger.

Along with the anti–Catholic movement, the anti-immigrant, or nativists, emerged. No doubt there was a relationship between the two, for certainly the same intolerant spirit dominated both groups. America had indeed become the world's "melting pot," and vast numbers wanted to improve their lot in life by coming to her shores. Irritations and real conflicts often existed between the immigrants and American citizens. Both became indignant and resentful.

These feelings against Catholics and immigrants came at a time when the crisis over slavery was being intensified. Such unsettled times provided a fertile field for prejudices to multiply. A new party, the American Party, or the Know-Nothings (so named because members when questioned about their organization would reply, "I know nothing"), was formed in an attempt to counteract the growth of the Catholic church and the influence of the growing immigrant population. At about the same time, another new political party, the Republicans, was formed, whose principal aim was to oppose slavery. Ex-president Fillmore decided he would attempt to regain the presidency as a member of the American Party, or Know-Nothings. The effort was doomed to failure, perhaps from the beginning.

A new secret society which called itself the "Order of the Star Spangled Banner" gave leadership to the anti-immigrant movement. They used passwords, the signs and grips of a secret organization, and gained a large following. James W. Becker developed the Order into a potent political organization. Fillmore joined the Order as a means of gaining a political base to run for office again. He hoped to gain the support of what was left of the old National Whig Party (he had been a Whig president) and combine it with the American Party to improve his chances for winning the presidency.

There are those who feel that Fillmore knew he had no viable chance at winning the election of 1856. However, the writer would take issue with this position. Fillmore's actions were those of a shrewd political strategist who was making a genuine run for victory. He knew it was in the realm of the possible for the final election of the president to go to the House of Representatives, which he hoped would return him to the White House.

Fillmore made two extensive tours of the country in 1854, all in the guise of a sight-seeing tourist. As he traveled he conferred with what was left of the Whig organization. In an attempt to build his political strength, he also sought out the important political leaders wherever he visited. His tours took him to most of the major cities of the nation.

The former president, turned politician again, also used an old but fairly effective political ploy. He left for a European tour in the spring of 1855 and was gone for 15 months. While out of the country he would not have to answer the hard questions about the slave issue, especially the turmoil it was causing in Kansas, for any position he took would certainly alienate a large number of voters.

Fillmore's European tour was a great success. He visited with many of the prominent people of the continent, including a number of the crowned heads of Europe. No doubt his prestige was increased at home to be received by kings, queens, prime ministers, and families of wealth and power on the continent.

There is little doubt that a good share of the leadership in the Know-Nothing organization had looked to Fillmore for several years as their candidate for 1856. The campaign of 1854, a nonpresidential election year, brought undreamed of success to the Know-Nothings. They carried the states of Massachusetts and Delaware. Together with the remnants of the Whigs, they also carried Pennsylvania. Seventeen new American (Know-Nothing) Party congressmen and a host of state officials were also elected. The new party was making real gains in the South as well.

The future looked good for the Know-Nothings in 1856. If the Democrats of the North and the South continued to split over the slave issue, and the new Republican Party would further split the Northern antislavery forces, the American Party would be the only truly national party in 1856. Fillmore was overwhelmingly nominated by the Know-Nothings while he was still in Europe. He then hastened back to New York City where he received a tumultuous welcome. The campaign was in high gear.

A number of Fillmore's friends were somewhat surprised when he joined a political party whose major appeal was to the racial and religious prejudices of the voters. He tried to explain his position by pointing out that there were other important issues involved, chief of which was the preservation of the Union. There is a considerable amount of material in his letters, speeches, and public statements to show interest in issues other than race or religion. In fact, several of the leaders of the American Party felt that Fillmore was not sufficiently emphasizing the initial positions of the Know-Nothings. It is not difficult to find passages from his speeches which seem to differ with the Know-Nothing stand on nativism and church.

At Newburgh, New York, Fillmore declared, "I have no hostility to foreigners.... Having witnessed their deplorable conditions in the old country, God forbid I should add to their sufferings by refusing them an asylum in this."[2] However, even with these sentiments he did not like to see foreigners hold high office or have them controlling America's destiny as a nation. As to the Catholics, Fillmore only mentioned the name once in the campaign. His daughter had gone to a Catholic school in Buffalo, and he had contributed toward the purchase of the bells of St. Joseph Church in that city. He had been received by the Pope in Rome in 1855. His chief concern on that occasion seemed to be that he might be expected to kiss the hand or the foot of the Pope.[3] Fillmore very openly denied that he disliked any religion or creed. But he did oppose any mixture of religion and politics.[4]

The chief plea in his campaign in 1856 was for the preservation of the Union. He decried sectionalism in all its manifestations. The concern he showed began when he was president and had to solve the problems related to the Compromise of 1850. Quite clearly he saw the possible dissolution of the Union over the issue of slavery. No doubt he felt some kind of a call to do his part to save the Union.

The ex-president explained why he entered the race for the White House in 1856 in terms of his love for the Union. He wrote to Dorothea Dix about the reasons for his action. "When I saw the Whig party demoralized, and efforts made to convert it, at the North, into a sectional, abolitionist party, I advised my friends to unite with the American or Know-Nothing party, and maintain a national organization in favor of the Union."[5] But he refrained from taking a definitive stand on how to end slavery.

When the votes were counted in November of 1856, James Buchanan, the Democratic candidate, received 1,838,169 popular votes and 296 electoral votes. The Republican nominee, John C. Fremont, garnered 1,231,264 popular votes and 114 electoral votes. Millard Fillmore, the American Party candidate did not do nearly as well as he had hoped, gaining only 874,534 popular votes and only the 8 electoral votes from Delaware.

The election over, and with no definite plans for his future, Fillmore sought for a way to occupy his time productively, and hopefully to secure an income. His financial situation, while not desperate, could not provide a life-style to which he had become accustomed. As a former president he felt that he could hardly enter the work force as an ordinary citizen. The solution to his problem came in an unexpected way when he found a rich, attractive widow to marry. The former president, still a strikingly handsome figure of a man of 58 years, married Caroline Carmichael McIntosh of Albany. She was the widow of the late Ezekiel C. McIntosh, who had been a prominent, respected, and wealthy businessman in Albany.

They realized that they had become very fond of each other, but there were certain details which had to be worked out before they could become man and wife. One of the problems was where they would reside. She preferred to live in Albany where her roots were. He wished to reside in Buffalo where he was its most important and well-known citizen. Eventually she agreed to move to Buffalo.

Another problem to be solved was what to do about her wealth. She was not quite ready to put it all in his name as was the custom of the day. As a result they made a marriage contract that left all her property and investments in her name. The husband would manage the estate for a modest fee of $10,000 a year, making him strictly accountable to his wife for the management of her estate.

The Fillmores were married in Albany on February 10, 1858, in the old Schuyler mansion where Mrs. McIntosh lived. (They were married in the same room where Alexander Hamilton had made Elizabeth Schuyler, the daughter of General Schuyler of Revolutionary fame, his wife.) The couple bought and refurbished a spacious mansion built by John Hollister on Delaware Avenue in Buffalo. It was Tudor Gothic in design, with the usual elaborate ornamentation of the Elizabethan era. The mansion fronted on Niagara Square and had as neighbors a number of the wealthiest families of the city. Here the Fillmores entertained such guests as President-elect Abraham Lincoln, President Andrew Johnson, and other nationally important figures. A number of distinguished guests from abroad also came to the Fillmore home. Mrs. Fillmore's genteel sophistication and gracious manner endeared her to Buffalo society.

For the remainder of his life Fillmore lived in Buffalo as its first citizen. Both the ex-president and the city seemed to enjoy the role he played in civic affairs. Until his death in 1874, few major events in Buffalo failed to have his participation.

The former president was most concerned when he saw the Civil War approaching. He felt that President Buchanan should have taken a more decisive action against the movement of Southern states to secede from the Union.[6] Fillmore was asked by some Northern leaders to go to the South to try to discourage the secessionist movement since he was generally well liked in the South. Fillmore plainly said, "I can not do any good."[7] Quite openly he urged the North to fully abide by the terms of the Compromise of 1850. He also asked the North to repeal certain laws he felt unconstitutional, such as the "personal liberty laws" in which some states prohibited their officials from helping to enforce the Fugitive Slave Law which was passed by Congress and signed by Fillmore when he was president. Few were influenced by what he said.

As chairman of the Committee of Public Defense in Buffalo, Fillmore organized a home guard, the Union Continentals, when war actually came. He knew those of military age and fitness were likely to go to war, and that the local population would have to protect itself. When he considered the vulnerability of the Erie Canal, so vital to Buffalo's prosperity, he was much concerned. He felt that the Union Continentals could help give protection to this vital artery of commerce. In many ways he showed his support of the war effort and tried to help those who were hurt by the war. He was seemingly indefatigable in his work for the Union cause.

However, he did express his opinions. Often he was quite forthright in his criticism of the conduct of the war. When the election of 1864 came, he did not support Lincoln but endorsed and voted for General George McClellan, feeling a change of leadership was needed.

When Lincoln was assassinated, a most unpleasant incident occurred in Buffalo. Fillmore was out of town when the news of Lincoln's murder came. As a result he had not draped his door with the appropriate black ribbon. A critical passer-by, angry at this supposed neglect, smeared black ink on the house. When the ex-president arrived at his home, he displayed the proper black ribbon. However, that made little difference to those who disliked him. A few went so far as to openly call him a traitor. Through it all he maintained an outward equanimity and made no response. The incident was soon forgotten.

When peace came, Fillmore settled down again to his best-loved role as "First Citizen of Buffalo." The list of his activities is indeed impressive.

A few of his projects included the barge project (designed to help businessmen by aiding water transportation); developing an excellent public library; creating the University of Buffalo, which included a fine medical school; opening a famous art museum and recognizing local artists; establishing one of the best historical societies in the nation; building and organizing the Y.M.C.A. of Buffalo; constructing and equipping Buffalo's hospital; and helping the American Indians of the area.

Millard Fillmore's health continued to be excellent. However, Mrs. Fillmore gradually became very frail and stayed more and more in her home, seldom going out. In the fall of 1866 she and her husband went to Europe, hoping that a change in surroundings and climate might restore her to good health again. The couple stayed in Europe for a few months, spending most of their time in Paris and Madrid. Her health did not improve, so they returned to Buffalo. In spite of her ill health, she survived her husband by seven and a half years.

During the years following his presidency Fillmore had kept in touch with most of his old and close associates in Washington. One of these friends, William O. Corcoran, invited the former president to meet with the surviving members of his cabinet for a dinner and reunion in Washington in April of 1874. However, on the morning of February 13, Fillmore was stricken with a stroke as he was shaving. He seemed to realize that he was gravely ill for he remarked, "This is the beginning of the end."[8] After a few days he was able to be up part of the time, but he was stricken again on February 26 and became much worse. On Sunday evening, March 8, he lapsed into unconsciousness. Shortly after eleven that night he died.

The Rev. N.R. Hotchkiss of the Baptist Church, together with the Rev. Dr. John C. Lord of the Presbyterian Church, conducted a simple service in the Fillmore home. On March 11 the body lay in state at St. Paul's Episcopal Cathedral in the city of Buffalo. A great throng paid final respects to their old friend and neighbor. President Grant, the governor of New York, congressmen, and other notables attended the elaborate funeral service. But somehow the feeling lingers that the tribute paid him by his neighbors and longtime Buffalo friends would have meant the most to him.

The 14th, Franklin Pierce

The One None Remembers, 1857–1869

Franklin Pierce (1804–1869), perhaps the least known American president (1853–1857), was also one of the most tragic figures ever to occupy the White House. Pierce was a Northerner from New Hampshire who opposed the Civil War, and at times was openly accused of being a traitor. His only living child, a son, was killed in a railroad accident a month before his inauguration. His wife suffered from lifelong depression and was in bed much of the time. After the death of their son she remained in inconsolable grief for the rest of her life.

Tragedy continued to stalk him after his presidency. He saw the union which he dearly loved disintegrate before his eyes; he had to stand by as the Northern troops invaded the South, an action he thought unconstitutional and immoral. One of his best friends, Jefferson Davis, became president of the doomed Confederacy. The federal government imprisoned a number of his friends for opposing the war. He was considered a security risk in the eyes of the secretary of state because of his Southern sympathies. The public turned against him; a mob gathered at his home and threatened him. It took fifty years for his home state to remember him with any sort of memorial.

Pierce had been in politics for a number of years, but he resigned from the United States Senate in 1842 because of a drinking problem[1] and entered the private practice of law. The Democratic convention in 1852 voted 49 times before they named Pierce their candidate for the presidency. Although he was elected president by a big majority, his administration was such a failure that there was no chance of his being renominated. He was the only elected president who was denied renomination when he openly sought it. Abraham Lincoln said that Pierce was "thrown aside as unfit for further use."[2] Stuart Holbrook in his *Lost Men of American History* called Pierce "a nonentity."[3]

When fellow Democrat James Buchanan was elected in 1856 to succeed him as president, Pierce felt that his own administration had been vindicated. Most of the nation did not see it that way. Many did not vote for Buchanan as much as they voted against Fremont, the nominee of the new Republican party which many felt was run by the abolitionists.

After Pierce left office, he and his wife stayed in Washington for a number of weeks as house guests of his secretary of state, William L. Marcy. There was real reluctance on the part of the former president to return to his home in Concord, New Hampshire, for he feared the kind of reception he might receive at the hands of his fellow townsmen. However, his fears were groundless, for the citizens of Concord turned out in friendship to greet him. There were welcoming speeches and a gala party at Depot Hall. Many did not approve of the way he had seemed to defend slavery in the Kansas territory when he was president, but they liked him as a man and accepted the idea that he had done what he considered right at the time.

The former president made his first public appearance after leaving the White House when he spoke at an anniversary dinner of the Ancient and Honorable Artillery Company in Boston on June 1, 1857. The speech was a strong statement calling for America to support the Constitution, pointing out that it was just as necessary to recognize the rights of others as to demand one's own rights. In the context of the place and background of the speech it was a defense of the right of the South to have slaves and take them into the territories. The speech was met with very mixed reactions. Jefferson Davis, his former secretary of war and a Southerner, warmly congratulated Pierce for his speech in a personal letter, praising him for his stand. Many in the North severely castigated him for it.

The next several years were spent in traveling about, trying to improve Mrs. Pierce's health. While not wealthy, the ex-president was well off financially and could afford to travel. He felt he could not settle down to the practice of law until his wife's health improved. At about this time Mrs. Pierce's close personal friend and chief confidante, Abby Means, died. She was devastated. Pierce thought that a warm climate would help her, so they wintered on the island of Madeira. They both enjoyed the island, but she grew restless, so they went to Europe, visiting Portugal, Spain, France, Italy, Austria, Germany, Belgium and England. Most of the summer was spent in a leisurely stay on the shore of Lake Geneva. Nathaniel Hawthorne, the former president's best friend, joined them in Italy for the winter (1858–59). The next summer they returned to America, as Mrs. Pierce's depression and accompanying physical symptoms did not improve. She carried with her locks of hair of her "precious dead," including those of her son and Abby Means. "Sorrow so assiduously nursed could not be dispelled."[4] Hers never was.

In October after their return to America, John Brown carried out his raid on Harper's Ferry. Many saw it as a stroke for freedom. Others looked on it as an invasion of a sovereign state and deliberate murder. Pierce, along with many conservatives, agreed with the latter position. They felt that Virginia would never give up her right to decide the issue of slavery for herself without outside intervention.

As the year 1859 ended, Pierce and his wife made plans to go to Nassau for the winter. However, shortly before he left he sent a letter to Jefferson Davis that was to haunt him the remainder of his days. In the letter Pierce stated that he considered Davis to be the best candidate for the presidency in 1860. The ex-president stayed in Nassau for five months and then returned to the United States only to find the nation in the worst kind of political turmoil. The Democratic party was split into the Northern and Southern wings, Abe Lincoln was about to be nominated by the Republicans, and John Bell of Tennessee was the nominee of the Constitutional Union Party. A few suggested that Pierce run again for president. However, no leader of stature in the nation seriously considered this suggestion. Pierce rejected it out of hand.

Abraham Lincoln of Illinois was elected president in November of 1860 with no electoral votes from the South. Pierce did not take part in the campaign nor did he publicly support any of the four candidates for president. No one knows whether he bothered to vote.

The election results left the former president very discouraged and apprehensive. He spent much time in thought and in discussing with his friends ways to save the Union and prevent a war. He actually formulated several plans, one of which was for all five of the ex-presidents (Van Buren, Tyler, Fillmore, Buchanan and himself) to meet and present a plan that could save the country. The idea found little support, and open rejection by Van Buren.

Pierce was in a real dilemma. He did not feel the South could be coerced to give up their slaves or their right to take them into territories; neither did he feel that the North could force the South to stay in the Union by military action as obviously they were planning to do. In the end he decided that if war came he would defend his native state, New Hampshire. Yet he was violently disturbed by Lincoln's call for volunteers, and would soon quite openly oppose the war. In an effort to keep Virginia from going to war, Pierce wrote Governor Letcher, "To this war . . . which seems to me to contemplate subjugation I give no countenance — no support to any possible extent."[5] When several of his friends including James G. Berret, the ex-mayor of Washington, were imprisoned because of their oppositon to the war, he protested vigorously. This upset Secretary of State Seward who sent Pierce a rather blunt letter questioning his loyalty to the country. Although Seward did later apologize for the letter, the damage to Pierce's reputation was already done. Pierce also condemned the Emancipation Proclamation, questioned the purposes of the war, and openly wondered how the people stood for it all. Few feel that Pierce committed open treason, but he did speak his mind and became very unpopular in the nation he served as chief executive.

Pierce wrote his wife, "I will never justify, sustain, or in any way or to any extent uphold this cruel, heartless, aimless, unnecessary war. Madness and imbecility are in the ascendant."[6] On July 4, 1863, he made a speech on the steps of the New Hampshire state capitol in which he attacked Lincoln personally, charging him with seizing too much authority. He even felt democracy might be doomed in America.

A few months later, on December 2, 1863, his wife of almost 30 years died. Nathaniel Hawthorne came to him immediately and stood by as her emaciated body was lowered into the grave on that cold, gloomy New England winter day. She had never been happy and had never learned to handle the melancholy that constantly beset her. The depression at times was very deep and no doubt hastened her death. It seems that there was more sorrow than joy in the life that Franklin Pierce and Jane Appleton had together.

Yet another death came to trouble Pierce. In the next spring, 1864, Hawthorne, one of America's best known and loved authors, and the former president's closest friend, was traveling with Pierce in the mountains of New England when very suddenly he collapsed and died. New England had a number of famous writers at that time. Most of them came to bury one of their own — Longfellow, Lowell, Whittier, Alcott, Agassiz, and the most famous of them all, Emerson. Even in this situation politics intruded. Pierce was not included among the pallbearers. Feelings ran deep in New England.

Tragedy still stalked the former president. The letter that Pierce had written to Jefferson Davis in 1860 came back to beset him. In 1864 it was found by invading federal troops. Pierce genuinely liked Davis, and the letter he wrote was totally nonpolitical, warm, and personal. Many felt it betrayed the United States and gave comfort to the enemy. Copies were circulated all through the North, especially in New England. Again Pierce was accused of using federal troops in an effort to allow slavery in Kansas, and not standing by his country in time of war.

Several politicians wanted to make Pierce the Democratic candidate in 1864, in the midst of the war. Pierce would not hear of such a thing. The Democrats did run on a platform which held that the war was a failure. General George McClellan, who had lost so often to General Robert E. Lee, was nominated by the Democrats. Fortunately for the country he lost to Lincoln.

After Lincoln was shot at Ford's Theater on April 14, 1865, and died the next morning, news soon reached New Hampshire and a crowd gathered at the capitol. After expressions of sorrow and indignation, it was suggested that they see if all the houses were showing flags or signs of mourning. Then someone said they should go to see if Pierce's house showed a flag. Pierce was ill and in bed. He had not displayed any sign of grief. However, a lad who had been living in the ex-president's home heard the remark and raced back to tell Pierce that the crowd was coming. As they neared his home, Pierce came to the door holding a flag in his hand. The crowd demanded a statement from Pierce. He replied, "It is unnecessary for me to show my devotion for the stars and stripes by any special exhibition upon the demand of any body of men."[7] The bluntness of his statement, the force of personality, and the power of his speech took the crowd aback. The people scattered and left Pierce alone on his own doorstep. Certainly this action on the part of Pierce is something of a testimony to the courage of the former president, and of the power of speech still to be found in the aging man in a time of real danger.

Perhaps it was inevitable, but the lonely, almost friendless and rejected leader turned to alcohol for comfort, and for a time he seemed held in its grip. Although he did not make a public spectacle of himself, those near him realized that he had come to rely more and more on the bottle to get through the day. Several episodes of illness came at about the same time. Late in the year 1865 illness threatened his life and few expected that he would survive. But he did recover, and with the recovery came victory over his addiction to alcohol.

One reason for this abrupt change in his outlook may have been his return to religion. For many years he followed the lead of his wife in church attendance. Her family was deeply religious, while his gave it scant attention. She was a devout Congregationalist, while he followed no particular church. When the war came he was greatly disturbed as the Northern church took up the demand for a vigorous prosecution of the war. The violent mood of much of the clergy in denouncing the South seemed to Pierce out of keeping with the overtones of the doctrine taught in the Scriptures. However, he came to respect and admire Dr. Eams, rector of St. Paul's Episcopal Church at Concord. The rector avoided all political issues, but rather emphasized the personal religious life of the individual. Pierce was able to identify with this stance and became a regular attendant at the church. On Sunday, December 3, 1865, the former president presented himself for baptism for the first time in his life. In the spring of 1866 he went a step further and was confirmed by his old friend, Bishop Chase. In this setting he seemed to have found a personal peace that had eluded him all his life.

Pierce became ill in the late summer of 1868. Recovery came slowly, but he could again travel some and began to engage in the life around him. In the spring of 1869 he made his last trip when he journeyed to Baltimore to deliver a speech at the triennial convention of the Order of Cincinnati, an organization he respected and loved for its undeniable patriotism. Yet in this, his last speech, he called to remembrance those who, like the Howards of Baltimore, were imprisoned for their beliefs rather than for any overt act committed against their country. Earlier, he had defended the president of Dartmouth College for his opposition to the war. Pierce firmly believed that evil could not be stamped out by resorting to arms.

Pierce spent most of the summer in his cottage at Little Boar's Head by the sea. He became less and less active, and began to drift off into semiconsciousness much of the time. His death came early in the morning of October 8, 1869. The ex-president's body lay in state at the New Hampshire capitol. Then the simple, short Episcopal service of committal was performed at St. Paul's. Burial in the family plot in the local cemetery at Concord ended the earthly career of Franklin Pierce, the fourteenth president of his country.

Other tragic figures have occupied the White House. But Andrew Johnson lived to see himself vindicated as did Herbert Hoover, Warren Harding died before the public knew the extent of his failure, Ulysses Grant was never personally excoriated or held in contempt by the public. Franklin Pierce had none of these advantages, if advantages they be.

In her 1984 visit to New Hampshire for the presidential primaries, Journalist Linda Ellerbee drove around the state asking people if there had ever been a president from New Hampshire. Almost no one was certain. She finally found a man who said, "Yes, there was Franklin Pierce. He was from New Hampshire, but really he was out of his league as president."[8] A few blocks from his grave in Concord she asked where he was buried. No one knew.

Franklin Pierce remains America's least known and perhaps most tragic president.

The 15th, James Buchanan

Search for Vindication, 1861-1868

William Shakespeare wrote, "Some are born great, some achieve greatness, and some have greatness thrust upon 'em."[1] There are also those who have had an opportunity to rise to greatness, but have let it slip through their eager fingers. Such was James Buchanan (1791-1868), fifteenth president of the United States (1857-1861). He was in office during one of the most critical periods in American history. The Southern states had begun to secede from the Union and were forming their own nation, the Confederacy. Buchanan tried but utterly failed in his attempt to preserve the Union. The problems were so momentous that he seemed almost paralyzed, unable to take any action whatsoever that would stop the seemingly inexorable tide of events. After he left office he spent the rest of his life in a frantic but vain effort to vindicate his administration.

Unfortunately, Buchanan possessed neither the force of personality nor intellectual capacity to deal with the new problems facing the nation, for it seemed some basic issues could not be settled until a bloody, vicious war was fought. (Out of a population of 31 million, 600,000 were killed — more Americans than were lost in all of World War I, World War II, and the Korean War combined.[2]) Buchanan lived several years after the Civil War ended, but he died still believing and maintaining he had made the proper decisions. His opinion was that the South did not have the right to secede, but he also believed that the Constitution did not give the chief executive the authority to use force to prevent the secession of states. After he left Washington, the ridicule and abuse heaped upon him were unmerciful. From his isolated country estate in southeastern Pennsylvania he attempted to answer these charges in a series of letters, papers and articles, as well as in a book. Even at the time, the rush of events was more than ever clearly proving his error.

Ironically, he confidently went to his grave with the inner assurance that the judgment of history would vindicate him. History did judge him, but it found him wanting. Not that he lacked ability, or a sense of morality and decency, but that he did not measure up to the demands of his high office at that critical time.

State after state left the Union, seizing federal property as they did so. Buchanan was frantic in his efforts to stem the erosion of the Union, but the Southern states had determined that their interests, especially the "peculiar institution" as they called slavery, were in jeopardy if they stayed in the Union. There were days when Buchanan did not dress or leave his private chambers in the White House, so distressed was he by the events that were transpiring. He did send messages to Congress, he did communicate with state governors, he did hold long and lugubrious cabinet meetings, he did get military advice, but there was no firm hand at the top with a well-formulated policy, and the whole nation sensed his indecision. Is it any wonder that in all likelihood he was the president who most gladly turned the reigns of government over to his successor. At the inauguration of Abraham Lincoln, Buchanan said, "Sir, if you are as happy in entering the White House as I shall feel on returning to Wheatland [Buchanan's Pennsylvania home], you are indeed a happy man."[3]

Buchanan made every effort to assist Lincoln and the new administration. The two had exchanged social calls with proper protocol and hospitality. Harriet Lane, Buchanan's niece who acted as his housekeeper and official hostess (Buchanan was a bachelor—the only bachelor to become president) and who was not impressed by Mr. Lincoln's rather awkward appearance nor Mrs. Lincoln's loud and unrefined manner,[4] had so enjoyed her central role in Washington's society that it was with reluctance that she returned to Wheatland.

The outgoing president was beset up to the last moment as chief executive. Just as he was about to enter the coach that was to take him to pick up Lincoln before they went to the Capitol for the inauguration, a note came from Major Anderson, heroically trying to hold Fort Sumter, telling Buchanan that he would need 20,000 men to hold the fort from the expected attack of South Carolina, which had already left the Union.

The outgoing and incoming presidents entered the Senate chamber arm in arm, to witness Hannibal Hamlin sworn in as vice president. They then went to the east portico for Lincoln's swearing-in by Chief Justice Taney.[5] For the first time in almost 50 years Buchanan was out of public life. But even after he was no longer in office, he met twice with his old cabinet in order to get papers ready that he needed to turn over to Lincoln, including the note from Major Anderson in beleaguered Fort Sumter.

A number of old friends accompanied Buchanan to the train that took him to Baltimore, where he made a short speech and was cheered by a large crowd. He tried to convey an optimism he did not really feel.

The next day, March 6, Buchanan and his niece, along with a few friends and aides, arrived by train at Lancaster. The train had stopped briefly at York and Columbia, Pennsylvania, where the citizens provided a big welcome for "Old Buck" in both places. When he reached Lancaster, the town outdid itself in its wild welcome by firing the "Old Buck Cannon" as well as a 34-gun presidential salute, by ringing church bells, and by marching in a parade from the train to the center of town and then on to nearby Wheatland.

During the first months of his retirement at Wheatland, he was constantly honored by various callers and groups who came to serenade him. Old Buck savored the first moments at home walking his land, seeing that supplies were brought in, examining his new team of horses, fixing up the little fish pool in front of the house, and making a few changes in the house itself, giving special attention to his upstairs study and bedroom. The old dressing gown came out, his supply of cigars and Madeira were replenished. In fact, he was ready for the leisurely life of a respected country gentleman.

The good feelings he enjoyed as he came home would shortly be sorely needed. The abuse he received from the press and politicians was soon beyond anyone's wildest imagination. The Republicans and the South blamed him in large part for allowing the national crisis to get out of control. The Southerners were angry because he had not seen the extent of their problem and had failed to help them. Many felt that if he had acted decisively the South might not have seceded.

At first Buchanan tried to settle back into something of a normal life. He passed many pleasant hours at the Grapes Tavern with old friends and townspeople. Frequently he passed the time along "Lawyer's Row," chatting with fellow professionals about the events of the day. But his leisurely, peaceful retirement soon turned ugly. Some said openly that he should not show himself in town. Day after day the mails brought threatening letters. Anonymous notes were found near the back door stating that the house would soon be the target of arsonists. Even "Miss Hetty," Harriet Lane, was the object of threats. The former president was too proud, too indignant, to hire a guard to protect himself though he was urged to do so. The Masonic Lodge at Lancaster, his own Lodge #43, pledged to the last man to protect his person and property. For many months the Masons posted a guard at Wheatland.

The former president was harassed by bill collectors who tried to recover alleged debts which he supposedly left unpaid in Washington. No proof was ever produced, and he and his legal counsel resolutely denied the validity of the debts and refused to pay them. Such charges were repeated many times in the press of the nation.

It got even worse. Several stores displayed bank notes which showed an obscene vignette of Buchanan with red around his eyes, a gallows situated above his head, a rope around his neck, and on his forehead the word "Judas."[6] Several newspapers pointed out that Andrew Jackson had

forced South Carolina to obey the law when they had threatened nullification during his administration. This was in sharp contrast to Buchanan's
indecisive actions. Although it failed, a resolution of censure against him
was introduced into the United States Senate by Senator Garrett Davis of
Kentucky on December 15, 1862, charging that Buchanan "...from sympathy with the conspirators and their treasonable project, failed to take
necessary and proper measures to prevent" the war.[7] These attacks made
Buchanan physically ill, and he was never again a well man. Any chance
for a peaceful, leisurely retirement was destroyed.

In an effort to explain what had happened in his administration,
Buchanan began to write letters to some of those who he felt had
misunderstood the situation. In a number of cases he asked former
associates to put their remembrances in writing and send them to him so
he could defend himself. As time went by he increased the number of letters
he wrote. Congress then stooped so low as to abolish the franking privilege
of ex-presidents, just to punish Buchanan.[8] But the incident which upset
him the most was probably an article written by Thurlow Weed that was
published by the *London Observer* in February 1862. The article so distorted
the facts about a cabinet meeting as to raise questions of Buchanan's loyalty
to the United States. No retraction was ever published.

At first the former president tried to answer the worst of these charges.
However, every effort to present his point of view was met with such scurrilous retorts that he finally gave up the effort. For the most part, even
though he kept his silence, he supported the war effort and his country
wholeheartedly. However, he did begin to collect relevant material about
his administration for a book he hoped would defend his acts as president.
The book was completed and entitled *Mr. Buchanan's Administration on
Eve of the Revolution,* and was published a year after the war was over.[9]
The book received scant attention because the nation was so caught up with
President Andrew Johnson's fight with the Radicals in Congress that few
cared about something that had lost its relevance.

However, many of the maligned ex-president's friends stood by him.
A constant stream of visitors came to Wheatland. Buchanan was a considerate and genial host and liked to entertain. The same elegant life-style
that had always characterized him was continued in retirement. He used the
best crystal, china, and silver in serving food and wine to his guests.

There was a special relationship between Harriet Lane and her "Uncle
James." Since he had no family of his own, she to a large extent took the
place of the children he might have had. She had been an excellent hostess
at the White House. By the standards of the day she was reputed to be a
beauty. Although she missed the glittering social life of Washington, she
spent most of her time at Wheatland trying to brighten the days of the
depressed former president. In January of 1868 she married Henry E.

Johnson, a banker from Baltimore. Buchanan was conspicuous at the wedding, enjoying the gala occasion as much as anyone. After the marriage she kept in close touch with the "country gentleman" at Wheatland.

The story of Buchanan's lost love is rather tragic. As a young man he was engaged to a beautiful young woman. There was a lovers' quarrel , but she died before they could be reconciled. When young Mr. Buchanan attempted to attend the funeral, he was rudely turned away.[10] He never again seriously thought of marriage. After his death a packet of letters tied with a ribbon was found among his personal effects. A note was attached which asked that the letters not be opened but destroyed. His wishes were respected.[11]

Many politicians visited Buchanan and sought advice on political matters, but he never again played an active role in partisan politics. In many ways he was unhappy about the election of 1864. As a former president and lifelong Democrat, he did not support Lincoln in his bid for reelection. However, he was not pleased with the position of the Democratic party, which held that the war was a failure and should be stopped.

Buchanan remained at Wheatland during the war. Gettysburg was not very far away, and the war did come within ten miles of his home. He refused to flee for safety even when the Confederate army came near. No doubt he did not quite comprehend what tragedy it would have been for the North to have an ex-president fall into the hands of the Confederates.

Along with most of his fellow countrymen, he was relieved when the Confederate army surrendered and the war was finally over. When President Lincoln was assassinated he was deeply moved, although the two men were not personal friends. During Buchanan's presidency he had known Andrew Johnson, who succeeded Lincoln as president, and felt that Johnson could give effective leadership to the nation. In no way did Buchanan support the Radicals in their fight against Johnson during Reconstruction.

Buchanan was never hard pressed for money. He was a lawyer who had received substantial fees for his services. While he was in public office he managed his own finances carefully and wisely. In fact he ran the financial affairs of most of his brothers and sisters, such confidence did they have in him. The story is told that once when he sold a farm, the sum given him was ten cents short of the agreement. He asked for and received the dime. When he died his net worth was something over $300,000, a fortune in those days.

While Buchanan had always been a religious man, he did not join a church. He had sought membership in the Lancaster Presbyterian Church during the war years, but his request was delayed over doctrinal issues. However, upon a personal confession of faith made before the ruling elders of the church, he became a communicant member on September 23, 1865.[12]

During much of the time after he returned to Wheatland from Washington, the former president suffered from various digestive complaints and also from gout. He had a number of short illnesses, became easily fatigued, and showed that the years bore heavily upon him, but no one considered him to be seriously ill. In May of 1868 he caught a severe cold which became progressively worse. After a short illness he died at Wheatland at half-past eight on June the first. It was a Monday morning.

The day before he died he said, "I have always felt and still feel that I discharged every public duty imposed on me conscientiously. I have no regret for any public act of my life, and history will vindicate my memory."[13] History vindicated James Buchanan as a gentleman and a patriot, a man who cared about his country. But he was a man who seemed to be a powerless victim of forces beyond his control.

The 16th, Abraham Lincoln

A Time to Die, 1865 *

On April 14, 1865, the city of Washington was in a festive mood. The famous Confederate General Robert E. Lee had surrendered to Union General U.S. Grant, in effect ending the Civil War. However, the surrender of the last pocket of Southern resistance under Confederate General Joseph E. Johnston to Union General William T. Sherman was a few days away. President Lincoln (born 1809; in office 1861–1865) was most relieved, and happier than anyone could remember.

Yet in another way the president was more troubled than he cared to admit. He had experienced a very strange dream in which he came down the White House stairs to hear weeping, but could see no one. When he arrived in the East Room he saw a catafalque with a body resting on it. He asked one of the soldiers on guard who was dead. He replied, "The president was killed by an assassin."[1] Lincoln did not believe that dreams foretold the future, but this dream, repeated the next night, was so vivid that he could not dismiss it from his mind. When he told his wife Mary about the dream, she was very upset.

His good friend Ward Lamon was equally concerned when Lincoln recounted the dream to him. Lamon wanted Lincoln to stay away from crowds. The president reminded Lamon, "For a long time you have been trying to keep somebody — the Lord knows who — from killing me."[2] Lincoln then tried to dismiss the whole affair by saying, "Well, let it go. I think the Lord in His own good time and way will work this out right."[3]

On this Good Friday, 1865, breakfast at the White House was a happy occasion. The Lincolns' oldest son Robert was home from the war. His parents invited him to accompany them to an evening at the theater, but he declined, saying he was tired. One story has it that he wanted to visit a

---

It is difficult in a brief account of Lincoln's assassination to include all significant details, so much is known. Also, many so-called eye witnesses are at variance with one another on crucial details. The writer has given credence to those who were in the best position to know.

girl in the city. President and Mrs. Lincoln were scheduled to attend a play at Ford's Theater, *Our American Cousin,* as a part of the general festivities over the ending of the war.

After breakfast the president went to his office and lit a fire to take the morning chill from the air. He had scheduled interviews with several people. At eleven o'clock a cabinet meeting had been called. The victorious General Grant was invited to attend. Secretary of War Edwin Stanton was late as usual, and made a grand entrance. The major topic of discussion was how to deal with the South now that the Confederates had lost the war. Stanton's plan was to treat them as conquered provinces, and in a power grab he wanted to divide the Southern states into military districts and govern them by the army. Secretary of the Navy Gideon Wells opposed the idea vigorously. The battle lines over Reconstruction were already forming. Lincoln did not accept Stanton's plan, but tried to keep the acrimonious situation within bounds by suggesting that Stanton, after further study, reduce these ideas into writing and bring them back to the cabinet. The meeting adjourned with no further disagreements. When the others had left the room, Grant stayed for a few minutes and told the president that he and Mrs. Grant could not accept the invitation of the first couple to accompany them to Ford's Theater that evening. The Grants were going to take a quick trip to see their daughter who was in school in New Jersey.

In the afternoon the Lincolns had planned to take a ride together about the city — just the two of them. But as they were ready to leave, word came to the president that a black woman said she must see Mr. Lincoln. He could not turn her away. She told him that her soldier husband's pay was not reaching her and that she and her family were destitute.[4] The president gave instructions for attending to her problem. Then he and Mrs. Lincoln left for their planned carriage ride, the first they had taken by themselves in some time. Lincoln talked to his wife about returning to Illinois after his term was up and resuming the practice of law in Chicago or Springfield.

After the evening meal the president walked the short distance to the War Department to get any possible news from General Sherman and his army in North Carolina. William Crook, one of the president's bodyguards, accompanied him. The two men observed several drunks near the path they were taking. Nothing happened, but Lincoln commented to Crook that he thought there were some men who wanted to kill him.[5] When Crook and Lincoln reached the War Department they learned that there was no message from Sherman, but the president stayed to talk with Stanton for awhile. On this occasion, the secretary of war urged Lincoln not to go out that evening because it could be dangerous. Lincoln said he had already given his word and would have to go.

At this time the president asked the secretary of war if he might have Major Thomas T. Eckert accompany him, and commented how he had seen the major break a poker over his arm. In the event of trouble, Eckert would be a handy man to have around. Secretary Stanton said that he needed Eckert for some work and could not spare him. The president repeated his request, this time to Major Eckert himself. The major was afraid to cross the secretary, his boss, so declined the president's request, pleading that he was needed to work for Stanton. The president let the matter drop. But it is interesting to note that there is good evidence to indicate that neither Stanton nor Eckert worked that evening, though there seems to be no good reason for Stanton suddenly to decide not to work.

On the way back to the White House, Lincoln told Crook that he would take Major Henry R. Rathbone and his fiancee Clara Harris, who was the daughter of Senator Ira Harris, with him that evening. As Lincoln and Crook parted for the day, Crook offered to accompany the Lincolns to the theater, but Lincoln replied that another guard had been secured. As they separated Lincoln said, "Goodbye, Crook." Crook thought about it on the way home, for Lincoln had always said, "Good night, Crook." He wondered why Lincoln had said goodbye.[6]

There was good reason for caution the night of April 14, 1865. Rumors had circulated in Washington that the president's life was in danger. Threats had been made openly against him, and letters containing similar threats had come to the White House a number of times. A plot to kidnap the president had almost succeeded just a few weeks before. An actor named John Wilkes Booth was at the center of the plot.

In the afternoon of the day Lincoln was shot, the *Whig Press* of Middleton, New York, had published the news that President Lincoln had been assassinated. The paper gave no source for the story,[7] in what is in some ways the strangest detail of the assassination.

After returning to the White House, Lincoln conferred with Speaker of the House Schuyler Colfax and one or two others. At about eight-fifteen the White House carriage received the nation's first couple as they set out for the evening. The coachman was Francis Burns and the valet footman was Charles Forbes. En route to Ford's Theater the White House carriage stopped at Senator Harris' home for Miss Harris and Major Rathbone. At about eight-thirty, or shortly after that time, the carriage drew up in front of the theater. The presidential guard for the evening was John Parker, a somewhat irresponsible member of the Washington police department. He was three hours late in reporting for duty and had walked from the White House to the theater. Consequently there was no armed guard for the president as he rode from the White House to the home of Senator Harris and then to the theater.

While Lincoln did not have an especially heavy schedule of activities on April 14, he was tired and would have preferred to stay at home. But to John Wilkes Booth, the day was filled with frenzied activity as well as

intense personal pressure. He was constantly in touch with the other con-
spirators who were planning the most dastardly deed in American history.
It seemed that his whole life was pointing to the performance at Ford's
Theater.

The primary conspirators besides Booth were Lewis Paine (sometimes
spelled Payne), George Atzerodt, and David Herold. Booth was a 26-year-
old celebrated actor of considerable talent and experience, an unstable personality with a monumental ego, a man given to excessive drinking and
high living. But he had an undeniable charm and a charismatic appeal.
Women were unusually attracted to him. He was of medium build and
height with black hair and eyes. In his dress he chose flamboyant styles.
There was in him a consuming devotion to the Confederacy, and he had
tried several times to form conspiracies against the leaders of the Union.
On one occasion he almost succeeded in kidnapping Lincoln in an effort to
hold him for ransom in exchange for Confederate prisoners of war. (The
Confederacy had no knowledge of his efforts on their behalf, nor did they
give him any assistance.) There is little doubt that this devotion to the South
was his major motivation for the assassination.

None of the other conspirators were persons of note. Lewis Paine was
a 20-year-old giant of a man with great physical strength. His father was
a Baptist minister of no outstanding reputation or ability. The son was dull-
witted, easily led, given to strong emotions, and cursed with a violent
temper. Booth gave Paine the responsibility of killing Secretary of State
William Seward, a task he came fearfully close to accomplishing.

George Atzerodt was 33, older than the other conspirators. A carriage
painter by trade, he had difficulty in finding steady employment. Of German extraction, he was a small, dark-complexioned man, unremarkable in
appearance. He lived in Port Tobacco along the Potomac River. His assignment was to kill Vice President Andrew Johnson, but just before the appointed time to shoot the vice president, he suddenly decided he wanted no
part of the murder and unsuccessfully attempted to get out of the city of
Washington before being arrested.

The most pitiable of the four conspirators was 23-year-old David
Herold. At times he served as a part-time drugstore clerk. For some reason
he seemed very attracted to Booth, giving him obsequious devotion, and
became a willing partner in the conspiracy. Herold was talkative and
friendly. Booth directed Herold to lead Paine to the home of Secretary
Seward, then to the Navy Yard Bridge so that Paine could take the same
escape route out of the city as Booth. Some have referred to Herold as
feebleminded. The writer has trouble reconciling that evaluation of his intelligence with the responsibility that Booth, who knew Herold well, gave
him on the night of April 14. Booth met with his fellow conspirators at eight
o'clock for their final rendezvous. Earlier he had rented a fast horse which

was to be waiting at the rear of the theater for his getaway. All seemed in readiness.

Lincoln, the object of these plans, arrived at Ford's Theater at eight-thirty with his wife and their guests. They were warmly greeted by the waiting crowd. Their box was to the right as one faced the front of the theater, and extended over part of the stage. The audience of over 1600 interrupted the play to stand and cheer as soon as they realized that the president had arrived. His coming had been well advertised, so the audience was expecting him. The orchestra played "Hail to the Chief" while Lincoln stood and acknowledged the audience. He then sat down and the play was resumed. The performance was not especially good, but it was entertaining and the chief executive was relaxed and enjoyed the production.

Booth had prepared well. In the afternoon he had come to the theater to get ready for his part in the drama, which seemed to be inexorably running its prescribed course. Booth bored a hole in the wall that separated the box from the passageway behind so he could clearly see what the people inside were doing. At the same time he blocked the door that would have allowed anyone to go from the passageway to the back of the theater, thus effectively cutting off that avenue of pursuit. Booth planned to shoot Lincoln at about ten-fifteen, the same time Paine was prepared to kill Seward, and Atzerodt to assassinate Johnson. Booth arrived at the theater at about nine-thirty. Everything seemed to be going according to plan, so he went to Taltavul's saloon next door for a drink to "fortify his spirits."

Some days before, Booth had purchased a one-shot derringer which fired a good-sized bullet, a deadly weapon at close range. During the afternoon he had carefully cleaned and checked the gun and loaded it for the evening. Also, he had provided himself with a large Bowie knife which he carried in a sheath. Both weapons were on his person as he set out for his last evening in Washington.

Unfortunately John Parker was the president's only guard that night. He had been reprimanded several times for dereliction of duty while a member of the Washington police department. No one has given an adequate explanation as to why he was made the president's guard that night. Parker had the last opportunity to prevent the assassination of the president, for he had been ordered to be armed and stay at the entrance of the president's box during the performance. The exact time is not known, but sometime after nine-thirty Parker was seen having a drink of ale with Burns and Forbes at Taltavul's saloon. As a result, there was no guard to prevent anyone from entering the theater and walking directly into the president's box. Security for the president seems to have been a succession of errors.

Booth walked unnoticed to the door of the president's box a little after ten. He watched those inside through the hole he had made in the wall. Knowing the play as well as he did, he timed his deed for the moment when there was only one actor on the stage and when the audience would be laughing. He planned to jump from the president's box onto the stage (a drop of about nine or ten feet) and make his getaway. He was sure no one could intercept him as he left by the back entrance. Booth stepped into the presidential box, raised his derringer, and at point-blank range shot Lincoln in the back of the head near the left ear.

Most of the audience did not realize that a shot had been fired. Even those in the president's box did not at first comprehend what had happened. Major Rathbone was probably the first to take it all in. As a result, when Booth was making his way to the rail of the box preparing to jump to the stage, the major grappled with him in an effort to prevent his escape. But Booth had dropped the derringer on the floor and had drawn his large knife. When Rathbone approached him, he lashed out and inflicted a large wound on the major's left arm. When the major dropped back, his arm bleeding profusely, Booth climbed over the rail of the box and jumped to the stage below. But as he dropped, the spur on a shoe caught a flag that was hung in front of the box. His fall was broken and he landed heavily with his left foot crumpled under him, breaking one of the bones in his left leg just above the ankle.

As he hobbled across the stage some say he shouted *"Sic semper tyrannis,"* the Latin phrase which means "Thus be it ever to tyrants."[8] Others contend that he also shouted, "Revenge for the South,"[9] as he headed for the back door. Harry Hawk, who was the only actor on the stage at the time, recognized Booth but made no attempt to stop him. Hawk obviously did not realize what had just happened. Booth went out the back door and jumped on the horse that stagehand Johnny Peanuts had been told to hold for him. He kicked Johnny hard in the stomach and spurred his horse to make his getaway. A Major Steward, who had been watching the play from the first row in front of the orchestra, rushed on the stage and out the back door of the theater and was almost able to grab the bridle of Booth's horse as he sped down Ninth Street and then toward Pennsylvania Avenue toward the Navy Yard Bridge.[10]

At almost the same moment Booth was in the act of shooting President Lincoln, Lewis Paine and David Herold arrived at Seward's house ready to kill him. Herold sat on his horse and held the bridle of Paine's horse as he went to the door of the secretary's home. William Bell, a young black boy in a white coat, opened the door to Paine's knock. Paine said he had some medicine for the secretary from Dr. Verdi. Bell refused to let Paine in, saying he would take the medicine himself. "Out of my way, nigger," Paine shouted as he pushed his way in and ran up the stairs toward Seward's room. Seward's son Frederick had come to the head of the stairs and refused Paine's demand to see the secretary. Paine pulled a pistol, pointed it directly at Frederick and pulled the trigger, but the gun misfired. Paine then pistol-whipped Frederick into unconsciousness, rushed to the secretary's room, drew his knife and three times attempted to slit Seward's throat. But a metal brace, which Seward wore as a result of a runaway horse accident, turned the assassin's blade away from his neck. While horrible cuts were made on his face and chest, no vital organ was damaged. The secretary's daughter Fanny was knocked unconscious, and another son Augustus was injured, though not seriously, when they rushed to their father's aid.

The severely injured secretary had fallen off the bed against the wall, no doubt saving his life. By this time Sergeant Robinson, a male army nurse, and a Mr. Hansell, a state department messenger, had entered the room. Paine turned to attack them and after slashing Robinson, plunged his knife to the hilt into Hansell's chest. Paine then fled down the stairs and out the front door. When Herold heard the commotion, he tied Paine's horse to a tree and fled the scene, leaving Paine to make his own getaway. Because he did not know the streets of Washington, he wandered about the city and made no escape.

Atzerodt went to the boarding house where Vice President Johnson was rooming. In all probability he had already decided not to try to kill the vice president. It is difficult to say whether his conscience was suddenly aroused or he simply lost his nerve. In any case, he did not attempt to assassinate Johnson. Even when Johnson knew that Lincoln had been shot, he refused to accept the protection which was offered.

Meanwhile, all was confusion at Ford's Theater. A few moments after Booth dropped onto the stage from the president's box, Mrs. Lincoln uttered a piercing scream which was heard by all those present. At that moment she had just realized what had happened to her husband. Rathbone cried, "Stop that man!" Someone screamed, "He shot the president!" A group of men tried to force open the little white door that led from the aisle back of the president's box to the rear of the theater. But Booth had blocked it too well that afternoon. Finally, under the wounded Rathbone's direction, the door was opened from the other side. Within the group around the president's box, a man called, "I am a doctor," so they let him in. It was Dr. Charles Leale, a 23-year-old assistant surgeon of the army.

In front of the theater a man cried, "I'm glad it happened." In a few moments he was stripped of his clothes and beaten by the crowd. It took several policemen with drawn guns to rescue him from certain death.[11]

Dr. Leale had the president placed on the floor of the box. He skillfully began to examine the fallen chief executive. Finding blood on the back of Lincoln's head, he searched and found the hole made by the bullet. He gently probed the wound with his little finger and determined that the bullet had traveled toward the right eye. Then he carefully examined the right eye and saw that there was no exit wound. Concluding that the bullet was still in the president's brain, he realized that the wound was fatal. Quickly he reached into the victim's mouth and pulled the tongue up and forward to save him from suffocation. Leale put his own mouth on that of the president and breathed into it. Soon the president's labored breathing began again. The doctor then uttered the now famous words, "His wound is mortal. It is impossible for him to recover."[12]

Some wanted to take the president to the White House, but Leale insisted that he could not survive such a trip. It was then decided to move Lincoln to a house nearby. When they looked for a place to take the dying president, they noticed a light in the Petersen boarding house across the street from the theater. A soldier on leave, William T. Clark, was in one of the downstairs rooms. He was roused and told to go elsewhere, that the president needed the room. Clark left in his nightgown, carrying his clothing with him. The president was so tall that they had to place him diagonally across Clark's bed. His head was propped up so that he might breathe more easily. The room was small, only about fifteen by ten feet in size.

By this time Dr. Joseph K. Barnes, the surgeon general of the army, joined several other doctors who had arrived. All the doctors could do was try to keep Lincoln warm, administer occasional stimulants, put the ever-present mustard plaster on his chest, and keep the wound open and free of blood clots so pressure would not build up inside the brain. Sometime during the night, Dr. Phineas D. Gurley, pastor of the New York Avenue Presbyterian Church where Lincoln most often attended, said a prayer. The vigil of death had begun. It lasted until 7:22 the next morning, Saturday, April 15, 1865.

Several times during the night Mrs. Lincoln came into the room for brief periods, once throwing herself on the bed beside her husband. Robert, the president's oldest son, was either by his father or trying to comfort his mother. All manner of governmental personnel came and went during the night. In all, some 53 people came to the dying president's bedside. Secretary of War Stanton took charge. No one questioned his authority, even though Vice President Johnson made a brief call during the night. Stanton and city officials directed the search for Booth and the other conspirators after Booth was identified as the assassin.

Stanton was in the room when Lincoln breathed his last. According to most writers it is he who made the comment that millions have seen written in large letters just behind the Lincoln tomb in Springfield, Illinois — "Now he belongs to the ages." However, some do not give credit to any particular person for this dramatic statement.[13] One person very near the dying president maintained he heard no such comment. At least one other person equally close to Lincoln said Stanton's comment was, "Now he belongs to history." No one can be sure. It is the writer's opinion that Stanton probably did make this famous comment.

After Lincoln died, his body was taken to the White House where his coffin was placed on a catafalque. Hundreds of floral pieces surrounded the body of the fallen president. Senator Charles Sumner of Massachusetts, a close personal friend of Lincoln, made the funeral arrangements. More than 25,000 people passed by the open casket in the East Room on Tuesday, April 18.

The next day the funeral was conducted in the East Room by Dr. Gurley assisted by four other ministers. During the service Robert, Lincoln's son, stood at the foot of the casket and General Grant sat at the head. Grant broke into sobs as the service began. Mary Lincoln was so distraught that she was unable to attend the service.[14] Some feared for her sanity. The black maid, Elizabeth Keckley, seemed to be the only one who could calm her. Tad, their 12-year-old son, was deeply distressed. Lincoln and Tad had been very close. The emotional condition of his mother made the loss of his father all the more devastating.

After the service the body was taken to the Capitol by a long procession led by freed slaves who had fought in the Union army. The mass of humanity was so great that the procession was able to move to the Capitol only with great difficulty. Tens of thousands more passed by the open casket in the Capitol rotunda. Throughout the North, church bells in every city, village and hamlet rang for the slain leader. Countless masses of people gathered in open churches to pray. In their grief they poured out perhaps the greatest demonstration of love in the nation's history.

On April 21 the funeral train left Washington to take the body back to Lincoln's hometown of Springfield, Illinois, for burial. The same railroad engine that had brought Lincoln as president-elect to Washington pulled the funeral train back to Springfield. The body of little Willie, who had died in the White House earlier in Lincoln's administration, was placed by his father's casket to be buried by his side. The funeral train traveled through Baltimore, Harrisburg, Philadelphia, New York, Albany, Buffalo, Cleveland, Columbus, Indianapolis, and Chicago before it reached Springfield. Millions viewed the body in the open casket. Elaborate ceremonies were held in the cities visited by the train. At its final stop in Springfield on May 3, 1865, the body was taken from the railroad car to Oak Hill Cemetery, where it was placed in a vault at the foot of a hill. Matthew Simpson, Methodist bishop of Washington and a good friend of Lincoln, said the final words over the body.

Charges have continued through the years that there was a conspiracy within the administration to put Lincoln out of the way and have the radical "hard-liners" direct Reconstruction. Lincoln, some felt, would be too easy on the South. There were many charges and countercharges; a few will be briefly noted here. Secretary Stanton is most often accused. Perhaps that is because he took charge so quickly that fateful night. It is hard to see how anyone in the government could have planned everything as it actually happened without discovery. The writer can find no hard evidence to tie Stanton to the assassination. Some noted the apparent agonized look on Stanton's face as Lincoln was dying. The comment Stanton made about Lincoln's place in history, which several swear he made, seems sincere enough. These witnesses were not beholden to the secretary. Again, Stanton did not gain anything personally by the death of Lincoln. In fact, he was soon out of government, fired by President Johnson. Certainly he did not gain money or position for himself from Lincoln's death.

It is distinctly possible that Stanton saw the assassination of Lincoln as but the beginning of a massive terrorist attack against the government in Washington by the South, and therefore was reluctant to spend too much energy and strength going after Booth and the other conspirators when all possible resources might be needed to protect the city of Washington. Grant's and Sherman's armies were some distance from Washington, leaving the city ill-prepared to defend itself against a large number of individual acts of terrorism.

No one would deny that Stanton was petulant, sullen, and irascible, with a transcending ego and a force of will matched by few in his day. A man of deep passions, he had very few friends. Many harsh things could truthfully be said of this volcanic man, but his contribution to the success of the Union armies was monumental. Apparently he and Lincoln had worked out some sort of strange understanding that kept the war machine of the North moving. However, some felt that when the war was over Lincoln could not be trusted with the direction of the nation. This theory would place Stanton in the center of a terrible conspiracy to remove Lincoln.

Some very interesting but unproven accusations have been leveled at Stanton. In 1977, a Joseph Lynch of Worthington, Massachusetts, claimed to have discovered the missing pages of Booth's diary in which Stanton is implicated in this act of murder. Without ever examining the so-called missing pages of the diary, many reporters, columnists, television personalities, and individuals in the motion picture industry began to repeat Lynch's bald statement that Booth's diary clearly implicated Stanton. Typical of these accusations was the book, *The Lincoln Conspiracy,* by David Balsiger and Charles E. Sellier, Jr. However, Stephen B. Oates, a careful and gifted historian, calls Lynch's claim a hoax and bluntly says that the so-called "missing pages" never existed.[15] The writer agrees that Lynch's findings lack substance and cannot be taken at face value.

Were the charges made of whole cloth? Of course not. Some facts could be construed to make Stanton culpable. He refused to let Major Eckert accompany Lincoln to Ford's Theater that fateful night. No doubt Eckert would have made a most capable bodyguard. It is charged by some that after the assassination Stanton isolated the city of Washington for more than two hours from the outside world by crippling the telegraph system. A technical malfunction was probably to blame. Also, it is charged that Stanton delayed going after the conspirators. There are some unanswered questions, but no evidence exists that Stanton delayed the pursuit of Booth in order to let him escape. The Navy Yard Bridge was apparently the only way out of the city at the time Booth was escaping. Booth was challenged by the guard at the bridge but allowed to cross the river. Also, one of Stanton's men shot and killed Booth several days later before there was an opportunity to question him. Was this done to prevent Booth from talking? The charge cannot be completely refuted, but neither can it be proved.

Otto Eisenschiml sees these as serious charges against Stanton in his book, *Why Was Lincoln Murdered?*, published in 1937. This work is most interesting, but it did not change the basic opinion of historical writers that Stanton was not a traitor.

When the conspirators had been arrested they were tried as civilians behind closed doors by a military tribunal. They were never given adequate counsel nor sufficient time to prepare a defense. The trial was one of the most flagrant cases of violation of civil rights ever seen in all of American history. Several hundred people were arrested and questioned with no real evidence against them. Countless irregularities occurred during the trial. Some of the prisoners were tortured.

Four persons were hanged, including Mary E. Surratt, a 48-year-old boarding-house owner, perhaps the first woman to be hanged in the United States. The charge that she was linked with the conspirators has never been proven. At the time of her trial almost everyone felt she was a part of the conspiracy. Emotions ran so high and the conduct of the trial was so irregular that few if any of those in authority actually examined the so-called evidence against her. She and her husband had owned a plantation with numerous slaves in Maryland. Also, several of the conspirators had been in her boarding house. Her son John was no doubt involved in Booth's scheme to kidnap the president. Guy W. Moore, who has studied the case exhaustively says, "As more and more facts have come to light her guilt has become more uncertain."[16] Moore concludes his work by saying her guilt, "was never more than a guess."[17]

Lewis Paine, George Atzerodt, and David Herold were also hanged. No doubt Paine had knowledge of the total conspiracy, and Atzerodt was a part of the plot, though he became afraid and did not attempt to kill Vice President Johnson as he was scheduled to do. Herold went with Paine in his attempt to kill Secretary Seward. He also accompanied Booth on his escape from Washington.

Dr. Samuel A. Mudd, who cared for Booth's broken leg, was sentenced to life imprisonment but was pardoned four years later, as was

Edman Spangler who, as a stagehand, had helped Booth escape. It is not certain that Edman knew what was going on.

For years tragedy stalked the lives of many of those who were involved in the events of April fourteenth. Major Rathbone and Clara Harris were married some time later, but disaster overtook them. The major killed his wife and spent the remainder of his life in an insane asylum. Ex-Senator Preston King of New York, who kept Mrs. Surratt's daughter Anna from seeing President Johnson to beg for her mother's life, committed suicide by tying a bag of shot around his neck and jumping off a ferry into the water. Senator James Lane of Kansas, who with King had prevented Anna Surratt from seeing President Johnson, shot himself.[18] Stanton, named to the Supreme Court at his own request by President Johnson, was on his death-bed when the appointment arrived.[19]

Mary Lincoln was no doubt the most pathetic figure of all those who were a part of the events of that Good Friday. Never could she find peace although she sought it as she moved to New York, Europe, and Chicago. On many occasions she was completely out of control. Her son Robert signed the papers that sent her to a hospital for the insane. She was released about a year later and returned to the home on Jackson Street in Springfield, which she and the promising attorney Abraham Lincoln had shared with their growing family. It is likely she was psychotic. Her last years were filled with dread and terror as she lived behind the closed shutters of her home, seldom ever venturing out of the house, never dressed in anything other than the clothes of mourning. Tad died in 1871, a sickly lad to the end. Robert became a member of President Garfield's cabinet and died in 1926 at 83.

Some years after the burial, criminals attempted to kidnap Lincoln's body and hold it for ransom. The special tomb that had been erected to house the body was not massive enough to prevent the kidnappers from easily opening the crypt. They were attempting to pass the body through a window when waiting police who had been alerted arrested them. To prevent another possible attempt to kidnap the body, it was quickly buried in the sand inside one of the work sheds in the cemetery. Today the body lies beneath tons of reinforced concrete in a magnificent tomb in Springfield.

Some have expressed the thought that had Lincoln only lived out his term of office, the period of Reconstruction would have become a time of healing not only between the North and South, but also between the various bitterly fighting factions within the government.

The writer cannot accept that theory. Already the Radicals were organizing to have their vindictive way in the Reconstruction. They were not reluctant to express the view that if the president got in their way they would run over him and reduce him to a political cipher. Reconstruction might have broken the spirit of the man of compassion who lived in the White House. He had borne so much. Perhaps it was his time to die.

The 17th, Andrew Johnson

Impeachment and Vindication, 1869–1875

Few presidents, if any, have had a term of office filled with more
malevolence, turmoil and violent politics than Andrew Johnson
(1808–1875). Elected as Abraham Lincoln's vice president, Johnson succeeded to the nation's highest office upon the death of Lincoln, just a little
over a month into his second term. Serving from 1865 to 1869, Johnson was
a man of integrity, courage, and probity. However, he was also sensitive,
proud, rude, crude, irascible, vindictive, and combative by nature. Put
such a man in the explosive situation that existed just after the Civil War,
and "all hell" is apt to break loose. It did. His enemies impeached him, but
he escaped conviction by one vote and stayed in office. Perhaps there was
more bitterness in this period than at any other time in America's history.

In spite of all the turmoil of his administration, the city of Washington
had come to rather admire the doughty chief executive. The White House
witnessed many social events that were very well received. Some even called
them brilliant.[1] These occasions set a high standard that many of his successors could not equal. This despite the fact that Mrs. Johnson was an invalid and only once left her sick room while she lived in the White House.
The Johnson's daughter, Martha Patterson, their oldest child, very successfully acted as first lady. As a result, many of the nonpolitical citizens
in Washington felt a sense of loss when the Johnsons returned to
Greeneville, Tennessee, their longtime home. On March 3, 1869, hundreds
came to the White House to bid farewell to the Johnsons. The Washington
press carried a number of stories extolling the simple virtues of the depart-
ing president.

Johnson was one of the few outgoing presidents that did not accompany the newly-elected chief executive to the Capitol for his inauguration.
Perhaps the reason can be found in an entry in the diary of Gideon Wells,
Johnson's secretary of the navy. "After the silly, arrogant and insolent
declarations of Grant that he would not speak to his official superior and
predecessor, nor ride nor associate with him, the President could not

compose a part in the pageant to glorify Grant without a feeling of abase-
ment."[2] The president bid goodbye to his cabinet in his White House office
and they all quietly left the mansion at noon on March 4. Mrs. Johnson had
already gone to be a guest of Mr. and Mrs. J.F. Coyne. Johnson then joined
his wife at the Coyne home. Coyne was editor of the *Intelligencer*.

The outgoing president declined a number of invitations, among them
a European tour, in order to return to his home. However, the one invitation he did accept was to a reception in his honor in Baltimore on March
12. Many places of business closed as the day became a public holiday. The
Baltimore and Ohio Railroad took Johnson to Baltimore in a special car.
In the afternoon a reception was held in the rotunda of the post office. Hundreds passed by to shake hands and to wish him well. In the evening a glittering banquet was held at the Barnum Hotel. If the toasts given at the dinner were any indication of the feeling of the people of that city, Johnson's
fight against the Congressional program of Reconstruction was much appreciated by the city of Baltimore. A number of the toasts openly predicted
that history would vindicate Johnson.

In the days immediately after leaving the White House, Johnson and
his daughter Martha were busy buying furniture and fixtures for their home
in Greeneville. The former president had not seen his own house since he
fled the town in 1861 to escape the Confederates. The Southern army had
left his home in shambles after using it as quarters for officers, a storage
place, and even as a Negro brothel.[3] Many of the windows had been
broken, some of the doors were missing, the walls were dirty and scarred,
and the floors needed repair. Johnson's daughter, Mary Stover, had supervised the repair of the house and the restoration of the grounds, garden,
and fences.

Johnson and his family started by train for Greeneville on March 18,
stopping frequently along the way. Each of the towns they went through
wanted to show him their affection and respect. One of the stops was at
Lynchburg, Virginia, where he had earlier been shot at and burned in effigy.
Now the town turned out to welcome him. It was the same at Watauga,
Nolichucky, Johnson City, Jonesboro, and Carter Station. At Bristol,
where they entered the state of Tennessee, a delegation from his hometown
boarded the train and escorted him home. When the train reached
Greeneville, almost the whole town was there to welcome him. The former
president responded with feeling and warmth. When a reporter asked him
if he might enter politics again, Johnson replied that there was a lot of life
left in him yet. The banner across the main street read, "Welcome Home,
Andrew Johnson, Patriot." A banner in the same spot in 1861 had read,
"Andrew Johnson, Traitor."

Now he was a private citizen for the first time in thirty years, a man
respected in his own community. While he was not wealthy, his financial

resources were more than adequate for his rather simple life-style. He was anxious to enter the life of his native state again. The chief note of sadness was that his son Robert died soon after their return, probably by his own hand.[4] Robert had acted as his father's secretary for several years before. Johnson himself was ill part of the first summer after he returned to Tennessee, but made a full recovery.

In all probability Andrew Johnson did not intend to enter politics again when he first came home from Washington. But his burning desire for personal vindication overcame his early reluctance, and soon he was completely immersed in politics. Few believe that he deserved the treatment he received at the hands of the Reconstruction Congress. His desire for vindication was perfectly natural. The wonder is that at his age he had the courage and the physical stamina to enter the rough and tumble of Tennessee politics again. Early in the summer of 1869 Johnson made a grand tour of the state. He met old friends and tested the political waters as he talked issues and politics. What he found on this tour made him feel that it was entirely possible for him to win an election again.

He had been in politics most of his adult life, serving in the House of Representatives for ten years, then as governor of Tennessee for two terms, and as a member of the United States Senate from October 8, 1857, to March 4, 1862. He refused to support the secession of his state, even remaining in the Senate after Tennessee seceded. As a result of his devotion to the Union, Abraham Lincoln named him the military governor of Tennessee with the rank of brigadier general of the volunteers. From this post he was named candidate for the vice presidency by the Republicans in 1864. The Republican victory made him Lincoln's vice president.

The Civil War had changed Tennessee in many ways. The carpetbaggers from the North and their Southern henchmen, the scalawags, had seized control of the state. Corruption, violence, and social upheaval had followed. True, a large part was due to the necessary abolition of slavery, but unprincipled men took advantage of the situation to "line their pockets" to the harm of both the newly freed slaves as well as the mass of the middle and lower class whites who had never been a part of the plantation system. The Radicals in Congress and in the state governments were raping the South. Johnson could not fit into this sort of government, neither could he ally himself with what was left of the old political machine and its so-called "Confederate brigadiers" who had run the state of Tennessee for so long. He had to start with no power base and little to help him except the force of his own personality. His successes were evidence of his tremendous ability as a politician and a speaker.

Johnson participated in four political campaigns after he returned from Washington. In a matter of a few months he was stumping the state for W.C. Senter who was running for governor. Senter was a capable, honest, hard working official who was attempting to take a moderate position in this very explosive situation. Great crowds came to hear the former president and it was obvious that he had lost none of his fire and ability to sway a crowd. Senter was elected governor. Large gains in the state legislature were also made by the moderates.

Then the name of Andrew Johnson began to be frequently mentioned as a candidate for the United States Senate. (State legislatures and not the people elected the senators at that time.) Johnson then announced his candidacy for the Senate, and another campaign was launched. The ex-president seemed the leading candidate. However, President Grant did not want Johnson in the Senate, so the influence of the federal government was used against him. A considerable amount of out-of-state money came in to oppose Johnson. When his campaign manager, Edmund Cooper, double-crossed Johnson, Cooper's brother Henry was elected to the Senate instead of Johnson. Even so, the former president came within two votes of gaining the Senate seat. One of Johnson's associates had an opportunity to buy these two needed votes, but the ex-president indignantly refused to engage in a deal of this sort.[5]

In 1872 Johnson ran for the newly-created position of Congressman-at-large. In a boisterous campaign Johnson boldly attacked the secessionists, upheld the Union, and defended the Constitution, which he said the Radical Reconstructionists had flagrantly violated. General Cheatham was the Democratic candidate, Horace Maynard the choice of the Radicals. Johnson ran as an independent with little organized support. It was a rough, disorderly campaign. In attacking the old-line secessionists and supporting the Union, as well as pointedly criticizing the Radicals who were in control of the Congress, Johnson had only a very narrow group that would actively and openly support him. Horace Maynard won the three-cornered race.

Several times Johnson's life was threatened. On numerous occasions rowdies attempted to prevent him from speaking. He was lied about and viciously attacked by pamphlets that were widely distributed. Yet he pursued his course in a calm, forceful manner, never getting involved in the numerous brawls nor descending to name-calling. He had not expected to win, but his main purpose was accomplished — to break the power of the old-line Democrats (Confederate brigadiers).

The next year a bad epidemic of cholera came to Tennessee. Many fled the state. Johnson had the means to leave if he desired, but he chose to stay and help his fellow townspeople. In the process he contracted the disease himself. His life was despaired of, but he recovered. However, he was never as strong and robust as he had been before. The effects of this illness followed him the rest of his life.

When he lay critically ill, not expecting to live, he reaffirmed his belief in God in rather poignant words when he said, "Approaching death to me is a mere shadow of God's protecting wing . . . where the great fact will be realized that God is Truth, and gratitude the highest attribute of man."[6]

In the Panic of 1873, Johnson lost $73,000 when the First National Bank of Washington failed. He felt compelled to announce to the public that he was not "broke" and would continue life just as he had before. He still had a small fortune.

In the midterm election of 1874 the Republicans lost considerable power. A Democratic House of Representatives was elected, the first since the Civil War. Of more interest to this account is that the state legislature of Tennessee would meet early the next year to elect a United States Senator. Johnson was determined to run again. He felt that the "brigadiers" had been weakened and that he had a good chance of winning his old Senate seat. He opened a strong campaign as an independent, especially attacking Governor Neil Brown, one of the Radicals. The old-line Democrats supported General Bates. Johnson's vigorous swing around the state produced gratifying results. He kept attacking the Radicals and telling how the Cooper brothers had betrayed him in his last run for the Senate. When he was scheduled to speak at Columbia, the home of the Coopers, word came to him that if he discredited the Coopers he would not live to get out of town.

The courageous ex-president went to Columbia as scheduled. When he arrived, he discovered that the opposition had seized the courtroom, leaving him no place to speak. Hurriedly his followers found packing boxes and constructed a crude platform under the window of the room where the Coopers and their followers had gathered. A crowd soon assembled and Johnson defied the Cooper faction to attack saying, "These two eyes have never yet beheld the man that his heart feared."[7] The Johnson followers expected the Cooper people to start shooting. So, just as Johnson issued his challenge, his followers could be heard cocking their pistols and pointing them at the window of the room where the Coopers were. His opponents did not fire, so there was no fight.

The Tennessee legislature gathered on January 4, 1875, to begin its session with the election of the United States senator the chief item on the agenda. The legislature was comprised of 92 Democrats and 8 Republicans. The voting began on January 19. Johnson had 10 more votes than anyone else on the first ballot. Brown and Bates, though both Democrats, developed a bitter rivalry. So sharp was the controversy that Brown withdrew, leaving Bates to battle Johnson. On the forty-fourth ballot, Bates was just one vote away from victory, but he never could gain that one vote. Finally, on the fifty-fifth ballot, on January 26, Johnson won the Senate seat by one vote. The former president would return to the body that had almost removed him from the presidency. His vindication had been won.

The city of Nashville turned out to celebrate Johnson's victory. He was the popular choice, though the people could not vote for senators. Johnson responded to the cheers in a careful and conciliatory speech. He assured his audience that he would go to Washington with no bitterness or hostility and would work to see that the Constitution was upheld and the Union strengthened. A few, in the euphoria of victory, declared they would return him to the White House.

Most of the press congratulated him on his victory. The big New York City newspapers, the *Times, World,* and *Tribune,* gave Johnson much favorable comment. Even some of the Radical newspapers praised his honesty and courage. The reaction in the South was on the whole favorable. The *New York Herald* maintained that "In the Senate he will be of greater use to the country than he was in the Presidency," for he would have an independence as a senator that he could not have as president. The *Herald* went on to state that the charges against Johnson when he was impeached (but not convicted) were without substance.[8] Congratulatory telegrams poured in from all over the nation. The Republicans were somewhat apprehensive about having to deal with Johnson again, while the Democrats enjoyed the discomfiture of the Republicans. One thing was certain, Johnson would be his own man.

Under normal conditions Johnson would have taken his Senate seat in December. However, President Grant had called the Senate into extra session to ratify a treaty the United States had made with King Kalakaua of the Sandwich Islands. On March 6, about noon, Andrew Johnson walked into the Senate chamber to take his seat. A large crowd of his friends, as well as the curious, crowded into the galleries and the halls of the Capitol to witness one of the very dramatic incidents of United States history. As he entered the Senate chamber, Johnson looked vigorous and healthy. One reporter noted, "There are neither hard lines nor deep wrinkles in his face, but his expression is a mixture of sadness and earnestness."[9] The vice president who swore him in was Henry Wilson, leader of the impeachment move against Johnson in the House, and who had said many scurrilous things against him. The personal feelings of both of these men is not difficult to imagine.

Of the 35 senators who in 1868 had voted to convict Johnson, only 13 remained in that body. It was of considerable interest to observe how these 13 would react when the former president took his seat. Johnson, neatly dressed in a broadcloth suit, advanced to his seat and discovered it was covered with flowers. A cheer went up from the gallery, and a number of senators stood up to show respect. Senator Edmunds of Vermont, who had voted against Johnson, was addressing the chair. When he saw Johnson come in, he abruptly took his seat and in the process knocked over a stack of books. Senator Rosco Conkling of New York pretended to read a letter, but observed all that went on out of the corner of his eye. Senator John Sherman had the dignity to come forward and shake Johnson's hand in welcome. Vice President Wilson came down from his chair and shook hands with Johnson. Oliver Morton showed some embarrassment when he saw Johnson. (Morton had first defended Johnson, but in the end yielded to pressure and voted against him.) When Johnson saw this, he went over to Morton and shook his hand. Morton gladly took it. Johnson showed only magnanimity and conciliation. Of the seven courageous Republicans who had voted for Johnson in the trial, none was there to welcome him. They had all died, or had lost their positions for voting their convictions against the pressure of the Radicals. Grimes, one of the most courageous of Johnson's defenders, was dead. Johnson confessed that one of his deepest feelings was that of missing his old friends. One of his finest statements was, "I have no enemies to punish, nor friends to reward."[10] Tears were seen in his eyes when he returned to his seat after taking the oath of office.

Johnson in that Senate session would have one occasion to tell the nation what was occurring in some of the carpetbag governments in the South. Some Radicals in the Senate introduced a resolution to approve President Grant's action in sending federal troops to aid the carpetbag government in Louisiana. The situation in that state was unspeakably vile and corrupt. The two worst villains were probably Henry Warmoth and William P. Kellogg. Warmoth was a carpetbagger who had come to Louisiana with the federal troops. He got himself elected governor of the state by promising the black voters that he would "invent a machine to pump the black blood from a Negro's veins and replace it with white blood."[11] In his two-year term as governor, the state's debt went from six million to fifty million dollars. In the same period Warmoth's bank account went from zero to about $70,000.

A little later Warmoth set up what he called the "Returning Board" to judge election returns. Kellogg's election as governor had been secured by these tactics. There was enough open resistance to this arbitrary action that the Radicals feared a riot might result and called for federal troops to protect them. The government responded with soldiers and warships, and by force established the Kellogg administration. Many Northern newspapers and national leaders vigorously objected to this use of force. The Radicals in Congress supported the Kellogg regime and felt they needed Congressional support for their action.

Senator Andrew Johnson arose and attacked the administration in the most vigorous manner. He made a long speech in which he documented each allegation of corruption in Louisiana. He indicted Grant for his arrogance and the ruthless manner in which he was seeking a third term as president, as well as for his vindictiveness and arbitrary use of power.

It is not the writer's intention to say that Grant knowingly perpetrated these outrages. Grant was naive and had such a poor knowledge of government that he probably did not know the actual situation himself. He was so bereft of understanding that he was influenced by those who glibly told him what he should do. This in no way relieves his administration of responsibility for the many instances of corruption in the federal government, but suggests that Grant was not guilty of criminal intent.

At the end of the special session, after serving for about two weeks, Johnson returned to his Tennessee home feeling very good about what he was able to do. He seemed in much better health than he had been in several years. He relaxed and looked after his local affairs until the heat of the summer became very oppressive. His daughter, Mary Stover, lived in the mountains of Carter County where it was much cooler, so he decided to spend some time there and escape the heat. He boarded the train at Greeneville, got off at Carter's Station and walked to his daughter's home, less than a mile away. He ate a substantial lunch and spent some time with his granddaughter, Lillie Stover. As she was leaving the room she heard a noise and looked back to see that her grandfather had fallen to the floor. A stroke had overtaken him. His daughter put him to bed, but he refused to let a doctor see him. He seemed to be resting comfortably in the afternoon of the next day when he suffered a second stroke which left him unconscious. Several doctors were soon at his side, but he was beyond help. He died the same day, July 31, 1875.

The family received requests from Knoxville, Nashville, and Memphis to have Johnson buried in their city, but he had already chosen the site for his tomb, a spot on the little hill of the Greeneville cemetery. It is easily seen as one enters the grounds, a simple obelisk with a figure on top. He had personally planted a willow from his yard which grew from a cutting of a tree near Napoleon's earliest tomb at St. Helena.[12]

In a speech several years earlier he had suggested he would like to be buried with the "Stars and Stripes" for a shroud and the Constitution for a pillow. In accord with these expressed sentiments, his body was wrapped in a flag and his own copy of the Constitution was placed under his head. The procession to the cemetery was more than half a mile long. Officials came from Washington and Nashville. The mayor of Greeneville, Blackstone McDannel, led the mourners. But the greatest number of those who came to honor this ex-president were the people from the towns around the state, many of them hill folk with their distinctive dress and manners. The Masonic Order took part in the service—the same chapter that had included Andrew Jackson as one of its members. The Master Tailor's Association asked the privilege of erecting the monument that stands today. The invalid wife of the ex-president followed him in death just a few months later.

The 18th, Ulysses S. Grant

A Race with Death, 1877-1885

General Ulysses S. Grant (1822-1885) came out of the Civil War the most popular living American. Four years after accepting Lee's surrender at Appomattox he moved into the White House. Although his presidency (1869-1877) was not an outstanding one, the public generally forgave him for his failures, and continued to regard him as the general who saved the Union. But the account of General Grant's heroic struggle against business reverses and terminal illness after he left the presidency is a dramatic one. He desperately needed to finish his memoirs in order to save the family from financial ruin. It seems that he held off death itself until his book was completed, for once his writing was finished, he died within a week.

President Grant retired from eight years in office on March 4, 1877, and, with his family, took a two-year triumphant trip around the world. While he was out of the country, the general's friends on their own initiative, and led by Boss Rosco Conkling of New York, began a campaign to nominate him for a third term in the White House. If Grant had received 72 more votes in the Republican Convention of 1880, he would have been nominated for a third term. However, he could not gain the necessary support, and James A. Garfield was nominated by the Republicans on the thirty-sixth ballot of the convention. Garfield went on to win in November of 1880 by a substantial majority. Grant was deeply disappointed at not winning the presidency again. He felt that he had learned by his previous experience as president and would make a much better chief executive if elected to a third term.

Upon losing his bid to return to the White House, the most immediate reality for Grant was that he now had to find a way to make a living for himself and his family. He had no profession other than the military and no experience in or capacity for business. He lived briefly in his modest Galena, Illinois, home, but to him that was too much of a loss of status for a person in his position, so he decided to live in New York City. In spite of his limited financial resources, he was not destitute. He had some real

estate, and some investments and savings. Also, at the suggestion of George
W. Jones, the editor of the *New York Times,* the general's friends raised
a fund of $250,000 for him. The money was not given to him directly, but
was invested and the income from the fund given to Grant. Unfortunately,
the trustees of the fund made poor investments and the monies the general
received were small. It was not long until the whole fund had been
dissipated by mismanagement, poor choice of investments, and lengthy
legal action. The general was left with very little.

In yet another way the friends of the general tried to help him. George
W. Childs and A.T. Drexel raised a fund and bought the Grants a home
in New York City. Although not ostentatious, it was more than adequate
for their needs. Furthermore, it was located at 3 East Sixty-sixth Street, a
very proper address for a man of affairs in New York.

Meanwhile, Grant's son, Ulysses S. Grant, Jr. (or "Buck," as he was
called), had joined forces with a bright, energetic young businessman
named Ferdinand Ward. The two young men formed a brokerage firm
called Grant and Ward that soon began to show very good profits. Because
of his name, the young Grant was a good front man, although he did not
know very much about the workings of big money on Wall Street. (Some
regarded Buck as not overly bright.) But he earned $36,000 a year for his
work as contact man for Grant and Ward. Buck was happy with the ar-
rangement and so was his famous father. In 1883, the general was invited
to join the firm, and managed to raise $100,000 to invest in the company.
Eventually the two Grants invested a considerable amount of money in the
enterprise. Ward brought stocks and bonds of questionable value as his
share of the capital in forming the new firm.[1] Ward explained that all his
ready cash was tied up in his many other business interests, so he would
contribute his share of capital to the firm by contributing "gilt-edged"
stocks and bonds. It is significant to note that the public generally assumed
the name Grant in "Grant and Ward" was the general's, when indeed it was
that of his son, Buck.

Many of the methods used by Ward in running the firm's business were
highly illegal. Two sets of books were kept, but the Grants only saw one
of them. Furthermore, the relationship between the Marine National Bank
of New York and the firm of Grant and Ward was most irregular. Ward
presented many worthless promissory notes to the bank for discounting
and the bank promptly accepted them. For example, Ward had one of his
messengers sign a promissory note for $80,000. The note was taken to the
Marine National Bank, immediately discounted, and the money given to
Ward.[2] "Ward was rehypothecating [a limited pyramid scheme] the
securities of the firm improperly by pledging the same stocks to support
more than one bank loan."[3] All this was accomplished with the knowledge
and cooperation of James D. Fish, president of the Marine National Bank.

No one warned the general of his son's partner's character. Many of Grant's friends suspected Ward of improper conduct, but no one bluntly told the general what was going on. His friends found it difficult to tell a former president of the United States that his business associate was a thief and a swindler.

The firm of Grant and Ward apparently was making a great deal of money. The general and his son were well satisfied with the good success of their business. But on Sunday morning, May 4, 1884, with no previous hint of trouble, a very agitated Ward came to see the general. Ward told him that the Marine National Bank was, for the moment, in a difficult position. The City of New York had suddenly withdrawn about $300,000 of its funds, leaving the bank short of cash for Monday's opening. Ward pointed out that the bank had a large amount of Grant and Ward money on deposit, and that if anything happened to the bank it would seriously embarrass their own business. The plain fact was that the firm of Grant and Ward was overdrawn at the bank. Ward concluded by pointing out that the bank was sound enough, but was just a bit short of cash for the next morning. Ward then asked the general to borrow $150,000 for just a few hours. The money would be returned no later than Tuesday morning.[4]

The general agreed to help out. He traveled the few blocks from his own home to that of William H. Vanderbilt, one of the most wealthy men in New York, and in the name of the firm Grant and Ward requested a loan of $150,000. Vanderbilt, who understood the situation, replied that he would not lend a cent to the firm of Grant and Ward or the Marine National Bank, but would lend the requested sum to General Grant personally, which he did with a check for the full amount. Grant returned to his home and gave the check to Ward. That was the last he saw of the money. It was not deposited in the account of Grant and Ward at the Marine National Bank, but was cashed by Ward personally. This left the general with a debt of $150,000 to Vanderbilt which he was honor-bound to repay.

The Marine National Bank was unable to meet its obligation to the clearing house on Wednesday, May 7, so it had to close its doors. They never reopened. The same fate came to the firm of Grant and Ward. They had many outstanding obligations which could not be met. Their own books showed they had over $600,000 deposited in the Marine National Bank, but the bank's books showed they were badly overdrawn. Ward had withdrawn large sums without the knowledge of either of the Grants or without recording the withdrawals in the firm's books. When Ward saw that he was discovered, he tried to leave the country, but was apprehended and brought back. Both of the conspirators, Ward and Fish, were brought to trial, convicted and sent to prison. But there was no way either of the Grants could recover their money.

The failure of both the Marine Bank and Grant and Ward left the

Grant family in dire straits. They could not even pay their household bills. When the family took stock of the total available money, the general had $80 in cash, and Mrs. Grant $130.[5] The day before the couple would have estimated their fortune at about one-and-a-half million dollars. Had not two friends given them $1,000 each, they could not have purchased the bare necessities for very long. Charles Wood of Lansingburg, N.Y., sent the Grants $1,000 saying the money was "on account of my share for [your] services ending April, 1865" (the date of the end of the Civil War).[6] Don Marías Romera of Mexico called on the general and left a check for $1,000 on the table which the Grants did not discover until after he had gone. Both of these gifts were accepted as loans and subsequently were repaid.

The general was intensely concerned about the money he had borrowed as a personal loan from Vanderbilt. Immediately he began to secure the loan. Grant had houses in Galena, Philadelphia and Washington, a farm near St. Louis, and property in Chicago. These were consigned to Vanderbilt as well as the war trophies and ceremonial gifts that Grant had received on his world tour. Vanderbilt offered to return the mementos to the Grants, but the offer was refused because they feared that some other creditor might take them. The trophies and gifts were then given to the government and placed in a Washington museum. Vanderbilt considered that the general's debt to him had been satisfied. A few who had lost money in the firm Grant and Ward tried to link the general with these losses, but the court agreed with Grant that he was a special partner and not one of the general partners, and thus was not liable for anything except the money he had invested in the bankrupt firm. At least Grant was now free from the most pressing obligations resulting from his business failures although his financial problems continued to be embarrassing to Grant. Perhaps they even shortened his life, for in just a little more than 14 months he was in his grave.

In June 1884, the Grant family went to their summer cottage at Long Branch on the New Jersey coast. Long Branch was a popular, if not exclusive, summer resort. Their cottage was adequate, pleasant and congenial. A number of Grant's friends also summered at Long Branch. It was here that Robert Underwood Johnson, one of the editors of *The Century,* a popular magazine of the day, found General Grant.[7] *The Century* had already published a number of articles by generals of the Civil War telling about their war experiences. Johnson knew that of the two most important generals of the war only one remained alive. Lee had died in 1870, leaving no written record of his part in the long and bloody struggle. The editor saw clearly the need of getting Grant's remembrances in writing. So Johnson came to Grant and asked him to write several articles for *The Century* about his war experiences. Before Johnson left Long Branch, Grant had agreed to write one or two articles for the magazine. The first would be about the Battle of Shiloh, and the second about the conflict at Vicksburg.

Grant had a way of remembering and telling interesting incidents of the war which Johnson wanted to capture. No doubt the $500 fee the magazine would pay the general for each article prompted him to agree to do the writing. Grant had no previous experience as a writer, but his military orders as general and memos as president were classic examples of exactness and clarity of expression. His article on what happened at Shiloh was well received, and the one on Vicksburg soon followed.

Now several other publishers became interested in getting the general to write his memoirs. *The Century* offered Grant a 10 percent royalty but no advance payment. The most this offer would bring Grant was between $30,000 and $50,000 which would be a godsend to the Grant family, but would not solve all their financial problems. Neither would it have taken care of Julia (Mrs. Grant) if the general died first.

Samuel Langhorne Clemens, who wrote under the pen name of Mark Twain, had long been involved in publishing as well as writing, and since he was a great admirer of the general it was natural that he would become interested in publishing his memoirs. Clemens was sure he could do much more for Grant than *The Century* had offered, so he made a counter-offer for the memoirs Grant had yet to write. After considerable discussion and negotiation, the offer by Clemens was accepted, and the general began the difficult task of writing. He completed the memoirs in less than a year — the last word was written less than a week before his death.

The returns for his memoirs more than solved the Grants' financial needs. Clemens gave the general a substantial advance and eventually paid the family almost $450,000 in royalties.[8] The royalty fee of $200,000 paid to Julia Grant on February 27, 1886, a partial payment for the memoirs, was the largest royalty check paid out to that day, and was more than enough to care for Julia and her family until the time of her death on December 14, 1902.

For a time it seemed likely that his new career as a writer would end very quickly. On June 2, 1884, shortly after the Grants had arrived at Long Branch for the summer, the general had eaten a large midday meal and was eating a peach when suddenly he felt a sharp pain. Julia thought there was a hidden insect on the fruit that had stung him as he ate. The distress was in the back of his mouth, although he was not quite sure exactly what had happened. It seemed that there was a sore spot on the back of his tongue that the bite of peach had irritated. Although he continued to be bothered by certain fruits, he regarded it as a matter of small moment. However, the pain still bothered him enough so that he mentioned it to George Childs, his friend and neighbor at Long Branch. So when Dr. Mendez DaCosta, a friend of Childs, was visiting at the Childs' cottage, the doctor was asked to look at the general's throat. This the physician did, leaving a prescription for some medicine and the advice to see his family doctor as soon as possible. The Grant family doctor, Dr. Fordyce Barker, happened to be in Europe on a vacation, so Grant did nothing further during the summer about his ailment.

However, the annoying discomfort in the back of his mouth did not disappear. It began to interfere with his sleep, and to bother him during the day. When he finally saw the family doctor, the concerned Dr. Barker immediately sent the general to Dr. John H. Douglas, the leading throat specialist in the area. The physician took the history of the case and then looked into the throat through a newly invented mirror that doctors still use for throat examinations. The doctor was not pleased by what he saw. When the preliminary examination was concluded, the general knew by the doctor's manner that something was wrong. "Is it cancer?" he asked. The question put the doctor in a difficult position. If he bluntly told Grant what he suspected, it might adversely affect the patient. Yet he knew that if he did not tell the general the truth the patient would lose all respect for him as a physician. So the doctor replied, "General, the disease is serious, epithelial in character, and sometimes capable of being cured."[9]

At last the general was in good medical hands. Dr. Barker, the family doctor, was a leader in his profession, and was the first American doctor to use hypodermic needles in his practice. Dr. Douglas was recognized as the leading practitioner in New York City in his specialty. Furthermore, Grant and the doctor were old-time friends, for Douglas had served in the Union army under General Grant as a medical officer, and a genuine friendship had developed between them. Grant never questioned what his doctor told him or the treatment that was prescribed.

When the first doctor examined Grant at his beach cottage, the lesion on the back of the tongue was the size of a pea; by the time Grant saw Dr. Douglas it was nearly the size of a plum.[10] At that time it was possible to surgically remove parts of the soft palate, but Grant's cancer had grown much too large for that procedure to be effective.

Obviously a microscopic examination was necessary to fully confirm Dr. Douglas' diagnosis, so he sent the general to Dr. George F. Shrady to confirm his findings, not telling Dr. Shrady his own opinion, or who the patient was. In his laboratory Shrady confirmed the diagnosis of the other physicians.[11] The growth was cancerous, and there was no cure for the condition. All the doctors could do was to make the patient as comfortable as possible so he could continue with his writing. Cocaine and Iodoform were administered locally to relieve the pain. Swabbing helped to clear the throat of the discharge that came from the lesion and the mucous from the surrounding tissue. At least with these measures the general could eat and sleep in more comfort. He began seeing the doctor twice a day, going to the physician's office on the streetcar as a matter of economy.

When Grant did not confide to the family the seriousness of his illness, his wife, Julia, and his son, Fred, made a visit to the doctor and learned the truth for themselves. However, neither the general nor his family used the word *cancer*. Dr. Douglas and Dr. Shrady both estimated that their patient would live about a year after their diagnosis. He did not live quite a year.

It was during this last summer at Long Branch, when he was 62, that Grant made his last public appearance. The occasion was a reunion of the Civil War's Christian Commission, an organization designed to assist the soldiers, much as the chaplain corps would in today's army. They met at Ocean Grove, a large Methodist camp meeting site just south of Long Branch. Grant was invited to attend by George R. Stuart, a wealthy Philadelphia businessman who was active in Christian projects, and a friend of Grant. There were about ten thousand in attendance. As Stuart helped Grant onto the platform, the whole audience rose and gave a great cheer. When Grant was introduced to the audience, he was so overcome with emotion that he could hardly speak and great tears rolled down his cheeks. Never again would he stand before an audience or say anything in public.[12]

At first when he worked on his memoirs he would have a cigar in his mouth, a habit he had acquired during the war. After he captured Fort Donelson and one of the newsmen described him as an inveterate smoker who was seldom seen without his cigar, people from all over the nation began to send him boxes of cigars which he gave away by the hundreds. When not smoking he often chewed unlighted cigars. Lighted or not, the cigars seemed to give him comfort. But the doctors told him that he must limit his cigars to no more than three a day. (Many medical people today believe that Grant's use of cigars caused his cancer.) One day in November, 1884, while he was visiting a friend, he pulled out a cigar and said, "This is the last cigar I will ever smoke."[13] He meant just what he said. Only a man with an iron will could have done this, or have finished his writing when he was so ill.

On October 2, 1884, Grant wrote to Adam Badeau, who had served on the general's staff in the war and during his presidency, and asked him to come to New York to assist in writing the memoirs. Badeau, who was now a professional writer, readily came to work for Grant as a salaried aide. He had already written a military history of the Civil War and seemed well suited to the task of helping Grant. Most of Badeau's time was spent in editing Grant's work and preparing the manuscript for the publisher.

Unfortunately, the *New York World* ran an item to the effect that Grant was not writing his own book, that the real writing was being done by Adam Badeau. Immediately Samuel Clemens issued a hot denial and threatened the newspaper with a lawsuit. Grant issued a statement that the work was entirely his own and that Badeau had served only as editor and researcher. The general then dismissed Badeau and continued his writing with the help of a secretary and his son Fred.[14] After the death of the general, Badeau tried to collect a part of the profits from the book, but the court threw out the claim as groundless. A number of competent literary critics have examined Grant's memoirs and the published writings of Badeau and have come to the conclusion that the styles are so dissimilar that the two could not have been written by the same person. Edmund Wilson, who wrote the well-known book about the literature of the Civil War entitled *Patriotic Gore,* agrees completely with this position.[15] The fact that the portion of Grant's memoirs written before Badeau came to work for him and the portion written after Badeau was dismissed show no change in style is significant. Later Badeau himself basically admitted Grant's authorship.[16] However, the whole incident did prove to be a source of irritation to the general at a time when he could ill afford to be beset by such matters.

N.E. Dawson was employed to take dictation when the general's voice was strong enough to speak for sustained periods of time. At other times Grant would use a pencil and a pad of paper and write in longhand. His work was well organized and he had a great facility with the language. He seldom repeated himself or had to rewrite his text. On the days when he was physically able, he turned out a great quantity of pages. Often he wrote or dictated as many as ten thousand words in one day, by any standard rather extraordinary. Many of these handwritten pages are still in existence. But without the help of Fred Grant and N.E. Dawson, who researched many specific items in the army's official records of the Civil War, the general could not have finished his work.

Grant's greatest difficulty came in trying to eat, sleep, and talk. At first he was able to get several hours of continuous sleep through the use of drugs of various kinds. But as time went on it was increasingly difficult for him to sleep for more than an hour or two at a time. Soon it became impossible for him to sleep lying down. He had a favorite overstuffed chair in which he slept. By putting another chair in front of him for his feet he was able to get in a more or less comfortable position. On occasion as he slept his throat seemed to constrict in something of a spasm, and for a few moments he would be unable to get his breath. He was worried that he might strangle. However, the doctors assured him that in such a case he would first become unconscious, then the muscles would relax and he could breathe again. But these assurances were not of much comfort.

Swallowing became most painful, water worst of all. Often the only food he seemed able to swallow was a mixture of milk and eggs. This would be put in a bowl and he would very quickly swallow several mouthfuls before the pain forced him to quit. Small wonder he became very thin and weak. There were times when he could not talk at all, so he always had a pad and pencil close by to write his messages. However, there were times even toward the end when he could talk and on occasion could dictate for several hours.

Late in March 1885, Grant became so ill that his death was feared. At this time he felt that he might not finish his book, but at other times, although in pain, he was genuinely optimistic. The doctors expected the worst. On one occasion he seemed so far gone that the doctors injected brandy directly into his veins. This procedure was repeated several times. Whether or not from the brandy, he did rally, improving dramatically. Also, during this time he had several severe attacks of coughing, and on one occasion coughed up a mass of tissue from his throat. He did get better after this very real crisis. Going for drives in his coach were times of real enjoyment. On occasion he visited friends again. Most important to him, he could work with more vigor on his book. In May he did most of his writing at night for there were fewer interruptions, and as daylight dawned he often fell into a much needed sleep. But the improvement was short-lived.

The press dutifully recorded the progress of his disease and the general's condition was a front page item. Several newspapers assigned reporters to cover the story. Some took rooms near the Grant home and recorded all who entered or left the house. It is fairly easy to trace the progress of his fatal illness from the front pages of the *New York Times*. Not all the stories were completely accurate, but most were based on fact. The general and his family, long accustomed to dealing with the press, cooperated. Some of the reporters were very critical of the physicians attending the general and at times ridiculed them. This was especially true when, on March 31, the doctors told the press that the general was dying, after which he made a dramatic improvement. The public took great interest in Grant's condition. Crowds stood in the rain for hours in front of the Grant home.

The religious life of Grant has often been a point of interest. The general had not been a very religious man, though he did respect the clergy and help church causes. Although tolerant of all creeds, he never espoused one of his own. Julia, however, was a very religious person. During her husband's crisis of March 31, Julia's longstanding clerical counselor, the Rev. J.P. Newman, was in the home several times. Realizing that Grant had never been baptized, Newman performed the religious rite.

Some who were in the room thought that the general was unconscious at the time. However, not all those present were of that opinion. Newman's diary was discovered in 1951 and in it the clergyman tells how Grant looked directly at him during the ceremony and afterward said, "I intend[ed] to take that step myself."[17] It is certainly possible that no one else caught the faint whisper that Grant would have used at that time.

During Grant's illness, many people from all walks of life called on him. Few were ever turned away, although most were not allowed to stay for more than a few moments. Grant was especially glad when former army associates remembered him. Among these were General Ely Parker, a full-blooded Indian, John C. Fremont, called the "Pathfinder" because of his Western exploits, and John A. Logan, Civil War general and vice presidential nominee for the Republicans in 1884. Some high ranking confederate commanders also called to express their concern. General P.G.T. Beauregard who opposed Grant at Corinth and Shiloh came. Perhaps the most touching was the visit of Simon B. Buckner, a classmate of Grant at West Point, and the Confederate commander at Ft. Donelson who surrendered to Grant in 1862. Buckner became governor of Kentucky and later the Democratic vice presidential nominee in 1896. The sons of Robert E. Lee and Albert Sidney Johnson called on Grant.

When Grant became president he had resigned his commission in the United States Army, because as president he became commander-in-chief of all United States military forces. However, many of his fellow officers had not resigned, and were on the army retired lists receiving substantial pensions. Several times friends of Grant had tried to place his name on this list so that he too could receive a pension. On February 16, 1885, the House of Representatives failed by 16 votes to provide the necessary two-thirds majority to sustain the action already taken by the Senate to provide a pension for Grant. The fact that there were almost 25 former Confederate officers in the House who voted against Grant, angered many.

Some journalists were prompt to say that this group could not defeat Grant on the battlefield, but they did so in the halls of Congress. An editorial in the *New York Times* of March 3, 1885, thundered in rage: "The House of Representatives has only one day in which to vindicate its own character for decency by passing the bill to place General Grant on the retired list of the army without any other unseemly discussion. . . . It would be an absolute disgrace if the present House . . . should fail to lay aside every contention . . . and vote with dignity and decency for the proposition."[18]

Though Congress was in the act of adjourning for the inauguration of Grover Cleveland, Speaker Samuel J. Randall called the House into session on March 4, the inaugural day of the new president, and they quickly passed the bill which enabled President Cleveland to sign the commission restoring Grant to the retired list of the army with the rank and pay of general.[19] To Grant this action was very meaningful both emotionally and financially.

As spring came to New York City and the days became warmer, Grant became more uncomfortable and decided to go to a cooler climate for the summer. Few, if any, expected him to return to his Sixty-sixth Street home.

A friend of Grant, Joseph W. Drexel, offered his mountain "cottage"— twelve large rooms, and spacious porches on three sides—at Mount McGregor, New York, to the Grant family for the summer. Although the cottage was just 12 miles from Saratoga Springs, New York, the most fashionable mountain resort in the nation, the only way of access to Mount McGregor was by a narrow-gauge railroad up the mountain.

In the city the weather was muggy and humid with a temperature of about 100 degrees. William Vanderbilt lent the Grants his private railroad car for the trip to Mount McGregor on June 16. The general stood the trip fairly well, considering how hot the railroad car became. He was awakened as the train passed West Point so he could see one of the places he loved. To the cheers of the crowd that had gathered, he somehow managed to walk to the smaller narrow-gauge train from the private railroad car. When the Grants got to the cottage, he walked up the steps, went into the house, and changed his clothes. Then in a dress coat and top hat came back to the front porch to be photographed and to visit with those who had gathered. In a little over a month he would be dead.

The move to the cottage proved to be a very good one for the general. The accommodations were more than adequate for their needs. Grant, Julia, and Harrison Tyrrell, the black valet who meant so much to the general in his last days, all had downstairs bedrooms. The large parlor, or front room, accommodated visitors. The six upstairs bedrooms housed the rest of the family. They took their meals at the adjacent Hotel Balmoral as guests of Mr. Drexel. The weather was almost perfect, rarely above 80 degrees during the day or below 45 at night, and the view was breathtaking. Visitors who wished to see the general could easily come by rail.

The Grants settled into something of a routine. Helping the general to finish his writing seemed to be the basic motivation of the entire household. A doctor was usually within calling distance. Henry McQueeney, a male nurse, was always nearby. Grant made several walks about the place, and on a few occasions even left the cottage briefly. Reporters were always present, often questioning visitors as they left the cottage and often taking photographs of the general and his visitors. From time to time Grant would don a dress coat and his top hat.

But he was in great pain. Frequent use of morphine and cocaine did help, but unfortunately when he was eased by these drugs he was not as effective in the writing of his book. As the end approached, the doctors on occasion injected brandy directly into his veins to stimulate his faltering heart. He still slept in his easy chair which he had brought from New York, and still had considerable trouble speaking and swallowing. Grant fought a constant battle to keep working even though his weakness and lack of strength grew more and more pronounced.

The last picture of the Grants all together was taken on July 19. Grant wore his dress coat and top hat. He had just written the last words of his memoirs. The struggle had ceased. On July 21 he had a bad episode of hiccups which sapped his strength considerably. All day of the 22nd he was very low, yet he managed to speak a few words. Julia was constantly at his side. During the night of July 22 he wanted to lie down and was put to bed for the first time in many months. His breath was shallow, his pulse weak, his hands cold. By 7 a.m. on the 23rd, it was apparent that he was dying. At 8:08 a.m., without a struggle, he simply stopped breathing.

The *New York Times* put a note in its window at 8:14 a.m., and now the world knew of the general's death. Within the hour the flags in the city were at half-mast. The fact that by 4 p.m. Bloomingdale's store had sold a hundred thousand yards of black and white ribbon[20] shows something of the public's response to the passing of the president and general.

Though the family had lived with his impending death for more than a year, when it finally came they were in no way prepared. No specific plans had been made for the burial, and neither the funeral director nor the burial site had been selected. Ohio, St. Louis, Chicago, Galena, Illinois, as well as Washington, D.C., were all considered, but Riverside Park on the banks of the Hudson River was chosen as the general's final resting place. A temporary edifice had to be hastily constructed until a fitting final memorial and tomb could be built. Grant died on July 23 and was not buried until August 8. The embalmers took two days to do their work, and it took five days to decide where the body would be buried.

Most felt that Grant should have a large military funeral. "The pomp and pageantry of the funeral which followed surpassed anything ever seen in America."[21] On August 4, a first service was conducted at Mount McGregor, where the Rev. Newman spoke for an hour and 25 minutes. The body was then moved to Albany, capital of the state of New York, where it lay in state. On August 6 the body was moved to New York City to lie in state at the city hall where more than 250,000 passed by the coffin on the catafalque. As the funeral train passed West Point, on the way to New York, the cadets presented arms. Interestingly, the cadet captain on this occasion was John J. Pershing, later supreme commander of the Allied Expeditionary Force in World War I.

On Saturday, August 8, the final burial took place, though even the temporary tomb was barely ready to receive the body. The funeral procession of 45,000 marchers and 200 musical groups was two and one-half miles long. More than a million people lined the streets. The customary riderless horse, boots backwards in the stirrups, followed the catafalque that bore the body. At about five o'clock the bugle finally played "Now the Day Is Over."

The 19th, Rutherford B. Hayes

The Reformer, 1881–1893

Few men in the nation have been involved in as many civic and reform movements as was the nineteenth president of the United States, Rutherford B. Hayes (1822–1893). Although there was little to distinguish his four years (1877–1881), his educational and humanitarian projects after he left the White House were remarkable.

Hayes' election as president was hotly disputed. Two days before the new president was to be inaugurated there was uncertainty as to whether Hayes or his opponent, Samuel Tilden, would be sworn in as the nation's chief executive. To this day it is not clear that he won the election, for a great many have regarded this as a stolen election. The dispute has never been resolved.

Strange as it may seem, Hayes was perhaps at the height of his limited popularity just as he was leaving office. By that time he had shown the American people that he was a man of integrity and character. In spite of the fact that the South was Democratic and he was a Republican, Hayes sincerely tried to help the South in their postwar problems, and during his administration the terrible Reconstruction period ended. Also, he was responsible for instituting reforms in the federal government, especially in civil service.

As the administration came to an end, the first couple hosted a number of successful social events. Both Hayes and his wife Lucy basked in this rather short period of popularity.

The political pressures on the president had been tremendous, so it was not unexpected that he announced he would not seek another term. In fact he felt that no man should have two terms in the White House. In all probability had his own administration been more popular, he might well have wanted a second term. Very few successful presidents have rejected a second term as chief executive.

Hayes tried to avoid getting involved in the politics of choosing a candidate to succeed himself. Privately he seemed to favor the candidacy of

Secretary of the Treasury John Sherman for the Republican nomination in 1880, but he led fellow Ohioan James Garfield to feel that he would be glad to see him as president. However, Hayes quite positively did not want former President Grant to be elected to a third term. Hayes was openly opposed to what came to be called "Grantism," or the obvious corruption in government that took place in Grant's administration. Some feel that Hayes personally tried to talk Grant out of seeking a third term. If so, Hayes completely failed, for Grant did seek a third term in 1880. In the end Hayes was gratified that a man like Garfield would succeed him in office. However, he was not so happy to have Chester A. Arthur as the new vice president.

On January 1, 1881, Hayes wrote to his close personal friend, Guy Bryan, stating his readiness to retire from office. He also expressed personal satisfaction at what his administration had achieved.[1] Another incident clearly shows Hayes' feelings. When William Dean Howells and his wife Eleanor were guests of Hayes in the White House, she commented to the president, "Well, you will soon be out of it." "Yes," he replied, "out of a scrape, out of a scrape."[2] He later characterized his return to private life as an escape from bondage into freedom.

Hayes felt very gratified when Alexander Stephens, former vice president of the Confederacy, and then a congressman from Georgia, called at the White House to wish the retiring president well and made the remark that he had never seen an administration go out of office so well regarded.[3]

The night of March 4, 1881, saw the new president in the White House and the retiring president and his wife as guests in the Washington home of the retiring Secretary of the Treasury John Sherman. The next day, in a cheerful mood, Rutherford and Lucy Hayes boarded a train for their journey back to their home in Fremont, Ohio. Near Baltimore the train carrying the former president, his party and honor guard, collided with another train. Two passengers were killed and another 20 were injured. Neither Hayes nor his wife was hurt, but some of his party were injured. The accident delayed his arrival home, but the city of Fremont waited to give him a rousing welcome. Hayes said he only wanted to resume his private life and do his part in useful work.

Hayes owned an estate on the edge of town which he called Spiegel Grove. The house was enlarged and refurbished with all the modern conveniences of the day. The wide piazza was 80 feet long. Spacious halls, a large parlor and dining room made the home well suited for parties and large receptions. There were about 20 rooms with ample bedrooms for the family and friends when they came to visit. (Two of the five living Hayes children were minors in 1881.) The large library contained many impressive historical sets of books and remembrances of the owners' stay in the White House.

An upstairs room housed curios and souvenirs from the presidential days, and came to be called "the Smithsonian." A middle-aged black woman, Eliza, ran the household with an efficient and firm hand. Also, there were Jack Ryan, gardener and handyman, and Jefferson Patterson, the coachman who tended the five horses. Altogether it was an impressive estate set in a spacious grove adjoining two small lakes.

The family settled quite easily into a daily routine that suited their various interests. The ex-president rose early and tried to get the disagreeable tasks completed before breakfast. Both he and Mrs. Hayes were college graduates and had rather cosmopolitan intellectual interests, ranging from authors Emerson, Browning, and Byron, to history, biography, and education. Hayes carried on an extensive correspondence with politicians, scholars, businessmen, clergy, philanthropists, and "average citizens." At the same time he kept in touch with his neighbors and fellow townsmen. He participated in an astounding number of community affairs and projects.

Several aspects of Hayes' retirement merit attention. In addition to his involvement with educational and humanitarian projects, he tried to keep in touch with and help his fellow veterans of the Civil War. He also began to study the political philosophy of various reform movements, and became interested in some of the so-called "leftist" causes. Hayes came to some startlingly liberal conclusions for a man who had been a conservative president.

The Peabody Educational Fund had attracted his attention for some time. Soon he added an interest in the Slater Fund. Both of these funds were for the purpose of educating southern blacks. Hayes felt that only education could raise the level of the freed slaves. Rarely did he miss a board meeting of either of these organizations, and during the years after the presidency he closely followed the work of these funds. On one occasion he spent time in the South visiting and evaluating the projects these funds were supporting. He also presided over a conference at Lake Mohonk designed to aid blacks in achieving economic independence.

Among the promising and bright young men who received scholarships from the Slater Fund while Hayes was its president was W.E.B. DuBois, who later developed into a national figure, a noted speaker, historian, and intellectual. DuBois became the leader of the National Association for the Advancement of Colored People, and openly opposed the moderate views of Booker T. Washington. DuBois attended Fiske and Harvard where he made brilliant records in both schools.

Public higher education captured Hayes' interest, and he became a member of the board of trustees of Ohio State University and of Ohio Wesleyan University. Countless tasks were assigned to him by both of these schools. Unless he was ill or unavoidably detained, he faithfully attended every meeting of these boards. Over and over again he explained and defended their efforts to give Ohio young people better educational opportunities. One of his most-often-used speech topics was his promotion of manual training for all youth. He felt that every young man should know how to do manual work.

Seldom could Hayes resist the call when Civil War veterans gathered. He joined the local Grand Army of the Republic chapter, and soon was in a position of leadership in Ohio, then in the nation. In 1888 he became the national commander of the Military Order of the Loyal Eagles, an organization of Civil War officers (modeled after the Society of the Cincinnati of the American Revolution).

About a year before his death he attended a large soldiers' reunion in Washington. Although an old man by then, he insisted on marching with his men in the parade, and made many speeches to various soldier groups. On other occasions he pled the cause of individual soldiers who needed assistance from the government in their illnesses or old age.

Hayes was a good public speaker and made countless talks all over the nation. He gave many messages centered around the value of education. He also insisted that each citizen had the duty to aid the community and country. His diary and letters give ample evidence of how freely he gave of money, time, and effort to causes which he espoused.

The fate of the prison population absorbed a considerable amount of his attention. In 1883 he became president of the National Prison Reform Association and presided over the annual meetings of this organization for almost ten years.

Hayes was very much involved in the work of the Fremont Methodist Church, where his wife was a devoted member. The former president headed drives for money to construct new buildings, and was involved in the men's work of this church. Few were as active as he in the causes the church supported, yet he never did join the church nor make a public confession of faith. It is certain that he believed in God, lived what he considered a moral life, and regularly attended public worship, but for some reason never saw fit to assume church membership.

Hayes said little publicly, or for that matter, to his personal associates, about his private religious feelings. He trusted to his diary thoughts he did not, or dared not, openly state. In his diary under the date of January 8, 1893, just nine days before he died, he did give his religious views: "I am a Christian according to my conscience in belief, not of course in character and conduct, but in purpose and wish; not of course by the orthodox standard. But I am content, and have a feeling of trust and safety."

Eventually he called himself a nihilist. His concept of nihilism was expressed in his diary: "It is the doctrine of the Declaration of Independence and of the Sermon on the Mount . . . I use it to mean all opinions to show the wrong and evils of the money-piling tendency of our country . . . giving all power to the rich and bringing in pauperism . . . and wretchedness like a flood."[4] When he talked about crime and prison reform he maintained that the problem was ". . . one that grew largely out of poverty."[5] Hayes was a part of the thinking that led to the rise of populism,[6] for the new stirrings in the land had captured the ex-president's attention. Many of the former abolitionists and early Republicans began to think along these new lines also. They now fought industrial slavery instead of the old chattel slavery of the South.

Hayes came to feel that hanging those involved with the killings in the so-called Haymarket Riot (a labor uprising in which a number were killed) was a gross miscarriage of justice. Hayes saw in the Fourteenth Amendment not only the provision for freeing the slaves, but also a means whereby the wealthy could protect their own interests. He saw industrialism and the resultant wage slavery as a curse rather than as progress, and a danger to free institutions. He pled the causes of labor and the blacks. Is there any wonder that there was no room for him in the new Republicanism of the 1880s? In James G. Blaine, Republican candidate in 1884, Hayes saw a man not to be trusted, lacking both sincerity and honesty. However, he was very fond of William McKinley, and presided over his inauguration as governor of the state of Ohio in January 1892.

Despite his liberal leanings, Hayes did not favor women's suffrage or the Prohibition cause. (His wife had banned all alcoholic drinks in the White House while she was first lady, and in derision she was often called "Lemonade Lucy.") Hayes himself never drank except a very few times when he did so for its medicinal effect, but he did not feel that it was the prerogative of the government to keep a person from taking a drink.

As time went by Hayes began to feel the infirmities of age. His hair and beard became very white, his once keen memory began to slip, he gained weight, and his step slowed along with his vigor. As his friends and family began to die, he felt increasingly alone. William Wheeler, his vice president, died, as did Winfield S. Hancock, the Democratic candidate of 1880, a man he admired very much. Hayes was very grieved when his grandson and namesake, Rutherford, the son of his own son Birchard, died of croup. Justice Matthews, a close friend, died in March of 1889.

The cruelest blow of all came on June 23, 1889, when his much-loved wife Lucy died at 57 years of age. As the former president left for Columbus on June 17 to attend to some university business, Lucy seemed in perfect health. When he returned home to Fremont, he was met at the railroad station with the agonizing news that Lucy had suffered a sudden stroke. She had lost the power of speech but seemed to recognize her husband. She soon became comatose, and in two days she died. Her death was a blow from which he never recovered. In spite of his sadness, the ex-president continued his active life, but things were never the same for him. When he traveled, his daughter Fanny often accompanied him.

On October 25, 1892, Caroline, the wife of President Benjamin Harrison, died in the White House. Although not a close personal friend, Hayes knew how the president must have felt. With no hesitation Hayes journeyed to Indianapolis to attend the final rites of the first lady, and then accompanied the president as far as Columbus on his way back to Washington.

December of 1892 was a busy month for Hayes. He spoke and presided at an alumni meeting for Kenyon College, his alma mater. Again he turned to one of his favorite topics, the value of manual training, as he spoke to the Ohio College Association. After the holidays, on January 9, he traveled to Columbus to a meeting of the trustees of Ohio State University, staying for a few days to visit with old friends. Thursday afternoon he took the train to Cleveland, where he was a guest of Linus Austin, a relative and close friend. His son Webb was living in the Austin home at the time. The affairs of Western Reserve University occupied his time on Friday. On Saturday afternoon he was with his son Webb at the Cleveland railroad station waiting for his train to take him home to Fremont when he suffered a heart attack.

Brandy relieved the discomfort somewhat, and though Webb felt his father should return to the Austin home, Hayes wanted to go back to Fremont. "I would rather die at Spiegel Grove than live anywhere else," he told Webb.[7] He insisted on boarding the train. In spite of the pain he seemed to stand the trip fairly well. At seven that evening the train pulled into the Fremont station, where he was met by the family physician and taken at once to Spiegel Grove. Although he lingered for three days, it was not long after his arrival that the doctor had given up all hope for his recovery. The patient knew he was dying, but talked freely, and surprisingly enough, seemed cheerful. At eleven o'clock on Tuesday, January 17, 1893, Hayes made his last statement, "I know I am going where Lucy is,"[8] and died.

From all over the nation and foreign lands messages of condolence poured in to Spiegel Grove. President Benjamin Harrison was too ill to travel to Fremont, but he sent four cabinet members as personal representatives to the funeral. Grover Cleveland, soon to be inaugurated president for the second time, attended the service. By his presence Cleveland hoped to heal the hurts caused by the disputed election of 1876. Hayes respected and trusted Cleveland, and the feeling was mutual. Governor McKinley of Ohio, later to be a president himself, brought his whole staff to show his respect for the ex-president. Thousands gathered around the home where the funeral was conducted. The service was simple and very short. There was no sermon or eulogy.

The entire group then went for a brief service to the family plot of Spiegel Grove where Lucy had been buried. The Sons of Civil War Veterans fired a salute, and taps sounded as the body was laid to rest.

As president, Rutherford B. Hayes will be little remembered, but as an ex-president, his undaunting crusade for reforms in the nation are secured in the annals of history.

The 20th, James A. Garfield

Eighty-Day Struggle for Life, 1881

James A. Garfield (1831-1881) was the second of the four American presidents to be assassinated, though there have been several unsuccessful attempts on others. For a modern civilized nation, the United States has experienced an unusual number of attempts to assassinate its leaders. John F. Kennedy died almost instantly after the assassin's bullet hit his skull, Abraham Lincoln lived a very short time, William McKinley lived eight days, but James A. Garfield struggled for 80 days before he lost his valiant fight for life.

Garfield came to the presidency in March 1881 from an active and very successful career. In the fall of 1880 he was a congressman, a senator-elect, and president-elect, all at the same time. This was possible because at that time the state legislatures elected United States senators, and the legislature of Ohio elected Garfield as senator before the November election which sent him to the White House. He was in office barely four months when he was shot.

Garfield's days in the White House had been difficult from the start. There were bitter intraparty fights and hordes of office-seekers who were most persistent and obnoxious. John C. Ridpath back in 1881 said that "they swarmed like locusts around the capital."[1] The glamour of the nation's highest office soon wore off for Garfield and he was anxious to get away for a long summer vacation.

On July 2, 1881, Garfield and two of his sons were at the Baltimore and Potomac railroad station in Washington waiting for a train that would take them to Long Branch, New Jersey, where they would join Mrs. Garfield and the rest of the family. Their vacation would take them up into New England to visit Williams College. A few days would be spent on the Cyrus Field estate on the Hudson, then on to his much loved farm in Mentor, Ohio. Tragically none of these plans materialized, for two bullets fired by a psychotic named Charles J. Guiteau mortally wounded President Garfield.

Guiteau was a misfit and a failure at everything he ever tried to do — factory worker, lawyer, theologian and minister, lecturer, politician, writer, salesman, and businessman. His last attempts had been to get a post in the diplomatic service, but no one in official Washington gave him the slightest attention. Guiteau began to imagine that promises of appointments had been assured him. When no job offer materialized he became unreasonably bitter and vindictive. He came to feel that God was leading him to "remove" Garfield. In this frame of mind he began to make careful plans to carry out this mandate from heaven. He borrowed $15 and began to stalk the president, having purchased a small .44-caliber "British Bulldog" pistol, a pearl-handled weapon he felt would look splendid in a museum as the gun that had killed the president.

The would-be assassin was very patient. He studied many possibilities, even considering shooting the president while he was in church on a Sunday morning, or while the chief executive was taking a walk. However, he eventually rejected these possibilities. On one occasion he followed the president and his wife to the Washington railroad station, but she looked so frail and dependent that he could not bring himself to shoot Garfield. (Mrs. Garfield lived another 36 years after the death of her husband and died in 1918 at almost 86 years of age.) Finally the appropriate time for Guiteau came on the morning of July 2. He approached the president from the back and fired two bullets at point blank range. Guiteau had even hired a hack to be ready to rush him to the local jail to save him from being lynched, a fate he expected unless he could make his getaway to the jail and safety.

In the railroad station all was confusion. The president lay on the floor in his own blood and vomit. Soon medical assistance was summoned. He was placed on a mattress and taken to the second floor of the station. Secretary of State James G. Blaine, who was with the president when he was shot, took charge. Several doctors arrived quickly and were soon busy assessing the seriousness of the wound and deciding what treatment should be administered. One of the bullets had only grazed his arm, but the other had entered the body a few inches from the spine in the lower back.

The doctors probed with unwashed hands and instruments, but experienced great difficulty in following the path of the rather large bullet. Their assumption was that the bullet had entered the abdominal cavity. Such wounds were almost always fatal. None of the physicians believed that the patient could live another day. When asked if the president would live, within the hearing of the fallen victim they replied that his chances were one in a hundred. Secretary Blaine was weeping openly. Finally the president himself told them to take him home to the White House. An express wagon from the railroad was secured and several mattresses placed on its floor. The president was then lifted onto the wagon bed, and a very slow, careful journey was made to the White House in this horsedrawn vehicle. The physicians began to give what medical help was available in those days while heavy security was placed around the executive mansion.

The wounded president asked that his wife be summoned as quickly as possible. Lucretia Garfield and her daughter Mollie, visiting friends in New Jersey, were contacted by telegram but they were not told how serious the president's condition was. A special train was placed at the disposal of the first lady, and she and Mollie started at once for Washington, arriving late that evening. With some apprehension the president's aged mother was told the news. Two of the president's sons, Irwin and Abe, were secretly brought home as quickly as possible, and soon the whole family was together again.

When the doctors finally were able to make a careful assessment of the patient's condition, they found that the bullet had shattered the thirteenth rib as it entered the body. They could see that the spine had been damaged but that the spinal cord was not severed. It was surely a medical tragedy: because they could not locate the bullet, they could not decide upon the proper treatment.

Doctors were surprised that Garfield lived through the night, for if the bullet had entered the abdominal cavity the president would have been close to death or would have already died. Most surprisingly, the president slept a good share of the night, and his pulse, temperature and bodily functions were near normal. Considering everything that had happened to him, Garfield was quite alert and cheerful. The most troubling symptom was the vomiting which continued to be a major problem during the whole of his ordeal. The president chose as his chief physician Dr. D.W. Bliss who was well-known in Washington. For his day and time Bliss was a competent practitioner and should not be blamed that his patient did not recover, nor should, considering what the medical profession knew at the time, the doctors be harshly judged for their treatment of the president.

News bulletins on the president's condition were released frequently — 10 in the first 24 hours, the first at 11:30 a.m. on July 2, the day of the assassination, and 9 during the second 24 hour period, but soon these were reduced to morning and afternoon bulletins. These many and lengthy accounts of the 80 days of Garfield's struggle are available to the researcher and make for rather lugubrious reading. For example, the pulse rate was 108 per minute on the third day and 120 the fourth day. On the sixteenth day it dropped to 94, never to be so low again. After the fourth week, and during the almost twelve weeks of life that remained, the pulse was never below 100 and usually over 105, going up on occasion as high as 130 and once to 140 per minute. Also, Garfield almost always ran a temperature of over 100 degrees though it seldom exceeded 104 degrees. The symptoms all indicated a pessimistic outlook — the high pulse rate, the elevated temperature, and the continual loss of weight, down to 135 pounds from his usual weight of 200 pounds.

The White House physicians were optimistic after the first 24 hours. Some even freely predicted a complete recovery. However, the press usually took a pessimistic view, issuing many conflicting reports. For example, on the sixty-first day four reports are recorded: "Almost out of the woods," "On the high road to recovery," "The valley and the shadow" (of death), and "The end at hand."[2] As late as September 8, two of his medical attendants announced his convalescence.[3] Dr. Bliss announced on the seventieth day that the "favorable symptoms would continue."[4] Only at the very end were the official bulletins foreboding.

Garfield had two surgeries, one performed without anesthetic, in an effort to obtain better drainage of the wound. These procedures helped temporarily. During this time he also developed an infection of the right parotid gland which caused real concern. The doctors were much too optimistic in their bulletins. There can be little doubt they should have seen that the patient could not recover.

Almost without exception, the nation responded with love and affection. Many prayers were made in churches and in private homes for his recovery. Not only was Garfield a popular figure, but many were troubled at the prospect of Chester A. Arthur, a product of the unsavory New York Conkling machine, succeeding to the presidency. Fortunately, history proved that these fears were unfounded, for Arthur became a president of integrity. However, the problem still remained as to who was actually running the government. Blaine wanted the cabinet to declare Garfield temporarily unable to fulfill his duties as president and make Arthur the acting president. However, Arthur was not willing to take that step.[5] As a result, each cabinet member ran his own department as he saw fit. Robert Lincoln, son of Abraham Lincoln, and Garfield's secretary of war, made a rather astute observation when he said that the government was "running along, every man running his own department and thinking he is doing so well that he may be President some day."[6]

The disabled president tried to the limited extent of his ability to follow the affairs of government, but it was not a very productive effort. He managed to hold one short cabinet meeting in his sickroom, but not much of real substance was accomplished. He could read but little, and only once did he attempt to write. After securing a pencil and a pad he wrote, "Strangulatus pro Republica," a Latin phrase meaning "tortured for the republic."[7] Garfield was a student of the classics, familiar with Greek as well as Latin. On occasion to amuse his friends the ambidextrous president would write in Latin with one hand and in Greek with the other.[8]

Alexander Graham Bell, the inventor of the telephone, devised an instrument that he hoped might help locate the lost bullet in Garfield's back.

The device was basically an electromagnet which surrounded the body of the president and hopefully would indicate the bullet's location by a buzzing sound. Although the device was tried a number of times, the large piece of bullet was never located.

However, in another way science was able to come to the aid of the wounded president. Summers are hot and humid in the city of Washington. Some navy engineers with the help of Simon Newcomb devised what was perhaps the first air conditioner in an effort to make the ailing chief executive more comfortable.[9] Air was forced by a blower over a large chest of ice, then dried as it passed through a box of filters. The air which was forced into the president's room was about twenty degrees cooler than that outside.[10]

As Garfield showed no improvement, it seemed to those around the president that a change in environment would very likely help him. He longed to go somewhere near the sea where he could watch the ocean and be cooled by its breeze. It was finally decided to move him to the New Jersey coast at Elberon. A Mr. Francklyn owned one of the finest dwellings in the resort community and he offered his cottage for the president's use. George C. Wilkins of the Pennsylvania Railroad arranged transportation to Elberon and ordered the tracks to be cleared of all moving traffic. Three hundred men worked around the clock to lay the necessary 3200 feet of temporary track in order to take the wounded chief executive to the very door of the cottage in which he was going to stay.

The move was made on September 6, one of the hottest days of the year, but Garfield stood very well the 233-mile trip which took seven hours to complete. The president's improved condition and outlook seemed to justify the risk involved in the move—certainly he was in better spirits. His symptoms seemed to improve as well. Dr. Bliss boldly announced that the patient was convalescent.[11] It is difficult to imagine how this could be said just ten days before the president died. Even the next day there was fear that blood poisoning might be developing. On the following day, September 11, there was considerable concern over a discharge from the patient's mouth which was felt to have come from his lungs. Yet two days later the report was, "Still gaining slowly."[12]

Saturday, September 17, was described as a "day of deep anxiety." Garfield suffered a deep chill, his temperature rose rapidly, and the word "rigor" crept into the medical report. On Sunday, September 18, the patient was critically ill. On the following day the pulse rate was rapid and thready and his breathing was shallow. Death was just hours away, yet at least outwardly Dr. Bliss remained optimistic. A little after ten o'clock that night the patient suffered acute pain in his chest. He was gone in three or four minutes.

The autopsy showed how badly the doctors had misdiagnosed Garfield's condition. The bullet was lodged in the large back muscle lower than they thought. Much of the tissue below the actual site of the bullet was destroyed by infection. The doctors had thought that the swelling caused by the infection indicated the location of the bullet. Death came from a burst aneurysm that developed in the abdomen from the wound and subsequent infection.

After a brief funeral service at Elberon, the same train that had brought the president to the cottage now took his body back to Washington where it lay in state at the Capitol for two days followed by an elaborate funeral service in the rotunda. The body was then taken to Garfield's home community for burial in the Lakeview Cemetery in Cleveland, Ohio. Though Congress should have paid the burial expenses of an assassinated president, they failed to make an appropriation, and the funeral director was never paid for his services.[13]

While Guiteau was in the Washington jail waiting to be tried, he received hundreds of letters and telegrams commending him for his act. The trial of Guiteau was but a legal formality — many had seen him fire at the president. However, it took an inordinately long time to hold the trial. The prisoner acted the fool at his trial, insisting that he had done God's will. The jury took less than an hour to convict him. There had been several attempts to lynch Guiteau before he was hanged on June 30, 1882, before a vast crowd which, through some sense of the macabre, wanted to see him die.

The 21st, Chester A. Arthur

A Fatal Illness Kept Secret, 1885–1886

President Chester A. Arthur (1830–1886) was terminally ill with Bright's disease (a name in that day given to a variety of kidney disorders) during the latter part of his administration (he served 1881–1885). But he managed to keep the fact from the press and the public—a testimony not only to the loyalty of the White House staff and his own family, but to Arthur's courage and determination to insure the image of an active, healthy president.

Arthur, who had succeeded to the presidency upon the assassination of James A. Garfield, was fearful that if the public believed that the new president might not live to the end of his term, his effectiveness as the nation's leader would be destroyed. In 1881, the country had seen three presidents in less than seven months: Hayes, Garfield, and Arthur. Instead of permitting an aura of gloom to pervade the White House, Arthur filled it with lively parties and social events. In fact he was criticized by some for having too much social life. To give the picture of a vigorous leader, Arthur went so far as to make a half-hearted attempt to gain his party's nomination for the presidency in 1884, although he knew he could not run.[1] Arthur did survive his term of office, but he lived for only a year and a half after he retired to his home in New York City.

There are those who criticized the Republican party for not renominating Arthur in 1884. His honesty and freedom from domination by any political machine had brought him well-deserved praise. But they did not realize how ill Arthur was during his last year in office.

In addition to his serious illness, the president had yet another major personal problem. The wife he adored died just a year and a half before he became chief executive, and he came to the White House a 50-year-old widower with two children, 17-year-old Chester A., Jr., and 10-year-old Ellen Herndon. Fortunately for both the children and their father, two sisters of the president, Mary McElroy and Malvina Hayes, spent most of their time in the White House caring for the children and helping manage the mansion. Mrs. McElroy, in fact, acted as the hostess of the White House.

For most of his term Arthur managed fairly well in the performance of his duties. He did not neglect the constitutional obligations of his office, although at times he felt the effects of his disease. However, during the last six months of his administration his condition became much worse. Some of those around him were concerned that he might not be able to finish his term of office. He was given physical therapy daily, and the doctors visited him at regular intervals. A personal friend described his health as "deplorable."[2] There were many days when he had great difficulty meeting all the personal demands upon him. By this time he tried to avoid as many public appearances as possible.

As the time approached for Arthur to leave office, some of his loyal supporters attempted to get him to run for the soon-to-be-vacant Senate seat from his home state of New York. When these overtures to Arthur were discovered, a number in the reform element of both parties began to accuse Arthur and his administration of not being interested in reform. Arthur assured the politicians that he did not care to run for the Senate seat, but they persisted in their efforts. To quiet the political tempest, he finally issued a formal statement on December 20, 1884, to the effect that he did not now and never had had an interest in a Senate seat. Although he realized the seriousness of his disease, neither the press nor his own party had knowledge of the extent of his illness.

Arthur's last formal speech as president was made when he helped to dedicate the Washington Monument. For many years the work on the monument had stopped, and for more than twenty years it was but a pile of stone and debris, until Congress finally appropriated the funds to complete the structure. Late in the year 1884, the 3,300-pound capstone was finally put into place. The monument was dedicated on Washington's birthday in 1885. The president read his speech to an appreciative audience, though a number of observers noticed that he did not appear to be a well man. That evening Arthur held his last public reception.

Arthur's last official act as president was to sign a bill that put former President Grant on the list of retired army officers as a full general, enabling him to obtain the pension of his rank. (At that moment Grant was seriously ill and in an extremely difficult financial situation.) A few hours later Arthur accompanied the incoming President Grover Cleveland to the Capitol for the inauguration ceremony, riding in a horse-drawn carriage. A great crowd of about 50,000 cheered Cleveland as he made his inaugural address. Both Arthur and Cleveland watched the long parade, then went to the White House where Cleveland was the guest of honor at a luncheon given by the retiring president. Both the incoming and outgoing presidents attended the inaugural ball that night. Arthur remained in Washington for a few days to conclude some personal matters and then went to his home at 125 Lexington Avenue in New York City.

The wonder was that Arthur ever became president. His nomination as vice president by the Republican convention in 1880 was something of an afterthought. Garfield became the presidential nominee only after the convention had voted 36 times. Arthur was quickly named as Garfield's running mate, largely to placate the Conkling organization in New York. There was consternation in many quarters when Arthur became president, for he was the product of the crooked Conkling machine. When he was in charge of the New York Customs House, he was removed from that office because of the corruption there.

However, one of the most surprising character changes ever witnessed in American political life occurred, for as president, Arthur became an honest, upright public servant who tried to represent all the people. "He was the president of no faction."[3] Special interest groups had no standing with him. He vetoed "pork barrel" legislation, defied party bosses, pushed civil service reform, and vetoed the Chinese Exclusion Act. He prosecuted illegal acts in government such as the Star Route fraud in the post office, and worked for tariff reform. Arthur did not make many friends among professional politicians, but maintained his positions in spite of strong and spirited opposition.

In March after he left office, Arthur made the announcement that he was returning to his old law firm in New York to resume the practice of law. An elaborate suite of offices was made ready for him. It is interesting to note that he hung a picture of Grant behind his desk. He and Grant were both members of the old-line conservatives who were often involved in the political machines of that day. However, Arthur's poor health prevented him from taking any major share in the caseload of the firm. Only routine matters were assigned to him, and often he was not able to come to the office. Yet the firm paid him a salary of $1,000 per month for the little he could do in order to have his name included among its members.

After returning to New York he was able to attend the funeral of a friend in Washington, and that spring he attended the graduation ceremonies of his son from Princeton University. His last public appearance was in December of 1885, when he presided over a ceremony honoring the retiring Supreme Court Chief Justice Charles P. Daily. At this time Arthur could get about the city and attend to some of his own personal affairs, but his capacity for sustained productive work had ended. It is also probable that he had developed a heart condition, but the diagnosis and treatment of cardiac diseases were rather primitive at that time.

While Arthur was not a man of wealth, he was comfortably situated. It is not possible to state his total worth accurately, but it is estimated that he had assets totaling something in excess of $150,000, a substantial sum in those days. He owned stock in several companies, and some valuable pieces of real estate in New York City and in New Jersey. He had managed his money carefully. As a result he had no real financial problems in his retirement, even though there was no presidential pension in those days. Most of his $50,000 a year salary as president had been spent on maintaining the White House. Arthur's life-style in the White House showed that he liked the finer things in life. He was one of the best dressed chief executives. He had some 80 pairs of trousers in his wardrobe, with outfits to match.

Some have suggested that his ill health was the result of over-indulgence in food and drink.[4] However, there is little to substantiate such an assertion. While it is true that he lived well, liked fine food and drink – at times he served 14-course dinners that took his guests two and a half hours to consume – yet he never had an alcohol problem nor was he excessively obese.

In February of 1886 his illness became critical. He made out his will, and attempted to put his affairs in order. At times he did rally, but it seems that nothing the doctors could do was able to reverse the deadly progress of his kidney disease. Often a little milk was the only food that he could take. Two of his sisters, Mary McElroy and Regina Caw, came to his home and took over the task of caring for the former president. In April they feared for the worst, but he improved sufficiently to be moved to rural Connecticut, hoping that the change in climate might help him, but it did not. He stayed in Connecticut until October 1, then returned to his home in New York. Most of the time he was bedridden or propped up in an easy chair. On occasion he was able to have visitors, among whom were former President Hayes and Chief Justice Waite.

Just a few days before his death he directed the burning of all his papers. A variety of reasons have been suggested as to why he did so. He admitted there were things in his political career that he wished were different. He even advised his son never to go into politics, for the price demanded of him had been far too high.[5]

On the morning of November 17, his nurse found him unconscious. He died early the following morning of a massive cerebral hemorrhage. There was no public funeral. However, thousands came to pay their respects. It took several hundred security guards to keep the crowds away from the Church of Heavenly Love in New York City where private funeral services were held. Among those present at the short, simple service were President Cleveland and former President Hayes, Chief Justice Waite and several associate justices, as well as a number of senators and representatives. The body was taken in the private railroad car of Cornelius Vanderbilt to the Rural Cemetery in Albany, New York, where it was buried beside that of his wife. An impressive marker was placed over his grave in a lovely spot overlooking the countryside.

The nation's press had many words of praise for Arthur. The Democratic paper, the New York *Sun,* said of him, "It is not too much to say he was one of the most successful and meritorious in our whole list of Presidents."[6] Historian W.E. Woodward wrote, "He was the first modern president, in that he governed for all sections, regardless of party."[7]

The 22nd & 24th, Grover Cleveland

Escape to Princeton, 1897–1908

The second term of Grover Cleveland (1837–1908) as president (he served 1885–1889 and 1893–1897) was so beset with personal difficulties and tremendous national problems, that this period is commonly called "Cleveland's Luckless Years." He was faced with unprecedented labor strikes, acute controversies over foreign policy, and disputes with foreign governments. He had to borrow money from Wall Street to keep the gold reserve in the treasury up to the legal requirement, the nation was faced with a major financial panic, and the attacks on him by the press would shame even present-day investigative reporting. His very serious cancer surgery was performed on E.C. Benedict's yacht to escape the reporters who hounded the ill president.

No wonder he longed to leave the White House and its onerous burdens. He sought out a small town where he could literally drop out of sight, and though he was past 60, finish raising his young and growing family. Earlier he had visited Princeton, New Jersey, and chose it as the ideal location.

Frances Cleveland, 27 years his junior, whom he had married during his first term in the White House, made the final selection of the house which they purchased for $30,915 shortly after the election of 1896. The property contained a large colonial mansion and spacious grounds. For their convenience some needed changes were made on the house. A study and a library for the former president's many books were provided on the second floor, and a billiard room added to the back of the house. In addition, the barn and the grounds were redesigned for the new occupants. The estate was named "Westland" in honor of Professor West of Princeton, who had helped the family find their home.

According to previous plans, the retiring president went immediately from the inaugural parade of his successor to a nearby yacht that took him and several companions to the shore of North Carolina for a few days of much-needed fishing and duck hunting, for the last days of his administration had virtually exhausted him. One of his companions, Leonard Wood, described how the ex-president appeared dead tired as he came aboard the boat and sat down heavily upon entering the cabin.[1] But a few days of rest and relaxation did wonders for his body and his spirit. Mrs. Cleveland and their three daughters went on to Princeton to begin the process of settling their new home. Cleveland arrived at Westland on March 18, 1897, relaxed and anxious to be with his family.

The Clevelands spent the next several months settling into their new home. It was a time of anticipation and fulfillment for them all. A new pony came to delight the girls. One evidence of Cleveland's affection for his home was seen in his effort to protect the song birds that made their home on his estate—he would have the servants go out on the grounds and drive the cats away. Friends, both old and new, dropped in frequently. The neighbors and the university people welcomed the newcomers with wholehearted affection and made them feel very much at home. But when the warm June days came, the Clevelands retreated to their summer home, Gray Gables, on the shores of Cape Cod. There the days were filled with picnics, general socializing, beach fun, and of course, fishing.

Of all the recreational activities in which Cleveland participated, fishing was the one that he enjoyed most. As one reads his letters written after he left the White House, it is evident that he was an inveterate angler. Fully half of his letters mention fishing in some way. Almost every spring he would travel south for the thrill of trying new tackle with his fishing companions, trips which often took several weeks or more. He was also fond of duck hunting, but found it a poor second to the excitement of "wetting his line." Cleveland continued fishing and hunting until the last few months of his life when he became physically unable to continue.

The former president tried to avoid publicity or public appearances, feeling that the people had turned against him. In retirement he once used the expression, "my old battered name."[2] As far as he was concerned, the public did not appreciate his difficult struggles to do what he thought best for the nation in critical times. When asked to make a speech in 1899 he commented to Judson Harmon in a letter dated April 17, 1899, "The announcement that I was to address my fellow countrymen on any subject whatever would be the signal for coarse abuse and ridicule."[3]

Gradually his feeling of rejection began to disappear, but it never completely left him. As he interacted pleasantly with the professors at Princeton, and received callers who were national figures, the sense of his own acceptance increased. In 1901 he was made a trustee of Princeton University. After being appointed a special lecturer at the university, he began to give lectures to students and faculty. On occasion he accepted some outside speaking engagements and also began to write magazine articles. Gradually the public began to accept and respect Cleveland.

At times he was sharp in responding to those whom he felt were trying to use him or his name. For example, he replied pointedly to William Randolph Hearst in a telegram dated March 4, 1898, "I decline to allow my sorrow for those who died on the *Maine* to be perverted to an advertising scheme for the New York *Journal*"⁴ (Hearst's newspaper).

It was evident to those around them that the former president and his young wife had a most successful marriage. His letters constantly showed his affection for Mrs. Cleveland, the former Frances Folsom. She saw to his comfort and health needs as he grew older. To the very end his family was the center of his life. His delight in his children comes through clearly in his letters. When his 12-year-old daughter Ruth died of diphtheria on January 7, 1904, he was very distraught. "It was the heaviest blow since the death of his mother, and his diary shows that he reeled under it."⁵ Eight days after her death his diary recorded, "God has come to my help and I am able to adjust my thought to dear Ruth's death with as much comfort as selfish humanity will permit."⁶

The three girls, Ruth, Esther, and Marian were born in 1891, 1893 and 1895, before he left the presidency. His two sons, Richard Folsom and Francis Grover, were born in his retirement, in 1897 and 1903. His younger son was not quite five years old when Cleveland died. In a letter to Charles Hamlin, he called this son "the most wonderful baby in the world."⁷

Cleveland did not have serious financial problems; he was worth about $300,000 when he left the White House.⁸ That was a large sum of money in those times, although he always worried that it might not keep his family comfortable after his death. He became something of an expert on investments, but relied on the advice of his good friend, E.C. Benedict, before making significant financial moves. In the end he let Benedict handle his entire portfolio, and the skill of Benedict's hand was seen in the steady rise of Cleveland's assets.

Cleveland earned some money by writing magazine articles and delivering a few lectures. But his best money-making enterprise was his work with several life insurance companies in New York. There had been corruption in the companies, and to restore public confidence Cleveland acted as trustee, for which he was paid $12,000 a year. He also accepted the position of referee between several insurance companies, and became chairman of the Association of Life Insurance Presidents, which earned him an additional $12,000 a year. This part-time job made his last days free of financial worries.⁹ Andrew Carnegie offered to give Cleveland a gratuity as a remembrance for his presidency, but he felt it would be improper to accept money in this way.

The former president did express the opinion that the federal government should provide an adequate pension for chief executives, though he had enough income to live comfortably in his retirement. He owned a fine home in Princeton, and was able to afford a very adequate summer place on Cape Cod. Later the family went for their summers to a place called "Intermont" at Tamworth in the hills of New Hampshire. The Cleveland family was adequately provided for after the death of the former president, although they would not have been considered wealthy.

Cleveland made it clear when he left the White House for the second time that he would never seek public office again, but many Democrats kept urging him to seek a third term, especially after the severe defeat they suffered in 1900. However, he did not lose his interest in politics when he retired, and kept in constant contact with his former political associates. Grover Cleveland was the only president to serve two non-consecutive terms as chief executive. After a lackluster first term, he was defeated in November 1888 by Benjamin Harrison. In the next election, 1892, the candidates were the same but the results reversed.

One finds abundant references to politics in his letters. To his friends in private there was little hesitancy in stating his own views, but he seldom spoke out in the public arena. Never for a moment did he personally entertain the idea of running again, but his conservative friends kept bringing up the prospect that he could be elected and that for the good of the party he should run for the presidency once again.

Cleveland had strong opinions about political figures of his day. He did not like William Jennings Bryan, who opposed one of Cleveland's deepest beliefs, sound money. Bryan had been nominated in 1896 by the Democratic national convention which had repudiated Cleveland while he was still in the White House. At times Cleveland worked with Tammany Hall in New York City, but he was never a part of that organization. At first Cleveland had good things to say about William McKinley, but in a short while criticized him for being too close to "big money." And the former president was aghast at the quick way he felt McKinley went to war with Spain. He felt "Teddy" Roosevelt was too ready to play for popularity, and too hasty in his decisions.

Perhaps the occasion that meant the most to him was the applause he received in St. Louis in April, 1903. He had been invited, along with President Theodore Roosevelt and other prominent Americans, to attend the Louisiana Purchase Exposition. Cleveland went by train from New York to St. Louis. In many places along the way large crowds gathered at railway stations to cheer and get a glimpse of the former president. Roosevelt gave greetings to the immense crowd at the exposition and received generous applause. But when Cleveland was introduced, the crowd gave a spontaneous and unexpected ovation. So great was the applause given Cleveland that Roosevelt felt slighted, or even affronted. *Electra,* a Texas newspaper, said that Cleveland "overshadowed the President in popular applause."[10] Certainly the "thunder of applause was balm to his wounded spirit."[11] To a lesser degree this acceptance by the public was duplicated many times. On his last several birthdays he was given adulation by the press in many words of commendation. Several tried to get him to write his autobiography, but he chose not to do so.

However, Cleveland did not escape criticism in his last years. Such a luxury is seldom, if ever, afforded any retired president. The Suffragettes were very pointed and vocal in their dislike for Cleveland. He did not support their cause nor did he approve of the way they conducted their campaign for the vote. The former president was never the friend of "free silver," and the scurrilous attacks from the West never abated. Bryan, the spokesman for the West, and three-time Democratic presidential nominee, continued to censure Cleveland for his "sound money" policy. A popular history of the last years of the nineteenth century by Harry T. Peck, *Twenty Years of the Republic—1885–1905,* published in 1907, was openly critical of Cleveland's views and in places held him up to ridicule, but never attacked his character.[12]

As time passed, Cleveland's health problems increased. He suffered from what was called rheumatism which frequently incapacitated him and at times put him to bed for weeks at a time. On occasion he was forced to cancel fishing trips, so it must have been painful. He was often bothered by indigestion. After 1900 he frequently carried a stomach pump.[13] The letters of his last years mention ill health rather frequently although none of the ailments seemed of a serious nature. Yet his continued loss of weight and vitality did concern Mrs. Cleveland.

He celebrated his last birthday, his seventy-first, on March 18, 1908. The Cleveland family had gone to Lakewood on the New Jersey coast for a brief vacation and to give the former president a change of scenery. A few friends joined the family for the occasion. The president was feeling better and in good spirits. He was able to take walks by the ocean again. However, in April he became ill and wanted to return to his home in Princeton. A mattress was placed in the back seat of a friend's automobile, and Cleveland was driven to Princeton in secrecy.[14]

Word reached his friends that he was quite ill (from digestive disorders and complications), but they were glad to see that the press included an item saying he was better. However, the improvement did not last, and, with his family around him, he died at eight-forty on Wednesday morning, June 24, 1908. His final words were, "I have tried so hard to do right."[15]

He was buried on Friday, June 26, in the old Princeton cemetery where a simple granite tombstone marks the gravesite—a tombstone bearing only his name, and the date of his birth and death. There is nothing to indicate that he had been president of the United States. Even in death he had preserved the anonymity he so carefully had sought.

The 23rd, Benjamin Harrison

A Widower with a New Career, 1893-1901

Benjamin Harrison (1833-1901) was a skillful attorney. Some feel he was the best courtroom lawyer who ever occupied the White House. However, in no way could he be thought of as a great president (1889-1893). Though he had many fine qualities—he was always upright, honest, thoroughly patriotic, and understood the significance of the office he held—and was the grandson of President William Henry Harrison, he somehow never seemed to fit in the circle of the power brokers that so often have dominated Washington. At no time was he popular nor did he have a charismatic personality. His physical appearance was not in his favor, for he was short and heavy-set, with a large head and a loud voice.

Initially he had the misfortune of being elected by a minority vote. President Cleveland, his opponent in the election of 1888, actually received more popular votes than Harrison, who was chosen by the votes of the electoral college.[1]

Certainly Harrison did not particularly enjoy his high office during the four years he held it. In the summer of 1892, however, he allowed himself to be renominated by the Republicans who, if they had not done so, would have repudiated their own record.[2] In that day presidential candidates did not campaign with the same abandon as they do today. Several aspects of this campaign were nevertheless rather singular. In the first place, an incumbent president was running against a former president, Grover Cleveland, whom Harrison had defeated four years earlier. At no other time in American history has this occurred. Also, President Harrison's wife Caroline was terminally ill during most of the campaign, suffering from an advanced case of pulmonary tuberculosis.

The attending physician hoped that fresh, invigorating mountain air might help the ill first lady, so she was moved to Loon Lake in the Adirondack Mountains. For a time it seemed that the change was indeed helping, but the improvement did not last. President Harrison tried to divide his time between his wife and his official duties in Washington. Benjamin and

166

"Carrie" Harrison had lived together for 39 years and were devoted to each other. The separation caused by her illness distressed them both. The general public had no knowledge of the nature of her illness until it was revealed on September 14, 1892. Upon learning of her condition, the outpouring of concern was very moving. On September 21, 1892, at her urgent request, she was moved the 500 miles back to Washington. The president was observed close beside Carrie, his eyes red from weeping, as the ambulance took her from the special railroad car back to the White House.

The president was relieved not to have to divide his time between Loon Lake and Washington. To his daughter in Boston, Harrison wrote that, "Politics and business have been crowding me day and night, and with the anxiety about your mother, makes life now a burden and ambition a delusion."[3] Bulletins about the first lady were issued daily, but the family insisted on editing them. On one occasion the word "fatal" was changed to "uncertain." A short time before her death she developed pleurisy. Fortunately the medical team was able to keep her fairly comfortable. But the hemorrhages still came, as is usually the case with pulmonary tuberculosis, and her strength ebbed. She died on the morning of Tuesday, October 25.

On Thursday, a brief service was held in the East Room of the White House. The body was then taken to the waiting railroad car to begin the journey to Indianapolis and home. Thousands lined the route along Pennsylvania Avenue as the procession passed from the White House to the Washington railroad station. The final service was conducted in the First Presbyterian Church of Indianapolis where the Harrisons were members. More than 100 carriages took the mourners to the family plot in the Crown Hill cemetery. Former President Hayes and a host of nationally known figures came to pay their respects. The president and his entourage left for Washington shortly after the interment.[4] When Harrison returned to Washington, he wrote a warm open letter to the people of Indianapolis thanking them for their love and sympathy. He began the letter, "My dear Old Friends and Neighbors."[5]

The presidential election was just days away, leaving little time for the incumbent president to campaign. But the outcome hardly mattered to Harrison, for his grief was still too fresh. It should be pointed out that when he learned of Mrs. Harrison's terminal illness, Democratic candidate Cleveland announced that he would not campaign until Harrison could "return to the stump."

Harrison had not been a strong national figure before he ran for the presidency the first time, although he certainly was not an inconsequential politician. But with both James G. Blaine, who had almost won the presidency in 1884, and Speaker of the House ("Czar") Thomas Reed as part of his administration, Harrison had little chance to be recognized as the man in control. No doubt Blaine could have had the Republican nomination in 1888 had he wished, but he decided not to run, and backed Harrison.[6] After the election Harrison was compelled to give Blaine a high office and named him secretary of state. Speaker Reed dominated Congress. Harrison always seemed to give him preferential treatment, almost to the point of obsequiousness.

The nation was in the midst of great change as seen in the continued rise of big business, the growth of the immigrant population, and the shrill demands of the West with their clamor for "free silver," each making claims on the government.

The political cartoons of the day were brutal in their portrayal of Harrison. One showed him as a very small figure sitting in a gigantic chair which represented the presidency.[7] Another pictured him as a midget sitting behind an oversize desk with a bust of his grandfather, President William Henry Harrison, behind the desk, and a large raven with the head of Blaine[8] perched on the bust.[9]

However, Harrison was a magnetic speaker, able to sway large audiences. One writer states that Harrison "never made a flat or feeble speech, nor one composed of platitudes ... his oratory was marked by ease and finish."[10] Yet, he often offended reporters and other visitors when he encountered them personally. His managers therefore tried to limit the opportunities for people to see him up close. The president enjoyed speaking to large crowds, but he did not enjoy any other type of campaigning, nor was he very effective in it. There is doubt that Harrison ever mastered the art of "cut-throat politics."

The election of 1892 did not create a great stir of interest. Harrison had alienated labor and the western "silverites," and Cleveland held the solid South and gained much support from business. The major issue, as far as the campaign rhetoric was concerned, was the tariff. But few of the general public knew much about the tariff, nor did they care. As a result, Harrison's chances of reelection were rather small at best. In the electoral college Harrison lost badly, though the popular vote was much closer. Of significance was the large third-party (Populist) vote—8 percent of the total—which showed a marked distrust of the administration by the public. Harrison took his defeat with good grace, having few if any real regrets at leaving the White House. Often he expressed pleasure at not having the burdens of the presidency to carry any longer. He wrote to a friend, "the result [of the election] is more surprising to the victor than to me. For me there is no sting in it. Indeed, after the heavy blow the death of my wife dealt me, I do not think I could have stood the strain of re-election."[11] Harrison was depressed for some time after the death of his wife, and this depression colored every aspect of his last few months in office. However, he was determined to follow the customs of the presidential departure from office and to return with some personal dignity to private life in Indianapolis.

When a vacancy in the Supreme Court occurred shortly before the end of his term, some urged him to resign from office, then let Vice President Levi Morton, who would have become president, appoint him to the high court. Considering Harrison's great interest in the law and his mastery of legal matters, the position could have been a temptation. But to Harrison such a plan appeared entirely contrived and he would have nothing to do with it. Just as he was leaving office, Harrison received and accepted an invitation to deliver a series of lectures on the law at Stanford University.

Harrison returned to his home on Delaware Street with no fanfare. Only those close to him knew how hard it was to come back to the empty home that he and Carrie had shared for so long. Returning to law was the only way he saw to occupy his time constructively. There were none of the doubts that Hayes had about the propriety of a former president becoming a practicing attorney again. It is true that several members of the Supreme Court before which Harrison would practice had been his appointees. However, he felt that a member of the highest tribunal would not be influenced by his new role.

Harrison did not enjoy living alone in his large, and to him, empty house. At age 62, three and a half years after Carrie's death, he married again and began to raise a new family. Mary Lord Dimmick, a 37-year-old widow, and a niece of the first Mrs. Harrison, became the new mistress of the mansion on Delaware Street.

The former president and Mary Dimmick had known each other for many years. She had helped care for her terminally ill aunt, the first Mrs. Harrison, both at Loon Lake and Washington. She had also served as his secretary after the death of his first wife. They were married in a ceremony performed in New York City on April 6, 1896. The wedding was rather simple, although a number of nationally known people attended, including former Vice President Levi Morton. Former Secretary of the Navy Benjamin Tracy acted as best man. Harrison did not want to upset his children any more than was necessary, so the couple chose not to be married in Indianapolis.

Although the new couple seemed very happy together, Harrison's two children, Russell Benjamin Harrison and Mary Harrison McKee, were very upset by their father's remarriage. Russell was 41 and Mary was 36 at the time. They undoubtedly felt that money they should inherit would go to the new family. Harrison deeply loved his children and recognized their displeasure, but he said, "my life now, and much more as I grow older, is and will be a very lonely one and I can not go on as now. A home is life's essential to me."[12] He further pointed out that neither of his children lived near him, nor probably ever would. How his children expected him to continue his lonely existence is hard to understand. But Russell and Mary were never reconciled to their father.

The former president and his wife were delighted when a baby girl, Elizabeth, was born on February 21, 1897. Harrison was most proud of his new daughter and spent considerable time with her. A new social life opened for the couple, and they lived happily together for almost five years.

The rather unusual family situation caused Harrison to draw up a long and interestingly-worded will. He felt compelled to specifically state to whom the furnishings of the house should go, and which of his mementos he had kept should go to which child. The will was more concerned with the welfare of his second wife and their daughter than the children by his first wife. But considering the lack of concern showed by these two older children, Harrison left a sizable portion of his wealth to them and their children in a trust. The second Mrs. Harrison lived to be 90 and did not die until 1948, so the final disposition of all the terms of the will was not completed for some time after her death.[13]

A number of Republicans endeavored to involve Harrison in the election of 1896 but he had no intention of entering politics again, certainly not as a presidential candidate. A very few times he did make political speeches. When Levi Morton ran for governor of New York, Harrison journeyed to New York in 1894 and made a most effective speech on his behalf in Carnegie Hall. Also, he made a few political speeches in the Midwest. On February 3, 1896, he tried to distance himself from politics when he refused to be a delegate to the Republican National Convention that summer. William McKinley and Mark Hanna, who hoped to control the convention, were pleased when Harrison made his position of no involvement plain to the public. Nevertheless, Hanna persisted until Harrison agreed to make a speech for McKinley. The former president delivered a powerful address in August which received national acclaim, and was helpful in McKinley's race for the presidency.

The last five years of Harrison's life may well have given him his greatest personal satisfaction. He enjoyed his position as an elder statesman, his successful law practice, and his new family. He also extended his activities to include membership in the board of trustees of Purdue University. During this time he turned down many job offers including a professorship at the University of Chicago at an excellent salary, and the presidency of a large Indiana bank.

In Cleveland's second administration, a dispute arose between England and Venezuela over the boundary between British Guiana, a British colony, and Venezuela. Harrison was selected as the attorney to represent Venezuela in Paris before the arbitration tribune which was created to settle the issue. The tribune was composed of two Americans, two Britons, and a Russian. The hearings dragged on interminably. The case was long and complex, with many technicalities. Harrison had given his full attention to the dispute for a year and a half, and before the case was heard he was forced to take a complete rest. Harrison's turn to represent his case did not come until late in September of 1899, but in his plea which took five days, he gave a brilliant defense of Venezuela's claim.

When the hearings ended, the unanimous decision of the tribunal on October 3, 1890, gave England most of the territory, for they had many settlers there. However, Venezuela gained significant territory at the southern end of the disputed area and thus was able to control the course of their most important river, the Orinoco. In many ways the decision was more of a victory for Venezuela than for England. Harrison was somewhat disappointed by the decision, but he accepted the verdict with good grace.

Harrison, his wife and small daughter, his personal secretary Frank Tibbott, and two servants had sailed for Europe in June of 1889. After the decision of the tribunal, the Harrisons did not linger long in Paris. They visited Cologne and Berlin and briefly toured England and the Low Countries before leaving Europe.

After returning home Harrison argued cases before the Supreme Court of Indiana as well as the United States Supreme Court. He had all the legal practice he could handle. According to his own wish, life was moving at a somewhat slower pace for him now. In the spring of 1900, the Harrisons toured the northwestern part of the United States, spending some time in Yellowstone National Park. They loved the mountains, and usually spent the hottest part of the summer in their Adirondack cabin.

Harrison's interest in religious matters was expressed in his almost lifelong membership in the First Presbyterian Church of Indianapolis, where he was a faithful communicant and gave special support in helping the less fortunate of the community. Some called him "rigidly pious."[14] So much did Harrison believe God was directing his life that he felt Providence had made him president. When he refused Matt Quay's request for a post in the cabinet, surprising several of Quay's friends, one of whom made the comment that Quay had made Harrison president (a doubtful claim at best) and therefore was in his debt. Quay's reaction was that "Benny says that God did it."[15]

The winter of 1900–1901 was an active one for the former president, who was chiefly occupied with his legal practice and with writing. In March he contracted a severe cold, and in just a matter of a few hours, became quite ill with pneumonia. In two days his condition worsened. Several doctors were called in to consult with the family physician, but they found nothing that could help. In the late afternoon of March 13, 1901, he died in the arms of Mary, his much-loved second wife.

Many of the great of the nation, including President McKinley, gathered in Indianapolis to pay respects to the former president. Thousands of survivors of Harrison's old military regiment marched in the procession. James Whitcomb Riley, famous Hoosier poet, gave a tribute at the service held in the First Presbyterian Church of Indianapolis. McKinley paid Benjamin Harrison a most worthy tribute: "The country has been deprived of one of its greatest citizens. A brilliant soldier . . . a leader of the bar . . . an orator and legislator . . . [with] extraordinary gifts as an administrator and legislator and statesman."[16]

Ironically, it could perhaps be said that Harrison died at the time of his greatest success, for the satisfaction of his post-presidency years far exceeded those of his presidency. Yet it was fitting that the nation paused, if but for a moment, to remember the man Benjamin Harrison.

The 25th, William McKinley

The Operation That Failed, 1901

The Pan American Exposition in Buffalo, New York, was one of the best of the great fairs so popular at the turn of the century. It sought to emphasize the cultural and economic unity of the Western Hemisphere. The other nations of the Americas responded with displays of culture and art as well as scientific advances. There were many attractions at the exposition such as bullfights, the ostrich farm, a cyclorama of the Johnstown flood, and the large Electric Tower that heralded the new day of electric power.

The exposition was important enough to attract presidential attention, and William McKinley(1843–1901; in office 1897–1901) agreed to attend the fair for a two-day period, deliver a major speech on United States policy, and to greet a large number of those in attendance. Riding in a Pullman car of wood construction, McKinley and the presidential train reached the exposition on September 4 at about 6:30 p.m. As the train arrived in Buffalo it seemed as if all the whistles in the city were blowing their loudest. A brass band was there to welcome the president. A number of gun salutes were fired, one of them so close and so loud that it broke windows in a coach of the presidential train. The welcome was loud, boisterous and friendly.

The nation's first couple was to be entertained at the home of John B. Milburn, president of the exposition. Mrs. McKinley was well enough to accompany the president on this trip. She had epilepsy, suffered at times from depression, and had been confined to her bed much of the summer. The *New York Times* noted how well she looked and how she smiled at those who came to greet them.[1]

Thursday, September 5, which had been designated as President's Day, broke all attendance records at the exposition. McKinley's speech was well received. He called for reciprocity in trade agreements, aiming eventually at free trade between all nations. This was a striking and new stance for the president.

Friday, September 6, 1901, dawned with beautiful weather. The president looked forward to a more or less informal day, one in which he could become something of a tourist in order to enjoy the exposition. He visited the famed Niagara Falls, rode the trolley along the scenic gorge route, lunched at the International Hotel by the falls, and visited the exhibits. The public had been promised that the president would greet the people that afternoon at the Music Temple. McKinley liked to shake hands and had worked out a system so he could greet about fifty persons a minute. However, his secretary, George B. Cortelyou, was concerned about the president's personal safety during this part of the schedule. He had wired ahead to ask for more security. Several times earlier the secretary had asked the president to omit the handshaking, but McKinley would not consider it.

By four o'clock the line of those wishing to shake the president's hand had already formed. On schedule the people were admitted and filed by the president. Several cardinal rules for the protection of the president's person had been completely ignored, but no one seemed to notice. Suddenly, at ten minutes after four, the dreaded, unexpected happened. Two shots could clearly be heard. For an instant there was complete silence, then all was tumult and confusion. The president had been shot twice by a .32-caliber revolver which the assassin had hidden in his hand with a handkerchief wrapped as a bandage. McKinley stood stock still for a moment, then was led to a chair where he sat down. The *New York Times* account told how the president said, "I am not badly hurt, I assure you."[2] But a red stain was growing over his abdomen, and immediate steps were taken to get medical attention.

The assassin, Leo Czolgosz, was quickly overpowered. The *New York Times* described it like this: "With the leap of a tiger three men threw themselves forward as with one impulse. . . . In a twinkling the assassin was borne to the ground, his weapon wrenched from his grasp, and strong arms pinioned him down."[3] The Secret Service rescued Czolgosz and he was taken into custody. Had they not acted quickly it is very possible that he might have been lynched on the spot.

A motor-driven ambulance came and the president was placed on the stretcher. He was taken to the exposition hospital on the grounds, although there was a fine modern hospital in Buffalo. The small hospital was staffed by interns, medical students and nurses, and was equipped for emergency treatment only, not major surgery. When the president arrived, no one seemed to know which surgeon to call or what to do. In twenty-two minutes Dr. Herman Mynter, a former military doctor, arrived. McKinley had met him the day before and recognized him. Mynter's quick initial examination showed that the wound was deep. Other doctors soon arrived. They included Dr. Matthew Mann, a well-known gynecologist and surgeon, Dr.

Eugene Wanbin, and Dr. P.M. Rixey, the president's personal physician. The best surgeon in the area for gunshot wounds was Dr. Roswell Park of Buffalo, but he was in surgery himself at the time.

The first question to be decided was whether or not to operate immediately. The decision to operate quickly was no doubt the correct one, for recovery without surgery was not possible. The question of where the surgery should be done was answered when they decided to operate at the small exposition hospital instead of taking the time to move him to Buffalo General Hospital. At five-twenty the surgery was begun under less than ideal circumstances. Perhaps the touchiest question was who was to do the surgery. From the standpoint of experience and ability the choice lay between Mynter and Mann. Yet neither doctor had experience in abdominal gunshot wounds. It would only be second guessing now to say that Mann was not the right choice. He was essentially a gynecologist, but had done considerable surgery. His very confident manner no doubt helped him to be selected.

The first bullet hit the breast bone and was easily found and removed. The second entered the abdomen and went through both sides of the stomach, damaged the pancreas, and lodged in the large muscle tissue of the back. The path of the bullet could be traced through the stomach. These holes were successfully closed. However, the bullet's path could not be followed beyond that point, so the wound was closed leaving the bullet still inside the body. One very debatable decision was not to insert a drain. Perhaps the surgeon did not have the necessary skill to do so.

Several conditions mitigated against good surgical procedure. The president's large abdomen hindered the surgeons. The instruments that were available were pitifully inadequate. There were, for example, no retractors. The light was so poor that Dr. Rixey directed sunlight into the wound by means of a mirror that caught the rays of the setting sun. Finally, he devised a small electric light. The procedure was described as "operating at the darkened end of a big hole."[4]

After the surgery McKinley was taken to the Milburn home where he was constantly attended by doctors and nurses. Though the patient had shown signs of shock, he basically stood the operation rather well. The physicians were "cautiously optimistic"[5] and felt that McKinley might recover. The doctors and the president's secretary issued frequent medical bulletins on the patient's condition.

Vice President Theodore Roosevelt was notified and hurried to Buffalo. Several cabinet members came as did Senator Mark Hanna, a good friend of the president. A detachment of soldiers arrived to guarantee security, and the press set up special telegraph wires to keep the public informed of the president's condition.

The next day, Saturday, September 7, the patient seemed to be making reasonable progress. The *New York Times* announced that physicians and friends were hopeful of recovery.[6] Vice President Roosevelt was reassured that the president would recover. Without any specific invitation, Dr. Charles McBurney, a famed New York surgeon, came to Buffalo to see what could be done and thrust himself into the center of the activity, talking volubly and making conditions uncomfortable for Dr. Park, who had been asked by the president's personal physician to be in charge of the patient. McBurney quickly announced that he "found no sign of peritonitis,"[7] despite the continuing rapid pulse. McBurney even began to talk about moving the patient back to the White House. At the same time Mann and Mynter were suggesting a more cautious view.

On Tuesday (under a Monday dateline)[8] the *New York Times* said the president "has passed the danger point." So reassured was the vice president that he returned to his vacation with his family in the Adirondack mountains. The same day the *Times* boldly announced, "President Will Get Well."[9] On Thursday the *Times* told the public, "President's Blood Free From Poison."[10]

However, the afternoon and evening of the day the newspapers carried their most optimistic reports, the president began to experience difficulties. He had what was called a sinking spell and was given restoratives. Thursday night and early Friday morning his condition obviously worsened. Dr. Mann admitted there were "signs of slight intestinal trauma."[11] The pulse rate of the patient became more elevated and he was having difficulty digesting the little food that was given him. Of more importance, the heart sounds began to show signs of weakening. The doctors were concerned that McKinley had not had a normal bowel movement since he was wounded, so they administered castor oil and other strong cathartics which further weakened him. The doctors again gathered for consultation, and the Secret Service began a hasty search for Vice President Roosevelt, who was in the wilds of the Adirondacks more than twelve miles from the nearest point of contact with the outside world.

The next day saw further deterioration of the president's condition. Digitalis and strychnine were administered to assist his faltering heart, but much of the day saw the president in something of a coma. Dr. Edward Janway, a famous New York heart specialist, arrived and could only confirm what the local physicians already knew, that the end was near. The worsening of McKinley's condition was carried by the Associated Press wires. By late afternoon he roused and asked for his wife. Both knew it was their final time together. Among his last words were, "It is God's way. His will, not ours, be done."[12] He repeated several lines of one of his favorite hymns, "Nearer My God to Thee."[13] The president then lapsed into unconsciousness again. At 2:15 a.m. on Saturday, September 14, Cortelyou came out of the Milburn home and announced, "Gentlemen, the president has passed away."[14] The wire services soon carried the news to the nation.

So often in very important and sensitive situations someone blunders in and acts outrageously. Certainly this was the case when James T. Wilson, the county coroner, arrived at the Milburn home in his official capacity several hours before McKinley died. Dr. Mann angrily informed him that his services were not required.[15] It seems that the local district attorney had heard that the president had died and ordered the coroner to investigate.

An autopsy was performed on Saturday morning. It gave some answers, but some rather fundamental questions remained. A local pathologist performed the postmortem in the presence of a number of doctors. Gangrene had set in on the walls of the stomach and pancreas. This was the basic cause of death. The autopsy certainly did not uphold Dr. Mann's rather tactless statement that the president's sedentary life had so weakened his vitality that his body did not have normal healing powers.[16] Mrs. McKinley halted the autopsy before the bullet was found.

Despite the fact that the press was present when the assassin shot the president and during the eight days McKinley fought for life, and despite the fact that so many who were involved in the care of the patient have left accounts of the incident, there are a number of questions yet unanswered. Perhaps the best single account of how President McKinley was cared for after the assassination is found in the form of a scrapbook left by Dr. Charles G. Stockton, one of the attending physicians. Discovered almost by chance, the scrapbook came into the possession of Dr. Stockton's grandson, Dr. Stockton Kimball, dean of the medical school of the University of Buffalo from 1946 to 1958. Dr. Kimball died in 1958 leaving his grandfather's scrapbook among his many effects. Four years later it was rediscovered by his widow, who gave it to Professor Selig Adler of the State University of New York at Buffalo. He published the material in the March 1963 issue of *Scientific American*.

In 1921, twenty years after McKinley's death, the press gave special attention to the anniversary of the unfortunate incident. At that time the same Dr. Charles G. Stockton was still alive and was interviewed by reporters. He gave as his medical opinion that McKinley died because the injury had allowed the pancreatic secretions to flow into the abdomen, causing damage that could not be reversed. "He had no chance to recover," stated the physician.[17] The accounts by the press of the assassination in 1901 are also very useful. But it is difficult for the press to give the total picture, and the problem of conflicting observations of the same event is always present.

Many factors hastened McKinley's death. The so-called hospital, a mere first aid station, lacked proper surgical instruments and light. A surgeon who was not experienced in gunshot wounds performed the operation, and no drain was placed in the wound. No X-ray was used although the best of its day was close by. Considering that hospital laboratories, blood transfusions, intravenous feedings, and antibiotics were not even heard of at that time, it is scant wonder that the operation failed.

At first the doctors supported one another, but as time went by they engaged in open disagreements before the press and the public. The New York doctors charged that the provincial Buffalo doctors had grossly bungled the case. The Buffalo physicians angrily responded with unprofessional vindictiveness and rancor, ridiculing the big-city doctors who could produce no better representative than the fallible McBurney.[18] A lawsuit was somehow averted. If there was a comic figure in the drama it had to be McBurney. Without having witnessed any of the surgery, he had called it "the epoch of the century in surgery."[19] He apparently liked to talk to the press.

When McKinley's condition worsened, the Secret Service frantically tried to get in touch with Vice President Roosevelt. They did not even know in what area of the Adirondacks he was vacationing. Fortunately his Buffalo host, Ansley Wilcox, knew approximately where he was. It was after nightfall on Friday before a wilderness guide found Roosevelt and gave him the news that he must return to Buffalo immediately. A midnight ride down the mountain at breakneck speed, using three fresh teams of horses, got him to the special train that would take him to Buffalo. By midmorning on Saturday he reached the Wilcox residence. Roosevelt went to the Milburn home to offer his sympathy to Mrs. McKinley and to show his respect for the late president. Shortly after noon in the Wilcox home, the vice president took the oath of office. Roosevelt asked all the cabinet to remain in their respective offices. He also promised to continue unbroken the policies of the fallen president.

On Sunday morning a brief, simple, private funeral service was conducted in the Milburn home. The body was then taken to the city hall where it lay in state for the rest of the day. Tens of thousands of the public passed the black coffin on the catafalque. Monday morning the funeral train left Buffalo and began its journey back to Washington. The new president and the officials who had gathered in Buffalo accompanied Mrs. McKinley and the body of the slain leader. At 8:38 p.m. the train pulled into the railroad station in Washington, D.C. The hearse which took the body to the White House was drawn by six matched black horses, and was followed by the carriage of the new president. The coffin stayed in the East Room of the White House overnight, but in the morning was taken to the rotunda of the Capitol in a long funeral procession in a drizzling rain.

An elaborate funeral service consisting of many prayers, eulogies, elegant music, and a sermon, was conducted at the Capitol. At six-thirty in the evening the doors of the Capitol were closed though thousands still waited to pass by the body of the president. At eight-twenty the funeral train with its 20 cars began the journey to Canton, Ohio, the home of the McKinleys, where the body finally would be laid to rest. When the train reached Canton on Wednesday morning, September 18, the coffin was taken to the McKinley home, a modest frame house on North Market Street. Again, thousands filed by the open coffin. Following a long service at one-thirty the next afternoon in the First Methodist Episcopal Church of Canton, the last funeral procession wended its way to Westlawn Cemetery where the body was buried.

Feelings against Czolgosz were dangerously strong. He was identified as a shy man, a misfit who drifted from place to place, seemingly always involved in one cause or another. Apparently he had acted entirely on his own and for reasons that at best are obscure. Those who knew him never would have imagined he could assassinate the president. Many called for him to be lynched, including two United States senators who quite openly spoke of lynching Czolgosz. One boasted that he himself had aided in the lynching of several blacks, and called for this to be the fate of the assassin. However, Czolgosz was indicted on September 16 and duly brought to trial on September 23. The criminal was given two prominent attorneys as court-appointed counsel, but refused to cooperate in his own defense. Three doctors testified that he was not insane, but the defense offered no witnesses in his behalf. The jury took 35 minutes to find him guilty. Throughout the trial, Czolgosz showed no interest in the proceedings. He was sentenced to die by electrocution at the state penitentiary in Auburn, New York. The Tuesday October 29 edition of the *New York Times* carried a detailed account of the execution.

Prison officials decided that nothing of Czolgosz should remain. His letters—he received hundreds of them—were burned along with his clothing. The family was not allowed to claim the body. It was put in quicklime within the prison walls.[20]

The 26th, Theodore Roosevelt

The Symbol of an Era, 1909–1919

Theodore Roosevelt (1858–1919), or "T.R." as he was called, was described as "an overgrown personality . . . appearing once or twice in a century or an age."[1] With an awesome excess of energy, together with his natural talents, Theodore Roosevelt became the leader of an era in American history, an era that still bears his name as well as his imprint. Since Roosevelt was only 42 when he became chief executive after the assassination of President McKinley, he was only 50 after almost two terms in office (1901–1909). His energy could not be submerged in the workaday world of American life. It is inconceivable that such a man would not be constantly in the news and on the cutting edge of the developing American nation. Theodore Roosevelt played his chosen role to the hilt in his so-called retirement years. So it seems ironic that he died at the relatively young age of 60.

Roosevelt personally picked William Howard Taft as his successor. In order to give Taft a free hand to develop his own administration, as well as to satisfy the boy that still was present in the famous man, the former president went on an extended hunting expedition in Africa. The Smithsonian Institution supervised the scientific aspects of the expedition, sending a taxidermist to see to the care of the animals that would be collected, and displayed at the Smithsonian. T.R. had the army modify several of its Springfield rifles for his use. He also took several large double-barreled rifles to use on the largest game.

After shaking hands with more than 500 people who came to bid him goodbye, and dressed in the greatcoat of a colonel in the Rough Riders, T.R. took his place beside the ship's captain on the bridge. The ship left Hoboken on March 23, 1909, and headed for Africa. Accompanied by his son Kermit, T.R. bagged nine lions, eight elephants, thirteen rhinoceroses, seven hippopotamuses, six buffaloes, and several leopards.[2] For him it was sheer joy to be in the jungle, many miles from the nearest human habitation, facing the challenge of the untamed continent. The exultation he felt is seen in his letters, the articles he wrote for *Scribners,* and his book, *African Game Trails.* During the 11 months of the trip, the press reported details of Roosevelt's exploits until the expedition sailed down the White Nile to Khartoum, where it was disbanded in March 1910.

Before Roosevelt left the United States he had been invited to give lectures in England, France, and Norway. These he gladly accepted. Soon he had invitations to visit most of Europe. It is interesting to note that none of his lectures in themselves received great acclaim, but his grand tour of Europe was a huge personal success. Among the principal nations visited were Italy, France, Holland, Belgium, Germany, Denmark, Norway, and Austria-Hungary. He felt that the Germans accepted him less warmly than the other nations, while he was best received by the English.

In Italy he had a rather unpleasant experience. Roosevelt had an appointment to be presented to the Pope, but before he was to see the pontiff he was asked to give assurances that he would not visit a small group of Methodist missionaries in Rome who had referred to the Pope as the "whore of Babylon."[3] T.R. responded, "I must decline to make any stipulations which limit my freedom of conduct."[4] As a result he did not visit the Pope, nor did he attend the reception which the Methodists wished to hold in his honor. However, the Italian people gave him a warm and spontaneous welcome which he wholeheartedly reciprocated.

But perhaps he enjoyed the English the most. He loved English authors and praised the British democratic government. On May 6, 1910, while Roosevelt was in Norway, England's King Edward VII died and President Taft asked T.R. to represent the United States at the king's funeral. The former president found the pomp and circumstance connected with European royalty very interesting and at times amusing. Oxford and Cambridge were a delight to the famous visitor. He especially enjoyed the undergraduates who responded to him enthusiastically.

On June 18, 1910, he arrived back home in New York on the *Kaiserin Augusta Victoria.* A large crowd turned out to greet him. But he was distressed to find himself immediately drawn into a bitter political controversy. Taft was not the Progressive that had been expected. On a number of occasions he made executive decisions that went contrary to the feelings of the Progressives. Examples were the tariff issue, and the Ballinger controversy — related to conservation — which Gifford Pinchot personally journeyed to Europe to lay before Roosevelt. At first the former president said little and observed what he could. He said nothing to Taft, still maintaining friendly relations with the administration. But as time went by, T.R. became convinced that something was amiss, and slowly he began to take sides with critics of the Taft administration. T.R. could tell that the basic tincture of his Progressive movement was being lost.

By February of 1912, Roosevelt had decided to openly oppose Taft and seek the Republican nomination himself. With such a late start, and the party machinery in the hands of the Taft people, it would have been a major political miracle for him to have gained the nomination. As the convention approached, the tactics of the administration became clear. They would challenge the seats of many of Roosevelt's delegates to the convention, and then have the credentials committee, which was in the hands of the Taft people, give the contested seats to Taft. To this day there is no clear-cut answer to the question of whether or not the nomination was stolen from Roosevelt. William Allen White is sure that T.R. was the rightful choice of the Republicans; others are not so confident. However, it is clear that when the Republican voters had an opportunity to express their preference in primaries, T.R. was the overwhelming choice.

Immediately after the Republicans had nominated Taft, the Progressives got together in a hastily-called convention and nominated Roosevelt by acclamation. It was here that T.R. made his famous speech where he thundered, "We stand at Armageddon, and we battle for the Lord."[5] Both of these assumptions may well be questioned, but it was a tremendous battle cry. With two Republican candidates in the field, it was rather obvious that Governor Woodrow Wilson of New Jersey, the Democratic nominee, would win the presidency, but not by a popular majority. He received only 40 percent of the total vote.

The campaign was most unpleasant and bitter. As Roosevelt was preparing to deliver a speech on October 14 in Milwaukee, a man by the name of John Schrank shot T.R. at point blank range. The bullet went through the manuscript of his speech and his metal spectacles case, then lodged in his massive chest muscle. T.R. refused immediate medical attention, insisting he was going to make his speech "or die."[6] He dramatically proclaimed, "I have a message to deliver and will deliver it as long as there is life in my body." (Schrank, sometimes Schranck or Crank, was examined by five specialists in Milwaukee and declared insane. He was placed in a mental institution for an "indefinite time," and died in 1943.)

Roosevelt talked for an hour and a half with the bullet in his body.[7] The drama of the occasion is easily imagined. When asked how he felt, he asserted, "I feel as strong as a bull moose." From that time his party was known as the "Bull Moose Party." Small wonder that T.R. easily gained more votes than Taft in the election of 1912. But Wilson, who ran a strong campaign, outdistanced both T.R. and Taft. However, T.R. and Taft together easily received more popular votes than Wilson. One commentator aptly stated, "The only question is which corpse gets the most flowers."[8]

Roosevelt was not one to sulk in defeat. There were always new worlds to conquer, and he was eager to accept the challenges. He had been invited to Brazil to give an address, and determined that since he was going to

South America he might as well explore some of the unmapped jungle, especially the course of the "River of Doubt."[9] He and his son Kermit got the expedition together, leaving New York on October 4, 1913, and returning on May 19, 1914. Kermit recorded the adventure in his book *The Happy Hunting Ground*. T.R. could have easily lost his life on this expedition. The going was much more difficult than they had imagined for the river was filled with rapids, and the hostile jungle was always ready to swallow them up.

In attempting to get the boats over one of the rapids, Roosevelt sustained a deep cut in his leg. A serious abscess developed which never did heal properly. He also developed a fever which made him so ill that he had to be carried much of the way in his party's desperate effort to get him back to civilization and medical help. Never would T.R. be in really good health after this trip, although he was up and around in a few weeks.

At about the same time he was involved in two lawsuits. During the 1912 political campaign, a Michigan newspaper accused T.R. of being a drunkard. The item attracted wide attention though very few believed the accusation. However, T.R. brought suit for libel against the paper's editor. T.R. did not desire a monetary award, but wanted vindication. By awarding him six cents in damages, the jury satisfied Roosevelt.

In the other trial, Roosevelt was the defendant in a libel suit brought by William Barnes, Jr., concerning a statement T.R. had made about Barnes, New York's political boss. T.R. had said, "It is idle for a man to pretend that he is against machine politics unless he will openly and by name attack Mr. Barnes...."[10] The trial was a sensation. At times T.R. used the witness stand for political diatribes which the judge was forced to stop. In the end the jury thought T.R.'s comments were acceptable under the First Amendment and found for the defendant.

The former president who was independently wealthy, held no permanent position in the decade after his term was over. His time was spent in traveling, writing, and speech making. He was a contributing editor to a magazine called *Outlook,* wrote many editorials and articles for the *Kansas City Star* as well as for other publications. He also wrote a number of books. It was his custom to speak out on any issue he chose.

During the latter part of his life the issue that occupied most of Roosevelt's attention was America's military unpreparedness. As he observed Europe drifting into World War I in the autumn of 1914, he saw that his country was in no position to defend its rights if called upon to do so. The navy had been neglected and the standing army was pitifully weak and small. The supply of arms was dangerously low. Yet President Wilson, as T.R. saw it, did not take steps to remedy the situation, nor did he help the Allies sufficiently. T.R. was totally convinced of the justice of the cause of the Allies. He felt they were fighting for the principles his nation was founded on, and that the Allies were fighting alone. For more than two years he pled in language which could not be ignored for the United States to arm itself and to help the Allies. In the end he significantly helped move America from a rather lofty, self-complacent isolation to an involvement in the problems of Europe.

Perhaps the greatest service Teddy Roosevelt performed after leaving the White House was to make the American people consider issues they would have liked to ignore. On many occasions the public chose to disagree with him, but they could not ignore him. There was no subtlety in his approach. He hit like thunder from Mount Olympus. Three times he crossed the nation on speaking tours. He wrote a stream of editorials and magazine articles, and made a constant barrage of statements to the press. The theme remained the same. America should arm, and quickly. He unmercifully castigated and berated the occupant of the White House. The nation's weak foreign policy, as T.R. saw it, was also a subject of attack.

Among other demands Roosevelt made was that the nation should adopt a policy of universal military service. He decried the lack of a steady supply of airplanes, ships, and guns for the Allies. He pointed out that two big oceans could no longer be regarded as all the protection America needed. Advances in the art of war had changed so much that the nation could not afford to sit idly by while others armed. He charged that the president spoke "lofty words" but they were "followed by no action."[11] The rather mild response the United States made to the sinking of the *Lusitania* infuriated him, and he called Wilson a "demagogue."[12] He charged the administration with being "intellectually slippery."[13] When the United States did declare war, T.R. felt it should move faster in its prosecution. He ridiculed "broomstick preparedness" when soldiers were forced to use wooden guns to drill because there were no real guns available. T.R. used such words as "supine inaction," "flubdubs," and "mollycoddles."[14] In private his assessment of Wilson was that he was the worst president since Buchanan, with the possible exception of Andrew Johnson.[15]

So violent was his attack on Wilson that the Delaware state legislature nearly passed a resolution denouncing Roosevelt, and in the United States Senate he was openly charged with sedition and treason. When the administration took steps which would have placed limits on free speech, T.R. was beside himself. There was little surprise when President Wilson summarily refused T.R.'s request to form an army division and go directly to France and fight "the Huns," although he had made the petition in person. The former president was angry at the denial of his request. This, despite the fact he was almost 60 years old, blind in one eye, with other physical disabilities, and with no real military background.

The four sons in the Roosevelt family all became involved in the fighting. One of them never came home. Families with sons in the service placed banners in their windows with a star for each son in the war. The flag in the Roosevelt home on Sagamore Hill of Oyster Bay, New York, had four stars in it. Later when daughter Ethel's husband, Richard Derby, went to war the flag had five stars. Not many American homes could share that distinction. The oldest son, Theodore, Jr., or "Ted" as he was called, had risen to the rank of lieutenant colonel. He was gassed, and wounded in the leg. He recovered, but limped for many months. It was in World War II that he died of natural causes while with his men at the front in Europe.

Kermit entered the war with the British army before America was at war, earning the British Military Cross for gallantry in action. Later he transferred from the British army to the A.E.F. in France and became a captain in the artillery. Kermit was the only son not wounded in the war, but he contracted malaria and never completely recovered.

Archibald, or Archie, was severely wounded while at the front. One arm and one leg were badly hurt by an exploding shell. The arm was paralyzed for a time. Archie's wife Grace came to Sagamore Hill with their boy, "Wee Archie, Jr.," much to the joy of T.R., who spent hours holding his infant grandson. Finally Archie, who had been cited for gallantry, came back to the states and to Sagamore Hill to recuperate with his family.

Quentin, the youngest son, left Harvard and joined the air corps. He excelled as a pilot and was retained as an instructor for a time, but he asked for combat duty and was sent to France. Here he became a member of Richtofen's 21-member "flying circus" and engaged in many missions. When he brought down his first enemy plane on July 8, 1918, the *New York Times* reported the account. Somewhat later, "the colonel," as T.R. liked to be called, was working in his study when Associated Press reporter Phil Thompson appeared at the Roosevelt home with a telegram that simply told him to watch Sagamore Hill. Phil asked the colonel what it meant. T.R. quickly concluded something must have happened to one of the boys. He knew that both Ted and Archie were still recovering from their wounds, and that Kermit was not at the moment in a battle zone, so it must be Quentin. It developed that "Q," as Quentin was called, had not returned to his home field after a mission. T.R. insisted that Mrs. Roosevelt not be told until something more definite was known. The next morning they learned that "Q" had been shot down behind enemy lines.

At first it was hoped that he was still alive, but finally the news came that Quentin had been shot down and killed on July 14, 1918. T.R. told the A.P. reporter, "But Mrs. Roosevelt, how am I going to break it to her."[16] In half an hour both the colonel and his wife came out of the house, and T.R. read a brief statement to the press: "Quentin's mother and I are very glad that he got to the front and had a chance to render some service to his country and show the stuff that was in him before his fate befell him."[17] The Roosevelt family was deeply religious. They had taken communion together with Quentin at their local church shortly before "Q" sailed for France and the war. The family took communion in the same small church after getting the news of Quentin's death.

Roosevelt was never quite the same. Some of the intense fire he always carried with him had been quenched forever. He continued his active schedule, but something within had died. The public did not recognize this from his manner or behavior, but intimates were very aware of the change. Two days after he received the news that "Q" had been shot down, he was scheduled to deliver the keynote address at the Republican state convention at Saratoga. He insisted on making the speech. The convention cheered him until he had to ask for quiet so he could speak. It was hoped that his speech would help to unite the New York Republicans. The convention tried to nominate T.R. for governor of New York, but he refused to consider the offer.

Just 20 minutes before Roosevelt was to have received an important Japanese delegation, he received a personal telegram from President Wilson confirming the fact that Quentin had indeed been killed in action and buried by the Germans. It was a warm and sympathetic message. T.R. insisted on receiving the delegation, later giving expression to his grief. He had earlier expressed the fear that not all of the boys would come home. Somewhat later he would say, "If the war goes on, none of the boys will come back."[18] Fortunately the other three did come home, but only one without wounds.

The Progressives wanted Roosevelt to run for the presidency in 1916, but he knew that such a move would only ensure Wilson's reelection, so he declined and asked Republicans of all kinds to make an effort to elect Justice Charles Evans Hughes, the Republican nominee for president. Hughes lost to Wilson in a very close election. In fact, Hughes was declared the winner before all the California votes were counted under the assumption that California would vote Republican again. But at the last moment California voted for Wilson by a scant margin, ensuring his reelection.

When the midterm elections of 1918 approached, Wilson asked for a Democratically controlled Congress, even opposing Republicans who had consistently supported him and his programs. This strategy backfired. Roosevelt ripped into Wilson for a completely partisan approach in a time of national crisis, feeling that Wilson was "at heart a pacifist, cold-blooded and without a single scruple of conviction."[19] It is interesting to observe that both T.R. and Wilson are consistently listed among the nation's great presidents. The antagonism that developed between them was probably due as much to a difference in personality and style as to the issues and the positions they took.

Roosevelt was obviously the most important Republican in the country. It was assumed by many that he would seek the presidency again in

1920. He made it plain that if they backed his program and wanted him to run he would do so. Many feel that if he had lived and was physically able to run, he would have won in 1920. Only an imaginative historian could tell how the country would have fared in the 1920s had T.R. been in the White House instead of Warren G. Harding and Calvin Coolidge.

The public as a whole could hardly imagine that the hearty, vigorous colonel of the Rough Riders could have anything less than perfect health. Until the very last of his life, when he was hospitalized twice in the year 1918, the public did not realize that Roosevelt was not a well man. Few knew he had sustained a detached retina and lost the sight of one eye as a result of a blow he received in a boxing workout in the White House while he was president. Although he stood the African expedition very well for a man of fifty years, his expedition to the jungles of South America left him with disease and injuries from which he never did recover. The leg injury brought continuously recurring abscesses, which on several occasions made surgery necessary. Frequently he had difficulty in walking. The jungle fever he contracted in South America caused periodic debility, often confining him to his bed. Also, the inflammation in his joints, which they called "rheumatism," at times caused him severe pain. He made several speaking tours when he was in considerable pain, often spending most of the time in bed when he was not on the platform. Yet the public never suspected his difficulties.

In February 1918 he was a patient at the Roosevelt Hospital in New York City for a number of days with the recurrence of abscesses in his injured leg. At the same time he had an ear abscess that cost him the hearing in his left ear. Yet after this hospital stay he made two more long speaking tours. Before the November election in 1918, T.R. made the last national appeal for the Republicans at Carnegie Hall in New York City. It was an impressive, effective speech, challenging Wilson's leadership. No one realized this was to be the last speech of his life. He was in such pain that he went immediately to Sagamore Hill and to bed. On occasion he dictated a few letters, but often could not sign them. He managed to get out of bed on November 5 to vote.

The war was over and the Armistice signed on November 11, 1918. It was also the day he again entered Roosevelt Hospital in New York City. He remained a patient there until Christmas Day. When he was able to leave the hospital, the doctors warned him that he might be confined to a wheelchair for the rest of his life. He faced the fact, and though he got on his feet again, he never moved about freely. A chance comment tells how he felt. "I feel as though I were a hundred years old, and had never been young."[20] In spite of all the difficulties, the family had a joyous Christmas. The presence of several grandchildren, their son Archie, and two daughters-in-law made the occasion a memorable one. T.R. expressed the hope that all three of the generations would be together on the occasion of the next Christmas.

On January 5, 1919, the former president made his last public utterance in the form of an editorial for the *Kansas City Star*. In it he protested the attempts of the administration to limit war correspondents in their work in gathering the news. On the same day, T.R. did not dress and go downstairs as had been his custom since returning from the hospital. He was tired and stayed for the most part in his favorite upstairs room, the northwest bedroom. T.R. and his wife Edith took turns reading to each other. Edith wrote to Ted that his father loved the view from this room. A capable nurse had been employed, and with James Amos, the valet, they cared for the former president. His mood was optimistic, and he felt that the future was bright. Edith had spent the evening near his bed playing solitaire. He read, talked, and dozed. She told her husband goodnight and went to her room. James Amos came in and the former president asked him to put out the light. Sometime between four and five the next morning, January 6, 1919, a coronary embolism stopped the famous Roosevelt heart. Vice President Marshall said, "Death had to take him sleeping. For if Roosevelt had been awake, there would have been a fight." Archie cabled Ted and Kermit in France that "The Old Lion is Dead."[21]

The 27th, William Howard Taft

Professor and Chief Justice, 1913–1930

Of all the United States presidents, none held as many high positions as William Howard Taft (1857–1930). Perhaps equally significant was the fact that his contributions to the life of the nation extended far beyond his tenure as chief executive (1909–1913).

Before he became president, Taft held a number of important positions. At 33 he was made United States solicitor general, a position in which he represented the nation when the United States was party to a case in the Supreme Court. Soon he became a federal circuit court judge. For a time he was dean of the Cincinnati Law School. Next he was named president of the Philippine commission, then governor general of the Philippines, two very important and sensitive positions. He also served as special envoy to the papacy concerning claims to some land the Catholic church made in the Philippines when the islands were taken from Spain. President Theodore Roosevelt made Taft secretary of war. During this time he also served as provisional governor of Cuba.

From 1909 to 1913 Taft was the twenty-seventh president of the United States. When his term came to an end he was only 56 years old, far too young to retire. It was then that Taft became a professor at Yale University. As an ex-president and a professor at a prestigious university with a very busy speaking and writing schedule, he became one of the prime movers in the shaping of American public opinion. His final years were spent as chief justice of the United States, a position in which he largely reshaped the Supreme Court and significantly influenced the decisions of the Court in the critical post–World War I period in American history. Taft felt that his work as chief justice was the most important service of his life. No doubt he was correct in this assessment. Of all the other presidents, only John Quincy Adams made anything approaching the contribution that Taft made after leaving the White House. In many respects the presidency for Taft was only an incident in a long life filled with high positions of trust and responsibility.

As Taft reviewed the options open to him after he left the presidency, his first inclination was to return to the practice of law. But after careful consideration he realized that there likely would be a conflict of interest when he represented his clients in court, for 45 percent of the sitting federal judges were his appointees, and six of the nine members of the Supreme Court had been appointed by his administration. At this time Andrew Carnegie, the famous industrialist, offered Taft a lifetime personal pension of $25,000 a year,[1] an amount which at that time would have allowed Taft a life of luxury. He quickly declined the well-meant offer.

After Taft lost his bid for reelection in November of 1912, Anson P. Stokes, secretary of the Yale Corporation, felt that the school would be well served to have an ex-president as a professor, so he discussed the matter with Arthur Hadley, president of the university. A few days after the election, Hadley discussed the possibility with Taft. Immediately Taft showed interest in the position and assured Hadley that he would discuss the proposal with his cabinet and his family. Without exception the cabinet felt it would be an ideal position for an ex-president, one which would offer a challenging outlet for Taft's creative energy. Taft commented, "It is a dignified retirement, one which Cleveland had at Princeton, and one which would approve itself to the general sense of propriety of the country."[2]

Yale hired Taft as the Kent professor of law to lecture to senior students on constitutional law. He was also scheduled to teach at least one course on international law in the Yale Law School. The salary was $5,000 a year (quite a contrast to the presidential salary of $75,000, plus another $25,000 for expenses). But Taft had made substantial savings so that he could get along comfortably at Yale on that salary (the highest salary they paid a professor).

In rather characteristic fashion Taft publicly announced his acceptance of the Yale appointment in a letter to the *Yale Daily News,* the student newspaper. This letter expressed his sentimental attachment to Yale and his anticipation of returning to his alma mater as professor. "If I can help the men of Yale to know the value of our institutions ... I will be thrice content."[3] He added, "I think I shall be doing God's service."[4]

Taft's closing days in the White House were not very satisfying. As the outgoing chief executive he had very little political power, for the incoming administration was of the other party. The president sent several messages to Congress, including his annual message, but Congress paid them scant attention. Bitterness was not a part of Taft's personality, and he displayed an amazing serenity as he prepared to leave Washington. As with most retiring presidents, he felt a genuine sense of relief that he was leaving the White House. He and his wife boarded the 3:10 p.m. train for Georgia on March 4, 1913.

After a golfing vacation, the Tafts started for New Haven. The proposed welcome by the Governor's Foot Guard was vetoed by the former president as being too elaborate, but he did agree to let the students welcome him as they wished. The *Yale Daily News* carried instructions as to where the welcoming crowd was to be and what part they were to play in the grand parade. Rain would be no reason to cancel the welcome. Classes during the periods before and after the noon hour were cancelled. Fully half the student body joined in the celebration. At the sight of the Tafts pandemonium broke out, but finally they were safely in the auto that was to take them to Memorial Hall for Taft's address. The captains of the major athletic teams (baseball, football, the crew, and track) formed the honor guard. The famous Yale bulldog, "Beans," was also present. Taft's first words in response to the tumultuous welcome were, "Men of Yale, you will believe me when I tell you that I am greatly touched by this student demonstration."[5]

The next few days were spent in getting acquainted and in settling themselves in their new quarters. People seemed to be completely captivated by Taft's unassuming, natural charm. Two days after his arrival, Professor John Beach took him golfing at the country club. Beach was a small, quick man, and the former president huge and slow moving. This disparate twosome would become a familiar sight on the golf courses of New Haven.

As long as he was physically able, golf was one of Taft's great interests. He was relieved to be able to play a quiet game of golf and not have the press know with whom he golfed, what they discussed, and incidentally what score he had. Though the former president was a most enthusiastic golfer, his skill did not match his fervent spirit. Once, in 1909, he bet $1,000 that he could play the rather difficult Myopia golf course at Boston in under 100 strokes. He shot 98 and collected his bet.[6]

In the fall of 1913, after a summer at Murray Bay, Taft began his regular teaching duties in constitutional law and international law. As might have been anticipated, his classes were overly large, and he was forced to use a reader in grading tests and written assignments. But students found his lectures fascinating. His resource of personal experiences proved to be of great interest. In what other class could a student hear the teacher tell of a case the Supreme Court had ruled on, then comment that he had vetoed the bill which was passed over his veto, then declared unconstitutional by the Supreme Court. It should be noted that Taft required his students to memorize the Constitution.

The new professor needed some help in class management. At first he relied on recitation, but soon saw that lecturing was his strength. He worked out a system of giving a five- or ten-minute quiz over the assigned material as the class started, then he would begin his lecture. He discovered that an excessive amount of cheating went on during the quizzes, but never was able to solve the problem. Also, the college dean had to step in and tell the students they could not leave class until they had waited at least fifteen minutes, for it seems that the ex-president was tardy for class a number of times. But except for illness, the Kent professor did not miss a single class, unless he had first arranged with the dean to make it up.

Fellow faculty members found Taft to be friendly and very approachable, and enjoyed many conversations with the former president. From his girth one could conclude that he always had time for another cup of coffee and a piece of pie or cake with a friend. Often he gave freely of his time to students who had problems. Both students and faculty found him to be a caring and giving person.

Among his other responsibilities, Taft coached the freshman debating team. In their three-cornered meet with Harvard and Princeton, Yale came in last. Coaching debate proved to be an activity he did not continue.

The demand for Taft as a lecturer was far greater than he ever imagined. Eventually he was away from campus more than he was in residence. Probably he enjoyed visiting and lecturing on other university campuses more than any other speaking he did. Dozens of campuses invited him to lecture. Civic and charitable groups often called on him as a special speaker, as did many private clubs and organizations. Topics that he lectured on included the jury system, the power of the president, Prohibition, women's suffrage, and international problems. Before long Wendell W. Mischler, his secretary who had come to New Haven from Washington with him, had to set up something of a lecture bureau for the former president. While he made many lectures where he charged no fee, on most occasions his fees ranged from $150 to $1,000, the average about $400. Some amusing situations arose while he was out lecturing, one on April 2, 1919, in Detroit, when he ran out of money and walked a mile from his hotel to the city hall to get the mayor to cash a check for him.

Taft wrote a number of articles for a variety of magazines. His usual fee was $1,000. Needless to say, these fees helped to augment his much reduced salary at Yale.

When Taft moved to New Haven, he immediately became an involved citizen. The Y.M.C.A. and Boys Club both received his attention and support. He registered to vote and regularly exercised his right of franchise in city elections. On several occasions he identified with local causes for civic improvement and twice was publicly insulted for the stands he took.

Although the former president made it abundantly clear that he would never again seek public office, he remained vitally interested in what was happening in current affairs. This was especially true when World War I broke out. Taft supported Wilson's policy of neutrality and nonintervention in sharp contrast to Theodore Roosevelt's desire to get America involved in the conflict immediately. The League to Enforce Peace found in Taft an advocate and strong participant. But when Wilson finally took the nation into war, he had Taft's outspoken support for the move. In fact, Taft began to feel that Wilson was not as aggressively pursuing America's preparedness as he should.

Taft took a year's leave of absence from his teaching and speaking to serve his country as a member of the National War Labor Board, which investigated situations where there was labor unrest and attempted to bring about peaceful settlements. Although the board had no power to enforce its recommendations, many explosive confrontations found peaceful solutions under the board's direction. While most of the nation applauded the findings of the board, organized labor at times found fault with Taft's leadership, feeling it was too conservative.

Taft roused the ire of many of his conservative colleagues when he supported the League of Nations. His firm conviction was that the world had entered a new era where the big nations singly or in concert could not always preserve peace. While Taft was apprehensive concerning certain aspects of Wilson's League, he was convinced that the nations of the world would have to devise some sort of cooperative effort to preserve the peace.

Many attempts were made to get him to enter the political arena again, but he refused to consider the matter. However, Taft early supported Charles Evans Hughes for the Republican nomination in 1916. Both Theodore Roosevelt and Taft campaigned for Hughes, who lost a very close contest to Woodrow Wilson.

Taft was not directly involved in the election of 1920. However, when Senator Warren G. Harding was nominated by the Republicans, Taft felt Harding would be a better president than his detractors predicted. In this Taft was in error, for he often had difficulty in judging people. When the Harding scandals came to light, the former president was quite surprised and more than a little chagrined.

When the Republicans recaptured the White House in 1920 and Harding became president, there was speculation that Taft would be named chief justice of the Supreme Court. The sitting chief justice, Edward White, was in ill health and was expected to resign. In fact when Taft met with Harding in December of 1920 after the election, Harding told Taft he would put him on the Court, but did not mention the position of chief justice. After White died, Harding let weeks go by without naming a new chief justice. Taft felt that his chance to be made head of the highest tribunal of the land was minimal. Harding had told intimates that he was going to name Taft to the post, but the president seemed slow to take definite action. Finally, on June 30, 1921, William Howard Taft was nominated as chief justice. Senate confirmation was a foregone conclusion. Taft had realized the fondest ambition of his life.

The Tafts were at their summer home at Murray Bay, Quebec, when his appointment was made. On July 1, 1921, Taft sent hand-written letters to President James Angell and Dean Thomas Swan of Yale tendering his resignation as Kent professor of law. It was with some degree of sorrow that he left Yale. He had come to love the university, first as a student himself and then as a member of the faculty. Eventually he gave a large part of his library to the university. When he returned to Washington he kept in close touch with the university and his friends in New Haven. He visited the campus frequently, and continued to be an active alumnus. Taft's last appearance at Yale was in June 1928 when he spoke at the law school luncheon. Two days later he made his last public speech when he spoke at the alumni luncheon.[7]

Few undervalue the importance of the Supreme Court. All through the nation's history the Court has made far-reaching and important decisions. Beginning with the John Marshall Court and its famed *Marbury v. Madison* decision which gave the federal government more authority, to the Taney Court's Dred Scott decision, to the New Deal controversy, to the Warren Court's new dictums — including *Brown v. Board of Education* — to the Reagan Court with its first female justice, the Supreme Court has been an immeasurably strong force in government. The Taft Court was not as controversial as the above-mentioned Courts, but its effect was to be felt by the entire nation. He attempted to speed up the judicial process and to deal with the new problems of the day, especially those involving Prohibition, the new income tax, cases which grew out of the Great War, and the new types of labor cases. The position of chief justice was and continues to be probably the most important judicial position in the entire world. Taft was fully justified in feeling that it was far more important and demanding than his presidency.

In Washington the Tafts purchased a spacious home on Wyoming Avenue near 23rd Street, three miles from where the Supreme Court met. The home, which cost $75,000, had three guest bedrooms and a nineteenth-century gracious elegance that seemed to fit the man, his family, and his position. An elevator was installed to make climbing the many stairs unnecessary for the aging chief justice and his tiring heart. The third floor became Taft's study and library. Here he kept his law books, the Court reports, more recent English cases of law, and his history and political science library. On the walls were the pictures of the justices that were sitting on the bench during his tenure, as well as the portrait of his father, the late Alphonso Taft of Cincinnati.

By this time Taft was attempting to do something about his weight, even going so far as to visit a health farm where he frequently enjoyed horseback riding. (The writer could find no reference as to the size and strength of the horses needed to give the chief justice his exercise.)

When at home, he was usually up at five fifteen and began his work at six in his study. Breakfast was scheduled for eight o'clock, followed by nearly two hours of more work in his study before he walked the three miles to the Supreme Court. The Court sessions lasted from noon until four-thirty, after which he was driven home where he worked until seven, when dinner was served. Unless there was some special activity for him to attend, he would work from eight until he prepared for a ten o'clock bedtime. His work schedule was very demanding, but the new chief justice saw much that needed to be done. Later, as he approached the close of his career he did not spend quite so much time in his study.

The Supreme Court even worked on Saturday. At noon the justices met in conference at which time they examined the basic facts of the cases they were considering and sought to determine the relevant questions of law. Each justice, according to his seniority, discussed the case, presented his views, and cast his vote as to the disposition of the case. The chief justice then sent each member a memo giving the assignment of the cases for opinions.[8] Taft wrote a large number of opinions himself. In fact few chief justices wrote as many court opinions as did Taft.

When he assumed his new role as chief justice, Taft found the Court rather badly divided in its legal views and political philosophy. More troublesome were the personal animosities that had developed between several of the members of the Court. Perhaps what bothered Taft most was that the Court was not getting its work done. They were very much behind schedule in the number of cases still to be heard.

When one remembers that the president makes appointments to the Court with no advice from the Court itself, that these appointments are made for life, and that they are made for political and not professional reasons, it is easy to see how divided any Court could become. Several of those on the Court had been appointed by Taft himself while he was in the White House. It was especially distressing when the Court made split decisions, 5-4 and 6-3. Taft tried to bring a sense of unity to the court, but much to his regret there was no more unity when he retired than when he assumed its leadership.

However, Taft was able to speed up the judicial action. His more efficient organization helped to cut some of the routine details and get more cases before the Court. Taft backed the Judiciary Act of 1925 which gave the Court an opportunity to determine more adequately which cases it would accept for an in-depth study.

For the most part Taft got along very well with his colleagues on the bench. But there were several rugged and iconoclastic personalities on the Court who were always a problem to the others. In time Taft came to appreciate Justice Brandeis and effectively work with him. The Nestor of the court, Justice Oliver Wendell Holmes, became a close friend of the chief justice. Taft and Holmes often walked to the Court together. When Mrs. Holmes died, Taft took charge of the funeral, as Holmes had no children and no close family still living. Mrs. Holmes, like the chief justice himself, was a Unitarian. Taft remarked that one thing he knew how to do well was to run a Unitarian funeral. Justice Holmes was indeed grateful.

Often Taft was irritated by the large amount of time the cases relating to Prohibition took from the Court. Taft had never been a drinking man, though he had an occasional glass of wine, but he could not see how it was a function of government to keep a person from taking a drink. The chief justice was very open in this view, but Mrs. Taft supported the "dry law," and they had interesting conversations about the matter.

Taft's Court was regarded as conservative. Yet it should be remembered that the chief justice saw that American society was changing, and that new problems demanded new solutions. His Court did not hesitate to face up to new issues, and he did not waver in the writing of difficult opinions.

When Taft donned his judicial robes, much of the casual social life he enjoyed so much was ended. The number of dinner parties he could attend was strictly limited. Also, much to his sorrow, the times he could play a round of golf were drastically cut. No doubt the rigid schedule that he was forced to adopt was the most onerous part of his position. However, the pressures of presiding over the world's most prestigious judicial body did not cause him to lose contact with his family. One of the reasons for buying the spacious home on Wyoming Avenue was that there would be room for the family to continue its tradition of coming home to celebrate special occasions. The grandchildren loved the grand old man who was the master of the house where they gathered. There was a rich bonding among the family of the chief justice.

The health of the former president was seldom a concern. He was an active, affirming, optimistic person who never complained and seldom had a sick day. The most obvious problem that he faced was his excess weight. His only intemperance was his eating. At Yale, where as a professor he was called "Big Bill," one of the adjustments that had to be made was to provide larger and more sturdy chairs for the places where he would sit. The first faculty meeting that Taft attended was delayed until an appropriate chair could be found for the new staff member. Chairs in dentists' offices and in barber shops were also adjusted to care for his herculean frame.

Taft had played center on the football team, and no touchdown was ever scored over his position by the opposition. When he graduated from Yale he tipped the scales at 240 pounds. By the time he left for the Philippines he weighed 270 pounds. When he left the Philippines, his weight had climbed to 320, and when he left the White House it was up to 340. This excess weight was especially hard on his heart. When he went to Yale as a professor he worked with Dr. George Blumer, dean of the medical school, and by diet and exercise he lost sixty pounds. When he returned to Washington, he weighed a respectable 260 pounds.

Taft had no single serious illness in his last years, but as he grew older he seemed at times to have a general sense of uneasiness. By this time there was a continuing stomach disorder, but it did not appear to be of a serious nature. His heart seemed overworked and struggling at times. In the summer of 1927 at Murray Bay, just weeks before his seventieth birthday, he remarked that he tended not "to question the general accuracy" of the old saying that a man's allotted time was "three-score and ten."[9] It was true that his health did deteriorate after he reached seventy, but he remained fairly active despite his growing aches and pains.

His chief personal fear was the feeling that there was something wrong with his heart although the doctors did not find an immediate cause for concern when they examined him. His blood pressure was somewhat elevated and there was a beginning of hardening of the arteries. In 1929, just before the summer recess of the Court, he was hospitalized, briefly, primarily for fatigue. He hoped that a summer at Murray Bay would rejuvenate him, but it did not. When the Court opened in October of 1929, he found his duties very difficult to perform. Once, while he was reading one of his opinions, a colleague had to finish reading the case.

On December 30, 1929, his oldest brother died in Cincinnati. Against the advice of his physician he insisted on attending the funeral. It was a difficult trip, and Taft could not sleep in the Pullman car. When the train reached Washington, he insisted on going directly to the Supreme Court with no rest. He never recovered from the effects of this trip.

When the new year (1930) came, his doctors insisted that he take an extended rest, so he traveled to Asheville, North Carolina, for a vacation. Though the sun and the warm air were enjoyable, he grew weaker. At times he went for a ride, but those with him could see that he was a seriously ill man. There were occasions when he hallucinated and times he did not recognize visitors whom he knew well. The family insisted he resign, and his son, Robert A. Taft, later the famed conservative senator from Ohio, took the resignation of the chief justice to President Hoover.

The ailing statesman came back to Washington to pass his last days in the family home. When the train arrived in the capital, he had to be lifted bodily and placed in a wheelchair.

The doctors told the family it was only a matter of time, but he lived a month longer, gravely ill. Death came late in the afternoon of March 8, 1930. According to his wish he was buried in Arlington Cemetery, for he had been commander-in-chief of the nation's armed forces for four years. A spontaneous nationwide outpouring of love and respect came for the man who had given a lifetime of service to the nation.

The 28th, Woodrow Wilson

Death of an Idealist, 1921-1924

Most of the polls which attempt to rank the presidents place Woodrow Wilson (1856-1924) among the best. In office from 1913 to 1921, he had taken the country successfully through World War I and the peace treaty at Versailles. He was responsible for putting the Covenant of the League of Nations into the peace treaty. Wilson felt that he indeed was making "the world safe for democracy." But his victory turned to ashes when the United States Senate, led by the implacable John Cabot Lodge, refused to ratify the treaty. In an effort to force the Senate's hand through public opinion, at the end of summer in 1919 the president began a long and difficult speaking tour, principally in the Western part of the nation. It was toward the conclusion of this tour that his physical breakdown occurred, resulting in his slow decline and eventual death.

Doctor Cary Grayson, the president's personal physician, had strongly advised against the trip, but Wilson insisted on making it. Wilson had been so busy that he had not had time to prepare for even one major speech when he boarded the train. Joseph Tumulty, the president's private secretary, said that he had "never seen the President look so weary as on the night we left Washington."[1]

As the speaking tour progressed, the president appeared to be winning his fight, for the public gave him enthusiastic acceptance wherever he appeared, and the press favorably reported his speeches. The whole presidential party seemed to be optimistic. The very real concern of the group traveling with the president was that he appeared to be so fatigued and lacking in strength. Severe headaches continued to plague him. The last full-length speech that he ever made was at the state fair in Pueblo, Colorado. Wilson was so weary he allowed his personal bodyguard, Colonel Starling, to physically help him up the steps to the platform. During the speech Starling stood close to the president so he could catch Wilson if he collapsed, for the colonel did not expect the president would be able to complete it. At times Wilson stumbled and seemed to be searching for words. But it was an effective speech that gripped the audience, and many were moved to tears. Wilson himself even wept during its delivery, something he had never done before. When the speech was completed he was drenched with perspiration.

Tired as he was, the president could not sleep, so when the train stopped to take on water, as the old steam locomotives had to do, Wilson decided to take a short walk near the tracks. After the walk he did feel a little better. He returned to his suite on the train and fell asleep near dawn after Dr. Grayson gave him a strong sedative. Sometime during his sleep Wilson suffered a mild stroke. When he awakened later that morning he had trouble using his left arm and leg, and the left side of his face visibly sagged. He spoke with difficulty and had considerable pain. The president called his wife and she immediately summoned Grayson, who was concerned but did not think it was necessarily a critical situation.

Mrs. Wilson, Dr. Grayson, and Joseph Tumulty had a hurried consultation. It was obvious to them that the trip could not be continued. But getting the president to agree to cancel the remainder of the itinerary was most difficult. When it was suggested to the president that the trip be abandoned he replied, "No, no, no. I must keep on."[2] He felt that the public would see such action as an indication that he had given up the fight for the treaty and the League. Wilson could not bear such an idea. It was only at the insistence of Mrs. Wilson that the president agreed to cancel the rest of the trip and return to the White House.

As quickly as possible arrangements were made with the railroad to take the special train back to Washington, D.C., and the president started on the 1700 miles back to the White House. A pilot engine preceded the train, and its speed was as fast as thought safe, with no unnecessary stops. The press corps were glad to be going home. They had been away, living out of suitcases, for more than three weeks. Though it was still Prohibition, the whiskey bottles were uncapped and the press relaxed.

Tumulty and Grayson tried to reassure the reporters that the president's condition was not serious. A bulletin asserted that the president had exerted himself so constantly and been under such a strain during the last year, that he was suffering from a serious digestive reaction. The public was assured that the condition was caused by overwork and really began when he had a severe attack of influenza while he was in Paris at the peace conference. Indeed, the reporters had seen how hard the president had worked, what a strain he had been under, and how he had suffered physically, so they generally believed the story they were told. Basically it was the truth, though the diagnosis of his illness was incorrect.

Wilson actually improved on the trip back and the use of his left side returned somewhat. He was able to eat a little and get some much needed sleep. Upon reaching Washington, Wilson was able to make the long walk from the train to the waiting White House limousine. His daughter

Margaret met the train and the two linked arms so that no one, not even the press, suspected the difficulty he had in walking.

When the president reached the White House on Sunday morning, the staff was told that Wilson had collapsed and would not have a full schedule for a while. Ike Hoover, the White House usher, thought Wilson looked "a little peaked."[3] Mrs. Elizabeth Jaffay, the housekeeper, did not feel the president looked quite normal as he entered the White House. Wilson took lunch at the usual time in the accustomed dining room with his daughter Margaret and John Randolph Bolling, Mrs. Wilson's brother. The president had wanted to go to church that morning, but was dissuaded from going out. At times during the afternoon Wilson wandered aimlessly through the White House, unable to relax or settle down to do anything. However, late in the afternoon he did take a ride and felt much refreshed when he returned.

On Monday and Tuesday the president seemed some better, certainly no worse. He attempted to do no real work though he wrote a few letters and saw two or three people. On Wednesday, October 1, Wilson seemed much better. He attempted a game of billiards, saw a movie, and read aloud from the Bible to his wife. She felt his voice was "strong and vibrant."[4] The entire White House felt encouraged and optimistic about the president.

Mrs. Wilson perhaps tells the next story best in her book *My Memoir*. Although the president appeared to be sleeping normally the next morning, she went into his room at about eight and found him trying to reach the water bottle beside his bed. She handed it to him and noticed that his left arm hung loosely by his side. Her husband told her that he had no feeling in that hand. She asked if she could leave him long enough to call the doctor. She then went into her room to make the call. Hearing a noise she rushed back to her husband's room and found him unconscious on the bathroom floor. Mrs. Wilson put a pillow under his head and covered him with a blanket. Soon Dr. Grayson arrived and the two of them placed him on his bed. His left side was paralyzed. The date was October 2, 1919.

The president was desperately ill. Three medical specialists were called in for consultation, and nurses were in attendance around the clock. "For days life hung in the balance," his wife records.[5] Then the president developed an infection that for many hours completely blocked the flow of urine. The opinion of the consulting doctors was that the president could not live more than a few hours in his condition without surgery to relieve his distended bladder. However, Dr. Grayson was afraid that the president could not survive the surgery, so Mrs. Wilson refused to give permission for the procedure. Fortunately the president's own body soon took care of the problem.

During all of this time the public did not have any idea as to the true condition of their chief executive. There was never any intention of telling the public the real facts about the president's health. The bulletin given to the press by Tumulty and Grayson when the trip was cancelled in Wichita was vague and inconclusive, and reflected the type of wording in subsequent bulletins. A fair sample of the wording would be, "The condition of the president shows no very material change." "He still suffers from headaches and nervousness." "The President's condition is about the same."[6] Editorial comment from across the nation demanded more information as did the Congress and the cabinet. Vice President Marshall stoutly maintained that he did not know a thing. The president's brother, Joseph Wilson, a businessman in Baltimore, wrote to Tumulty suggesting that more information should be given to the public, noting the many rumors concerning the president's condition.

One rumor stated the president was insane and that bars had to be placed over his window to keep him from escaping. It is true that there were bars over some of the windows on the lower floor of the White House. However, they had been placed there to protect the windows from the active play of the children when Theodore Roosevelt was president. Apparently few had ever noticed the bars until they began to wonder about President Wilson's condition. Another rumor without substance was that Wilson had contracted syphilis by a casual contact while in Paris.

The president was definitely a very ill man, and as time went by he did not materially improve. His beard was not shaved for several weeks and with a white beard he certainly did not look like himself. Sleep was difficult and in the main he took "cat naps." Many times he required sedatives to sleep at all. His appetite was poor and it was hard to encourage him to eat enough. He found it difficult to concentrate for long on anything of a substantive nature, and he found it impossible to dictate for more than a few minutes at a time. Extraneous noises made him very uneasy. At times he could lose his temper at those who were doing the most for him, yet rarely toward his wife. A number of people noticed how his eyes would light up whenever she entered the room.

Although the medical personnel whom Dr. Grayson called in saw him on a regular basis, very few others were allowed to see the chief executive. Of course the immediate family could see him. Wilson was very fond of his daughters and their families, and they kept in close touch with him when they were not in Washington. Margaret, who was not married, was in Washington more than her sisters Jessie (Mrs. Francis B. Sayre) and Eleanor (Mrs. William Gibbs McAdoo). Joe Tumulty occasionally saw his chief, but there were whole weeks when he was denied access to his boss, and most of the time he was allowed to communicate with Wilson only through his wife. On occasion the president did see others—the king and queen of the Netherlands and the prince of Wales from England—although not once did he see Vice President Marshall. Governmental officials, even cabinet members, were kept at a distance. Needless to say, no one from the press was ever allowed in the family quarters of the White House, nor was information offered them about the ill man upstairs.

Who then was acting as president of the United States? The majority of writers dealing with this question seem to feel that it was his wife, Edith. Let Mrs. Wilson speak for herself, as she does in *My Memoir*. She tells that those closest to the president advised him not to resign from office, and that she and the president discussed the matter of resignation together and finally decided he should not resign the presidency. Dr. Grayson warned her that the president must be kept from most outside problems. "So began my stewardship," Mrs. Wilson writes. She would study the papers and matters sent to her husband and try to digest them and give their meaning to the president in capsule form. However, she maintains that she "never made a single decision regarding the disposition of public affairs. The only decision that was mine was what was important and what was not, and the very important decision of when to present matters to my husband."[7] Obviously she was beyond her depth. Hundreds of people wanted to gain the president's attention. She said, "Upon all sides I was literally besieged by those who 'must' see the President."[8] Much criticism came to her both from Washington and the country at large, criticism that hurt her deeply.

Questions as to whether the president was able to perform his duties as the nation's chief executive continued to arise. Should Vice President Marshall become president? Secretary of State Lansing did try to get a definitive answer as to the capacity of the president to perform his duties, but he was met with angry retorts from both Grayson and Tumulty. The Senate attempted to determine whether the president could act for himself. They decided to send two of their number to call personally at the White House to see President Wilson. Their visit makes a very interesting story.

Under the guise of conferring with the president about the Mexican situation, the Senate asked if two of their number, Senator Albert Fall, a Republican, and Senator Gilbert Hitchcock, a Democrat, could meet with Wilson. The two senators were granted a conference with the president at the White House that very day, December 4, 1919. The press carried news of the planned visit all over the nation and more than 100 reporters gathered at the White House that afternoon. The doctor placed the Senate's report of the Mexican situation by the president's good right hand so he could dramatically pick it up at the proper moment. When the two senators entered the room, the president gave Fall a firm handclasp and pointed to a chair where he could sit. Then in an off-handed manner Wilson said to Fall, "Well, Senator, how are your Mexican investments getting along?" And so the conference continued. When the two senators were preparing to leave the room Fall said, "Mr. President, I am praying for you." The president replied, "Which way, Senator?" Fall told the reporters that the president was mentally fit and that he had used both arms during the visit, although his useless left hand was under the cover the whole time.[9] Thus ended the attempt to have the president declared unfit for office.

No one can now say with certainty whether or not the United States should have ratified the peace treaty and accepted the League of Nations, but the fact is that the president would accept no amendments nor compromises concerning the treaty, and the Senate would not accept the treaty without changes which they called "reservations." This resulted in a stalemate and the treaty was rejected. Wilson was furious.

In the long view, it was Wilson's religious beliefs which finally helped to moderate some of his feelings of bitterness. He began to feel that perhaps some good was coming out of his losing fight, saying, "Perhaps God knew better than I did after all."[10] His religious faith was important to him during his term of office. In February of 1919 in Raleigh, N.C., at an occasion to honor the memory of Stonewall Jackson, Wilson said, "I do not understand how any man can approach the discharge of the duties of life without faith in the Lord Jesus Christ."[11] There was never a doubt as to his belief in or his own reliance upon God. He often read the Bible aloud to the family or his wife. In the last years of his life he carried a khaki-covered Bible that the army issued in World War I. His father had been a very effective and popular Presbyterian minister, and Wilson never left the faith of his father.

When Congress met in December of 1919, the matter of the constitutionally required annual message to Congress arose. Obviously the president was in no condition to write a state of the union address. So Mrs. Wilson and Tumulty had the various heads of departments and agencies submit short reports. These were then put together and sent to the Congress as the president's message. Certainly the report lacked the touch of Wilson's masterful rhetoric. Many were dissatisfied with the mesage and were bitterly critical of the procedure. Some even bluntly said that it was immoral for a president to use material that he had not personally written. How surprised these critics would be now to see the teams of writers every president has used since the time of Franklin Roosevelt.

Without the president's knowledge or consent, Secretary of State Lansing had called a number of cabinet meetings. Their only agenda was to have an exchange of views so that they might coordinate the work of their own departments with the others. But when the president heard about these meetings he was very upset and asked by whose authority the cabinet had been called together. The angry president promptly removed Lansing from his position and appointed Bainbridge Colby to be the new secretary of state. Colby had not been in the state department nor was he personally very knowledgeable about world affairs, and his appointment aroused a great deal of negative comment.

From the beginning Wilson had no real chance of recovering, though Grayson issued bulletins saying that they expected a complete recovery. But it became clear that Wilson was not himself. His behavior became erratic and bizarre. Frequently he ordered the White House car in which he was riding to chase down speeding autos, and ordered the Secret Service to pursue and apprehend them, which of course they never did. He even asked the attorney general if the president had the rights of a justice of the peace, feeling that he might personally punish speeders. As is often the case with stroke victims, Wilson's very personality seemed to have undergone dramatic changes.

For some time after his illness Wilson took little interest in partisan politics. The Democrats were to hold their national convention in San Francisco in the summer of 1920. As the time for the convention approached, the president did begin to take more interest in politics. He was able to meet with the leadership of the Democratic party, and to discuss with his associates possible nominees for president. It was quite natural that he would look at the coming election as a "great and solemn referendum"[12] on the treaty and the League. Wilson did not feel that the fight for his ideals had been permanently lost and he was anxious to continue the struggle.

There is some weight of opinion that Wilson desired the Democratic nomination for a third term. William Allen White, one of the most able political commentators of his day "saw unmistakable evidences that President Wilson, stricken as he was, hoped for a third-term nomination that would vindicate him and give him a chance to rescue his discarded and discredited League."[13] However, such an action was never seriously considered by the convention. The president himself did not know what he wanted. At times Wilson would tell Grayson that he should resign, and at other times he suggested that he would like to have a third term. "Cabinet members and Democrats close to the administration came one after the other to indicate tactfully to the President that he should step aside, but he would not respond to their hints."[14] Mrs. Wilson completely ignored the whole question. She did not accept the idea that her husband should run for another term.

It seems quite likely that Wilson's son-in-law, William Gibbs McAdoo, wartime secretary of the treasury, might have had an excellent chance for the nomination if Wilson had encouraged it. There are those who feel that Wilson did not endorse McAdoo because he actually hoped to win the nomination himself.

As spring came Wilson did gain strength, his appetite increased, and he spent less time in bed during the day. On April 14, 1920, he held his first cabinet meeting since August 1919, walking the 600 yards from his living quarters to the executive wing of the White House. The meeting was not very fruitful, but Wilson did call and preside over it. He also began to receive visiting diplomats and accept the credentials of new ambassadors to the United States. In mid-June he gave an in-depth four-hour interview to Louis Seibold, a reporter for the *New York World*. Seibold "was amazed at the president's vitality, 'mental vigor,' and by his 'saving sense of humor.'"[15] The article that Seibold wrote after the interview "gave the impression of a man well able to bear the strains of his office."[16] These facts may have given the president the idea that he might actually run and be reelected to office.

At the convention McAdoo showed the greatest strength of any of the candidates during the first several ballots. A. Mitchell Palmer, the attorney general, had a strong following, but neither McAdoo nor Palmer could gain the necessary two-thirds vote that the Democrats demanded for nomination. An acceptable compromise candidate therefore was necessary, and proved to be Governor James Cox of Ohio. It is interesting to note that the president had referred to the nomination of Cox as a joke just a few weeks earlier.[17] A young, impressive politician from New York, Franklin D. Roosevelt, was nominated for the vice presidency.

Governor Cox and Franklin Roosevelt called on the president at the White House. They realized that such a visit would be a political risk because it might tie them too closely to the president and his controversial League. But they felt that calling on the president was the only honorable thing to do. Then both Cox and Roosevelt endorsed the League and made it a campaign issue. This sanction of the League by Cox and Roosevelt sealed their defeat. Warren G. Harding, the Republican nominee, defeated Cox by about a two-to-one ratio. Until the last, Wilson steadfastly believed that the American people would not turn down Cox and the League. The people, however, were tired of war and international involvement, and Harding's slogan of "back to normalcy" sounded very good. The election of 1920 sealed the doom of the League of Nations, for without the United States it could never be the meaningful organization that Wilson had envisioned.

In the remaining four months of his term Wilson tried to fulfill his duties as president. Perhaps the most interesting event of his last days in the executive mansion was the awarding to him of the Nobel Peace prize. Albert G. Schedeman, the American minister to Norway, accepted the prize for the ailing president.

The Wilsons soon began to search for a place to live. After considerable discussion they decided to remain in the city of Washington, D.C. Finally Mrs. Wilson found a house at 2340 S Street that seemed just right to her. The house cost $150,000, quite a sum of money in those days, but ten wealthy friends of the president contributed $10,000 each to the purchase price, or the Wilsons could not have afforded it.[18] When the president saw that Edith liked the house so much, he went ahead without her knowledge, bought the house and gave the deed to her. Following an old Scots custom, he also presented her with a piece of sod from the property along with a key to the house. They made a few alterations in the house, installing an electric elevator, building a brick garage, and cutting a doorway in the side of the house for easy access from the automobile. An iron gate was placed at the entrance to the driveway and a few minor changes were made in the house. This home proved to be ideal for their needs.

As the Wilsons were preparing to leave, Mrs. Wilson invited Mrs. Harding, the incoming first lady, to come and inspect the White House. The Hardings were staying with the McLeans of the Hope diamond fame, and Mrs. Harding asked if she might bring Mrs. Evelyn Walsh McLean with her as she viewed the White House. Mrs. Wilson quickly responded that Mrs. McLean was not welcome at the White House. Mrs. McLean's husband owned the *Washington Post* and this newspaper had opposed the ratification of the treaty. Mrs. Wilson was not about to forget or forgive this offense.

February of 1921 was the president's last month in the White House. Both Mrs. Wilson and the chief executive seemed anxious to become private citizens again. The month was a busy one for the couple. Their furniture and personal belongings had to be removed from storage and taken to their new home. The president attended Keith theater for the first time in a year and a half. The theater had been one of Wilson's chief amusements, and he had regularly attended. Wilson's last cabinet meeting was held during this time. Cabinet members were invited individually to lunch at the White House, an act apparently appreciated by them. It was also at this time that Secretary of State Colby and the outgoing president agreed to open a law office in Washington. Both of them seemed quite elated at the prospect. However, although the office was opened and did a small amount of business, the project never proved practical and the partnership was dissolved.

Inauguration day 1921 was a difficult one for both of the Wilsons. The president was determined to go through the ceremony as far as he was physically able. He rode with the newly elected president in an open car to the Capitol. Wilson left the car and entered the Capitol through a small side door while Harding rode around the front of the building and walked up the long steps to the platform for the ceremony. The point of greatest tension came when Senator Lodge entered the room where the outgoing president waited and informed him that the work of the Senate was done. President Wilson received Lodge with icy correctness. All except the ill president went up to the platform to witness the inauguration of Warren G. Harding. With halting steps Wilson returned to the side door and was helped into the waiting car which would take him to his new residence. He would never return to the Capitol again. It is well to note that when Wilson was first sworn in as president in 1913, he was taken to the Capitol in a horse drawn carriage, but he made his last trip to the Capitol in a luxury automobile.

The Wilsons were very fortunate in securing two competent people to help them in their new home, Isaac Scott and his wife Mary. Isaac served as Wilson's valet and personal aide. Mary Scott helped Mrs. Wilson about the house and acted as her personal maid. Isaac Scott became very skillful in helping the invalid former president in the sick room. Mrs. Wilson commented that she did not see how they could possibly have managed without their help. The Scotts took only one vacation, and they cut that one short because they felt that the Wilsons needed them. Randolph Bolling, Mrs. Wilson's brother, came to the house and acted as Wilson's secretary.

Wilson tried to write, but it was not a successful effort. He did write one article for the *Atlantic Monthly,* but it was not up to the quality of the material that had become expected of the brilliant Woodrow Wilson. He tried to write a book, but only wrote the dedication paragraph, which was to his wife, Edith. Once he spoke on the radio. This was a new means of communication and Wilson had an aversion to it. He did not listen to the radio very often and had never talked over it. But a daughter of Bernard Baruch came to see the Wilsons, and prevailed upon him to go on the air in support of the League of Nations the evening of November 10, 1923, the day before the fifth anniversary of Armistice Day. The talk was to last only ten minutes, but the former president spent several weeks in preparation. Wilson developed a severe headache the morning he was to deliver the talk, no doubt brought on by nervous tension. He tried to memorize the text, but was unable to do so. He then decided to read it. The first few sentences could hardly be understood. It was difficult for him to read the words before him, and there were long pauses. But in spite of his difficulties, the radio talk did arouse public interest. Never again would he attempt to speak on the air.

While Wilson was living on S Street, handling the considerable amount of mail took most of the constructive effort of his day. His secretary, Randolph Bolling, would sort the mail and Wilson would indicate what sort of reply to make. Most of the letters were signed by Wilson himself. He did enjoy corresponding with his friends, but of special interest to him were the letters from ex-servicemen which were answered and signed, "Your War Comrade."[19] He also tried to answer letters from children. The variety of ways people tried to get opinions and comments from the ex-president were unbelievable. Randolph Bolling soon developed an evasive style in answering such letters. There were also a number of hate letters, but very quickly residents in the house on S Street learned to keep these from the former president.

One of the sad features of Wilson's later life was the fact that he broke with some of his old friends and refused ever to see them again. The two outstanding examples were Colonel Edward M. House and Joseph Tumulty. House had been the former president's closest confidant and personal friend. Some even referred to him as Wilson's "alter ego." Wilson felt that House had not handled matters as he should have when Wilson left Colonel House in charge of certain issues at the peace conference when the president had to hurry back to the United States in the summer of 1919. Wilson felt that House violated instructions by yielding to pressure from England and France, and the colonel was never forgiven. House repeatedly tried to communicate with Wilson and was completely ignored.

Tumulty also incurred Wilson's wrath. Tumulty had been Wilson's private secretary for ten years, and they were very close. Yet when Wilson felt that Tumulty had improperly used a letter of his, the former president cut him off completely. Tumulty tried to see Wilson during the final illness, but he was not allowed in the house when he came to the door.

The public did not forget their wartime leader. More than 20,000 came to his residence on Armistice Day 1923, to pay their respects. No effort was made to attract a crowd, but the people were impelled by their own emotions to say they still cared for and loved him. During the last several days of Wilson's life, when he lay dying, large crowds gathered in front of his house to pray, or simply to stand.

The family enjoyed the celebration of Christmas, 1923. But it was obvious to all that the former president was growing weaker. Mrs. Wilson felt that he would not last much longer, and Dr. Grayson confirmed her fears. Nothing dramatic happened. There was just a gradual weakening, loss of vision, declining appetite, a shorter attention span, and less awareness of what was going on around him. Every effort of medical science was made to forestall the inevitable, but nothing helped. The family gathered. The last recognizable word that he spoke was the name Edith. The end came quietly. It was 11:15 a.m. on February 3, 1924.

Dr. Grayson went to the front door of the home and announced the passing to the reporters who were waiting outside. As he began his statement to the press, Grayson was so overcome with emotion that he could hardly talk. President Coolidge was in church that Sunday morning when the news of Wilson's passing came to him. President and Mrs. Coolidge called on Mrs. Wilson as soon as it could be arranged. The newspapers immediately published extra editions which were soon on the streets. All of the embassies of foreign nations in the city of Washington flew their flags at half-mast as a sign of mourning—that is, all but the German flag.

As soon as it was apparent that Wilson's death was imminent, the family was called to Washington. Wilson's daughter Jessie, Mrs. Sayre, was in Siam, so could not come, but Margaret was close by and came immediately. Nell McAdoo was in California. She and her husband started immediately by train on the almost four-day journey to Washington.

However, the train was scarcely half way to the nation's capital when Wilson died. As a potential Democratic party nominee for the presidency in the election of 1924, McAdoo received much political attention during the period of mourning. Such recognition of Wilson's son-in-law upset Mrs. Wilson, and she made some rather strong statements about it to McAdoo. The relationship between Mrs. Wilson and McAdoo was never healed.

Mrs. Wilson could not forget the injuries of the past even in the presence of death. Mr. Wilson's longtime secretary, Joseph Tumulty, came a second time to the house during the final illness and tried to speak to Wilson for just a moment, but Mrs. Wilson would not hear of it. However, Dr. Grayson did arrange at the last moment for Tumulty to receive an invitation to the funeral, but the message did not get to him in time to attend the service. When Senator Lodge, bitter foe of the League, was scheduled to attend the funeral as a representative of the Congress, Mrs. Wilson sent him a curt note telling him not to come. Lodge replied in a brief but courteous note saying that he understood the situation and would not attend.

It was not immediately certain where the former president would be buried. The family considered places in Virginia and South Carolina, and decided to bury him in Washington Cathedral in the capital. Some have asked why Wilson, a lifelong Presbyterian, was buried in an Episcopal cathedral. While it is true the religious affiliation of the Washington Cathedral is Episcopal, the basic idea behind the cathedral was to have a place of worship that would represent the entire nation. Burying Wilson in a place of national significance appealed to Mrs. Wilson.

The funeral was held on Wednesday, February 6, 1924, at three o'clock in the afternoon. The family made all the arrangements for the private service. The federal government had no official part in the funeral although the president and many other officials attended. The body did not lie in state as might have been expected.

To this day many visitors go to Washington Cathedral to view the grave of a man who literally gave his life in the struggle for his ideals of democracy and peace.

The 29th, Warren G. Harding

A White House "Greek Tragedy," 1923

The Harding presidency (1921–1923) is often spoken of as a tragedy. So unbelievable were the events of this administration that it is frequently called "the incredible era."[1] The entire third decade of the twentieth century, commonly called the "Roaring Twenties," was a unique decade filled with intensely human and fascinating events. If there had to be a Harding in the White House, it almost seems fitting that it should have come in this decade.

Warren Gamaliel Harding (1865–1923) reached the presidency almost by chance. In the Republican convention of 1920 held in Chicago, two highly qualified and able men, Governor Frank Lowden of Illinois, and General Leonard Wood of World War I fame, were in contention for the nomination. Neither of them could quite get the necessary majority vote, so the convention turned to a third candidate, a "dark horse" by the name of Senator Warren G. Harding of Ohio, who was nominated on the tenth ballot. A Senate cabal had secured Harding's nomination because they hoped to control him and thus increase the power of the Senate. Prior to his nomination, Harding had been asked if there was anything in his background which would embarrass the party if he were nominated. Harding asked for a few minutes to pray, went into a room by himself for about ten minutes, returned and told them there was nothing of that kind in his background. In the light of subsequent events, one is prompted to wonder what sort of a prayer he offered.

Harding was most unfit for the presidency. At best his intelligence was mediocre and his experience in government was not outstanding. In state government he did work his way up until he became lieutenant governor of Ohio, but was defeated when he sought the governor's chair. Then Harry Daugherty, a master politician and good friend of the future president, succeeded in getting Harding elected United States senator from Ohio. As senator he did not sponsor a single piece of major legislation. When the Senate roll was called he answered to his name less than half the time.[2] He

210

enjoyed baseball, golf, poker and socializing too much to let his duties in the Senate take much of his attention. As president, he lacked the capacity to organize and lead his administration. In sum, he was unfit for the presidency emotionally, intellectually, and morally.

In almost every poll ranking the presidents according to their success in office, Harding was ranked either last or next to last. Ulysses S. Grant is the only other president to be rated so low. The sad fact is that Harding honestly wanted to be a good president. Few writers believe that Harding personally and deliberately perpetrated the many acts of corruption which his administration witnessed. He simply did not have the capacity to administer his high office effectively.

Harding was president for two years and 151 days. Many feel that he died in time to escape impeachment. Although he escaped the wrath of Congress, he was unable to avoid the shame that came to be associated with his administration. By the fall of 1922, Harding became vaguely aware that all was not well in Washington. By the spring of the next year he began to grasp something of the enormity of the corruption that was in his own government, and there is ample evidence to suggest that the situation caused him great concern.

Although the Harding administration was a failure, it still attracts the interest of scholars. So many unusual and strange events, so many inexplicable coincidences were present, that one is indeed prompted to agree with the old saying, "truth is stranger than fiction."

Warren Harding had married a rather domineering woman five years his senior, named Florence Kling De Wolfe. In that day she was openly referred to as a "grass widow" because she had been divorced. She was not physically attractive, but had a brilliant mind and the undeniable capacity to get what she went after. In all likelihood Harding never would have reached the White House had he not married her. However, Harding had several affairs with other women, the most publicized of which was his liaison with Nan Britton, although he never seriously entertained the thought of divorcing his wife, whom he referred to as the "Duchess."

Early in 1923, William Allen White, one of the leading political commentators of his day, was invited to the White House by the president. While there White talked with an old friend, Jud Welliver, one of the longtime secretaries in the executive mansion. Welliver commented, "Lord, Lord, man. You can't imagine what the president is going through. You see he doesn't understand it; he just doesn't know a thousand things he ought to know. And he realizes his ignorance, and is afraid. He has no idea where to turn." Harding had admitted his lack of knowledge to Welliver, then added, "This is a hell of a place for a man like me to be."[3] White further commented about Harding's fitness for the presidency, "The man was unbelievably uninformed."[4]

It is interesting to note that although the president had asked William Allen White to come to the White House, there were no momentous issues the president wished to discuss with him. It seems that all Harding wanted to do was to talk about the newspaper business. So Harding, owner of the *Marion Star,* and White, the publisher and editor of the *Emporia Gazette,* spent most of the morning talking about small newspapers and how to run them. White felt that Harding was simply lonesome and wanted to talk about the thing he knew and loved best – newspapers.

Other instances illustrate Harding's inability to deal effectively with the problems a president must face. Harding told his secretary, "I can't make a damn thing out of this tax problem. I listen to one side and they seem right – God – I talk to the other side and they seem just as right ... I know that somewhere there is a book that will give me the truth, but hell, I couldn't read the book."⁵ To Nicholas Murray Butler, the longtime president of Columbia University and Republican factotum, Harding confided, "I am not fit for this office and should never have been here."⁶

Harding could not stand up to his so-called friends. The last time that William Allen White was in the White House during Harding's term, the president could not refrain from commenting, "My God, this is a hell of a job. I have no trouble with my enemies. I can take care of my enemies all right. But my damn friends, my God-damn friends, White, they're the ones that keep me walking the floor nights."⁷ At first Harding felt that his old friends could be trusted and that they would not do anything that might hurt him. But when friends, especially those known as the "Ohio Gang," began to destroy his administration by their corruption, he did not know which way to turn or what to do.

The problem began with Charles R. Forbes and Charles F. Cramer who bilked the government of millions through the Veterans Bureau. Then there was the Teapot Dome affair where Albert Fall, secretary of the interior, allowed the oil interests to gain possession of rich deposits of oil on federal lands. Also, persons connected with the Justice Department, where Harding's mentor, Harry Daugherty, was attorney general, sold pardons and paroles to the highest bidder. Liquor permits for alcohol stored in government warehouses were obtained for a price during the days of Prohibition. As the beleaguered president began to learn of these matters, he became panicky. At times he seemed to have a sense of impending catastrophe. Dr. Joel T. Boone, the assistant physician to the White House, is sure these fears hastened Harding's death.

Back in the fall of 1889, at the age of 24, after a grueling political campaign, Harding suffered what in that day was called a nervous breakdown. His father, who was a doctor, urged his son to go to the Battle Creek Sanitarium in Michigan for treatment. This sanitarium was sponsored by the Seventh Day Adventists, and run by Dr. J.P. Kellogg, the inventor of peanut butter and corn flakes.[8] The young newspaper editor must have responded to the rigorous regimen of the vegetarian Dr. Kellogg, for he returned to Marion, Ohio, after several weeks, 20 pounds lighter and ready for work. Four more times, usually after periods of stress, Harding returned to Battle Creek for treatment.

As president, Harding tended to have high blood pressure and occasionally sugar in his urine, and he would tire easily. He often could not finish a round of golf. In 1922 his blood pressure went still higher and occasionally he had brief periods of discomfort in his chest. At about the same time, the famed heart specialist, Dr. Emanuel Libman of New York, saw the president at a dinner and remarked to a friend that he felt the president would be dead from a heart disorder within six months.[9] Arthur Brooks, the White House valet, told Colonel Edmund Starling, chief of the Secret Service detail at the White House, that the president could not sleep unless he was propped up on several pillows because he could not get his breath when lying down.

At the time of the great strikes in late summer and early fall of 1922, Mrs. Harding became seriously ill with a kidney ailment. A number of years earlier she had a kidney surgically removed and now the other kidney seemed on the verge of failure. The Hardings' personal physician, Dr. Charles E. Sawyer, was so concerned that Dr. Charles Mayo of the famed Mayo Clinic in Rochester, Minnesota, was called in for consultation. Dr. Mayo and the other consulting physicians advised immediate surgery. However, Dr. Sawyer advised against it, and Mrs. Harding herself refused surgery. Although she was critically ill for a time, the Duchess recovered.[10] Both the strike and his wife's illness put a great strain on Harding, and his own symptoms worsened.

In January of 1923, Harding had a difficult time recovering from flu. He was tired and did not feel well. The very wealthy McLeans of Washington invited the first couple on a Florida vacation to cruise on a houseboat, golf, fish, swim and sun. Everyone noted how tired the president seemed. After the three-week cruise, the Hardings spent an additional week in St. Augustine, Florida.

It was in the spring of 1923 that Harding saw Nan Britton for the last time.[11] According to sources within the White House, the president smuggled Nan into the executive mansion on a number of occasions. Once, only the alertness of a White House staff member kept the Duchess from interrupting a presidential romantic interlude.[12] Harding had managed clandestine meetings with Nan Britton numerous times, even in a Pullman car on one occasion. Many times the president sent her money, usually through a third party. After Harding's death, Miss Britton wrote a book, *The President's Daughter,* telling how she had a daughter by the president, and of their great love. The book, dedicated to "all unwed mothers," was a "bombshell," and became a best-seller. No one begins to believe all that she recorded in the volume, but there are very few writers who completely deny the Nan Britton story.

On a Saturday in early May, the president called Nicholas Murray Butler to come to the White House to talk about a matter which he felt could not be discussed over the telephone. Butler was scheduled to leave for Europe the next day, but changed his plans and went to the White House. Butler tells how Harding barely left him during the whole of the next day. "Evidently, there was something very much on his mind and he was trying to bring himself to tell me what it was. Several times during the morning, afternoon and evening he seemed to be on the point of unbosoming himself, but he never did so."[13] It is felt by most who are familiar with the situation that Harding wanted to discuss the corruption that was being uncovered in the administration, but could not face discussing it with a friend, even a man of Butler's integrity.

Added to all of Harding's problems was the fact that the Republican party had suffered setbacks in the midterm elections in November 1922, and seemed to be losing out in public opinion. It was the feeling around the White House and in the leadership of the party itself, that if the president traveled through the nation and talked with the people, public opinion would swing behind him and the party's political fences could be mended. Those who noted Harding's fatigue thought that a trip away from Washington would give him much-needed rest. Dr. Sawyer was opposed to the trip unless his patient kept to the very lightest schedule possible. But the politicos kept adding speeches and appearances to what was becoming a very full schedule.

No president had ever visited Alaska, and a trip there would take him over a large part of this important territory, give him high visibility, and create a favorable press. The proposed itinerary, as planned by Walter Brown, called for 85 appearances in six weeks. Dr. Sawyer became quite concerned and opposed the trip when he saw the final schedule. Harding called in Colonel Starling, and told him to cut the schedule wherever possible, but the damage was already done, and the president finally gave his consent for a crowded itinerary which included 18 formal speeches and innumerable talks and personal appearances.

The makeup of the presidential party was considerably different from that of previous trips the president had taken. None of the old "Ohio Gang" was included. Three cabinet members were invited: Secretary of Agriculture Henry C. Wallace, Secretary of Commerce Herbert Hoover, and Secretary of the Interior Hubert Work, a former physician. Also included were Speaker of the House Frederick Gillett, Rear Admiral Hugh Rodman, Harding's secretary George Christian, and Malcolm Jennings, a confidant. The wives were invited along with the usual entourage of functionaries, news correspondents and photographers. Doctors Sawyer and Boone were there to look after the physical needs of the group, and Mrs. Harding insisted that they have rooms close to that of her husband.

Harding called this trip a "Voyage of Understanding." He wanted to meet the people and prove to them that he was truly doing what was best for the country. Few doubt that Harding was sincere. The "Voyage of Understanding" began on June 20. At two o'clock in the afternoon the train bearing the presidential party pulled out of Union Station in Washington, D.C. It was a ten-car train that carried the party of 65 across the country. The president occupied the last car, called the "Superb." Since this was some time before air conditioning and the nation was in the midst of a heat wave, the whole group was hot and uncomfortable. At many of the towns, as the train stopped a moment, Harding would appear on the rear platform and say a few words to the people who had come to see their president.

In St. Louis, Missouri, Harding made his first major address of the trip. He spoke before an audience of 10,000 at the International Rotary Convention. In this speech he boldly stated that the United States should join the World Court, a rather audacious move because the nation was not in the mood for involvement in any more internationalism. The nation had enough of that with Wilson's League of Nations. But Harding firmly believed that the World Court would encourage world peace.

The president appeared fatigued as he began the trip, yet he could not relax. He seemed obsessively busy, either walking the train, talking with someone, or playing bridge, with games often beginning early and lasting until midnight. Those who could play the game were thoroughly worn out playing with the president. In it all he seemed preoccupied.

In Kansas City Harding delivered an address in Convention Hall. William Allen White was there and saw the president for the last time. Three times Harding told White that he wanted to have a long talk with him, but the conversation never took place. The next day Harding made a talk to some Kansas wheat farmers. Dressed in white shoes and trousers, a blue coat and a straw hat, the president briefly drove a wheat binder.

The trip continued to Denver and then through the West to Tacoma, Washington, where the president left the train and embarked on the *Henderson,* an army transport ship which was to take the presidential party to Alaska. It was in Tacoma that Secretary and Mrs. Hoover joined the party. Harding respected Hoover. Though he was an excellent bridge player, Hoover was most distressed at the interminable card games, and remembered them with distaste for many years.[14] It was on the ship that Harding finally talked about what had been troubling him, although he told Hoover only the bare outline of the scandals plaguing his administration. Harding bluntly asked Hoover, "If you knew of a great scandal in our administration, would you for the good of the country and the party expose it publicly or would you bury it?" Hoover replied, "Publish it, and at least get the credit for integrity."[15] However, Harding thought this would be politically dangerous, and did not heed Hoover's advice.

On July 4, the party again boarded the *Henderson* and the next day left port for Alaska. The *Henderson* was built in 1917 as a World War I troop transport. For its time it was a rather large ship, with a crew of 460 seamen in addition to its officers. In fact, it was the largest ship to go up the inland waterway to Alaska until that time. The presidential party was in a festive mood, but the interminable bridge games went on from breakfast until midnight. The route to Alaska from Tacoma took four days.

The ship landed at Metlakatla, Alaska, and was met by Governor Scott and a delegation of Indians who performed for the president. The party stopped at Ketchikan, Juneau and Skagway, and docked at Seward. The Alaskan Central Railway offered their best train, which the presidential party then took to Anchorage, McKinley Park and Fairbanks. On July 15, the president himself took the throttle and for 26 miles ran the engine himself. But Harding was becoming increasingly worn. The trip was cut short and the party returned to the *Henderson*. The few people the president saw came to his cabin so he would not have to make trips from the ship to shore.

On July 26, the *Henderson* arrived at Vancouver, British Columbia. It was the first time an American president had made such a visit to Canada. There was an official luncheon for the American party, following which the president played golf. But he played only the first six holes and then cut over to the 17th hole, playing that one and the 18th. In that way it was hoped no one would notice he had played less than half the holes. He rested for an hour, then went to a formal dinner and spoke for about 15 minutes. Usually he was very effective on such occasions, but he was not in his best form that evening. It was obvious to most that he was very fatigued. One reporter remarked that the president "is not just tired or worn out. He is beyond being merely fatigued. He is an entirely exhausted man, and the sort of rest he requires is not that of a day, or two or three, but of weeks."[16] A number of the group became concerned.

The *Henderson* left Vancouver that night and was expected to arrive in Seattle the next morning. However, fog delayed its arrival until the afternoon. In the fog, the *Henderson* rammed a destroyer broadside, but no one was hurt. After landing, Harding toured the downtown area of Seattle where thousands had gathered to see the president. Later he went to the football stadium of the University of Washington, and in the blazing sun, bareheaded, gave a major address. It was poorly delivered. Harding frequently misspoke, and once dropped his manuscript. Surprisingly the press gave no notice of his poor delivery.[17] By evening he returned to his private railroad car and immediately went to bed.

As the train moved down the coast, the president called for Dr. Sawyer, complaining of upper abdominal pain and nausea. Dr. Sawyer thought Harding was suffering from indigestion and saw no immediate cause for alarm. However, Dr. Boone was very concerned, as the patient had a pulse rate of 120 and a respiration rate of 40. Dr. Boone consulted Dr. Work, and he agreed that the president's heart was in difficulty.[18] The two doctors had Herbert Hoover call ahead to San Francisco and ask Dr. Ray Lyman Wilbur, president of Stanford, and a physician himself, to meet the train and to bring the noted heart specialist, Dr. Charles M. Cooper, with him.[19]

The train arrived in the city on Sunday, July 29, at eight in the morning. The president was able to dress himself. The doctors wanted to have him use a wheelchair, but he disdained it, walking to the limousine unaided. He was taken to the Palace Hotel where he was immediately put to bed. He remained very uncomfortable that day and was worse by nightfall. It was obvious to all the doctors, except Sawyer, that the president was in serious condition. An X-ray and blood count showed that he had bronchopneumonia,[20] but Harding refused to accept the fact that he was critically ill. The doctors treated the pneumonia, and administered the standard doses of digitalis and heart stimulants. On Tuesday, Dr. Sawyer proudly announced that the congestion in the lungs had begun to clear. On Wednesday, the patient's temperature was normal and the pulse under 100, the *New York Times* noted. On the same day Harding took some solid food and sat up in bed to read the newspapers. By Thursday the usually glum Dr. Boone was somewhat optimistic, but the president was kept under close medical supervision.

Harry Daugherty arrived in San Francisco on Wednesday and immediately saw the Duchess in the Palace Hotel. She told him he should have stayed in the same hotel with the president. Daugherty replied that he did not want to further burden the ill chief executive. He never did see Harding, but kept in touch with the Duchess every few hours.

Harding felt better on Thursday. He told his friend, Malcolm Jennings, that he was "out of the woods" but "so tired, so tired."[21] Dr. Sawyer even announced his intention to take a vacation soon since the president was recovering so well.

The rest of the story has often been told. On Thursday evening, the Duchess was reading an article from the *Saturday Evening Post* about the president. It was entitled, "A Calm Review of a Calm Man." The president was propped up in bed listening. He said, "That's good. Go on, read some more."[22] The Duchess finished the article and stepped across the hall to her own room. The nurse, Ruth Powerly, stepped back into the room with a glass of water to give Harding his medication. She saw his face twitch, then he slumped to the side, and was gone. In seconds the doctors were in attendance, but there was nothing they could do. The Duchess had arrived even before the doctors, and sat by the side of the bed just repeating his name, "Warren, Warren, Warren." It was 7:32 p.m.

Mrs. Harding refused to allow an autopsy, and the five physicians did not completely agree as to the exact cause of death. Dr. Sawyer felt that a cerebral hemorrhage was responsible. But Drs. Wilbur, Cooper, Work, and Boone were not so sure.[23] After some discussion they all signed an official statement that "death was apparently due to some brain involvement, probably an apoplexy."[24] This seems rather strange after previous medical opinion that his heart condition of long standing was his chief problem. Probably Dr. Sawyer insisted on this wording.

H. Gray and Company, funeral directors, prepared the body for burial. A brief funeral service was held in the Palace Hotel the next afternoon with the Reverend James S. West, pastor of the First Baptist Church of San Francisco, conducting the service. Only the official presidential party and a few newsmen were allowed to attend. A small funeral procession took the body to the Union Pacific Railroad station and placed it in the "Superb," the same car the president had used on his Western trip. The casket was placed in the last compartment, high enough so that it could be seen by people standing outside the railroad car. Dr. and Mrs. Sawyer, and Mr. and Mrs. Malcolm Jennings stayed in the "Superb" with Mrs. Harding. At seven-fifteen in the evening the train pulled out of the Southern Pacific Railroad station and began its four-day journey back to Washington, D.C.

The public's demonstration of grief was probably the greatest since the death of President Lincoln, for little did they dream of the corruption which had involved their president. One of the few jarring notes was sounded when Senator John Cabot Lodge exclaimed, "My God, that means that Coolidge is President."[25] The press and radio stations were filled with stories about the president and his death. Crowds of people stood silently as the train passed by. In Omaha, Nebraska, nearly 40,000 stood in the rain to view the train as it passed through at two in the morning. In Chicago a great throng turned out to see the train. The new president, Calvin Coolidge, and official Washington met the train as it arrived in Union Station.

Thus began a series of services and tributes to Harding, seldom seen, even for a great president. The body was taken to the East Room of the White House where the Duchess visited the casket for more than an hour during the night. At times she was almost hysterical. The next morning a brief private service was held in the East Room. The body was then moved to the rotunda of the Capitol where another brief service was conducted by the Reverend J. Freeman, pastor of the Calvary Baptist Church, and the Reverend James S. Montgomery, chaplain of the House of Representatives. In the next few hours thousands passed by the open coffin.

That afternoon, August 8, the funeral train left Washington for Marion, Ohio, Harding's hometown. Countless throngs stood by the tracks to catch a glimpse of the funeral train. The next day, President Coolidge, several close friends of Harding, the cabinet, and many high ranking officials, as well as representatives of the military and diplomatic corps, boarded a train to attend the funeral. Marion was crowded with visitors, as people from all over the nation came by the thousands to express their sorrow. Marion, Ohio, came to a stand-still as its citizens paid their last respects.

The body was taken to the home of the president's father, Dr. George Harding, on East Center Street. In the early afternoon the public was allowed to view the body as it lay in state. They walked by the casket, 36 a minute, until two in the morning. At nine in the morning a new line of people started to view the body. Three local clergymen led the fourth and last religious service. The president was laid to rest on August 10.

When the Duchess died in 1924, she was buried beside her husband. In the spring of 1927, a rather elaborate memorial to Harding was erected in Marion in which the bodies of both the Hardings were finally placed. But the dedication of the memorial was delayed until 1931. Both Coolidge and Hoover were reluctant to lead in the dedication and thus become even remotely linked with the Harding administration. However, in January 1931, President Hoover agreed to dedicate the memorial. Even so, the Quaker president alluded to the Harding troubles when he said, "Here was a man whose soul was seared by a great disillusionment ... Harding had a dim realization that he was betrayed by a few of the men whom he trusted."[26] Harry Daugherty was seated just a few feet from the president when these words were spoken.

In 1930, Gaston Means, a thoroughly discredited operative in the Justice Department during the Harding administration, published a book entitled *The Strange Death of President Harding*. In this book he charged that Mrs. Harding poisoned her husband as he lay ill in San Francisco. No one of any reputation gives the story credence, but it did create a sensation. Means died in a federal prison for one of his confidence schemes that backfired. In 1932, Harry Daugherty published a book entitled *The Inside Story of the Harding Tragedy*. This attempt to whitewash the administration of which he was a part did little to change the opinion of scholars.

The Harding presidency came at the time of immense social and moral upheaval which followed the Great War. Perhaps even a great president would have been unable to stem the rushing tide of events, but the man in the White House during this incredible era seemed confused and helpless.

The 30th, Calvin Coolidge

A Puritan Leaves Babylon,* 1929–1933

Some presidents are remembered for personal characteristics rather than for their performance as the chief executive. Such a president was Calvin Coolidge (1872–1933, serving from 1923 to 1929). Even when he went to Washington, his conservative, rather old-fashioned ways still clung to him. But rather than being a handicap, they seemed to endear him to people. He was concise, laconic, honest, not given to ostentation, and careful of money to the point of parsimoniousness. In private among good friends he was talkative and certainly not antisocial, but in public he was taciturn and something of an isolate. A "bluebellied Vermont Yankee to the core" is the way William Allen White characterized him.[1] Although he eschewed liquor, gambling and swearing, he was an inveterate cigar smoker. For these unique qualities — certainly a contrast to many of the public figures of the decade of the twenties — public interest followed him into retirement.

President and Mrs. Coolidge were packed and ready to leave the White House immediately after seeing the new president, Herbert Hoover, take the oath of office. They left Washington as quietly as they had come. Only once would he return to the nation's capital. Although a crowd of fellow citizens gathered at the railroad depot to see the Coolidges off, he simply said, "Goodbye," and waved his hand in farewell.

He had pointedly requested that there be no formalities of welcome when they returned to their home town of Northampton, Massachusetts. But as they got off the train they discovered that a large crowd had come to greet them. A band played "Home Sweet Home," and the mayor made the welcome official. The girls from Smith College cheered as the small procession passed their campus, and neighbors and friends lined the route taken from the railroad station to their old home at 21 Massasoit Street. Thus they returned to the house that had been their home since they set up housekeeping. The Coolidges were most relieved when the last of the

*Title taken from William Allen White's 1958 biography, A Puritan in Babylon.

photographers and reporters had left. They hoped once again to be simple private citizens, Calvin and Grace Coolidge. However, such anonymity could never come to a former president.

Their home was a seven-room duplex in a residential district not far from downtown Northampton. Coolidge had paid $32 a month rent on this duplex all the time he was in Washington just to save it as their home when they returned. A physician occupied the other side of the duplex. A considerable effort was required to put the many items they had acquired during their stay in Washington into this small home. Much had to go into storage. Mrs. Coolidge employed a cook and a maid, but soon found the house too small for even this staff. There was little privacy. Sightseers drove by the house, creating traffic jams on frequent occasions. Coolidge had anticipated sitting in his rocking chair on the front porch, enjoying the evenings, but he soon discovered that was an impossibility. So many of the curious drove by, often leaving their cars to try to shake his hand, that the former president could no longer sit and enjoy the afternoon sun or the coming of dusk.

The Coolidges grew exceedingly tired of public scrutiny and soon began to look for another home. Finally, after considerable searching and due deliberation—the Coolidges did nothing precipitously or quickly—they purchased a very fine 12-room home, well hidden from view, with spacious grounds, and with a view from the back porch of the Ox Bow, a part of the Connecticut River. Because of the trees the home was called the Beeches. There were stone pillars at the entrance and an iron gate. The home ideally suited their needs. They could comfortably entertain out-of-town guests, have considerable privacy, room for the ex-president's thousands of books, grounds where they could enjoy nature and walk the dogs, and still be near town and Coolidge's office. Also, for the first time in their marriage, Grace Coolidge could have a workroom in her own home.

As the Coolidges looked to retirement, Mrs. Coolidge was somewhat apprehensive as to how her husband would occupy his time. He was only 57 years old and had held the world's most responsible position. She said to their friend Frank Stearns, "What can I do with him?"[2] She need not have worried. Some suggested that he could return to the practice of law. But it had been a number of years since he had represented a client in a court of law. Also, he had doubt as to the appropriateness of an ex-president appearing in a court before a jury. However, he did decide to occupy his old law office in Northampton, located in an old four-story brick office building in the so-called Masonic Block on Main Street not far from the railroad station. On the second floor was the door with the words COOLIDGE AND HEMENWAY / LAW OFFICE / WALK IN.

Calvin Coolidge and Ralph Hemenway, attorneys-at-law, had shared this office space for many years before Coolidge went to Washington.

When Coolidge returned to Northampton the office space was enlarged to care for his new needs. He hired a private secretary to manage the office and handle the considerable quantity of mail that came in, and to very politely say "no" to the countless requests for speaking engagements. The former president's plain oak desk with a flat top occupied one corner of his office. There were several bookcases filled with law books, two chairs for visitors, and on the walls facsimile copies of the Declaration of Independence, Shakespeare's will, and the warrant for the execution of Charles I of England. Nothing in the office suggested that it was occupied by a former president, and it was here that Coolidge did most of his writing. A door opened into the hall so that he could leave his office without going in front of anyone who might be in the outer office demanding to see him.

Although he had not given much thought to writing as he left office, he had received an offer from Ray Long of *Cosmopolitan* to write the story of his life. At first Coolidge declined, but Long persisted and in January 1929, just before he left Washington, he agreed to meet Long in the Oval Office and discuss the proposed writing. The president handed the representative of *Cosmopolitan* a short manuscript and sent him to the cabinet room to read it, telling Long if he was still interested in having him write for the magazine they would talk. The president added that if the material was not satisfactory nothing would be binding. The magazine was very much interested, and Coolidge agreed to write his autobiography, which would be carried in installments by the magazine. Later it was published as a 250-page book by the Cosmopolitan Book Corporation. The biography as written was rather stilted, and shed little light on the personality of the ex-president or told incidents not previously known, but it did sell well and Coolidge received good royalties from the sale of the book.[3] He also wrote several articles for the *Ladies' Home Journal* and *American Magazine*.

The writing which took more of his time and effort than he expected was the daily paragraph of about 200 words that the former president agreed to write for the McClure Syndicate in 1930. For a year's contract he received $200,000.[4] The daily paragraph hopefully was to sound like a modern Ben Franklin, but it was filled with platitudes and stolid, conservative, middle-class observations and reflections. Though he was never late for one installment, Coolidge found this daily paragraph to be an onerous task. In the evenings he would make a few notes on a pad, take the paper to the office the next morning and dictate his feature to Herman Beaty, his secretary. On occasion he might ask for help in a place or two, but not often. He was thoroughly relieved when the year was up and the last installment written. He always wrote the daily paragraph for the newspaper as soon as he arrived at the office, then took care of his correspondence. After that he received any visitors who had appointments. He regularly read the

New York Herald-Tribune and the *Boston News Bureau*. During the course of the morning he usually smoked two or three cigars.

Mrs. Coolidge wrote articles for *American Magazine* and *Good Housekeeping*. She realized the publishers wanted her writing only because she had lived in the White House, but she enjoyed doing it nevertheless. Her husband encouraged her and at times became an active partner in her project. It might be noted that the Coolidges were the first president and wife who both had earned college degrees.

The Coolidges daily routine was always simple. Meals were almost as regular as the rising of the sun. Breakfast was at seven-fifteen, lunch at twelve-thirty, and dinner at six. The dogs were fed on schedule as precisely as the family. Coolidge liked to arrive at the office around nine in the morning. He would have preferred to walk to the office, but he could not tolerate people staring at him, so he was driven there by his secretary or the male employee who did a variety of jobs about the place. Although the Coolidges had bought one of the cars that they had used at the White House, he never learned to drive it.

Since lunch was served promptly at twelve-thirty, he would be driven home about noon. A daily nap was a ritual. Only something very unusual would deprive him of his after-lunch siesta. At two-thirty he would go to his office for a short work period, returning home about four o'clock. In all but inclement weather he liked to take the dogs for a run on the nine-acre estate before dinner. Tiny Tim, a red chow, and Beauty, a white collie, were always ready for the daily exercise with their owner. After dinner the Coolidges enjoyed a leisurely evening. They were both fond of books and often read to each other as the radio played quietly in the background. When he was writing his regular feature for the newspaper he would at some point in the evening make some notes, but his writing was seldom a topic of conversation between husband and wife. She never knew what he wrote until she read it in the paper. They retired early and were early risers. Mrs. Coolidge liked knitting and needlework. On a summer afternoon she often listened to the ball game on the radio as she worked, being a fan of both of the two major league teams in Boston at that time.

The Coolidges had two sons, John and Calvin, who were 17 and 15 when the family moved to Washington. Calvin died in the White House about a year after his father became president. His death was caused by an infection which resulted from a blister he developed on his foot while playing tennis on the White House courts. In the days before antibiotics the doctors could do nothing to save young Calvin. Those close to the president felt that he never recovered from this loss.

John Coolidge attended Amherst as had his father. While in college he met Florence Trumbull, daughter of the governor of Connecticut. They first met on a train going to Washington in March of 1925. She was a tall blond with a vivacious personality and they saw each other regularly after that. Though he was often a guest in the Trumbull home, they were able to keep their interest in each other from the press. Even when the press realized that there might be a story about the two young people, Florence was very adroit at evading their direct questions. All she ever admitted was that they enjoyed being together. They were very much in love and would liked to have gotten married much sooner than they did, but the president insisted that the prospective groom be able to support a wife before they went to the altar.

Mrs. Coolidge liked Florence immediately and made her most welcome at her frequent visits to the White House. It took somewhat longer for Florence to feel perfectly at ease around the president, who did not seem to know how to relax with this prospective member of the family. But before long Florence appreciated his off-beat humor and his shy manner. John graduated from Amherst in 1928 and found a position with the New York, New Haven and Hartford Railroad. The marriage took place in September of 1929 in the Congregational Church at Plainville, Massachusetts. John was 23 and Florence, 24. Mrs. Coolidge regarded this occasion as perhaps the highlight of her life in retirement, and many guests noted that on that day Grace Coolidge looked beautifully radiant. The Coolidges gave the newlyweds colonial furniture for the bedroom of their four-room apartment in New Haven. When asked some questions by the press at the occasion, Coolidge replied in his taciturn manner, "I do not choose to say."[5]

During the summer Northampton was often hot and humid, so the Coolidges would return to his family home in Plymouth, Vermont, where the weather was comfortable and the small New England town suited the former president's tastes. He knew and loved the people there and the feeling was reciprocated. Since the house was very old and lacked many modern comforts, Coolidge arranged for and supervised the addition of six rooms without upsetting the basic design of the home. While no architectural masterpiece, it did make a very comfortable summer home and took him back to his roots.

Few have ever observed that Coolidge was a compassionate, caring individual. Bruce Barton was a personal friend of the Coolidges and was a frequent visitor in their home. He tells an interesting story about the relationship between Calvin Coolidge and Frank Fasano, a "bootblack" of Northampton. Coolidge and Barton were on a morning stroll and the ex-president said, "I'll blow you to a shine." Barton protested that his friend did not need to do that, but Coolidge was quite firm. When they reached Fasano's shop it had not opened yet. The former president said, "We'll wait, he [Fasano] has five children. He would not like to have us go away."[6]

During the Depression a bank where Coolidge's law partner, Ralph Hemenway, did business failed, and for the moment Hemenway was in financial difficulty. The ex-president wrote a check for $5,000 and left it on his partner's desk one morning before Hemenway came to the office. The check was accepted, but only as a loan.

The Coolidges did take one extended trip after leaving the White House. This pleasure trip took them West to California by way of New Orleans. They traveled on to Hollywood and the usually quiet, unexpressive former president and his wife met with stars such as Douglas Fairbanks and Mary Pickford. William Randolph Hearst was their host for several days as they visited San Simeon, Hearst's castle-like mansion. Mrs. Coolidge was using the elevator when it got stuck between floors. She yelled, sang, and pounded on the walls of the elevator, but it was some time before anyone heard her so she could be rescued. The experience did not upset her nearly as much as it did Hearst. Unfortunately the Coolidges were confronted constantly by the media, and never again attempted such a trip.

There was a dry, often-missed sense of humor with Coolidge, which could at times become abrasive. For example, as he passed a nearby house on a morning walk, the neighbor in all good humor called the ex-president's attention to his very colorful lily pond. Coolidge looked at it and commented, "I never liked stagnant water."[7] After he had delivered the last major speech of his life at Madison Square Garden in the fall of 1932, a woman came up to him and told him how much she liked it, adding that she had stood up during the whole of the speech. The unsmiling ex-president responded, "So did I."[8]

Coolidge was involved in a number of activities in retirement. He was a member of the board of his alma mater, Amherst College. He accepted membership on a national committee to study the transportation problem, principally shipping and railroading. It was during this time that he became a friend of Al Smith. Another of his interests was the American Antiquarian Society and for some time he served as its president. In retirement he joined the very prestigious Northampton Literary Club which dated back to the Civil War and retained an exclusive all-male membership. The only position that brought any monetary remuneration was his directorship of the New York Life Insurance Company. He always went to the quarterly meetings and, somewhat against his usual habits, lived and traveled in style.

His wife did not always accompany him on these trips, but it was his custom to write to her while he was away. On his last trip he wrote what was perhaps his last letter to her. In it he reminded her that she had "borne with my infirmities and I have rejoiced in [your] graces. We thought we were made for each other."[9] No presidential couple in modern times more obviously still cared deeply for each other and were more dependent upon each other. It is possible that, as the old saying goes, opposites attract. She was gracious, outgoing, constantly cheerful, very sensitive to the needs of others, and a good conversationalist, while her husband was pessimistic, at times very blunt, and often seemed dour or even disgruntled.

The Coolidges regularly attended the Edwards Congregational Church of their town. Mrs. Coolidge participated actively in church work and the ex-president helped to raise money for the missionary budget. He probably considered their young minister too liberal for his views, but said nothing. When his old friend and classmate, Charles A. Andrews, had supper with Coolidge one Sunday in January of 1933, Andrews thought that Coolidge was somewhat depressed. The former president commented that nothing seemed permanent but religion which outlasted elections and depressions and is "the same yesterday, today and forever."[10]

Coolidge seldom talked about his health. His wife had to observe him and guess as to how he was feeling. He seemed much older than his years when he left office at 57, and was easily fatigued. His wife often caught him unobtrusively checking his own pulse. His friends suspected that his heart bothered him. In his last years there were many occasions when he appeared to be in some discomfort. Often he would drink a little bicarbonate of soda in water. Sometimes he declined to participate in activities that he normally would have enjoyed because he was too tired. At times he seemed to walk hesitatingly and on occasion his color was ashen.

About a month before he died he had sought help from the family doctor because of continued fatigue. The physician examined him carefully, paying especial attention to his heart, but could find nothing specifically wrong with him. However, there were several small indications of illness. On New Years Day, just five days before he died, Coolidge told Charles Andrews, "I am very comfortable because I am not doing anything of real account. But any effort to accomplish something goes hard with me. I am too old for my years ... but I am very comfortable."[11] He was 61.

Northampton was cold and clear on January 5, 1933. Coolidge arose as usual, but for some reason neglected to shave. He ate his breakfast on time, went to the office at nine o'clock and for about an hour did odd jobs at his desk. He then told his partner that he did not feel well, but there was no specific complaint. Harry Ross, his secretary at that time, drove him home. As they entered the grounds of the Beeches they passed Mrs. Coolidge who was on foot going on an errand. When the ex-president asked her if she did not want the car, she said "It's such a nice day I'd rather walk than ride."[12] These were the last words they exchanged. After he reached the house he read for a time then went to the basement to get something. When he came back he said to Ross that he had forgotten to shave and was going upstairs. That was the last time he was seen alive.

Mrs. Coolidge came home and began the preparation of lunch. She then went upstairs to summon him to eat. When she went to their room she found him lying on the floor of their dressing room in his shirt sleeves. She ran downstairs and told Ross that her husband was dead. He had complained for several days of indigestion which had become more or less chronic. Over the past months he had gradually stopped eating several types of food, feeling that they were hard for him to digest, and his wife worried because she feared he would not get enough nourishment. But no one believed him to be in any real danger.

News of the death of a president travels fast. The announcement was made that he had died of a coronary thrombosis instantly and painlessly.[13] John and Florence came immediately to be with Mrs. Coolidge. The radio flashed the news as did many newspapers whose extras quickly reached the streets. Flags were flown at half-mast and many shops and stores closed. Guns were fired at regular intervals across the nation.

Grace Coolidge quickly decided against an official funeral in Washington or Boston. She felt that her husband would have wanted the simplest kind of funeral. Plans were made for burial in the Plymouth, Vermont, cemetery where his father and mother, his son Calvin and five generations of ancestors were buried.

The young pastor of the Edwards Congregational Church of Northampton where the couple attended conducted the simple, short service. The day was dark with the falling rain. The service included Scripture, Chopin's "Funeral March," and the popular "Goin' Home." There was no sermon or eulogy.

President Herbert Hoover called at the Beeches before the service. Mrs. Coolidge told the president that he should not risk the icy roads to Plymouth for the burial, and he followed her wishes. Many great and near great were at the service, including several cabinet members, Chief Justice Charles Evans Hughes, senators and diplomats.

All along the route taken by the funeral procession, war veterans, Boy Scouts, and ordinary citizens lined the sides of the road and stood at attention as the cortege passed. Many factories stopped work as the cars moved by in the rain and mist. As they reached Plymouth, the rain, now mixed with hail, pelted down on the solemn group of mourners. The family followed in single file while the bearers struggled to carry the heavy bronze casket up the steep path to the gravesite for the simple burial service.

The 31st, Herbert Hoover

The Longest "Retirement," 1933–1964

When Herbert Hoover (1874–1964) left the White House at age 58 amidst a barrage of personal abuse, his policies disparaged by most of the press and a majority of the people, he was a defeated man, his term in office, 1929–1933, discredited. But before he died he was honored and praised, and had risen to a high state of public veneration. While Hoover never did hold public office again, as did former presidents John Quincy Adams, Andrew Johnson, and William Howard Taft, he made several significant contributions to his nation and the civilized world. He was the American who did the most to feed the world's hungry, especially the children, and he served two presidents as the chief officer of the commission to reorganize the machinery of government. Some feel he rivals John Quincy Adams and William Howard Taft in the contributions made to his country after his retirement. Hoover lived 31 years after leaving the White House, longer than any other former president. Only John Adams lived a longer life than Hoover, and that by only six months.

As one studies Hoover's personal life, it is quickly seen that there are far fewer intimate anecdotes told about him than most who held this high office. He was a very private man, predictably proper and reserved. Few, except for several intimate friends, penetrated the invisible but very real barrier behind which he usually took refuge when dealing with those not close to him. Much of this personality trait may have been due to the fact that he was left an orphan at an early age. His father died when he was six, and his mother when he was nine. It is difficult to know what the desperate struggle to survive as a person did to this lonely boy.

The Great Depression haunted Hoover's administration as well as the years of his retirement. He had been overwhelmingly elected in 1928 on the tide of peace and prosperity. When the nation is at peace and is prosperous, the party in office usually is kept in power. All the signals of a great administration seemed to be present when Hoover took office. Suddenly, just seven months after his inauguration, the Depression hit with little or no warning. No prominent economist, business leader, or governmental official predicted any such disaster. Though a very few isolated voices had given a warning that the bulls on Wall Street would not indefinitely run unchecked, the great bulk of American business leaders and government officials were completely surprised by the stock market crash and the following business slump that turned into the Great Depression. The effects of the business reversals were catastrophic. Countless multitudes were ill-housed and destitute. Bread lines appeared everywhere, and millions of people cursed the name of Herbert Hoover.

At first both business and government talked in platitudes about a period of adjustment or a healthy leveling off of too much speculation. "Prosperity is just around the corner" was an oft-repeated expression. Hoover did try to make governmental adjustments, and business began to consolidate or to simply retrench, but the plight of millions only became worse.

Quite naturally the Democratic party saw the major campaign issue of the century and began to use it. The Democrats could claim just two presidents since the time of Lincoln—Grover Cleveland and Woodrow Wilson. In 1929 John J. Raskob of General Motors, who had been Alfred E. Smith's campaign manager in 1928 and was now the chairman of the national Democratic committee, hired Charles Michaelson to head a national campaign to discredit the Hoover administration, an effort that has often been called a smear campaign. In his biography of Hoover, Richard Norton Smith tells a very interesting story of how Charlie Michaelson "backed by a million-dollar bank roll cranked out dozens of vituperative speeches and . . . a column called 'Dispelling the Fog' for use by anti-administration spokesmen. Charlie boasted the table was spread, all we have to do was eat."[1] These attacks continued unabated for years.

Twenty years after the arrival of the New Deal, Leland D. Baldwin, considered something of a liberal in his day, commented in his American history textbook, *The Stream of American History*, "In 1929 John J. Raskob, the [Democratic] party chairman . . . set up a propaganda mill headed by two shrewd and unscrupulous operators whose business it was to attack Republican policies, but particularly Herbert Hoover in person."[2]

Even Will Rogers joked that if someone bit an apple and found a worm in it, Hoover would get the blame.[3] While Hoover did not admit publicly that these attacks upset him, those close to him knew better. The photographs of the president during the closing days of his administration show a very harried, distressed man.

Hoover did begin a number of measures to stimulate business and help the economy. Some of these were retained by Roosevelt's New Deal, and several were claimed by the New Deal as their own. In all sincerity Hoover felt that if his policies had been put into practice the Depression would have run its course and normal times would have returned. It is needless to point out that most economists and historians do not share this view. For many years most writers still held Hoover responsible for the Depression. Even Harry Truman used the Depression as a campaign issue when he ran for president in 1948. In the 1952 Democratic convention, the writer was listening to Sam Rayburn speaking to the convention. Chet Huntley, one of the NBC news team commented, "Rayburn is in his usual form. He has been talking less than two minutes and he's already running against Hoover."

Fortunately for Hoover, he lived long enough to see the perception the public had of him change dramatically. Present-day writers picture him quite differently than those in the days of the Depression. There was no dramatic shift in the opinions of political analysts, but when those who were not personally involved with that era began to reexamine the data from the distance of time, they did not single out Hoover as the villain. Even John Nance Garner, Franklin Roosevelt's vice president for eight years, commented at the close of his life that he had fought Hoover with everything he had. Yet he considered Hoover a wise statesman in world affairs and domestic problems. Hoover is generally seen as a man caught up in a worldwide economic maelstrom which he did his best to stop.

The honors and acclaim which came to Hoover in the latter part of his life were numerous. He wrote a number of books and many magazine articles. His speaking schedule was a crowded one which took him into all parts of the country before varied groups of people. However, to the end there remained a note of bitterness about the way he felt the media had betrayed him, and to a certain extent, the way his own Republican party had failed him.

In 1932 the Republicans renominated Hoover with little enthusiasm. In a closely contested convention the Democrats nominated Franklin Delano Roosevelt. Long before the November election it was fairly obvious that Roosevelt would defeat Hoover. For the remainder of his life Hoover felt humiliated and bitter, and would never quite understand how it all happened. Until his last days he vigorously defended his administration.

After Hoover lost his attempt at reelection, he sought the cooperation of the president-elect in making plans for governmental action to help the economy, but FDR never responded favorably to these requests. At one point Hoover sent a personal letter to Roosevelt pleading for joint action on some very pressing questions. Roosevelt waited three weeks before answering the letter.[4] A number of the working press felt that FDR was not meeting Hoover halfway in these matters.[5]

However, there are two sides to this question. It is true that many felt FDR simply wanted to make Hoover look bad. On the other hand, it has been cogently argued that FDR could not politically afford to take any part in deciding issues that he had not initiated, that he must wait until he had been inaugurated president so he would be entirely on his own before the responsibility became his.

It is evident to a number of observers that FDR bore bitterness toward Hoover long after the election of 1932. The Roosevelt administration tried a number of times to find scandal in the Hoover tenure of the White House, but nothing irregular was ever uncovered. Hoover's Secretary of the Treasury Andrew Mellon was thoroughly investigated. Charges against Mellon were presented before the grand jury but were dismissed as having no substance. Later, Tax Commissioner Elmer Irey told reporter William J. Slocum that "the Roosevelt administration made me go after Andy Mellon."[6]

Hoover's own family was attacked. Allan Hoover, the former president's second son, had agricultural interests in California. Roosevelt's secretary of agriculture, Henry A. Wallace, charged that Allan had drawn $20,000 from the Agricultural Adjustment Administration for the purpose of curtailing crops. As a matter of fact, Allan was by formula entitled to draw only two dollars, an amount which he immediately rejected. Allan Hoover vigorously attacked the New Deal for these fallacious charges.[7]

In another instance, Charles F. Andrews, who had been Hoover's secretary of the navy, was attacked by a Democratic member of Congress who gleefully announced that Andrews held stock in a number of firms doing business with the navy.[8] Although it was subsequently proved that an entirely different Charles F. Andrews, not related to the secretary, was involved, no apology was ever offered.

When the high dam was built on the Colorado River it was named the Hoover Dam in honor of the president who had invested considerable effort in its planning and building. The new administration changed the name of the dam to Boulder Dam less than sixty days after Hoover left office. Hoover was not even invited to the dedication of the structure later in the year. After FDR's death the name subsequently was changed back to Hoover Dam. Most writers feel that the change from Hoover to Boulder was another attempt by the Roosevelt administration to discredit Hoover.

The question is often asked, why did FDR dislike Hoover? Surely most presidents have not held personal grudges against the other candidate for the White House after the votes are counted. Some writers admit that they do not understand this feeling of bitterness which FDR carried toward Hoover. One plausible explanation is offered by Hugh Gregory Gallagher in his recent book, *FDR's Splendid Deception*. As Gallagher points out, when the Governors' Conference of 1932 was held in Richmond, Virginia, President Hoover invited the governors and their wives to the White House for a reception. Governor and Mrs. Roosevelt of New York attended and attracted much attention. They came early to the White House to give the disabled governor time to slowly make his way to the East Room. President

Hoover was delayed for some time in meeting the governors, and the severely crippled New York governor had to stand for a long period of time with his steel braces and Eleanor's arm keeping him upright. White House ushers twice offered him a chair, but each time he refused. He did not want to show any physical incapacity in this setting while he was looking toward the presidency himself.

Both FDR and Eleanor went to their graves feeling that Hoover had deliberately placed him in this painful and awkward position. Roosevelt was known to hold grudges and not to forgive slights, fancied or real. The writer is of the opinion that this incident could have contributed to FDR's longstanding dislike for Hoover.

Eugene Lyons tells of a most interesting incident between Hoover and FDR that could have fueled the feelings of animosity between them. On November 23, 1932, President-elect Franklin Roosevelt came to the White House at Hoover's invitation to discuss certain rather important issues facing the government. Hoover wanted FDR to work with him and present a united front on these issues. When FDR decided there was nothing else to discuss, he gave the signal to his group to leave. Hoover icily reminded him, "Nobody leaves before the President."[9] Roosevelt was stung by this pointed reproof.

Hoover's last days in office were filled with great tension. The banks were in a deplorable condition, and the incoming president did not offer any cooperation with the president in office. Castigation of Hoover from the press and radio continued unabated. Few, if any, defended the beleaguered president. With great relief his troubled administration finally came to an end. Hoover and his family tried to leave town as quietly as possible. The former president went with his son Allan to New York so he would be near Washington for a few weeks. Lou Henry Hoover, the former president's wife, went to their home on the campus of Stanford University with their son Herbert, Jr.

It had been the custom of the inaugural band to play while the outgoing president was leaving the platform. For some never-discovered reason this courtesy was not given outgoing President Hoover, nor did the new president furnish any protection for the outgoing president even when it was requested. Railroad detectives provided safety for the outgoing president as he boarded the New York-bound train. Several thousand people gathered at the Washington depot to show their support of Hoover. The demonstration encouraged him at a time of deep personal turmoil. Once the train reached New York City the chief of police, who could not understand the absence of a presidential Secret Service detail, came personally and escorted Hoover to the Waldorf Astoria Hotel.

The former president predicted that he would sleep a day and a half when out of office. Actually he slept for 24 hours. The next day he motored

without any police protection to visit his friend Edgar Rickard in Connecticut. At daybreak he and his secretary Lawrence Richey walked alone from
the Waldorf to Central Park, also with no protection.

After Hoover and his wife returned to their home on the campus of
Stanford, he purposefully kept out of the public eye as much as possible.
However, his days were not idle. There was much to do with the papers
from his administration. The Hoovers traveled some, read a great deal, and
renewed old friendships. Their mountain retreat, the Bohemian Grove en-
campment, was a place of refuge. Fishing again occupied a part of his
leisure time.

As he left the White House he said he would wait for two years before
saying anything about the New Deal. He broke his silence in March 1935
in a speech at Sacramento, California, when he attacked the New Deal as
being economically unsound, and deplored the erosion of American
freedoms under the New Deal laws which regulated private lives. In June
he gave the commencement address at Stanford where he attacked the New
Deal in a very formal but pungent and forceful manner. A number of his
speeches that year were carried coast to coast by radio.

Herbert Hoover was among the most politically active former
presidents in American history. While he was never again a candidate for
any office, he wielded considerable influence over the issues and candidates
of his party. However, almost all of his activity was carried on behind the
scenes in letters, phone calls, and personal advice.

There are those who feel that Hoover might have responded to an
authentic draft and allowed himself to be nominated for the presidency in
1936. Certainly he would never have voiced such a feeling to anyone.
However, there is nothing of a factual nature to show that he was remotely
interested in the nomination of 1936. But the absence of a firm statement
that he would in no case run again has led some to suspect that he secretly
wanted the nomination. It is clearly evident from his correspondence that
he felt the Republicans should have defended him more than they did
against the attacks of Democrats during the Depression. And there is ample
evidence to show that Hoover considered himself the head of the
Republicans. One writer calls him the "Titular Leader,"[10] another[11] refers
to him as "Leader of the Loyal Opposition." But the old guard Republicans
never accepted him wholeheartedly. To them he remained an outsider, and
something of a liberal, strange as that may seem today.

Just after Hoover left the White House there was a power struggle for
the leadership of the Republican party, but Hoover did not emerge as the
undisputed leader in the party councils. When he urged that the party defend his administration, his plea fell on deaf ears. Somewhat reluctantly
Hoover was invited to address the Republican convention of 1936. Subsequently, however, he would address every convention through 1960, seven

in all. When the 1964 convention was held he was just days away from death.

Alfred Landon, the governor of Kansas, was not Hoover's first choice as the party's candidate in 1936, and only late in the campaign did Landon accept Hoover's offer to speak for him. On the surface all was amiability between Hoover and Landon, but that was not Hoover's innermost feeling. Even so, after Landon was nominated Hoover hoped very much that he would defeat FDR. Landon carried only two states in the November election of that year.

In 1940 Hoover opposed Wendell Willkie as the Republican nominee. He did not feel Willkie had the necessary background; nor did he favor Dewey in 1944 and 1948. Senator Robert Taft was his personal choice. In the very hard-fought contest between Taft and General Dwight Eisenhower in 1952, Hoover worked assiduously for Taft. But in every case he supported the party's candidate and offered to assist in each campaign. Although his services were not often used, he did deliver several very effective speeches. As time went by the party welcomed his talents, even though the Democratic candidates still played on the old refrain of "look what Hoover and the Republicans did to us in the Depression."

In 1960 Hoover felt that Richard Nixon would make a good candidate although he was not personally very fond of the vice president. He did not wish to see John F. Kennedy win the White House, but found he rather liked the youthful, newly-elected president. John Kennedy's father, Ambassador Joseph Kennedy, and Hoover often talked together, occasionally visited one another, and seemed genuinely to like each other. Joe Kennedy suggested that in the interest of unity Nixon and John Kennedy should meet informally to help unite the country after a bitter campaign and election. Hoover liked the idea, but it was not an easy task to persuade Nixon to agree to the proposal. Eventually the historic meeting took place in Florida.

By 1964 Hoover was too aged and feeble to become deeply involved in politics. However, before the Republican convention he pledged his support to Senator Barry Goldwater who was his choice over Governor Nelson Rockefeller.

Hoover's humanitarian efforts took much of his time and effort during his retirement years. After World War II broke out in Europe, Hoover, having witnessed the terrible destruction in Poland by the Nazis, tried to procure food for the starving Poles. It was Hoover's plan to ask both sides in the conflict to permit food to be delivered to the suffering people. Neither Germany nor the Allies would consider such a plan, nor did FDR push the idea.

With the death of FDR in the spring of 1945, and the swearing in of Harry S Truman as president, the attitude of the administration toward

Hoover changed dramatically. It was not long before Hoover was a guest in the White House. For more than 12 years he had not set foot in the executive mansion. Not many anticipated that Hoover and Truman would get along together so well. One writer called them the "oddest couple."[12] Hoover performed a number of services for President Truman. First, he headed the Famine Emergency Commission. In this capacity he flew to Europe, Asia, and Africa determining the relative need for food in the war-torn parts of the world. He was able to gather a substantial amount of food to send to the most needy areas. There is little doubt that he saved many thousands of lives. He was most concerned with the needs of the children, for the infant mortality rate in the war zone was staggering. Hoover also helped to feed the hungry in Japan and Korea.

These trips were made in the nonpressurized cabins of slow, propellor-driven planes. The housing and food that he himself received on these trips were very poor. For a man more than 70 years of age, his efforts were monumental.

Again the next year, 1946, Truman sent Hoover on what was called the President's Economic Mission to Germany and Austria. On the return flight he suffered considerable discomfort from the constant changes of the air pressure in the plane's cabin, and he developed an ear infection that permanently damaged his hearing.

The sudden growth of governmental activity during the war left an overlapping morass of offices and officials. "Between seventy and a hundred agencies, boards, and commissions reported directly to the President, many of them 'temporary' but tottering with old age."[13] Truman got the idea that if any man alive could bring some order out of the chaos in Washington it was Herbert Hoover. On September 27, 1947, Hoover began to work on the problem, serving as chairman of what was commonly called the Hoover Commission. Dean Acheson was the vice chairman. Other important persons such as Secretary of Defense James Forrestal, former Ambassador Joseph P. Kennedy, Arthur S. Fleming, Owen D. Young, and Dr. William Menninger also served on the commission, which included an equal number of Democrats and Republicans. Both houses of Congress had a hand in selecting its members. More than 300 specialists were chosen by Hoover to help in the work.

The former president's personal physicians advised him to slow down, but he did not know how. A typical day, according to his secretary, began by a brisk walk, breakfast, and steady work until the so-called quitting time of 10 p.m. However, it was quite a common thing to see him working until midnight. His associates constantly marveled at his drive and energy. As could have been expected, Hoover was the hub around which the whole project moved. During the work of the commission, Hoover developed a painful case of shingles, but he did not slacken the pace of his work schedule.

The Hoover Commission report was presented to Congress on February 7, 1949. Nineteen separate sections were submitted. Hoover wrote 16 of them himself. President Truman was most pleased with the quality and extent of the report. It has been estimated that about 70 percent of the recommendations were adopted by Congress.

When Dwight Eisenhower became president, he asked Hoover to do the same kind of task for his administration. In spite of the protests of his doctors, he accepted the assignment and began the work of the Second Hoover Commission. This body did not achieve the monumental success of the first one; neither did Eisenhower support it to the degree that Truman had.

Another area of Hoover's contribution lies in the establishment of the Institution on War, Revolution and Peace at Stanford University, later to be referred to as the Hoover Institute. It houses an incredibly large number of documents in 89 languages from governments and nations all over the world. It is not a propaganda instrument, but rather a repository for documents and a place for research in the areas of its holdings. Hoover's influence and labor in establishing and maintaining this facility were enormous. In 1941 the Hoover Tower that houses the institute was dedicated on the campus of Stanford. Alexander Kerensky, of Russian Revolution fame, was a frequent visitor at the institute.

Hoover's wife, Lou Henry, was a great source of comfort and stability to him. She never sought the limelight or any publicity, but was constantly by his side. It fell to her to provide the needed warmth that her husband seemed to lack, as well as to maintain their social life. Yet it seems strange that the media did not give her more recognition and credit for her husband's success than they did. Their life together spanned 45 years, ending with her death on January 7, 1944. Hoover was very distraught. He immediately left their home on the Stanford campus that she had planned, feeling he could not live there alone.[14]

Mrs. Hoover had gone to a concert in midtown Manhattan with the former president's secretary Bernice Miller. The two women started to walk back to their apartment in the Waldorf Tower. Lou Henry complained of suddenly feeling very tired, so they took a cab the rest of the way home. She went to their apartment, waved to her husband, and went to the bedroom. A little later Hoover stopped by to tell her goodbye before going to an evening appointment with Edgar Rickard. He found her on the floor, dead of a heart attack. It was not a front page story in the *New York Times.*

Lou Henry died late on Friday. The funeral was held Monday morning at St. Bartholomew Episcopal Church near the Waldorf. The service was short, according to the tradition of Friends (Quakers). The widow of Benjamin Harrison was in attendance. So were 200 Girl Scouts, Joseph

Kennedy, Mrs. Wendell Willkie, Eddie Rickenbacker, and Edgar Rickard. President and Mrs. Roosevelt sent a message of sympathy. In the afternoon the train bearing the body of Mrs. Hoover started for California and burial in Alta Mesa Cemetery at Stanford. (In 1966 the body was reinterred in West Branch, Iowa, by the side of her husband.)

Hoover said of his wife, "I had lived with the loyalty and tender affection of an indomitable soul almost fifty years."[15] After her death there was never any further consideration of returning to their old home on the Stanford campus. It had been her home and too closely related to their life together for him to return to it alone. From that time his permanent address was Suite 31-A, Waldorf Tower.

Someone once remarked that for Hoover, work was his leisure activity. He could seldom simply relax. He looked for something specific that needed to be done. As a writer he was productive, although none of his books were best-sellers. The better libraries of the country have these works in their stacks. They are worth reading, but in many places the writing is pedantic to a fault, and often the reading is dull even to an academician. The magazine articles, and he wrote many, were much more readable, and in the opinion of the writer, much more to the point.

One of his major efforts, *Freedom Betrayed,* was never published. Those close to him felt he was too outspoken, that libel suits might result, and that the book showed considerable bitterness against those he felt had acted against the obvious best interests of the nation. Today the manuscript is locked in the vaults of the Hoover Institute.

During his last years, Hoover usually went to California for a couple of months each year, visiting friends and spending time at the Hoover Institute. Also, he never ceased to enjoy his visits to the Bohemian Grove not far from Stanford, which was for a good many years a retreat for the Hoovers. After Lou Henry's death, Hoover used it as a place to invite guests just to talk, usually on a few timely topics. It was an honor to be invited to this mountain hideaway, by then a retreat for male camaraderie. Hoover usually did a substantial part of the cooking. It was here that he invited Harry Truman on occasion. Hoover's and Truman's friendship was similar to that which developed between Thomas Jefferson and John Adams after they both left the presidency more than 125 years before.

Until 1962 Hoover visited a fishing club at Key Largo, Florida, for his annual session of bone fishing. It was one of the most enjoyable times of the year for him. When he feared his physical condition would not permit him to return, he presented his fishing gear to his guide who had the foresight to remark that if Hoover ever returned he could borrow it back.

Hoover had been born into a Quaker home and he remained loyal to the church of his heritage all his life. Lou Henry commented that it was her husband's faith in God that helped him through the dark, bitter days of the

Depression.[16] On occasion he would speak at religious gatherings such as the Christian Endeavor. He was never one to talk about his personal faith, but morality, honesty, and the need for Christian virtues in the country were often mentioned. He was indeed a man of deep Christian faith, although his world contacts caused him to respect any other person's honest views about religion. It might be pointed out that in at least two particulars he departed from Quaker practice as to his life-style. His speech at times was a bit too salty for most Quakers, and he used tobacco and a little alcohol.

No doubt the change in the public's regard for him was most welcome. However, he had gone through such disfavor that he fully realized how transitory public adulation can be. His inner resource, stability of character and purpose, never left him. His work in relief of the world's hungry and the Hoover Commission had now made him a popular figure. His friendship with Truman and Joe Kennedy seemed very natural, never contrived. When he celebrated his seventy-fifth birthday on August 10, 1949, his public acclaim had never been so great. The press honored him. Some even pronounced him one of the greatest men in American history saying he had lived "a life of superb usefulness and public service."[17] Lyons says, "Never before had a living former president been the object of such a vast and sentimental outpouring."[18] Congress also joined in the celebration. The focal point of the occasion was his return to Stanford where thousands turned out to honor the former president.

His eightieth birthday called for an even greater celebration. He returned to West Branch, Iowa, at the invitation of the governor and legislature of the state. Thousands came to see their favorite son. In an unusually personal comment Hoover said, "I am glad to come to West Branch. My grandparents and my parents came here in a covered wagon. In this community they toiled and worshipped God . . . My roots are in this soil."[19] Another celebration was held in his honor on his eighty-fifth birthday. At eighty-five he still kept a staff of six to eight busy, for his literary production was considerable.

On his eighty-eighth birthday the Hoover Presidential Library was dedicated at his childhood home in West Branch. The former president flew to Iowa for the occasion, while about 500 people from New York paid their own way to be with Hoover on this memorable occasion. Among those were some who had been with him when he fed so many hungry in Europe during and after World War II. For the dedication, about 45,000 gathered in West Branch, whose population was barely 1,000. The library was turned over to the National Archives and became a part of the presidential libraries. Truman came in person and spoke. (Hoover attended the dedication of the Truman Library.) Eisenhower sent greetings from Europe. President John F. Kennedy sent a warm personal message. Visibly an aging man, Hoover said a few words though he could not stand during all of the few minutes he spoke. He did not feel well when he arrived at West Branch. He soon became ill and left the ceremony before it was over, and was flown to a New York hospital. His illness was diagnosed as anemia, and a malignancy in the colon.[20]

Hoover's first overnight stay in a hospital had occurred during his seventy-eighth year when he was bone fishing at Key Largo, Florida, but he had soon gone back fishing. His last years witnessed surgery several times including once for a gallbladder problem, and a continual battle against the ailments associated with his advancing years. The last months of his life found him frequently in a wheelchair and working only five or six hours a day. On another occasion he had internal bleeding that required heroic medical treatment. It was at this time that the new president, Lyndon Baines Johnson, called at Suite 31-A in the Waldorf. Jacqueline Kennedy also called soon afterward.

Herbert and Lou Henry Hoover had two sons, Herbert Clark, Jr., born in 1903, and Allan Henry, born four years later. Both were born in London while their father was working in Europe. Though Hoover was a world figure, their parents always tried to keep them out of the public eye. After the death of Lou Henry in 1944, Hoover lived alone for over twenty years, and came to rely on his sons and their families. Herbert, Jr., was involved with mining and oil, spending considerable time in the Middle East. President Eisenhower appointed him under secretary of state for Middle East Affairs. The elder Hoover gave his son some advice when Herbert, Jr., took this sensitive position. "Herbert, keep a bottle of whisky in your bottom drawer, and after the day is over, when you're tired and before you start for home, take a swig ... it'll pep you up."[21] Herbert, Jr., lived in New York and stayed close to his father during Hoover's last years, often taking and sending messages for the former president. Allan did not often appear in the news, for he worked in the private sector after earning his degree in economics from Stanford. He managed his father's California farm for a number of years, and was involved in the banking industry before he turned his attention to mining. Allan, like his brother, lived near his father. He spent the night in Apartment 31-A at the Waldorf after the assassination of President Kennedy, knowing how upset his father would be.

Hoover's final illness began in February, 1964. A recurrence of the internal bleeding and pneumonia showed that the sands of his hourglass had about run out. But he was still aware of the happenings of the world about him. He sent a personal note to General Douglas MacArthur, ill in Walter Reed Hospital. A message from Hoover was read at the Republican National Convention in San Francisco. Barry Goldwater called at Suite 31-A in August. A new color television set helped him to enjoy the World Series.

On October 16 he suffered a massive abdominal hemorrhage, but flatly refused to be hospitalized. He lapsed into a coma before death came on October 20, 1964.

Tributes poured in from the great of the nation and the world. Both members of the Johnson-Humphrey and Goldwater-Miller presidential tickets attended the short Quaker-type funeral held in the same church that had witnessed the last rites for Lou Henry more than twenty years earlier. Among the 400 that gathered to remember Hoover were Jean MacArthur (the general's widow), Eddie Rickenbacker, John Connally, and Jim Farley. Seventeen thousand New Yorkers passed by the casket before the doors of the church were closed. The body was then taken to the rotunda of the Capitol where another service was conducted.

On October 25, a Sunday, the plane bearing the casket landed at Cedar Rapids. Along the 30-mile trip to West Branch it seemed his own kind of people gathered at every crossroad to stand in a silent, final tribute to their friend and neighbor. A crowd estimated to be 75,000 to 90,000 gathered at Hoover Park in West Branch. Dr. Elton Trueblood, a lifelong friend and the leading Quaker minister of his day, said the final words of eulogy at the grave near the Hoover Library. The national guard band played "Fight the Good Fight," and "Battle Hymn of the Republic."

Herbert Hoover had met death with the same resolution and courage that had sustained him during a disastrous presidency, years of public abuse, and ultimate triumph.

The 32nd, Franklin D. Roosevelt

The Final Portrait, 1945

Those who were listening to the radio on April 12, 1945, reacted with stunned disbelief when they heard the news, "The president is dead." To the young it seemed impossible to think of anyone else as president, for Franklin Delano Roosevelt (born 1882) had been in office for twelve years (1933–1945) and had led the country through depression and war. America's shock and grief were deep. Roosevelt had collapsed in Warm Springs, Georgia, while Madame Elizabeth Shoumatoff was painting his portrait.

It was well known that FDR had been crippled by an attack of polio in 1921 and could not walk unaided, but that made no particular difference to most. In a way he seemed indestructible. Americans almost felt that they knew him personally. Certainly all instantly recognized that clear, magnetic, resonant voice on the radio when he began his famous fireside chats with the words "My friends. . . ." It seemed impossible that this voice would never be heard again.

During the campaign of 1944, when FDR was running for an unprecedented fourth term, rumors were afloat that the president was in poor health and would not live out a fourth term if he were reelected. Comments about the president's health began to appear with some regularity in the press, on the radio and in magazines. However, to the average American these stories seemed more like political gossip than fact. Nothing from official Washington even suggested there was anything seriously wrong with the president. That FDR had a chronic and bothersome sinus condition was freely admitted. Pictures of the president swimming in the White House pool or at Warm Springs had been a common sight for many years, all testifying to his vigor and good health.

But as 1944 wore on, "Washington watchers" began to see pictures of the president that showed him looking quite a bit thinner, tired and worn. In the days before television, the newsreels at the movies were the most popular way to get the news in pictures. The view the people got of the president in mid-1944 showed a man failing in strength and vitality.

241

A possible factor in the president's health was the severe mental depression that at times hindered his ability to execute the duties of his office during the last 16 months of his life. By 1944 FDR had apparently little if any interest in the management of his health. A number of those close to him observed that he had somehow lost much of the ability to make vital decisions quickly, for he began to waver among the conflicting options that were presented to him. The attention that he gave the briefing papers which constantly crossed his desk declined noticeably. In the midst of making significant decisions he once remarked to his son James, "The whole thing doesn't matter a damn."[1]

Members of his family commented that FDR seemed lonely. Missy LeHand, his secretary and confidante, had left because of illness, and his wife Eleanor was seldom at home. At times his daughter Anna (Mrs. John Boetiger) was with him and seemed to be a great comfort to him. His doctor ordered that he should retire before the evening meal which he usually ate alone in bed. His problems of chronic fatigue, loss of appetite, and recurring indigestion could not be attributed solely to his chronic sinus infection. His responsibilities were crushing and there was little in life to give him a sense of personal joy. The increasing residual effects of polio and the diminution of physical strength could easily bring a state of depression to the most robust personality.

Ironically, the most important people often do not receive adequate medical attention. So many individuals become involved with an illness of a president that it is hard to fix responsibility, and too many of them have hidden agendas so that the medical care of the patient often suffers.

The public was given little information about the health of Roosevelt. Such things as blood pressure or the results of X-rays were never released. Many of the generalized statements about FDR's physical condition turned out to be misleading at best. It should be remembered that in the forties it was not customary for a president to release information regarding his health. The public had certainly not known the true condition of Woodrow Wilson or Warren G. Harding when they were ill during their terms in the White House. Both the president's wife Eleanor and daughter Anna were concerned about Roosevelt, especially after the Teheran Conference in late 1943. Both had attempted to get some definitive statement from the president's private physician, Admiral Ross T. McIntire. However, his answers were vague and unsatisfying. The physician talked in very general terms about the aftereffects of influenza, a sinus condition, and the fact that FDR was overworked. There is always the question as to whether McIntire was qualified for his sensitive position or even for the practice of medicine. At times he seemed to sacrifice the president's health for political expediency. Perhaps Admiral McIntire recognized that Roosevelt would lose some of his effectiveness if the public knew the true condition of his health.

In late March of 1944, Admiral McIntire finally did order a complete physical examination of the president at Bethesda Naval Hospital. Lieutenant Commander Howard Bruenn, a brilliant young naval doctor, was to conduct the examination giving especial attention to the heart and lungs. The results of the examination were to be treated as top secret information. Dr. Bruenn was ordered to report his findings directly and only to Admiral McIntire. Bruenn was not to discuss them with anyone else, not even the president himself. To further the secrecy, Dr. Bruenn did not know until nine o'clock in the morning that it was the president he was to examine at eleven that same morning. Interestingly enough, the famous patient did not ask Dr. Bruenn a single question that morning or on any other occasion.

Roosevelt did not like physical examinations, but when Admiral McIntire finally told him that it was time to go to the hospital for his "check-up," he went along without complaining. When Bruenn asked Roosevelt how he felt the morning of the examination, the president is said to have responded that he felt "like hell." Some say that while FDR never once mentioned it, he realized that he was in failing health.

As the examination began, the doctor noted that his patient was extremely fatigued, that there was a bluish cast to the fingernails and lips, that any exertion left him breathless, and that there was fluid on both lungs. These findings depict a man suffering from heart failure. Also, the heart was considerably enlarged, and the blood pressure was moderately high, 186/108. (In two months' time it would be 218/120.) Bruenn made a diagnosis of hypertensive heart disease. He also found severe iron deficiency and chronic bronchitis. It was the doctor's private opinion that the patient might live several months or several years, depending upon how much care was given his physical condition.

Commander Bruenn gave the report to his boss, Dr. McIntire, who called a secret consultation of six eminent physicians to hear from Bruenn. The two most prestigious were Dr. Frank Lahey of Boston and Dr. James A. Paullin of Atlanta. None of them could believe that the situation was as serious as Bruenn stated. Both Lahey and Paullin agreed to examine FDR the next day, and confirmed Bruenn's diagnosis. As a group they agreed not to tell Roosevelt or his family the actual nature of their findings, but instead to give the patient digitalis, a heart stimulant, and try to get him to limit his work day and rest more.

It might be well to compare what McIntire and Bruenn recorded in their medical notes about Roosevelt after this examination. McIntire wrote "a moderate degree of arteriosclerosis [hardening of the arteries], although no more than normal in a man of his age; some changes in the cardiographic tracing; clouding in the sinuses; and bronchial irritation."[2] However, when Bruenn recorded his findings he spoke of "hypertension;

hypertensive heart disease; cardiac failure and acute bronchitis."[3] It should be remembered that the consulting physicians basically agreed with Dr. Bruenn. One could wonder if McIntire and Bruenn were examining the same patient.

A few days after the president's examination at the naval hospital in Bethesda, McIntire made a statement to the press as to the chief executive's health. John H. Crider of the *New York Times* reported that according to Roosevelt's personal physician, the president's health was regarded as "satisfactory." Crider further reported that FDR had been suffering from a head cold, bronchitis, a sinus disturbance, and quoted McIntire as saying that Roosevelt had a "respiratory infection." There was no mention of a heart problem.[4]

After the physical examination the doctors recommended a period of almost complete rest for the president. Bernard Baruch, one of America's elder statesmen, had invited FDR to spend time at Hobcaw, his large South Carolina estate, and in early April 1944 Roosevelt went there for rest and relaxation. For a month the president slept twelve hours a night, sat in the sun, fished, read detective stories, and tried to relax. He returned to the White House on May 6, tanned and feeling better, but his basic physical problems had not significantly improved. The White House staff gave the public the story that the president had gotten over his sinus infection and was well again.

The year 1944 was a most demanding one for Roosevelt. Several major problems had to be addressed, the war effort perhaps the most pressing. The invasion of France at Normandy on D-Day in June was an emotional strain on the president. Keeping Japan at bay, and the constant demand for war matériel were persistent problems. America's foreign policy and the planning of an international organization to keep the peace occupied much of Roosevelt's attention. Also, FDR was not only the president, he was also the titular head of the Democratic party. The issues of a fourth term and who would be the vice presidential candidate were very much on the president's mind. All of these problems together were placing a severe strain on an ill and very tired chief executive.

How the nation prosecuted the war and cooperated with the Allies is a well-documented story. However, the political narrative is not as well understood. There is no good evidence that FDR ever seriously considered not running again in 1944 for a fourth term. In all probability he did not feel that there was anyone else who could accomplish what he thought necessary. There are many who would fully agree. When FDR made no statement about his political plans there was little else the Democratic convention could do but renominate him.

The question as to who would be Roosevelt's running mate was another matter. Henry A. Wallace, FDR's third-term vice president, was too far to the left to gain the support of the South or many of the old professionals of the party. Jimmy Byrnes, another strong contender, did not have the support of labor or the more liberal wing of the party. The Democratic convention was on the verge of selecting a vice president in Chicago, when at the last moment Roosevelt and the party leaders secured the nomination of Harry S Truman.

During much of the Chicago convention Roosevelt was en route to San Diego by train. While in San Diego the president made a radio address directly to the convention and the nation in which he accepted the Democratic nomination for president. The speech was made from his private railroad car parked on a siding in the rail yards. The pictures of the president delivering his acceptance speech clearly showed a tired old man. Even Jim Farley, essentially the man who made FDR president in 1932, commented that he did not think Roosevelt could live through a fourth term.

From San Diego the president sailed to Hawaii to confer with General Douglas MacArthur. After meeting with the general, Roosevelt came to the naval shipyards at Bremerton, Washington, and made a short speech about the war effort. James Bishop, author of *FDR's Last Year,* believes that the president had a heart attack while delivering this talk. Though there was a slurring of words and a loss of attention several times, most observers did not feel that there was anything resembling a heart attack at this time.

During 1944 the president did not campaign in his old style of meeting people face to face. He would visit military installations as the commander-in-chief of the armed forces, let himself be seen, make a few short remarks about the war and move on. Clearly he was running for reelection as commander-in-chief. It was a simple, effective way to campaign and conserve his strength. However, many of his advisers felt that low-key campaigning was not adequate to defeat a young, articulate, vigorous Thomas E. Dewey, governor of New York, especially since Dewey kept referring to the "tired old men" in government.

As the campaign dragged on, FDR saw the need of more direct contact with the people. On October 21, Roosevelt was scheduled to make several appearances in New York and ride through the streets of the city. The president's private railroad car arrived at the Brooklyn army base at seven-thirty in the morning in a veritable downpour. His staff and family tried to dissuade him from going through with his plans. But the Dewey challenge had gotten the president's competitive spirit up, and he was determined to make a strong appeal directly to the people.

At nine-thirty that morning, the procession left the army base. The president sat in the left rear seat of the open car and began his tour. He stopped at Ebbetts Field and in the driving rain, bareheaded and without his great navy cape, gave a speech before more than 70,000 cheering citizens. Along the way he stopped at a coast guard station to change his clothes and get warm. He was wet to the skin even though he wore special underwear designed to protect him. Roosevelt then went on through Queens, and then Harlem, stopped at Hunter College, continued on down Broadway and Seventh Avenue, by the Empire State Building, and down to Washington Square where he stopped at Mrs. Roosevelt's apartment to again change clothes and rest. He had driven more than fifty miles in a crowded city and was seen by more than three million people.

That night he delivered the major foreign policy speech of the campaign at the Waldorf Astoria Hotel before a packed house. His delivery and articulation were good. The press commented that it was the Roosevelt of old. The public's reaction was, "No sick man could do that." He did it again six days later in the rain in Philadelphia. On October 28, at Chicago's Soldier Field, in 14-degree weather with a freezing wind off Lake Michigan, he spoke effectively to more than 100,000 in the stadium and 150,000 outside. For the general public the issue of the president's health was settled. Roosevelt defeated Dewey 25.5 million to 22 million votes. However, this was the smallest percent of the total vote Roosevelt ever received.

Less than a month before the election of 1944, Admiral McIntire issued a statement about Roosevelt's health. "The President's health is perfectly okay. There are absolutely no organic difficulties at all."[5] Some of the press were not quite convinced. Several asked why Dr. Bruenn, a heart specialist, always accompanied Roosevelt. No reasonable answer was ever given to this question. Most of those who saw the president on a regular basis continued to be deeply concerned about how ill he looked. The immediate family was worried but accepted McIntire's assurances that all was going well. However, Anna tried to get a second opinion, but was blocked at every turn.

By this time the president's work schedule had been reduced. He usually got up at eight in the morning, arrived at his office at half past ten, took a rest at noon, returned to his private quarters between six and seven, and was in bed sometime between seven-thirty and eight. After his evening meal he would see the family, staff or friends for a short time before going to sleep. But on those occasions when the situation demanded, he could still rise to the occasion and perform more or less as expected.

Roosevelt spent Christmas 1944 at Hyde Park with the family. But he was so tired that he spent more time in than out of bed. He was not even up to opening many of his presents until well after Christmas Day.

It is rather difficult to know what really happened on the day of his fourth inaugural, January 20, 1945. Held on the south portico of the White House before a small invited audience, the ceremony lasted only fifteen minutes. The weather was cold but FDR took the oath of office and delivered his inaugural address without a coat or a hat. His hand shook so much that some wondered if he could hold his very brief address long enough to read it, and that it was with considerable difficulty that he got back inside. Some have even gone as far as to say that he had a heart attack during the inaugural ceremony, but this is doubtful. It is known that he saw very few visitors that day. Eleanor Roosevelt and the Trumans greeted the guests in one of the largest receptions ever held at the White House.

A plausible explanation for FDR's absence was that he was preparing to leave two days later for the Yalta conference and did not have time to greet guests. A number of his family and staff wondered if he was physically up to traveling such a distance and enduring the strain of meeting with Stalin and Churchill.

The president had asked that all of his grandchildren be at the White House during the time of his last inauguration. Mrs. Roosevelt thought that having all of them there at one time might tire him too much, but the president insisted. In her autobiography Eleanor Roosevelt says, "Early in January, realizing this would certainly be his last inauguration, perhaps even having a premonition that he would not be with us long, Franklin insisted that every grandchild (thirteen) come to the White House for a few days over the 20th."[6]

The Yalta conference took a deadly toll on the president's dwindling reserve of strength. Some have felt that it was the worst experience of his whole life. In the official photograph taken at the conference, Roosevelt is described "holding a cigarette in his right hand . . . his caved-in face is the face of a dying man."[7] His staff had noted that usually after a sea voyage he bounced back and seemed in better health. But this did not happen on the way home from Yalta. Grace Tully, his private secretary, observed the decline in the health of "the Boss" during Yalta. Of course Eleanor Roosevelt noticed it. Merriman Smith, the journalist who for years followed the president later wrote, "It seemed he had aged ten years in ten days."[8] Vice President Truman saw him after Yalta and was shocked by his appearance.

When the president reported to Congress on the Yalta conference, he was sitting down. He joked about it, but his audience realized this was the first time he had not spoken to Congress from a standing position. Eleanor Roosevelt felt that in doing so he "had accepted a degree of invalidism."[9] Others noted that FDR's voice was weak and that he did not have his old effectiveness. In this speech he departed from the text he had before him almost fifty times and some felt he occasionally seemed lost in his manuscript.

On March 3, two days after his address to Congress about Yalta, the president went to Hyde Park to rest for a few days. He had hoped to work on his stamp collection, but his hands shook so that it was difficult for him to handle the stamps. He gave up his custom of always mixing cocktails before the evening meal. Also, Eleanor noticed that it was difficult to get him into serious conversation for any length of time. Mrs. Roosevelt confided to a friend about her husband, "I say a daily prayer that he may be able to carry on till we have peace."[10]

Unfortunately, when FDR returned to Washington after this short stay at Hyde Park he began to skip his midday rest too often and to work into the night. The attitude of Stalin bothered him acutely, for the Soviets kept demanding more and more from the Allies.

At this time Roosevelt sent for Robert Murphy of the State Department, his favorite troubleshooter. The president wanted to talk to Murphy about the critical Polish situation. When Murphy began his talk with Roosevelt he realized that the president was not himself. Murphy recalls that "his appearance was a terrible shock; he was a mere shadow of the buoyant man who had talked so confidently the previous September."[11] They spent an hour in small talk without addressing any of the problems which must have beset FDR.

On March 24 Roosevelt made his last trip to Hyde Park. Nothing especially significant happened while he was there. He handled the details of office and got as much rest as possible. The Soviets continued to cause him considerable concern for he felt that they were already violating the agreements made at Yalta. Roosevelt communicated with Churchill over the matter and then sent a fairly stiff note to Stalin from Hyde Park. The rest he took at Hyde Park did him no observable good. On the morning of March 29 Roosevelt left Hyde Park and returned to Washington, worked briefly in his office, and in the late afternoon boarded his special train for a rest at Warm Springs, Georgia.

Roosevelt had been planning this trip for some time. Warm Springs was perhaps his favorite place to go and just rest. His cottage, the "Little White House," was comfortable and suited his particular needs. He loved the people there and they returned his affection very openly. The president also enjoyed the ride to Warm Springs, ordering the train to go at a moderate speed so he could see the countryside and the people along the way. In his private car he could relax, read, talk, or sleep as he pleased.

The nine-car train traveled all night and well into the next afternoon before it arrived at the little town of Warm Springs. Roosevelt took only a small staff, and no immediate family member went along. Anna had planned to accompany her father, but the serious illness of her young son prevented that. However, two of FDR's favorite cousins, Margaret Suckley and Laura Delano, made the trip with the president. They were cheerful and full of good humor, made no demands on him, and he was genuinely fond of them. Only three reporters were allowed to accompany the president, one from each major news service. He expected to do as little as possible and rest as much as he could.

No one sensed the imminent death of the president. He was ill, but it did not appear to those around him that death was near. Mrs. Roosevelt was glad to see her husband go on a vacation. She felt he would recover some of his strength and gain a little weight. Admiral McIntire did not accompany him, but kept in touch with the president through daily calls from Dr. Bruenn who now traveled with Roosevelt everywhere he went. Bruenn saw the president several times each day and examined him at least once daily. William Hassett, one of FDR's secretaries, was the only one to put in writing his fears that the president did not have long to live. Hassett wrote in his diary the evening of their arrival at Warm Springs, "He is slipping away from us and no earthly power can keep him here."[12]

Many of the crowd of 600 who came to greet the president at Warm Springs noticed how worn, thin, and tired he looked. They also observed that he did not give them his customary hand wave. Roosevelt had a way of quickly moving from his wheelchair into the waiting limousine in which he was to ride. But on the afternoon of March 30 at the little railroad station, he could not help himself into the auto. Mike Reilly, chief of the Secret Service detail, usually helped FDR to make the transfer easily, but on Good Friday 1945 it took all of Reilly's strength to put the president into the limousine. In a few minutes the president and his entourage reached the Little White House and Roosevelt asked to go to bed.

Thus began Roosevelt's last stay at Warm Springs. He arrived on March 30 and died on April 12. During this period he seemed no worse than before. If anything he looked better and seemed to be enjoying himself. The routine was pretty much the same during his stay. He would wake up between eight and nine o'clock. Arthur Pettyman would bathe, shave and dress him. A leisurely breakfast followed. What little work he did was completed before lunch. He was supposed to take a nap after lunch, but did not always do so. In the afternoon he frequently shared a ride with a few intimates. After dinner he relaxed with his stamps, books, or conversation. On several occasions he called his wife and told her he was feeling better.

The housework at the Little White House was done by Daisy Bonner and Lizzie McDuffie, two black women of the community of whom he was very fond. They knew just what he liked to eat and cooked his favorite foods in an effort to help him gain weight. But by this time it was difficult to get the president to eat very much.

Few visitors were allowed at Warm Springs this time. The president very rarely went out except for a ride, although he attended church on Easter morning and listened to a sermon that was too long. Bill Hassett said a sense of "last times" permeated Warm Springs.

After the president had been at Warm Springs a few days, he was visited by a specially invited guest, Lucy Mercer Rutherford. Franklin's attention to Lucy had almost broken up Franklin and Eleanor's marriage when he was assistant secretary of the navy. During his presidency FDR had seen Lucy a number of times by asking his staff and his daughter to arrange meetings. Even now in their later years they still cared for each other. Lucy brought an artist, Madame Elizabeth Shoumatoff, to paint the president's portrait.

On the last evening of his life Roosevelt was visited by an old neighbor and friend, Henry Morganthau, who was also his secretary of the treasury. They had the evening meal together, waffles made on an iron that Morganthau had given Roosevelt. They spent the evening reminiscing about old times, the fun they had on the Hudson River as boys, the gossip about neighbors, and the people who were important in the lives of their youth.

At the same time another group was eating dinner in the capital. Sam Rayburn, speaker of the House, was dining with cronies. During the dinner the speaker commented, "The President is not a well man. . . . I think I'll have a talk with Harry Truman tomorrow. He's got to be prepared to carry a terrible burden."[13] They all understood the speaker perfectly. The next day Harry Truman became president of the United States.

A beautiful spring day dawned at Warm Springs on Thursday, April 12. The mail plane was held up by bad weather in Washington, so the president could have slept longer, but he was awake at the usual time. He was propped up in bed and began reading the *Atlanta Constitution*. The war news was good, Roosevelt was satisfied. The president wanted fried eggs, bacon and toast for breakfast. He shared his toast with his little dog Fala.

Commander Bruenn came in and performed his daily physical examination. The physician noted a slight cyanosis (blue coloring) on the fingernails and the lips. He once again saw the usual signs of advanced arteriosclerosis, and took a blood pressure reading of 180/110. The president complained of a slight headache and stiffness in his neck.[14] As per instructions, Dr. Bruenn called the White House and gave Dr. McIntire his findings. He also explained that the president planned to attend an old-fashioned barbecue and minstrel show later in the day. The entry in McIntire's notes for April 12 contained the following sentence, "Every cause of anxiety seems to have lifted."[15] Either McIntire was not telling the truth, did not fully understand the physical symptoms, or perhaps could not emotionally accept the fact that the president was dying.

Laura Delano, Margaret Suckley, and Lucy Rutherford were in the living room of the Little White House with the president as he posed for his portrait, signed letters and documents, and chatted with Lucy. The president said to the artist, "Just fifteen minutes more." He fitted a cigarette into the holder, turned toward Lucy Rutherford, looked startled, and put his hand to his head. His hand dropped by his side. Margaret Suckley went to him. She thought he murmured, "I have a terrific headache."[16] The president slumped in his chair and was unconscious. The time was 1:15 in the afternoon, just as lunch was about to be served.

Dr. Bruenn was by his side in minutes. The president was placed on his bed. Bruenn and George Fox, a navy medic, immediately began working to revive Roosevelt. Bruenn phoned McIntire in Washington who immediately called Dr. James Paullin in nearby Atlanta who made a frantic drive to Warm Springs, arriving at the Little White House just five minutes before Roosevelt stopped breathing. The doctors pronounced the president dead at 3:35 on the afternoon of April 12, 1945. He was 63.

It took a little more than half an hour to let the world know the president had died. First, Mrs. Roosevelt had to be informed of her husband's death. She was at the Sulgrave Club participating in a fund drive for charity when she received the news and returned immediately to the White House. Only then could the shocking announcement be made that the nation's leader had died. Mrs. Roosevelt, Dr. McIntire, and Steve Early, the president's news secretary, began preparations for an immediate trip to Warm Springs, but they did not leave before Vice President Truman was sworn in as president of the United States. Mrs. Roosevelt arrived at the Little White House around midnight.

When a president dies, observing the necessary protocol is no simple matter. A whole night of preparation was needed to secure an undertaker, to inform the armed forces to have servicemen present for the honor guard, and to assemble the special train to take the body of the president to Washington. Nevertheless a little after ten the next morning, the train pulled out of Warm Springs and was on its way to the capital.

By mid-morning of the next day, Saturday, April 14, the special train arrived in Washington, D.C. A procession took the body to the White House. Only once was the casket opened before the simple four o'clock service in the East Room of the White House conducted by the Reverend Angus Dun, bishop of the Episcopal diocese of Washington. At about nine-thirty that night, the funeral train left Washington to take the president's body to the Roosevelt ancestral home at Hyde Park for its final resting place.

At 8:40 Sunday morning, the train drew up on the siding at Hyde Park, New York. The procession began its trip up the hill to the Roosevelt estate. The burial took place after a brief service at ten o'clock Sunday morning, conducted by the Rev. Dr. George Anthony, rector of St. James Episcopal Church at Hyde Park where the president had been a vestryman for many years. A simple white marble stone, designed by the president himself, marked the grave in the rose garden at Hyde Park.

Millions listened intently to the radio as descriptions of the funeral train and burial were sent out over the air. The nation mourned a leader, a friend, and, for many, a father figure.

The 33rd, Harry S Truman

The Modest Missourian, 1953–1972

The story of Harry S* Truman (1884–1972) in retirement is the account of how the world's most powerful figure left his high office (in which he served from 1945 to 1953) at 68 years of age, and returned to the small, rural midwestern town where he had spent the first fifty years of his life, as if little had happened except that he had been away from home for 18 years.

Truman and his wife Bess came back to the house at 219 North Delaware Street, Independence, Missouri, that was her mother's home, and where she and Harry had lived together until they went to Washington. The house was almost a century old, large and comfortable. They had never planned to live anywhere else.

High office had sought Harry Truman, not he the Senate or the presidency. Perhaps that is part of the reason the Trumans adjusted so quickly to their old home and community. Harry had come home from World War I and claimed Bess Wallace as his bride, the only girl he was ever seriously interested in. He failed in business and entered politics at the county level. In 1934, Tom Pendergast, the political power of the state of Missouri, chose Truman to be the Democratic candidate for the United States Senate. His selection came as much a surprise to him as it did to the citizens of Missouri. Truman won a close election and spent the next ten years in the Senate where he made a reputation for honesty and efficiency.

In 1944 President Franklin D. Roosevelt chose Senator Truman to be the Democratic vice presidential candidate. The selection of Truman surprised the professional politicians in Washington, for Truman had not been one of FDR's political intimates nor a particularly close personal friend. After less than three months in that office, Vice President Truman was catapulted into the White House by the sudden death of FDR. Truman did not reach the position of chief executive of the nation because of wealth, prestige, or power politics. Yet, after being momentarily stunned, he

*Truman had an initial but no middle name; the "S" is correct with and without a period.

moved into the White House with an inner confidence that surprised most of those who knew him.

Truman was not anxious to retire from his responsibilities. During the years he was in the White House he learned how to thrive in the "hot seat." He really meant it when he said, "The buck stops here." Had he been somewhat younger than his 68 years, it is entirely possible that he might have run for reelection in 1952. Truman was an uncomplicated personality, though neither naive nor simple, who could cut through to the key issues of a problem. He was neither a great intellect nor a charismatic leader, yet he handled the world's largest issues with dispatch. No president loved the practice of politics more than Truman. As he often said, "If you can't stand the heat, get out of the kitchen." Such a man could handle the pressures of 1600 Pennsylvania Avenue when a lesser spirit would have crumbled.

In most respects the Trumans' last days in Washington were happy and satisfying. There were the usual social and governmental functions that come at the end of an administration. The president as well as his wife and daughter Margaret thoroughly enjoyed these occasions. The attitudes of the media and the Washington pundits had noticeably mellowed in their treatment of Truman. Washington had come to like and accept the "little man from Missouri." They were going to miss him and said so.

The sad note in the Truman family's last weeks in Washington was the death in the White House of Mrs. Truman's mother, Margaret Gates Wallace, called "Madge," on December 5, 1952. Bess had taken wonderful care of her mother and had seen to all her needs during her last years. President and Mrs. Truman were both by her bedside when she passed away. At 90 years of age her body had simply worn out.

Packing to move back to 219 North Delaware was no emotional trauma for Harry and Bess. Being the Trumans they took life as it came with a positive, optimistic attitude. Bess was considerably more pleased than her famous husband about leaving the center of national politics. She had never participated in much of the social life of the capital, yet she always graced the position with poise and dignity. The Trumans were packed and ready to move out on January 20, 1953.

One situation marred Truman's last days in the White House—the personal, acrimonious feelings that developed between the incoming president, General Dwight D. Eisenhower, and the outgoing president. During the closing days of the presidential race of 1952, Truman had made a spirited whistle-stop campaign for Adlai Stevenson, the Democratic nominee. As could have been predicted, Truman made a vigorous attack on Eisenhower. In private he bragged that he had "skinned Eisenhower from head to foot."[1] The president attacked Ike's background, claiming that he did not represent the people and that he was guilty of duplicity. It was a direct personal attack filled with Harry's political hyperbole.

After the election of Eisenhower, Harry was ready to forget the campaign. But Ike was so personally offended that for many years he could not forgive Truman for questioning his integrity. Margaret Truman Daniel, the president's daughter, comments in one of her books that Ike's "skin was very thin," that these remarks were only campaign rhetoric and therefore a part of the political process.[2] Perhaps these divergent attitudes are entirely understandable on the part of both men. It was Ike's first campaign and he could not have been expected to hold the same kaleidoscopic view of national politics as did Truman, the veteran campaigner.

Truman wanted a smooth transfer of authority to the incoming administration. Eisenhower did visit Truman in the White House where they discussed the transfer briefly, but the meeting was neither warm nor even friendly. A number of meetings took place between the Eisenhower team and the outgoing administration, but they were not especially productive. At this time Truman distrusted Eisenhower and doubted his ability to govern, and Eisenhower saw Truman as a politician who would say anything to win an election. In large part both were wrong. As a result Ike refused Harry's invitation to lunch at the White House or to accompany Truman to the waiting limousine which was to take them to the inaugural ceremony as is usually done. Truman was furious and Ike icily polite as they rode side by side to the Capitol. On the way Ike told the president that the reason he had not come to Truman's inauguration in 1948 was that he did not want to attract too much attention. Truman, in clipped tones responded, "Ike, I didn't ask you to come – or you'd have been there."[3] The others in the limousine gasped and tried to change the subject.

Truman, experienced politician and realist that he was, did not let his tiff with Eisenhower during the time of the inaugural cloud the satisfaction he gained from the warm send-off he received in Washington. After the inauguration the Trumans went to a farewell luncheon at the Washington home of retiring Secretary of State Dean Acheson. Truman called it a "grand luncheon."[4] At least 500 people were waiting there to cheer the doughty outgoing president. When the Trumans went to the Washington railroad station to board the train that would take them back to Independence, there were 10,000 who had come to say goodbye. When the train stopped in St. Louis 4,000 people greeted them. A crowd of about 10,000 was at the railroad station in Independence, and another 5,000 at the Truman home to welcome them. Harry wrote in his diary, "Mrs. T. and I were overcome. It was the pay-off for thirty years of hell and hard work."[5] The Trumans quickly left the aura of the White House and settled into the routine of life in Independence. The people accepted them as before, with love and affection. As one of the citizens remarked, Truman "never got the big head."[6] Truman spoke to everyone he met, usually calling each by name. He was still interested in the things that were important to his neighbors. When a reporter asked him what he did the first day home, Harry responded, "I took the suitcases to the attic."[7] As yet there was no protection by the Secret Service for former presidents, so the police and the people of Independence assumed the responsibility of security for the family.

Truman obtained a small office in the Federal Reserve Bank of Kansas City where he could handle his large correspondence and begin his writing. Frances Myers and Rose Conway, in addition to the policeman which the city provided, comprised the total staff. Harry habitually went to the office every weekday and on Saturday mornings. When the Truman Library was ready he moved his office there and continued his daily routine until 1969 when age forced him to do most of his work at home. (He was 85 then.) Rose would bring his mail to him and take dictation for the letters he chose to answer. By this time the mail averaged about 40 letters a day. People would often send the former president money, but unless the donor stipulated that the money should go to the Truman Library or the National Democratic Committee, it was returned with thanks.[8]

Truman found it difficult to do such a simple thing as go out for lunch. He attracted so much attention that his lunch was frequently interrupted. Finally he accepted a solution, though not entirely satisfactory to him at first. Some had suggested that he join the Kansas City Club, a private club whose membership was mostly upperclass Republicans. At first he firmly declined, but as no other solution to his problem of eating out presented itself, he said he'd try it. To his surprise he was warmly welcomed by the membership who usually let him eat in uninterrupted peace. The club became a refuge when he did not eat at home or in the library. The idea of having a "brown bag lunch" never appealed to him.

Something of a daily routine developed. At five or five-thirty he arose, took his early morning walk, returned home, read the papers and worked on his mail until a little after seven when Bess came down and fixed breakfast. By eight he had driven to his office and begun the day's work. He would dictate forty or fifty letters and then have his lunch. After the library opened he usually walked the short distance to 219 North Delaware for his lunch. He was back by one or one-thirty to work on his papers and memoirs. At this time of the day he enjoyed reading the *Congressional Record*. As a rule he was home in time for a nap before the evening meal which was served sometime between five-thirty and six. After dinner he and Bess usually sat in their favorite chairs talking, reading, or watching television. Before ten he would be sound asleep.

The Trumans liked simple and substantial meals. When they returned to Independence they basically ate the same kind of food they had in Washington where Bess supervised their private meals and where they ate without uniformed waiters, elaborate place settings, or finger bowls. Of course at state dinners elegant gourmet meals were served. Harry to the end of his life preferred the simple food of the Midwest. When they were in Independence Bess selected the menus and had a hand in preparing the meals. Vietta Garr was a tremendous help to the Trumans in the kitchen, especially when Bess was suffering from arthritis in her hands. Eventually Vietta did most of the cooking.

One of the problems that constantly faced the Trumans was how to maintain their privacy. The several presidents before Truman had encountered the same problem. Herbert Hoover, being independently wealthy, could afford seclusion and private protection. But Woodrow Wilson and Calvin Coolidge, of modest means like Truman, found it hard to cope with the thousands of curious citizens who wanted to get a glimpse of a former president. At times there was danger from those who might do them harm. One mental patient who demanded to see Truman had a .45 revolver in his pocket when stopped by the police at the door of the Truman home.[9]

After coming back to Independence the former president "tried to do as other people did,"[10] but he quickly discovered this was quite impossible. For example, in their first summer of retirement the Trumans planned a motor trip back to Washington. Harry bought a new car and carefully planned the route they would take. Bess was always apprehensive about her husband's driving. She would ask him how fast they were going. He'd usually reply, "Fifty-five." She would then explode and say, "Do you think I'm losing my eyesight? Slow down!"[11] The Truman car would slow down. When motel managers and filling station attendants recognized them, local reporters would soon appear, and their trip was no longer private.

People would drive into the alley behind their house in Independence to get a glimpse of the famous family. When she was home, Margaret would on occasion berate them. Tourists often tried to get a souvenir from the grounds. The former president explained to the family that it was the American way to pick up souvenirs when visiting historic places.[12] While the Trumans were in the White House the government spent $5,400 to install a wrought iron fence around the house and yard in Independence. The family had expected to remove it when they moved back, but they soon found that the fence was still needed. Herbert Hoover had earlier told the president they would need the fence to protect the house.

Strange as it seems today, the federal government provided no protection for ex-presidents and their families until after the assassination of John Kennedy. It was then that the Secret Service men established themselves in a small house across the street from the Trumans. Special closed circuit television kept the home under surveillance on all sides. After Truman died, a Secret Service agent would spend the night seated in one of the downstairs rooms. Bess fought against the idea but was finally persuaded to accept the intrusion upon her privacy.

Though a number of ex-presidents have run into financial difficulty, Truman was never really embarrassed by lack of funds though they had to be conservative in their expenditures. But he found it difficult to keep an office open, to answer the letters that kept coming to him, and to pay for secretarial help out of his own resources. Seventy thousand letters came to the Trumans the first two weeks they were back in Independence. That amount of mail did not continue, but the quantity of mail he received was awe inspiring and expensive to answer. In 1957 the federal government did give aid to ex-presidents in maintaining an office, which was a substantial help to the Trumans. Bess was the one who watched the family finances, but no matter how carefully they tried to conserve, they were beginning to run short of cash before help came from the government.

Truman was offered many lucrative jobs, mostly perfunctory or ceremonial in nature. There was nothing illegal or degrading about these offers, but Truman felt that they were exploiting his name. Consequently he refused most of them. He made a few speeches for which he received compensation, but he did not want to become an itinerant lecturer, so he declined most of these opportunities. Even though the publishers paid Truman $600,000 for his memoirs, he gained comparatively little for his personal needs, for taxes took more than two-thirds of the total. The expense of arranging his papers so he could write his memoirs was considerable, as was the maintenance of his office and the hiring of a secretarial staff. The family was saved from financial embarrassment when a developer purchased the Truman farm and turned it into a shopping center. When Congress finally remembered the needs of former presidents, the family never again felt the pressure of insufficient funds.

No doubt Truman's chief interest after leaving the White House was his family. A quick look through his papers shows something of the care and attention that he and Bess gave their family. As well as taking care of her mother during her last days, Bess had repeatedly helped an alcoholic brother. Harry looked equally well after his own mother. Both mothers on several occasions visited the White House at the same time. Harry's mother died at the Truman farm home in 1947. Harry's sister Mary Jane, at past 80 years of age, insisted on living alone in her own home in Independence. His brother Vivian also lived in the community. They were a very compatible and close-knit family.

Harry and Bess had been "going together" for many years before they married in 1919. Harry had worked on the family farm helping his parents to remain financially solvent. When they might have married, World War I took Truman overseas and postponed the wedding. Harry wanted Bess to meet him in New York so they could be married immediately when he landed from France after the war, but Bess wanted a church wedding. Several weeks after his ship landed in New York the wedding took place.

Their marriage was filled with love, and life was a joint enterprise. No breath of scandal ever involved either of the Trumans. Both were positive, strong personalities, but they kept their differences to a minimum. Harry gives considerable credit to Bess for his success. In his memoirs he wrote, "I owe a debt of gratitude to Mrs. T. on whose counsel and judgment I frequently called." Near the end of their life together Bess burned all of Harry's letters to her. He was rather surprised and told her to think of history. Bess' tart response was, "I have."[13]

The Trumans' affection for their only child Margaret was obvious. How Harry wrote "hot" personal letters in his own hand to those who criticized Margaret's talents when she considered a professional career as a singer, is well recorded. The president knew his staff would never mail these letters so he wrote them himself and personally mailed them. They have become collectors' items and have brought high prices when placed on sale. Margaret had real talent, but was probably more suited for roles in musical comedy, for her sense of timing as a comedienne was superb. Although she did not regularly live at home after the president retired, the close relationship between parents and daughter continued.

The parents were delighted when Margaret married Clifton Daniel, an editor of the *New York Times*. Margaret and Clifton soon gratified her parents' wish for a grandchild. The day after Clifton Truman Daniel, their first of four grandsons was born, the proud grandparents were on a train headed for New York to greet the newest member of the family. All of the grandchildren were a real joy to the Trumans, though the long hairstyles of the grandsons did bother Harry and Bess at times. On occasion the grandparents "babysat" to let the Daniels get a little vacation together. More often than not the Daniels spent the Christmas holidays at 219 North Delaware.

The first major task the former president attempted after retirement was writing his memoirs. Truman had brought his personal papers back to Missouri and quickly began to supervise their organization by date and topic. Never would he tolerate others to ghostwrite, for he wanted his own style of rapid movement, cheerfulness and optimism to be reflected in his writing. Though he dictated the first draft himself, some polishing was done by a trio of editors and researchers. He remarked, "I want to fix things so they'll have my thoughts instead of their own." He added, "The lies [about his administration] are beginning to be solidified and made into historical facts. Let's head them off now while we can. The truth is all I want for history."[14] Truman, of course, thought he had the truth. Perhaps he did more often than not.

The memoirs were published in two volumes by Doubleday, *Year of Decision* in 1955, and *Years of Trial and Hope* in 1956. The work basically showed Truman's clear command of the language and expressed his point of view. Though he spent a disproportionate amount of time on the early part of his administration, the books sold well and are invaluable to anyone researching that period of American history.

The Truman Library occupied the majority of his time after he finished his memoirs. Since no governmental program exists for the building or the funding of presidential libraries, each one must be built by those interested in that particular president. The first problems Truman faced were the funding of the library, finding the best possible location, and making plans for the building itself. Truman's friends held benefit dinners all over the country as fund-raisers for the library, and he attended a number of them himself as the principal speaker. Many admirers and friends of means made substantial contributions to the fund. Altogether about $2 million was raised, some from thousands of citizens across the nation who contributed small sums for the project.

Several sites were considered for the library. Some wanted it to be built at Kansas City University in Kansas City, Missouri. The University of Missouri in Columbia made a very attractive offer in an effort to get the library placed on their campus. Most felt that the library should be close to Truman's home. At first he thought of building it on the old Truman farm at Grandview and even considered restoring the old farm house and moving there to live. Finally the question was solved when the city of Independence offered to donate a large part of Slover Park, a city park, for the library. To make the site more usable, an entire block adjacent to the park was purchased for $100,000. This additional land enabled the library itself to be placed on a slight rise of land, and provided more adequate space for parking as well as for the beautification of the surrounding area. This site satisfied all of the requirements for the library. Also, it was close to 219 North Delaware, near enough for the aging former president to walk to his office in the library most of the time. Perhaps more importantly it was easily accessible for tourists and interested citizens as they traveled through the area.

The ground breaking ceremony was held on Truman's seventy-first birthday, May 8, 1955. There were 150 invited guests, all of whom were asked to attend an old-fashioned country dinner at the Truman home. Bess made all the plans and arrangements for the dinner which consisted of smoked ham and turkey, vegetables, and of course hot biscuits. The guests ate on tables set up on the lawn. Fortunately the weather was beautiful.

Truman supervised every detail of the library plans. Thomas Hart Benton, the famous artist, drew a magnificent mural for the lobby. One room is a replica of the Oval Office during the Truman administration, another is dedicated to the World War I mementos of Captain Truman and Battery D as well as to the remembrance of the soldiers who fought in that war. All the official gifts to the president during the Truman administration from foreign nations and their representatives are housed in the library. One of the former president's autos helps to tell the Truman story. Included in the plans was an adequate auditorium, for Truman liked to talk to students — high school as well as college — about the American presidency, the Constitution, and the history of America. The library buildings surround a patio in which the bodies of Harry and Bess are buried.

The dedication ceremony was held on July 6, 1957, with Eleanor Roosevelt as the principal speaker. Some Baptist friends of the former president were concerned that a Catholic archbishop was selected to perform the actual dedication. Harry felt the occasion should not be sectarian, so in addition to a Protestant minister, Rabbi Thurman was invited to take part in the laying of the cornerstone. The library was turned over to the General Services Administration and is operated by the National Archives and Records Services of the federal government.

Truman's involvement in politics was lifelong — at times a passion — and continued in the closing days of his administration and into retirement. Although he was leaving the presidency, Truman took great interest in who would succeed him in the White House and looked for a suitable Democrat who could be elected in November of 1952.

Early he thought that Governor Adlai Stevenson of Illinois would make an ideal choice for the Democrats, but the governor was a reluctant candidate at best. He waited so long to show any real interest in the presidency that when the Democrats met in the sweltering heat of Chicago, the convention seemed leaderless. Only when Truman and Jim Farley arrived was there any real direction. The convention quickly nominated Stevenson with apparent enthusiasm, but Stevenson's campaign was run by amateurs. Stevenson completely changed the top personnel of the party and asked for no help from the president until late in the campaign. In fact he studiedly ignored Truman.

The fighting instinct in the president was aroused. Truman wrote a pointed letter to Stevenson saying, "I have come to the conclusion that you are embarrassed by having the President of the United States in your corner in this campaign.... Since the convention you have treated the President as a liability.... I have tried to make it plain to you that I want you elected.... But I can't stand snub after snub by you...." He further stated that he would go to the dedication of the Hungry Horse dam in Montana, make a speech, return to Washington and stay there.[15] Fortunately or not, at the last moment he did not mail the letter, but it is contained in his papers and clearly indicates how he felt.

When Stevenson mishandled a question put to him by a reporter from the *Oregon Journal* asking him if he could "clean up the mess in Washington," the Democratic candidate naively replied that he had cleaned up a mess in Illinois and he would do the same in Washington.[16]

The president was indignant, especially when Stevenson openly confessed that he had never wanted "the nomination and received it without commitments to anyone about anything — including President Truman."[17] Harry wrote a scorcher of a letter to Stevenson which he likewise did not mail but included in his papers. Like the good party man that he was, the president did not publicly express his feelings, and when belatedly requested, worked effectively in a "whistle-stop campaign" for the election of Stevenson.

In 1956 Truman was again upset because Stevenson showed so little interest in the Democratic nomination for the presidency. As a result, Harry openly supported Averell Harriman prior to the convention, but backed Stevenson when it became obvious that he had the necessary votes for the nomination. Harry's foray into Democratic politics bothered Bess. She got in touch with Tom Evans, a mutual friend who was at the convention and said, "Can't you do something to stop Harry? He's making a fool of himself."[18]

In 1960 Truman did not approve of the candidacy of John F. Kennedy, whose father he felt had bought the nomination for him, and asked Kennedy bluntly if he was ready for the presidency and if the country was ready for him. When the nomination went to JFK, Truman gave his full support to the handsome senator from Massachusetts. However, when Kennedy invited Lyndon Baines Johnson to be his vice presidential running mate, Truman strongly advised Johnson not to accept the nomination. For once Harry had not read the political winds correctly, but as always he backed the ticket and seemed happy about it. No doubt Truman's antipathy to Republican Richard Nixon made JFK's narrow victory all the sweeter.

Kennedy appreciated Truman's endorsement, for he had badly needed it in the cliffhanger contest with Nixon in November of 1960. The new president showed how he felt by immediately inviting the Truman family to be guests at the White House. The Trumans were pleased, for they had not stepped foot in the executive mansion for eight years. The visit seemed something of a vindication, especially when a Democrat was again in the Oval Office. When the dynamic young president was assassinated, Truman was greatly distressed. He recognized that JFK had had a rough time during the early days of his administration, but by the fall of 1963 felt that Kennedy was getting affairs in hand. The blow of JFK's death was somewhat lessened by Truman's confidence in the person and ability of Lyndon Johnson, the new president, who was a longtime friend. Within a few hours after LBJ took the oath of office he phoned Harry. Johnson visited the Trumans in Independence half a dozen times, and they were also his guests in the White House.

Harry Truman still had disdain and contempt for Republicans in general, Eisenhower and Nixon in particular. In a letter he referred to them as "Alibi Ike" and "Tricky Dick." On another occasion he called Nixon a "squirrel head."[19] Somewhat later the rift between Ike and Harry was repaired, although the hard feelings toward Nixon were only partially healed.

Harry and Ike did "bury the hatchet," if late in their lives. The rapprochement was no doubt sincere on the part of both men. Eisenhower called Truman, telling him that he was going to be in Kansas City in a few days and felt it might be a good idea if they "would negotiate a truce."[20] The aging former president was ready to forget the past bitterness between the two, and invited Ike to come to the library for a visit. They chatted pleasantly and both appeared to feel pleased that they had ended their misunderstanding. Ike was impressed by the Truman Library and sought advice as to how he might do something of the sort himself. Their reconciliation came none too soon, for in about a week they sat side by side on the front row of a little Baptist church in Texas at the funeral of Speaker Sam Rayburn. A rather famous picture was taken of Truman, Eisenhower, Kennedy and Johnson seated together during the funeral service.

Later there was further evidence of a genuine rapprochement. The morning of JFK's funeral Ike called Harry at the Blair House in Washington, where Harry and his daughter Margaret were staying, and suggested that he and Mamie stop by to take them to the cathedral for the funeral service. Ike waited on the phone while Admiral Robert L. Dennison, a former naval aide to Truman, went to ask Harry if that was agreeable. Truman gave instant assent. Neither the Eisenhowers nor the Trumans went to the graveside service, so when Harry was getting out of the limousine at the Blair House, he invited Ike and Mamie to come in for some refreshments. The Eisenhowers accepted, and soon they were, according to Admiral Dennison, "talking animatedly. They just kept on having another drink and talking. I thought it would never end . . . you'd think there had never been any differences between them."[21]

The Trumans traveled to Europe twice in retirement. They also visited Hawaii, enjoying the weather, the ocean and the people. The famous couple often visited New York, especially after Margaret's marriage. They visited Washington, St. Louis, Chicago and other major cities as well. On occasion the Trumans spent vacations in Key West, Florida, where Margaret and her family would visit them. Travel was an enjoyable interlude in the routine they had established in Independence.

In general the Trumans enjoyed good health. However, both of them had a few bouts with illness. In June of 1954 while they were watching a performance of the musical "Call Me Madam" in Kansas City, the former president became quite ill. His earliest symptoms were nausea and chest pains. Their personal physician, Dr. Wallace Graham, diagnosed the illness as an infected gall bladder which was successfully removed. Truman, now age 70, recovered very well except for a negative reaction to some of the medication. However, he was far from the ideal, long-suffering compliant patient. Bess for the first time allowed an air conditioner in the house to make Harry's recovery more pleasant. She had it installed in Harry's downstairs bedroom. The former president was not entirely sure he wanted one, but it proved to be very helpful.

In 1958 a tumor was discovered in Bess' left breast. She put off the surgery until she could attend the salute to Harry's seventieth birthday by the Democratic party in New York. She also wanted to see her second grandson for the first time. She then had the surgery. To the great relief of everyone, the growth was benign and successfully removed.

Early in 1963 Truman began to experience discomfort in his abdomen. The physicians diagnosed an intestinal hernia and immediate surgery was performed. For a man of 79 years he withstood the procedure amazingly well.

The former president had two falls in which he suffered broken ribs. He was upset at himself for the accidents. The first fall occurred more than a year after his gall bladder surgery when he slipped on some ice on the sidewalk as he was taking his morning constitutional. It was then that Bess laid down the law: no more morning walks if there was ice or snow on the sidewalks. Margaret commented, "For once he obeyed."[22] In his eightieth year he fell in the bathroom and fractured two ribs, broke his glasses and cut his eyebrow. His recovery time was somewhat longer than for his first fall.

By the end of 1970 those close to the former president began to notice that his health had discernibly deteriorated. No longer could he regularly take the early morning walks that he enjoyed so much. He moved about the house more slowly, read less, and took more time when he expressed himself. But he retained his optimism and found life a joy. By this time those who were allowed to visit him were from the group of close friends that had stayed in touch with him through the years. He still enjoyed his food, reading, television, and especially talking to Bess and his friends.

Though no immediate life-threatening physical ailment confronted him, health problems arose. He had occasional vertigo, his arthritis continued to give him pain, and his energy level had greatly declined. He no longer went to the library on a regular basis.

When he was 88 the doctors discovered some congestion in his lungs and he was hospitalized on December 5, 1972. At first he showed signs of improvement, but his heart was weakening and he developed cardiac instability from which he never recovered. Bess stayed with him at the hospital until her strength was almost gone and the family became concerned about her health. Bess spent all of Christmas Eve and most of the next day with her husband. Finally, on Christmas night Margaret insisted that her mother come home for a good night's sleep. By this time Harry had slipped into a coma. At almost eight o'clock in the morning of the day after Christmas, Dr. Graham called the home and told the family that the first citizen of Independence had slipped away.

The whole nation paid homage to Truman's memory. Hours of television time were devoted to his achievements as president, while messages of condolence came to the family from all over the world. President and Mrs. Nixon came personally to Independence and called on Bess and the family, as did Lyndon and Lady Bird Johnson. Thousands of his fellow Missourians stood in line for long periods, some for six hours, to pass by the casket as it lay in state in the library.

The final service in Independence was short and simple. Much more elaborate services are usually held when a former president is buried. Army officials had worked out an elegant five-day tribute to Truman which called for the body to lie in state in the rotunda of the Capitol in Washington. Mrs. Truman, as well as her daughter Margaret and son-in-law Clifton Daniel, declined the offer for they wanted a much simpler kind of tribute to their husband and father. They were very sure that was what Harry would have preferred.

Only 250 people could crowd into the auditorium of the library, so the family selected that number of guests. The body of the former president was laid to rest on the grounds of the library. Bess and Margaret stood the ordeal well, but all could see how moved they were, especially when the flag that had been draped over the casket was presented to the family according to army protocol. The old battery of Truman's service days, Battery D of the 129th Field Artillery, fired a 21-gun salute. The nation had paid its final tribute to a famous leader.

Only two presidents had lived longer—Herbert Hoover and John Adams. The Trumans lived together 53 years, the Adamses a few months longer—the only presidential couple to be married longer. The Truman record is all the more remarkable when it is remembered that he was 35 and Bess but a few months younger when they were married. Harry S Truman led an active life for just a few weeks short of 20 years after leaving the presidency. Only four presidents survived longer after leaving office— Herbert Hoover, John Adams, Martin Van Buren, and Millard Fillmore.

The 34th, Dwight D. Eisenhower

The General's Faltering Heart, 1961–1969

Few presidents have been so sure of their ability to do any task they attempted, so willing to make hard but necessary decisions, or enjoyed the office as much as did Dwight David Eisenhower (1890–1969). He was not eager to leave the presidency (1953–1961), as so many have who lived in the White House. But after fifty years given to military, educational, and governmental service, he looked forward to a time in which he could enjoy private life. He had been confident that he could win a war or direct the affairs of a great nation, and his innate talents and ability seemed equal to the challenges.

Probably no president in modern times has displayed such a range of activities in retirement as Eisenhower. Interestingly, he chose to begin his post-presidency years by purchasing a working farm in southeastern Pennsylvania, taking an active interest in agriculture and animal husbandry. Also, his continuing career as a writer, after his success with *Crusade in Europe,* attracted national recognition. He wrote three more major works, as well as many magazine articles, and as a speaker his schedule was full but selective. He spent what leisure time he had painting, golfing, hunting and fishing, and playing bridge, of which he was a strong player. While his scheduled activities filled most of his time, he was able to keep in constant contact with his close inner circle of friends. Yet his family came first in his attention and affection.

The last summer of Eisenhower's tenure in the White House tested his basic optimism and patience. His greatest problem was Nikita Khrushchev. When the Russians shot down the U-2 high altitude reconnaissance plane over Russia, the scheduled Paris summit with Khrushchev collapsed, and with it any hope of real progress toward disarmament. From his base in Cuba, Fidel Castro, with Russia's backing, was responsible for a high level of hemispheric tension. Disturbances in Africa and the Near East troubled the president. The Congo crisis sent shock waves all through Africa. The United States was stretched to its limit in trying to stop Communist advances in many parts of the world. Eisenhower had planned a trip to Moscow and Tokyo, but both of these were cancelled — the Russian trip because of the U-2 incident, and the Japanese visit because of the riots over Japan's signing of the mutual-defense treaty with the United States.

At home the Democratic victory in the November election of 1960 embarrassed the president. There is no doubt that Eisenhower wanted to see Richard Nixon succeed him in office, but his strategy was flawed from the beginning. He fumbled his support for Nixon before the convention, and afterward probably delayed too long his campaigning for the vice president. Even in his speeches he seemed more interested in showing the achievements of his own Republican administration than in selling Nixon to the voters. In any case, the president was keenly disappointed by the narrow Kennedy victory, almost feeling it was a repudiation of him personally, although the public opinion polls certainly did not indicate any erosion of his own popularity.

Following the election he took a short golfing vacation in Augusta, Georgia, and seemed to recover from his disappointment. While he still gave close attention to his duties as chief executive, he determined to begin no new programs or initiate any legislation which would bind the hands of President-elect Kennedy. In a real sense he presided over a caretaker government during his last three months in office.

Any president's final days in office are extremely busy, Eisenhower's were no exception. The newly-elected president, Senator John F. Kennedy, came to the White House for a long conference in order to make arrangements for the orderly transfer of the office of president. They discussed a wide range of subjects. Eisenhower was pleased at the way Kennedy grasped the scope of national and international problems. In fact, the president liked his successor personally much better than he had anticipated. It was here that the incoming president learned about the "bag man," the man who carried the device that could launch a military counterattack, the man who would shadow the president all through his administration. The day before the inauguration, Kennedy came to the White House for a long briefing session. That morning foreign affairs was the chief topic of conversation. When the young president-elect arrived, the aging Eisenhower waited hatless under the north portico to welcome Senator Kennedy to the executive mansion, though it was a cold, snowy day. The president carried this cordiality to the last moment. When the Kennedys and the Johnsons came to the White House before the inauguration ceremony, President Eisenhower invited them in for coffee.

Farewell parties and receptions were a part of the process that inevitably precedes a change of administrations. The Christmas party for the staff, White House employees, and advisors, was a warm and festive affair. The president gave everyone a color reproduction of one of his paintings as a memento of the evening. The Republican senators hosted a farewell reception for the president, as did the top military officials at the Pentagon. After their last meeting, the cabinet reenacted the traditional ceremony of presenting the chief executive with the chair he had used in presiding over their meetings. As commander-in-chief of the armed services, Eisenhower bid goodbye to the army in an emotional last review of the troops at Fort Gordon in Georgia. A weekend of golf at Augusta National Golf Course followed.[1] In mid-January the Eisenhowers spent a weekend in their home at Gettysburg arranging for their arrival there on January 20. At about the same time the president had written a letter to all the members of "the gang," as he called his close circle of friends, and asked them again to call him "Ike," his old nickname.

Eisenhower decided against delivering his last State of the Union address in person. At the suggestion of his good friend Norman Cousins,[2] he decided to deliver a farewell address to the nation on television and radio.[3] Not only did he say goodbye to the people of the land, he also discussed some of his concerns for the future of the nation, reminding them that they faced hostile ideologies, that they needed to protect the environment, and that decency in human relationships was vital to the integrity of the nation. However, the part of his address that caught the most attention was his warning of the danger of an ever increasingly powerful military industrial complex. If left unchecked, he felt, it could become a growing threat to the future of America.

He held his last press conference on January 18, 1961, the 193rd he had conducted in his years as president. In general the press and the president had gotten along well, and the reporters cheered him as the conference ended.

In January, under the leadership of Sam Rayburn, speaker of the House, and Lyndon Johnson, within days of concluding his career as majority leader of the Senate, the Congress restored Eisenhower's rank as a five-star general of the army. Aside from giving him an enormous boost in morale, it gave him the use of all the army medical resources as long as he lived.

Eisenhower viewed his final day in office with some misgiving. As he saw the platform for the reviewing stands being constructed in front of the White House he commented, "It's like being in the death cell and watching them put up the scaffold."[4] And there were some genuine apprehensions as to the direction the new administration might take, especially in the areas of a balanced budget and foreign policy.

However, his innate optimism exerted itself as he left the White House, and he looked forward to a bright future for the nation. The Eisenhower-Kennedy transfer of power was one of the most cordial ever seen in Washington. Eisenhower seemed cheerful as he saw John F. Kennedy take the oath of office. This was Kennedy's moment, so after the inauguration, the Eisenhowers quietly retreated to the F Street Club in Washington, where the Lewis Strausses hosted a farewell luncheon for the outgoing president. His car then took the now private couple over the very familiar route from Washington through the towns of Rockville, Frederick, Thurmont, Emmitsburg, and on to the Gettysburg farm entrance. The former president got out of the car and opened the gate himself.

January 20, 1961, had seen the oldest man who had served as president to that time succeeded by the youngest man ever to be elected to the presidency. The outgoing president was one of only four chief executives since Andrew Jackson, 124 years before, who was elected twice and who served two full consecutive terms in the White House. Of these four, Grant, Wilson, Franklin Roosevelt, and Eisenhower, only Roosevelt and Eisenhower left the presidency more popular than when they came into office.

However, the move to Gettysburg meant more of an adjustment to Ike than he expected. He himself had not placed a telephone call in the past twenty years. The first time he picked up the phone at the farm in Gettysburg he still expected to hear the voice of an operator say "Number, please."[5] He literally yelled for his Secret Service agent and then learned how to place a call. He hadn't driven a car since he left the states to fight Hitler. After some difficulty, he obtained a Pennsylvania driver's license, but never felt at home behind the wheel of a car. However, he had no difficulty in driving his motorized golf cart. The new experiences were challenging—shopping in a supermarket, going to a laundromat, visiting a modern drugstore, making travel arrangements for himself. He had no idea how to make a reservation or buy a train or airplane ticket, how to adjust a television set, or how to use the strange intricacies of the credit card system. And he never did learn the knack of determining how much cash he should have with him.

The house on the Gettysburg farm was a rural, square, two-story frame dwelling, typical of its day, and took considerable effort and money to change into a home fit for an ex-president. The renovated house had a colonial appearance on the outside, but all the modern conveniences inside. When it was completed it had spacious living quarters with guest rooms, porches, a sun room, space for Ike's paintings, work rooms for both Mamie and Ike, as well as space for large groups to gather. It was in an ideal location for the Eisenhowers, near Washington and New York City, and near the place Ike's ancestors had settled after coming to America from Europe. Only in the coldest part of the winter was the weather inhospitable.

When the Eisenhowers bought the estate it contained 246 acres of land. Soon Ike leased another 305 acres in order to more than double the working capacity of the farm. He hoped to improve the soil's fertility by establishing grazing land for the cattle, and by rotating the crops, which included barley, sorghum, soybeans, hay, corn, and oats. Ordinarily he kept more than 100 head of Angus cattle to sell for beef, and on occasion twice this number. He kept a few Holstein cows to nurse the calves. At times he sold a few of the best animals for breeding, but only the best, for Ike wanted to protect the reputation of the farm. A few dogs and riding horses completed the animal population of the estate. He usually employed about nine farm workers. In all likelihood the farm never earned a profit for its owner. The first several years it lost money, but the cash flow improved.

In the first several years of retirement, Ike spent more time in activities away from Gettysburg than on the farm. In the cold months the Eisenhowers went to California, and to Augusta, Georgia, with its famous golf course. Ike was again and again drawn to the hunting lodges, streams and lakes of North America, as well as to Europe, the scene of his wartime years.

Mamie did very little of the cooking at Gettysburg. She explained that as a girl she had never been allowed in the kitchen, so she never learned to cook. However, Ike enjoyed cooking and was often in the kitchen. When "the gang" was there he usually had a hand in preparing the food. Even in the White House, Ike would putter around the kitchen as a means of relaxing, often enlisting the White House staff to help eat what he had cooked.

Ike's own family was poor, and Mamie did not inherit wealth, so what money they had acquired came from savings and investments, and from his military pay. Even as a five-star general, Ike was not a man of wealth. By the time he became president his holdings were still relatively modest, but were effectively managed in a blind trust so there would never be a conflict of interest. Royalties from his best-seller, *Crusade in Europe,* made up the major portion of his monies. When retirement came, he was comfortably secure, and his farm at Gettysburg was paid for. (It is probable that some friends did help in buying this property.) The *U.S. News and World Report* of July 18, 1960, carried an article that estimated Ike's yearly income in retirement at just under $30,000, which included his pension and interest on investments.

He had the option of receiving a presidential pension or the salary of a five-star general. He chose the presidential pension, which included an office and a small staff, plus the mailing privilege. But he kept his military rank. He also had the use of "Mamie's Cabin," a cottage on the Augusta National Golf Course in Georgia. In all likelihood the winter quarters of the Eisenhowers in Palm Springs and Palm Desert cost them very little out-of-pocket money. The income from speech making and from his writings — magazine articles and three books — added substantially to his fixed income. Thus the general had few financial worries.

Ike needed an office in Gettysburg and was able to obtain the former campus home of the president of Gettysburg College. It was a stately stone structure about the size and location Ike wanted. Here he supervised his immense correspondence and did most of his writing in an upstair bedroom which was especially equipped for his needs. It was in this building that Eisenhower received most of his visitors. Only intimate friends or important guests were entertained at the farm. His work day began shortly before eight o'clock and ended before four-thirty.

In making plans for retirement, the writing of his memoirs became a high priority. His purpose in writing the story of his administration was to let the American people see exactly what happened from his point of view, and to demonstrate that he was aware of the problems facing the nation and had taken the proper steps to handle them. His son John, a career army officer, left the military service and directed the research needed for Eisenhower to write his presidential memoirs. He also supervised the revising and assembling of the manuscripts, leaving the writing to the former president. Most of the large publishing houses were anxious to secure the rights to the memoirs, but because of personal friendship, Douglas Black obtained the manuscript for Doubleday. Eisenhower was offered a million dollars for his memoirs. Taxes took about half of this, but the money that was left would be needed in the next few years.

Ike arranged to have his church membership transferred from the National Presbyterian Church of Washington to the First Presbyterian Church of Gettysburg. The *New York Times* ran the story on page one of their January 22, 1961, issue. When he had taken the oath of office on January 20, 1953, Eisenhower did not belong to any church, but a few days later, on February 1, 1953, he was baptized, made a confession of faith, and was received into the membership of the National Presbyterian Church of Washington — the only president to join a church for the first time while in office. Mrs. Eisenhower joined that church at the same time by letter of transfer, as she had been a lifelong Presbyterian.

Eisenhower was brought up by very devout parents who were part of a pacifist group called the River Brethren, whose roots went back to the European Pietists. As a boy he went to church with his family, but when Ike was in the army, he seldom attended church services. As he explained, this did not mean he did not have a belief in God, but the dogma of theology never interested him. He said his was a felt religion, not one reached through his intellect.[6] The Eisenhowers regularly attended the National Presbyterian Church in Washington, and he took an active interest in the building campaign when the church was enlarged.

In Gettysburg he was a regular church attendant when he was in the city. The writer interviewed the Rev. Robert H. MacAskill, who was pastor of the Gettysburg church at the time the Eisenhowers were in attendance there. He pictured Eisenhower as a devout man "with a strong faith in divine providence." The pastor pointed out the pew which the Eisenhowers occupied during worship services. Ike and Mamie sat just two rows back of the pew that Abraham Lincoln sat in when he attended worship in that church just before he made the famed Gettysburg Address in 1863. Both of these pews are clearly marked, and no one is permitted to use these seats. The pastor told of the active part Ike took as a member of the building committee when the church was renovated.

The writer heard the Rev. Dr. Billy Graham speak of General Eisenhower's faith[7] and tell of being invited to call at Walter Reed hospital shortly before the former president died. Eisenhower was interested in talking of heaven.

Ike had taken up painting as a means of relaxation during the vexing pressures of the presidency. While never a great artist, he seemed to have some talent. Among his best works are those which reflect the beauty he found in the European mountains and landscapes. Even when he tried to discard some of his less favorite pieces, miraculously they seemed to survive the garbage can and turn up in art shops for sale without his knowledge.

Ike was an excellent bridge player and enjoyed the game immensely, but golf was his best-loved hobby. Bob Hope was one of his favorite golfing companions, although he often golfed with many other celebrities. Word got around that on his better days he would shoot in the middle 80s. However, his scores were a well-guarded state secret. One of the better parts of his game was his short game. When he was near the green he often got "up and down" in two strokes. He participated in many charitable golf exhibitions.

Ike had great love for his family, and his activities reflected that. Seven boys were born to his parents, David Jacob and Ida Stover Eisenhower of Abilene, Kansas. One son, Paul, died in infancy; another, Roy, died of natural causes while World War II was in progress. Arthur, oldest of the boys, died while Ike was in office. When Ike left the presidency, he had three living brothers, Edgar, Earl, and Milton. Ike was probably closest to Milton, who was president of Johns Hopkins University, and who had often been an advisor to Ike during his term as chief executive.

Dwight Eisenhower, as a young career army officer, married Geneva (Mamie) Doud of Denver on July 1, 1916. He was 26 and she 19. They spent most of their lives together on army posts, and whenever possible she accompanied him on his various assignments. His diary is full of accounts of their activities. According to fellow army officers and their wives, Ike and Mamie got along well together. The young Eisenhowers had a son, Doud Dwight (Icky), born to them September 24, 1917, but he died of scarlet fever January 2, 1921, at Camp Meade, Maryland. His death was "probably the most tragic occurrence of Eisenhower's life."[8]

John Sheldon Doud Eisenhower, their second son, was born in 1923 in Denver, and spent his early years on army posts around the world. Young Eisenhower married Barbara Thompson at Fort Monroe, Virginia, in 1947, who became more like a daughter than a daughter-in-law to the Eisenhowers. When the Eisenhowers moved to Gettysburg, John helped to manage most of his father's business affairs.

Ike and Mamie spent much time with their four grandchildren. John and Barbara's three daughters often stayed for days with Ike and Mamie at Gettysburg. The grandchild most in the news was Ike's namesake, Dwight David Eisenhower II. Often Ike would take his grandson fishing. On one occasion while in office the president went to a sporting goods store to outfit his grandson for stream fishing. When the two had made their selection of items to purchase, a Secret Service agent picked up the packages, and the three started out of the store with the fishing gear. The nonplussed salesman did not know what to do, as nothing was said about paying the bill. Merriman Smith, a veteran newsman and White House watcher, was present and hastened to inform the clerk that the president never carried money or had a credit card, but that "if the bill was sent to the White House it would be paid."[9] Ike and young David spent many hours together fishing, playing golf, skeet shooting, and watching sports on television.

One of the most-followed romances in the nation was that between young David Eisenhower and Julie Nixon, daughter of Richard and Pat Nixon. Ike and Mamie watched the wedding by closed circuit television from his room at Walter Reed Army Hospital on December 22, 1968.[10]

Writing his memoirs, *The White House Years,* published in two volumes — *Mandate for Change* and *Waging Peace* — occupied much of Eisenhower's time and energy in retirement. He sought to point out that it was he, not his staff, who made the important decisions in the White House. Certainly those closely associated with the work of the White House realized that the president made his own decisions. The memoirs give a detailed account of his eight-year presidency. Reviewers found few misstatements of fact. Ike refused to evade most controversial issues such as the U-2 incident. However, some felt that he may have been deliberately brief and nondefinitive about his realtionship with communist-hunter Senator Joseph McCarthy, and in his discussions of nuclear testing and disarmament. Ike admitted his mistakes as a general when he wrote *Crusade in Europe,* but in the material on his White House years, few such admissions are to be found.

Mandate for Change reached the second spot on the best-seller list following its publication in 1963. *Waging Peace* was published in October, 1965. The *New York Times* had planned to publish excerpts from the book, but a newspaper strike intervened, so Ike held a press conference to publicize his book.[11] Ike's memoirs did not have the salty comments of Truman's, but they sold well and filled an important place in the understanding of American history.

Ike also wrote a very readable informal biography that he called *At Ease: Stories I Tell to Friends,* which received excellent reviews and sold well. In it a great American had shown his humanity. In *Life* magazine, John Steele tells how Ike started the book with a "list of 150 incidents that came to his mind." Recognizing that he was one of the outstanding figures of his time, Ike wanted to give some insight into his personal life. The same article describes the ex-president, "His face, still ruddy and pleasant, has retained that remarkable quality of reflecting so quickly his likes and dislikes. His eyes are clear and live, and his easy twangy voice rings loud and strong. He laughs with gusto. His enthusiasm bubbles forth."[12] Ike was 75 at the time.

The Eisenhower Library and Museum were officially dedicated early in May of 1962. The structure is plain in design, but possesses an elegance in the quiet setting of Abilene, Kansas. The Eisenhowers rode to the dedication in a private railroad car, and found thirty thousand people there to greet them. Ike was tanned, relaxed, and happy. The pageantry included cowboys, bands and an infantry parade. Vice President Lyndon Johnson, representing President Kennedy, came, as did many of Ike's White House officials. When the former president spoke, he praised the traditional values of America, and expresseed optimism for the future of the nation.

Eisenhower's participation in Republican politics began when he announced his availability as a presidential candidate in 1952, and continued throughout his post-presidential years. His outspoken views regarding government were well known — a balanced budget, adequate protection from outside enemies, morality in high office, true democracy, and the government's responsibility for all citizens.

When Nixon lost to Kennedy in 1960, Nixon did not seize control of the Republican party machinery. This left Ike in a particularly strategic position to influence the party, though he refrained from attempting to seize control of the Republican organization. Eisenhower did not agree with the so-called "old guard," feeling they were not moving with the times. However, he had the good sense to keep the infighting behind closed doors. After leaving the White House Ike tried to move some of his party to a more moderate position, and in an effort to do so organized a group called Republican Citizens, but it never influenced the party as he had hoped it would. Some accused him of trying to form a third party, but such allegations were unfounded. Eisenhower could have had an enormous political influence on the party, but he chose to use his prestige sparingly.

In the 1964 election Ike was not enthusiastic about either of the two leading Republican candidates, Senator Barry Goldwater or Governor

Nelson Rockefeller, but led no movement at the convention, and supported Goldwater when he was nominated. In 1968 it was a different matter. Ike strongly supported Richard Nixon, and publicly endorsed him. During the years of Eisenhower's retirement, he often spoke at Republican fund-raising events, and repeatedly came to the aid of Republican candidates whom he felt needed and deserved his support.

Both Kennedy and Johnson kept Ike regularly informed concerning matters of foreign affairs and the military, and Ike gave unstintingly of his time in advising them both when they requested it. During the Cuban missile crisis, Kennedy relied on Eisenhower's advice. On President Johnson's fifty-seventh birthday, Ike spent four hours with him and his top advisors discussing Vietnam. One writer maintained, "[Johnson] comes away from meetings with Ike convinced that Ike is a 'better general than my generals and a better diplomat than my diplomats'."[13] Ike was proving to be the elder statesman of his day.

When Eisenhower had his first major heart attack in the fall of 1955, his doctors had told him that he could run for a second term as president and even suggested that he had ten good active years ahead of him.[14] At the time Eisenhower left the White House in 1961, his physicians found him in excellent health. In November of 1965 when Ike was in Augusta for a week of golf, he remarked to Mamie that the ten-year period the doctors had promised him was up. The next day, while he was in "Mamie's Cabin," he suffered his second major heart attack. He was rushed to nearby Fort Gordon Military Hospital, and later moved to Walter Reed Army Hospital in Washington. He responded well to treatment and was home in Gettysburg by Christmas.

Between January 1961 and this second heart attack in Augusta, Eisenhower was admitted to Walter Reed 11 times. Each time the hospital used the word "check-up" to describe his visits, but no major illness was identified. However, after January 1966, Eisenhower began to experience major medical problems and was gradually forced to curtail his activities, though he continued to travel and golf. During 1966 and 1967 a series of illnesses beset the former president, and on May 14, 1968, he entered Walter Reed Hospital where he remained for the last 11 months of his life.

By 1966 Ike realized the unstable condition of his health and began disposing of his properties and providing for Mamie's future. He sold most of his large herd of cattle. In December 1967 he gave his 246-acre Gettysburg farm and home to the nation as a historical monument with the provision that he and Mamie could live there as long as they wished. Mamie's comment was, "Well, we're back in government housing."[15]

Following his second major heart attack, the Eisenhowers traveled to Palm Desert again for the winter. Ike played golf, but on a more limited schedule. However, bridge remained a real diversion for him. In June 1966

Ike and Mamie proudly went to the graduation of their grandson David from Phillips Exeter Academy, and on July 1, 1966, Ike and Mamie celebrated their golden wedding anniversary. It was this summer when Ike gave his large stamp collection to Cardinal Spellman for the Spellman Philatelic Museum at Regis College. In December Ike had gallbladder surgery, but recovered from the operation surprisingly well. Most of 1967 was spent in Palm Desert and Gettysburg, though Ike was a patient at Walter Reed for an intestinal disorder, and for a urinary ailment, as well as for his faltering heart. He still enjoyed seeing his friends, among whom was Billy Graham, the famous minister, who visited him at Gettysburg. In February of 1968 at the Palm Desert golf course, he hit his first and only hole-in-one, which was a source of conversation the rest of his life.

In April 1968 while in Palm Desert, Eisenhower suffered his fourth heart attack. He was taken immediately to the hospital at March Air Force Base in California, where he stayed until he could be moved to Walter Reed again. There he had three more heart attacks and many episodes of heart fibrillation. The doctors tried a pacemaker without success. The whole nation followed Eisenhower's medical condition during this tense period, and at least twenty people offered to literally give their hearts to him.[16]

The Eisenhowers had by now determined that they would be buried in Abilene in the meditation chapel, which was just west of the Eisenhower Library and across the street from the home of his youth, which is also a national monument. The body of their first child, Doud Dwight, was moved from Denver to the chapel and placed next to the space reserved for the graves of his parents.

Though very ill, Ike's interest in politics continued. He endorsed Richard Nixon well before the Republican convention met in Miami in August 1968, and addressed the convention on television from his hospital room at Walter Reed. However, within a few hours after this television talk, he suffered another heart attack. In February 1969, to save his life, the former president had abdominal surgery to correct a blockage of the small intestine. How his damaged heart withstood this surgical procedure is something of a medical marvel. Pneumonia followed the surgery, but to the amazement of his physicians, he recovered. For a time he appeared somewhat better, but his heart, scarred by seven attacks, recent episodes of fibrillation, and congestive heart failure, could not recover, and it was evident that death was near. At 2:15 p.m. on April 28, his last words expressed love for his wife, children, and country. He asked to be propped up higher, looked at his son John and whispered, "I want to go; God take me."[17] Mamie, John, David, and Julie were at his bedside.

The body was taken to Bethlehem chapel of Washington Cathedral for a prayer service. A horse-drawn caisson, followed by the riderless horse, then took the body to the rotunda of the Capitol where it lay in state, the eighth president to be so honored. (Blackjack, the riderless horse used in so many of the former processions, was no longer used, and Raven, a ten-year-old gelding, took his place.) Police estimated that as many as 100,000 people may have passed by the casket. President Nixon gave the eulogy during the service at the rotunda, the first time that a president gave the eulogy for a former president. The casket was then taken back to Washington Cathedral for the funeral service, where 18 heads of states and 75 representatives of foreign nations were in attendance.

Thousands of people lined the railroad tracks to pay their respects as the ten-car train passed by on the way to Abilene. The final service was held in the chapel of the Eisenhower center, and the body was buried in the spot selected by Ike himself.

Dwight Eisenhower was one of the best-loved figures in American history. He had won the hearts of the people as a military hero, leader of the Allied forces in Europe, and then as a successful president. But above all, he was a man whom they could love and respect.

The 35th, John F. Kennedy

Pandemonium in Dallas, 1963

Never before had Dallas, Texas, seen such confusion, such pandemonium, or such sheer panic as it did in the several hours after noon on Friday, November 22, 1963. John Fitzgerald Kennedy (1917–1963), president of the United States (1961–1963), had been shot down in their streets before thousands of horrified spectators. No one had anticipated, no one was prepared for this catastrophic event. The men around the president had no plan of action in case of an assassination attempt, especially away from Washington, nor had the local authorities in Dallas any plan or procedure in the unlikely event that a United States president would be struck down while a guest in their city. Certainly Parkland Hospital had no idea of how to deal with a dying president who would be brought in to their very competent trauma department. No one knew what to do with the vice president during the developing turmoil, nor how to adequately protect him until he could reach the comparative safety of Washington. No one knew when the vice president should take the oath of office as the new president, or even where a copy of the oath could be found, or when the new president should take charge from the staff that had served the late president.

Perhaps the most potentially dangerous situation to the nation was that the "bag man" (the man who carried the black bag which contained the device to trigger a nuclear response in the event of an attack on the United States) was out of touch with both the Kennedy aides and Vice President Johnson after the assassination. For many minutes it was not clear just who could issue an order for a retaliatory strike. An added factor to the confusion was the more than 100 media people who were in Dallas to cover the president's trip, all impatiently demanding information about the shooting so they could report the most shocking news story of the decade. They cluttered the halls of Parkland, tied up its communication system, and almost stopped the operation of the hospital. They descended on the Dallas police department in large numbers and intruded into the most sensitive areas of police investigation, making it most difficult to conduct any business, much less to apprehend the assassin.

For many months President Kennedy had been concerned about the strife within the Democratic party in Texas. The intraparty struggle between the group around Governor John B. Connally, an ally of his fellow Texan, Vice President Lyndon Baines Johnson, and the more liberal group led by Texas Senator Ralph Yarborough, was bitter and longstanding. The controversy was in part ideological—Connally the conservative and Yarborough the liberal—but perhaps more important, an old-fashioned struggle for political power. Kennedy had won the presidency over Richard M. Nixon by the narrowest of margins, and Texas loomed large in the president's mind as he made plans for his reelection campaign. A split Democratic party would hurt his chances in 1964. The young president hoped that a personal appearance in Texas would unify the party under his own leadership. However, Yarborough was upset because Connally had made most of the plans for the president's Texas visit, and he let his displeasure be known to the press.

The trip was important for the Texas Democrats as well as to the president. For this reason Kennedy was anxious for his wife Jacqueline to accompany him. The Kennedys always made an attractive, magnetic pair in their campaign contacts.

Thursday morning, November 21, 1963, had been a busy day in the White House. Aides were hurrying to get ready to leave Washington for Texas. Kennedy had very specific ideas about how things should be packed for the trip, and any who did not do their assigned job were the target of his displeasure. The president's wife had so recently given birth to their third child, Patrick Bouvier, only to see him die two days later of a lung disorder, that some feared she would not be able to take the trip to Texas. But she insisted that she was anxious to go in order to be with her husband. The Kennedy children, Caroline and John—or John John, as JFK called him—had been prepared for the absence of both of their parents, but John John wanted to accompany his father in the helicopter to Andrews Air Base near Washington where the president and his party would board Air Force One and fly to Texas. JFK kissed his son for the last time as they entered the plane.

Time in the air on Air Force One was not for relaxation. The plane in flight was virtually the seat of government. The communication system it carried connected the president with all of Washington, and in fact with the whole world. The presidential staff as well as the media were assigned to this plane. Quarters for relaxation and rest were provided, but John Kennedy was constantly in motion as he prepared for two days of intensive campaigning. He was still reviewing the several speeches that he would make, for the importance of this trip to his political future never left him.

At 11:05 a.m., Air Force One lifted off from Andrews Air Base on the way to San Antonio. They landed at Kelly Field at 1:23 p.m. (Central Time), to be greeted by Vice President Johnson, city officials, Texas congressmen, and other state leaders. JFK was given a warm, enthusiastic welcome, but Jackie's undeniable charm carried the occasion. The motorcade to and from the city passed thousands of cheering people and was without incident.

Air Force One was somewhat behind schedule in leaving San Antonio and did not arrive in Houston until 4:37 p.m., where the testimonial dinner for the veteran Congressman Albert Thomas was to be held. A crowd in Houston welcomed the Kennedys, but a number of anti–Kennedy placards were displayed, and the turnout to greet the motorcade was less than expected. Houston's Harris county had voted for Nixon in the last election by a substantial margin, and a less-than-unanimous welcome could have been anticipated.

The presidential party went to the Rice Hotel to prepare for the gala of the evening. Jackie was nervous about the few words she was to say. While she was practicing in another room, LBJ came to the president's room to discuss the Yarborough-Connally feud. One report has it that there was a loud argument between the two, while others hold that the animated discussion did not indicate a basic disagreement. There seems to be little evidence of sharp opposing positions, and certainly there was no break between the two men, for the next day (November 22) Kennedy let it be known that Johnson would be on the ticket in 1964.

The dinner for Albert Thomas was a success. As JFK was addressing the crowd, he stopped, turned to Jackie and asked her to say a few words. Conquering her ever present stage fright, she spoke to the audience in Spanish and literally "brought down the house." It was past nine o'clock before the group was ready to leave the hotel for Air Force One. Two more motorcades and a flight were to be made before they could get any rest.

Air Force One landed at Carswell Air Force Base near Ft. Worth at 10 p.m., and the motorcade into the city and to the Hotel Texas was made in a drizzle. Few had expected much of a turnout in the rain at that hour, but there were shouts for the Kennedys and for LBJ along the entire route.

The Hotel Texas was not as ornate as many that hosted the president, but was in the grand style of old Texas, and the Kennedys appreciated the warm welcome it represented. The Johnsons and the Connallys, having been guests at the hotel many times, had the feeling of coming back home. Jackie sent word to the reporters that "Texas friendliness was everything I'd heard it to be."[1] After the first couple retired to their suite of rooms on the eighth floor (805), the president had short conferences with several of his staff and prepared for bed, admitting that he was very tired. Young as he was, it was necessary to conserve his strength, for the adrenaline deficiency from which he suffered demanded careful attention from his physician. He still wore a back brace as a result of an injury sustained in the South Pacific in World War II. Kennedy was scheduled to talk to a large group the next morning in the parking lot across the street from the hotel. He told his wife not to get up when he did, but to be sure to be down to the Longhorn Room at nine-fifteen in the morning.

John Connally and Lyndon Johnson held court for several hours after they reached the hotel, LBJ on the thirteenth floor and Connally in the coffee shop adjacent to the lobby. Members of the Secret Service detail stood guard over the Kennedy and Johnson suites the entire night.

Kennedy had avidly followed the Texas newspapers and their reaction to the political situation. He did not like what he saw the next morning, for he found the biggest political story of the day was the feud between Senator Yarborough and Governor Connally. The Dallas *News* headlines read, "President's visit seen widening the state Democratic split."[2] Kennedy was disappointed and angry, for his visit was supposed to heal the rift between the two. It was then that he called his aide, Kenneth O'Donnell, and told him to insist that Senator Yarborough ride in Vice President Johnson's car in the motorcade the next morning as a show of political unity, and that he, the president, would not accept any excuses. O'Donnell and another aide, Larry O'Brien, got together and decided they would have to lay out the alternative for the senator: he would suffer presidential wrath if he did not cooperate. Johnson was agreeable to having the senator ride with him, but even at the last moment the senator almost got away. Two from the president's staff had to physically block his escape route or he might have avoided riding with the vice president.

The morning had been a great political success for the president and his wife. The large crowd in the parking lot gave him a resounding ovation. The rain had stopped just in time for his speech. Jackie had held the Texas audience spellbound at the breakfast that followed. The president commented, "Two years ago I introduced myself in Paris by saying that I was the man who had accompanied Mrs. Kennedy to Paris. I am getting somewhat the same sensation as I travel around Texas."[3] The crowd cheered.

At the breakfast Jackie was given a pair of western boots, and JFK a five-gallon hat. The president assured them that he would wear it Monday in Washington. Jackie planned to wear the boots at the LBJ ranch, which they expected to reach later the same day.

What the president did not see in the Dallas *News* until after the breakfast was a large ad run in the morning edition asking twelve questions which at best charged Kennedy with being too soft on the Communists and responsible for "the imprisonment, starvation and persecution" of thousands of Cubans.[4] Some handbills which were violently anti-Kennedy, with no signature or name of the printer, appeared in several places during the morning of November 22, 1963. The incidents made some of the president's associates feel concerned about his safety. Several directly asked him not to go to Dallas.

But in his heart the president had already faced the possibility of assassination. Before he ran in 1960 it was pointed out to him that every president since 1840 who was elected in a year ending in a zero died before his term was up. The president made the remark that "Any man who wants to trade his life for mine"[5] could find a way to do so. He may even have had something of a premonition of an assassination attempt. Once he asked Washington correspondent Charles Bartlett, "How do you think Lyndon would do if I got killed?"[6] After seeing the disturbing ad in the Dallas paper he muttered, "You know, last night would have been a hell of a night to kill a president."[7] When he made that statement, he had just three hours to live.

The other part of the unfolding drama was occurring in Irving, Texas, a small town just outside of the city of Dallas. On Thursday evening, November 21, Lee Harvey Oswald went to see his wife Marina and their two children, one a toddler and the other an infant. He was employed by the Dallas Book Depository and lived in a small rented room near where he worked during the week. His custom was to go to Irving on Friday after work and stay until Monday morning when he would return to Dallas. Since he had no car he was forced to arrange rides with others over the weekends.

The fact that Oswald visited his family on a Thursday night was unusual and attracted some attention. It was common knowledge that Oswald and his wife, a Russian national he had married in the Soviet Union and brought back to the United States, were having domestic problems. He may have tried to reconcile with Marina, but they quarreled bitterly. It would be their last night together. The world knows that Oswald would see John F. Kennedy through a gunsight the next day.

As the motorcade taking Kennedy from Love Field to the Dallas Trade Mart passed Dealy Plaza, three — it is said — rifle shots rang out. For a few seconds no one was exactly sure what was happening. Those who were hunters recognized the sound of rifle fire, and the instant reaction was to wonder where the shots came from and why they were fired. But in a few seconds the Secret Service and a number of others grasped the dreadful nature of those sounds.

President and Mrs. Kennedy were riding together in the back seat of the second car in the motorcade, a large open Lincoln Continental. Governor and Mrs. John Connally were also riding in the car, sitting on the jump seats just in front of the Kennedys. The first shot from the Dallas Book

Depository hit the street beside the press car and bounced to the curb and shattered, throwing up particles of cement and dirt. The second shot went through the president's neck, severing part of the windpipe and nicking the tie he was wearing. This wound alone might not have been fatal. The same bullet went through Governor Connally's chest, right wrist and left leg. The third shot hit the president in the back of the head, scattering pieces of his skull, brain tissue and blood over the car. Jackie noticed the peculiar expression that came to her husband's face as he grabbed for his throat. After the third shot he raised his hand as if to touch his head, but slumped to his right, over against his wife. Nellie Connally believes she heard Jackie say, "He's dead, they've killed him — Oh Jack, Oh Jack, I love you."* By this time Clint Hill, Mrs. Kennedy's special agent who had seen the back of the president's head blown off, ran to the big Lincoln, lunged at the step on the rear bumper, reached for the hand grip on the trunk of the car, but momentarily slipped and began to slide off the car. Jackie started to climb out onto the trunk and reached her hand toward Agent Hill. Their hands touched and Hill soon had a firm hold on the hand grip at the back of the car. He then gently pushed Jackie back to her seat. She has no recollection of this action, but it is recorded on the film taken by amateur photographer Abe Zapruder. Several times Jackie repeated, "They've shot my husband, they've shot my husband." Two of those nearby thought they heard her gently croon to her husband as she held his shattered body.

Governor Connally, a hunter from the plains of Texas, turned his head when he heard the first discharge of the rifle. The next moment he felt the impact of the second bullet as its force threw him forward and toward the door. The only words he uttered were, "No, no, no." Soon he was drenched in blood, and as the pain hit he began to scream. His wife, much as Jackie was doing, drew him to her and tried to comfort him as he drifted in and out of consciousness.

Agent Greer, who was driving the president's Lincoln, and Agent Roy Kellerman, who was riding in the front seat beside Greer, recognized the gravity of the situation in a moment. Kellerman called on the radio to Agent Winston Lawson in the lead car with Police Chief Curry, "We are hit. Take us to a hospital quick."[8] Kellerman yelled to Greer, "Move it out.... We are hit. Get us to a hospital."[9] It is not entirely certain when Chief Curry realized what had happened, but it is clear that he knew what to do, for he called on his radio to Greer to follow his car to Parkland Hospital. At 12:30 by the clock, the chief got in touch with the dispatcher at police headquarters and instructed him to tell Parkland Hospital to stand

---

*It is impossible to be sure what happened in every detail during the few minutes after 12:30 p.m. Exact words spoken may still be in doubt. The writer has attempted to state the facts as nearly as can be determined.

by. Why the hospital did not receive the call from the police until 12:33 is still unclear.

The third vehicle in the motorcade was the Secret Service car called "Half-back," driven by Agent Sam Kinney. Agent Hill had been riding on the left running board before he dashed ahead to aid President and Mrs. Kennedy. Four other agents were in that car, but Agent Emory Roberts was perhaps the first to grasp the fact that since JFK had suffered a mortal wound, the Secret Service's chief task was to protect the life and person of Lyndon Johnson. As agent Jack Ready was preparing to run ahead to the president's car, Roberts shouted at him, "Don't go, Jack!" Some say that Roberts pointed to the car ahead that carried the president and then to the car just behind them where the vice president rode. Roberts then told Agent Bill McIntyre, "They got him. You and Bennett take over Johnson as soon as we stop."[10]

Confusion had by now overtaken car number four, the Lincoln convertible that carried the Johnsons and Senator Yarborough. Agent Rufus Youngblood sat beside the driver, Texas Ranger Hurchel Jacks. When Youngblood heard the shots and saw what happened, he quickly assessed the situation and shouted to LBJ, "Get down," as he pushed the vice president to the floor of the car, shielding him with his own body.[11]

Car number five was the Secret Service back-up car for the Johnsons and Senator Yarborough. They immediately drew close to the vice president's car and followed it to the hospital. Mayor and Mrs. Earl Cabell's car was next in the motorcade, but they were powerless to assist in any way.

What happened in the next car, number seven, the press pool car, is scarcely believable. Merriman Smith of United Press International was the senior member of the group and was sitting in the middle of the front seat with the car phone in his hands. When he heard the shots and saw the immediate confusion ahead of him, he dialed the UPI office in Dallas and said, "Three shots were fired at the president's motorcade in downtown Dallas."[12] This report to the local UPI office was sent within the first few seconds after the last shot, and its cryptic message was on the UPI printer at 12:34, a full two minutes before the president reached Parkland Hospital. As Smith finished his first report to his office, Jack Bell of Associated Press who was in the back seat of the car stood up and demanded the phone for himself. Smith insisted on having his report repeated back to him, although the group felt they had heard the message being received correctly. The almost universal feeling among the journalists in the pool car was that Smith delayed overly long in giving his colleagues an opportunity to use the common phone. At that point Bell attempted to seize the phone, but Smith placed it between his knees. Bell, thoroughly angered by this time began to throw punches at Smith, although most of them seemed to land on the driver of the car and on Malcolm Kilduff, the president's press secretary on this trip. Smith finally let Bell have the phone, but at that moment it went dead; UPI had a real scoop.

The panic spread. The first three cars of the motorcade instantly increased their speed. As they reached the relative darkness of the triple underpass just beyond the Book Depository, they narrowly avoided a collision and almost crushed a motorcycle policeman. The race to the hospital had other moments of terror. At one time two large trucks nearly blocked the way. Greer, exactly gauging the available space, put the president's car between them with only inches to spare on each side. Chief Curry's car went around both trucks. At times their speed reached 80 miles an hour.

Racing to the hospital, the motorcade covered the four miles in just six minutes. Drivers of all six cars parked anywhere they could find space and rushed to find the hospital staff. To their horror there was no one to meet them.

True, Chief Curry had sent his message to police headquarters and had instructed them to alert Parkland, but the hospital did not receive the chief's message until 12:33. The operator at the police department blamed the delay on a technical malfunction, but some are inclined to feel the real reason was flawed human reaction in a desperate crisis. The message from the police department reached Ann Ferguson at the Parkland switchboard at 12:33. The word she received said, "Six-0-One coming in on Code 3, stand by."[13] When stripped of its technical wording, the message stated that the president was coming to the hospital in an extreme emergency, a call of the highest priority. Mrs. Ferguson set the wheels of the hospital in motion as quickly as possible, but a little less than three minutes was not enough time to have staff at the emergency entrance.

When the Secret Service agents saw there was no member of the hospital staff to receive them, two of the agents went looking for gurneys to take the president and the governor to the emergency treatment rooms. But within seconds several of the hospital staff arrived. Since the governor was in the jump seat just in front of the president, he had to be removed from the Lincoln first. Kennedy was wheeled into Trauma Room No. 1, and Connally to Trauma Room No. 2.

Two nurses began to cut away the president's clothing, leaving him clad in shorts and his back brace. It was quickly seen that he had no wound below the neck. By this time a second-year surgical resident of the hospital staff, Dr. Charles Carrico, arrived. In a moment Carrico found there was no blood pressure and no pulse, and that the desperate efforts of the president to breathe were failing. Carrico inserted an endotracheal tube down Kennedy's throat to aid his breathing. By this time Dr. Malcolm Perry, the assistant to the hospital's chief resident in surgery, reached the treatment room and assumed command of the hopeless effort to keep the president alive. Dr. Perry thought, "Here is the most important man in the world."[14]

He began to perform a tracheotomy in a vain attempt to restore the president's breathing. The incision was made just below the bullet hole on the front of the neck (necessary because the windpipe had been hit by the bullet). At the same time he called for three more doctors to join him.

Jackie had entered the treatment room, ignoring the determined efforts of nurse Doris Nelson who physically tried to prevent her from coming into the room. Very quietly Jackie said, "I want to be in there when he dies."[15] Only the assistance of Dr. George Burkley, the president's personal physician, got her past Nelson. Several times hospital staff tried unsuccessfully to get Jackie to leave.

The medical attention received by the president was nothing short of heroic. A blood transfusion and Ringer's solution were administered through catheters placed in a leg and an arm, two tubes were inserted into the chest to suction out fluids, forced oxygen was administered, and a tube was inserted into the stomach through the mouth to remove any substances that might remain. Dr. Perry began to perform heart massage through the chest wall. After about ten minutes, Dr. Kemp Clark, the hospital's chief resident neurologist who had come at Perry's request, looked up at Perry and said, "It's too late, Mac."[16] Clark then turned to Jackie and told her that her husband had a fatal wound. Nurse Nelson began to prepare the death certificate.

Just as the medical team gave up the struggle to save the president, three policemen were bringing a small, frail, 70-year-old Roman Catholic priest to Trauma Room No. 1. Seventeen minutes before, Jackie had asked for a priest. There is no reasonable explanation why a priest could not be found for the dying man. Father Oscar Huber had come on his own initiative to attend the stricken president. As soon as he heard that Kennedy had been shot and taken to Parkland, Huber immediately rushed to his car and began the journey to the hospital accompanied by Father James Thompson.

President Kennedy was a Roman Catholic by baptism and was a regular communicant. The priest realized how important it was for a dying Catholic to receive the last rites of the church while the soul was still in the body. Father Huber immediately put on his stole and began the time-honored ritual of the church repeating the phrases in Latin. *"Si vivis ego te absolvo a peccatis tuis. In nomine Patris, et Filii, et Spiritus Sancti. Amen."*[17] The priest then traced the sign of the cross in holy oil on the forehead of the president and said a blessing. As he had repeated the prayers, Jackie and Dr. Burkley, the only Catholics in the room, joined in the appropriate responses. The priest then gave comfort to Jackie, which she received with appreciation, especially when he assured her, "I am convinced that his soul had not left his body,"[18] realizing how important that would be to her. She seemed on the verge of fainting, so a nurse helped her to a folding chair by the door of the treatment room and placed a cold damp towel to her face and forehead. When asked if she wanted a doctor she declined any medical aid and refused the offer of fresh clothing. Not once did she express the slightest intention of changing clothes. She repeated a number of times, "I want them to see what they've done to him."[19]

As Father Huber left the hospital, one of the two Secret Service men accompanying him and Father Thompson pointedly emphasized, "You don't know anything."[20] The two priests nodded in understanding. However, as soon as the members of the press saw the priests leaving, they excitedly crowded around them. Neither of the priests had had experience with the pressing questions of the media and soon revealed that they thought the president was dead. Immediately the priests were quoted over the air, though nothing official had been said. Many of the press logically wondered just how much two parish priests would know.

When John Fitzgerald Kennedy was pronounced dead, a number of decisions had to be made by those who had been with the president— principally Kenneth O'Donnell and Agent Kellerman, and by the new president, Lyndon Baines Johnson. Decisions confronting them were when and how the announcement would be made to the world, when and how Johnson and the body of the late president would be taken to Love Field, and when and by whom the oath of office would be administered to Johnson.

Strange as it may seem, the new president had not been informed of the actual death of Kennedy for some 13 minutes after Dr. Clark had said he was dead. In fact, the Secret Service chief at the White House, 1500 miles away, knew of the death before Johnson who was just a few feet away. A number of explanations have been offered for this delay, but none are very plausible. It seems to the writer that there may have been hidden agendas which caused the delay in informing the man who was now the president. Perhaps there were those who wanted to make some decisions before the new president would have a chance to change them.

Lyndon Johnson had been hidden in the Minor Medicine area of the hospital on the chance that some conspirator might be stalking him as well. When Malcolm Kilduff was taken to the little room where Johnson waited, his first words were, "Mr. President."[21] The title caught Johnson unprepared and he looked strangely at the press secretary. Kilduff was ready to make an official statement of the death that moment, but the new president felt he should be out of the hospital for reasons of security before the announcement was made. Immediate steps were begun to take Johnson to Love Field. However, Johnson, now president, but not officially installed, did not feel like leaving Parkland Hospital until he had contacted the Kennedy people. He made every effort to be considerate and sympathetic to them, and especially to Jackie. Several times he inquired specifically about her, but when LBJ found that Jackie would not leave the hospital without the body of her husband, he sent Agent Emory Roberts to see Kenneth O'Donnell, now the spokesman for the Kennedy people, to discuss leaving the hospital and returning to Love Field. When Roberts asked O'Donnell about Johnson going "to the plane," O'Donnell, said Roberts, nodded his head. When O'Donnell saw Johnson for the one and only time they saw each other in the hospital, Johnson asked about going to "the plane," but did not indicate which plane. Johnson and those with him felt that O'Donnell was agreeable to Johnson's going to Air Force One.

Thus occurred a misunderstanding that was to mark the beginning of the long and bitter relationship between the Kennedys and Johnson. The conversation between LBJ and O'Donnell has continued to be a matter of dispute. It seems clear that O'Donnell and his group were disturbed — incensed is scarcely too strong a term — when they learned that Johnson had boarded Air Force One. They no doubt expected him to return to Washington on Air Force Two, the plane in which he had come to Dallas. It is their contention that O'Donnell had never agreed to Johnson's coming aboard Air Force One. Certainly the incident must be viewed in the context of the deep emotions of the moment. The Kennedy people were so devastated by their loss that they were perhaps blind to any other consideration. They wanted to be alone in their grief.

Contributing to the misunderstanding was the fact that once Kennedy was hit, Roy Kellerman, who technically was in charge of the Secret Service agents on the Texas trip, almost forgot about Johnson. On the other hand, Agent Youngblood, who was with LBJ when Kennedy was hit, saw clearly what was happening and instantly assumed the responsibility of protecting Johnson. Youngblood felt that Johnson should go to Air Force One, receive the oath, and assume the full powers of the presidency immediately. There was little coordination between Kellerman and Youngblood, each engrossed by the concept of what they felt was their responsibility during the crisis. Actually, both forgot about the "bag man," who hung around not knowing where to go or what to do. He finally did reach the presidential plane with his black bag.

When it had been decided to take LBJ from the hospital to Love Field, Lady Bird Johnson said she must see Jacqueline Kennedy and Nellie Connally before she left. The two wives of the men who were struck down were standing within a few feet of each other, but both were so consumed with the anxiety of the moment that they scarcely noticed the other. Lady Bird spoke first to Jackie and then to Nellie expressing her concern and affection.

Agent Lem Johns went to Chief Curry and requested unmarked cars to take Johnson and his immediate group to Love Field. Johnson wanted his associate Jack Valenti, his executive assistant Liz Carpenter, and his personal secretary Marie Fehmer to accompany him. Johnson was hurried out a side door of the hospital and entered the first car. Chief Curry was at the wheel. Lady Bird went in the second car. As they traveled, LBJ sat low in his seat, surrounded by the bodies of Secret Service agents.

It would seem that the best plan would have been for the cars going to Love Field to travel as quietly and inconspicuously as possible. However, someone turned on the siren until LBJ ordered it turned off. Upon reaching Love Field, the cars went immediately to Air Force One, and the party hurried up the back ramp into the plane.

Bill Moyers, a Texas Baptist minister and a Johnson intimate, was in Austin when he heard of the assassination, and chartered a private plane to take him to Dallas. When over Love Field, arrangements were made by radio for the small plane to taxi up to Air Force One. Johnson was most pleased to see Moyers.

Once Lyndon Johnson was out of the hospital, Kilduff called the members of the press into a room at the hospital and made the official announcement that President Kennedy had died as a result of a gunshot wound to the head. Some wept, some sat in complete immobility, while others were moved to almost a frenzy of activity. Dr. Perry came in to answer questions about the fatal wound of the president. At 1:35 p.m. in Dallas, the national news services let the world know that Kennedy had died. Three minutes earlier UPI had broadcast Father Huber's statement, "He's dead, all right."[22]

While LBJ was on his way to Air Force One, the Kennedy party began to make plans to move the body of their chief to the plane at Love Field. Very quickly Jackie declared, "I'm not going to leave here without Jack."[23] With this in mind, O'Donnell began giving the orders that would take his fallen leader back to Washington, and told Agent Hill to order a casket. Hill found Steve Landrigan, the assistant hospital administrator, and asked for help in finding a funeral home near the hospital. Landrigan dialed the Oneal funeral home and gave the phone back to Hill. When Vernon Oneal (owner of the establishment) answered, it took a few seconds for him to realize who needed a casket. When Oneal asked what kind they wanted, he was told to select the best that he had. Shortly after 1:30 Oneal arrived with the casket.

Meanwhile the hospital staff began to prepare the president's body to leave the hospital. When this was completed, Jackie came in and held her dead husband's hand and kissed him. After the body was in the casket, she took off her wedding ring and placed it on one of his fingers. (The Secret Service later recovered the ring and returned it to her.) During this time several people, including Lady Bird Johnson, tried to get Jackie to change her clothing. Later in Washington, this effort was repeated by others a number of times in Bethesda Hospital where the autopsy was conducted and the body embalmed. When the coffin was taken to the White House about four-thirty the next morning, Jackie still wore the same blood-soaked suit, gloves, stockings and shoes.

Just as the bereaved group was waiting in Parkland Hospital for the death certificate, a bizarre incident took place that defies imagination. A small "pale, freckled, walleyed man in shirt sleeves" entered Trauma Room No. 1 and imperiously announced, "This is Earl Rose. There has been a homicide here. They won't be able to leave until there has been an autopsy."[24] The man was the Dallas County Medical Examiner, and became a formidable obstacle to the removal of the president's body. As Rose was about to leave the nurses' station, Kellerman informed Rose that "this is the body of the President of the United States, and we are going to take it back to Washington."[25] A shouting match soon erupted with Kellerman declaring that they were taking the president's body immediately, and Rose loudly insisting they would not.

Soon Kellerman was joined by other Secret Service men, Dr. Burkley, and Kennedy staff personnel. The fact was that the small Dallas official had the technicality of the law on his side. John F. Kennedy was no longer the president and was actually under Texas law. But realistically the body of a president is not just another body and certainly could not be treated as such. Dr. Burkley shouted, "This is the President of the United States; you can waive your local laws."[26] Rose just stood in front of the casket and shook his head. Agent Kellerman threw down the gauntlet by saying, "Doc, you are going to have to come up with something a little stronger than yourself to give me the law that this body can't be removed."[27]

Rose responded by trying to find a justice of the peace to back him up. Finally, Justice Theron Ward came to the hospital (a justice of the peace in Texas had some of the authority that a regular judge has in many other states). Ward was an unimpressive looking youth in his early twenties. Kellerman addressed him courteously as "your honor" and appealed to his patriotism by referring to the unnecessary ordeal Mrs. Kennedy would have to go through if they lingered in Dallas. But after a moment of indecision, the young justice seemed to harden his attitude. By that time the group had moved down the hall a short distance. When Rose saw the casket in motion he jumped in front of it, and soon a policeman with a pistol and helmet joined Rose and Ward. The casket moved a few inches now and then, but the confrontation was growing more intense by the moment. Ward took a more aggressive stance by remarking, "It's just another homicide case."[28] However, Ward did have the foresight to get in touch with the district attorney of Dallas County who told the young justice that he had no objection to the body of the president being taken back to Washington immediately. When Dr. Rose learned of the district attorney's decision, his resolve to keep Kennedy's body in Dallas seemed to weaken. The officials reluctantly stepped aside, and the casket was pushed toward the door by a very determined and angry Kennedy party. However, Rose's objection had delayed the departure almost half an hour. Through it all Jackie just stood by, her hand on the casket.

Let it be said that Justice Ward did try to make amends for his behavior. In his official log of the incident he recorded a notation authorizing "the removal of John F. Kennedy, male, white."[29] He also signed the official death certificate when the one signed in the hospital by Dr. Clark was deemed inadequate.

A large crowd had surrounded the hospital entrance, and it took several minutes for Oneal and his men to place the casket in the funeral car. Jackie sat by the casket and was immediately joined by Dr. Burkley, Agent Hill, and General Godfrey McHugh, a Kennedy military aide. Agent Andy Berger took the wheel of the funeral car and led the four-car caravan. The body left the hospital at 2:28 p.m. and arrived at Love Field in about ten minutes.

A space in the back part of the plane had been readied for the casket by removing several seats. With great effort the 800-pound casket was lifted up the rear ramp and into the plane. Then for a few moments the group just stood silently about the casket.

When the Kennedy party reached Air Force One, most did not realize that the new president was already on board. The transition between administrations was further marred when O'Donnell wanted to get the plane airborne before some Dallas official might try to interfere again, but the new president had already decided to take the oath of office before they began the flight back to Washington. The arrangements for administering the oath were still being completed when the casket reached the plane. But General McHugh was so anxious to be off the ground that he ordered Colonel James Swindal, the plane's pilot, to take off. However, Kilduff, representing President Johnson, said that the plane could not leave until the oath was taken. To make matters worse, the air conditioning was not functioning at the time, and the heat in the plane was almost unbearable.

Johnson had twice called Attorney General Robert Kennedy, the late president's brother, to offer condolences and to ask where the oath should be taken as well as where he could find the exact wording of the oath. Two versions of this conversation have emerged. Johnson felt that the attorney general had given his approval for the oath to be taken in Dallas. On the other hand, Bobby did not feel that he had given his approval—he did not remember either approving or opposing the early oath-taking.

To the writer neither acted in a dishonorable manner. Bobby, no doubt for emotional reasons, would rather have delayed the oath until the body of the late president reached Washington. Johnson, on the other hand, laboring under the fear that there might have been a conspiracy against the government, wished the official transfer of presidential power to take place as quickly as possible.

Today most American historians and political scientists seem to feel that the sooner a new president is sworn in after the death of the sitting president the better for all concerned. Johnson's desire to show a continuity of administration and to demonstrate strong leadership is understandable.

The matter of which plane the new president used to travel to Washington, or whether the oath was taken in Dallas or the nation's capital, are not of great historical moment. However, they did, perhaps significantly, exacerbate the growing feelings of personal antipathy between LBJ and the Kennedy family.

Once the decision was made to have the oath administered in Dallas, the fact remained that no one could locate the exact wording of the oath. The attorney general called Deputy Attorney General Nicholas Katzenbach, but neither could immediately remember where the oath could be found. Then two people working independently found the oath in the Constitution itself. Katzenbach dictated the exact wording to Johnson's secretary on Air Force One.

Johnson had determined that the oath should be given by long time friend Sarah Hughes, a federal judge of Dallas. Although it took some time to locate her, she assured LBJ that she would hurry to Love Field, and soon arrived in her small red sports car. Having found a photographer as well as a recording device to capture the actual voices of the participants, the appearance of Judge Hughes meant that the ceremony soon would begin.

President Johnson asked Jackie to stand by him as he took the oath. As many as could crowded around President and Mrs. Johnson and Mrs. Kennedy in the cabin of the plane. O'Donnell and O'Brien, in their resentment of LBJ, carefully avoided being included in the photograph of the occasion. After the swearing-in ceremony, which lasted 28 seconds, Judge Hughes, Chief Curry, the photographer, and several others were hurried off the plane. A number gave muted congratulations to Johnson. Then the new president directed that Air Force One leave for Washington. Colonel Swindal had the plane off the ground at 2:47 p.m. Central Time, leaving the pandemonium and the terror of Dallas behind. The plane landed at Andrews Air Force Base at 6:05 Eastern Time after an emotionally charged but uneventful flight.

Perhaps a listing of the events as they happened on the afternoon of November 22, 1963, in Dallas would be helpful. Times are given in CST.

12:30 President Kennedy shot
12:36 President Kennedy arrived at Parkland Hospital
1:00 President Kennedy pronounced dead
1:05 Robert Kennedy informed of his brother's death

1:13   LBJ informed of JFK's death
1:26   LBJ left Parkland Hospital
1:33   LBJ boarded Air Force One
1:33   Kilduff made official announcement of death
1:50   Lee Harvey Oswald arrested
2:06   LBJ calls three Dallas lawyers to find oath
2:08   Body of JFK taken from hospital in Oneal's funeral car
2:18   Body of JFK on Air Force One
2:20   Katzenbach dictated oath to LBJ's secretary
2:38   LBJ sworn in as 36th President of the United States
2:47   Air Force One left Love Field
4:15   Networks announced Lee Harvey Oswald's arrest

During the afternoon and night of November 22 hundreds of media representatives arrived in the city of Dallas and demanded interviews with those who were in any way involved in the events of the day. Chief Curry tried to cooperate with the media, realizing the intense desire of the public for accurate information about the assassination. Police headquarters became a madhouse. Reporters probed everywhere and seemingly had the run of the building. However, there was only limited contact with Lee Harvey Oswald.

Much criticism has been heaped on the city of Dallas for the way the situation was handled. Many palpable errors were made, but it is the writer's opinion that the police did a very creditable job in apprehending Oswald as quickly as they did. Only 35 minutes elapsed between the murder of Patrolman J.D. Tippit and the arrest of Lee Harvey Oswald for Tippit's murder. The Dallas district attorney was able to indict Oswald for the assassination of Kennedy within 12 hours. Obviously Oswald should have been given heavier protection, but Jack Ruby's act in killing Oswald was so bizarre and unpredictable that the Dallas police cannot be entirely blamed for their failure to anticipate Ruby's presence in that crowded corridor.

On November 29, 1963, President Lyndon B. Johnson by executive order established the Warren Commission "to investigate the assassination on November 22, 1963 of John Fitzgerald Kennedy, the 35th President of the United States." The Warren Commission, made up of Americans of unquestioned integrity, labored carefully over the evidence that was provided by all the resources of the federal government and the state of Texas, and concluded that Lee Harvey Oswald, acting entirely alone, killed President John F. Kennedy by rifle fire in Dallas on November 22, 1963.[30]

When Jack Ruby, a Dallas night club operator, killed Oswald in the basement of the Dallas jail on national television, finding all the facts became impossible. Oswald had defiantly maintained his innocence in killing either the president or Officer Tippit. However, there were many inconsistencies in his story, including statements that were in direct contradiction to clearly demonstrable facts the authorities had in their possession. Few doubt that had Oswald lived, information elicited from him would have contributed to the investigation no matter how hard he tried to cover his involvement. No pertinent facts not already known were revealed by Jack Ruby who died of cancer in prison. No evidence has been uncovered that linked Ruby with any other persons, the underworld, or foreign governments, in the killing of Oswald.

Not long after the publication of the Warren Report, a number of writers took issue with its conclusions. Mark Lane in his *Rush to Judgment* probably received the most attention for his published disagreements with the Warren Report. The writer has studied these disagreements carefully and can find no adequate rebuttal to the Warren Report.

After many years the House of Representatives appointed another commission to reinvestigate the assassination. The new commission made its report in 1979, concluding that there was a conspiracy "possibly involving organized crime figures bent on revenge against the Kennedy Justice Department."[31] The commission also stated that there were "some grounds to suspect Cuba and Russia in the assassination."[32] The document continued that "new scientific acoustical evidence . . . established a high probability that two gunmen fired at President John F. Kennedy."[33] The House voted to adopt the commission's report. Terms such as "possibly," "suspect," and "high probability," however, raise too many questions for the writer to accept the second commission's conclusions as viable.

Certainly the major news services of the nation saw no clear conspiracy in Dallas. CBS spent vast sums investigating the assassination before they released their in-depth study which generally supported the Warren Commission. Though it is possible that the whole story may never be told, and the Warren Report may never represent the final conclusion, it seems to be the most reliable summary of the days of pandemonium in Dallas.

In retrospect it should be remembered that more than a hundred years later, serious questions still continue to be raised about the involvement of government officials in the assassination of President Lincoln. Historians probably know as much as they will ever know about the death of Lincoln. The same may well be true of John Fitzgerald Kennedy.

The 36th, Lyndon B. Johnson

Back to the Pedernales, 1969–1973

Who could have dreamed that four years after he had won the presidency by the largest majority of any modern chief executive, Lyndon Baines Johnson (1908–1973) would decide not to run for reelection? Who could have imagined that a sitting president (1963–1969), eligible for reelection and only 60 years old, would decline to run? Yet President Johnson announced in March of 1968 that he would not seek a second term.

The decision did not come quickly or easily for Johnson, but was preceded by months of agonizing. It seemed impossible for him to withdraw from politics, but equally difficult to continue as the nation's chief executive. Opposition to his Great Society was mounting, and the war in Vietnam had reached unprecedented resistance. Some saw the president as almost a prisoner in the White House, for demonstrators would follow wherever he was scheduled to appear. Antiwar activists hounded him until the day of his death.

Johnson could see no way to de-escalate the war as long as he was in office and seeking reelection. He hoped that by announcing the end of his political career, the public would recognize as patriotic and nonpolitical his efforts to end the war honorably and attain the goals of his Great Society.

It should not be thought that President Johnson simply withdrew at the clear evidence of his declining popularity, nor that he was afraid of the opposition in his own party. Despite a rather rough exterior, Johnson was a sensitive man who did not want to lead in a direction the nation clearly felt was wrong. He was also very well aware of the families whose sons, husbands and brothers were dying in the jungles of southeastern Asia.

Multitudes began to question the morality of the war. The president was also fearful that even if he began the peace process, the antiwar groups would continue such an all-out attack on him that it would be impossible to negotiate a settlement of the conflict.

However, Vietnam was not the only factor Johnson considered in making his decision not to run. A bid from Johnson for the nomination in

1968 would certainly have fragmented the Democratic party. The New Hampshire primary election showed that many Democrats did not want him to continue as president. The polls taken prior to the Wisconsin primary indicated a continued erosion of Johnson's strength. To the surprise of few, Bobby Kennedy announced his own candidacy in the caucus room of the old Senate Office Building on March 16, 1968, the same room from which his brother, John F. Kennedy, had made his own announcement when he ran for the presidency in 1960. Had Johnson decided to run for reelection, a most bitter campaign for the Democratic nomination would certainly have taken place. By this time the ill feeling between LBJ and Bobby Kennedy was well known. On occasion the president had referred to Bobby as "that little runt,"[1] and admitted that it would be very upsetting to see Bobby marching to "Hail to the Chief." There had been little overt dissension between LBJ and JFK, but after Kennedy's death Bobby steadily distanced himself from President Johnson.

Another factor in Johnson's mind was the matter of his health. In 1967 he had a secret actuarial study made to determine how long he was likely to live. The prediction was made that he probably would not see his sixty-fifth birthday.[2] He took the study seriously, and no doubt it helped him to decide not to seek reelection. Often he made comments to friends about his health. On occasion he openly suggested that he might not live out a second term if elected. At the time he announced his retirement he was not in worse health than he had been for the last year or so, but he was tired and obviously aged. To many in Washington Johnson's announcement not to run came as a distinct surprise. But his family and intimates knew that he had been seriously considering such a move for some time.

He was tempted to announce his withdrawal in his State of the Union address early in January 1968, but later made the official announcement on the same occasion that he declared a halt to the bombing of North Vietnam. The date was March 31, 1968.

Riots continued to break out in major cities, more often than not with racial overtones. Blacks often felt that the momentum toward the dreams of Martin Luther King, Jr., had almost come to a halt, and that the end of the civil rights era was in sight. They saw money that should have gone for jobs and inner-city development devoured by a vast and growing military budget feeding a war that was increasingly taking the lives of their own. They directed their rage at the president of the United States.

There had been bitter moments during his presidency. He once said, "I walk through the White House and I think about Lincoln walking through the same corridors. I remember when Churchill came here and stayed in the White House. He used to wear Mother Hubbard pajamas and wake Roosevelt at two or three in the morning to tell him how to run the war. I may not be so bad off after all."[3] Johnson saw a parallel between his own problems of Vietnam and the riots in the cities, and those faced by Lincoln and FDR. He continued the comparison by remembering that Washington, Lincoln and Franklin Roosevelt at times had troubles with unfavorable reactions by the press.

It was a personal blow to the president when the National Democratic Convention met in 1968 and did not urge his attendance. Too many feared that the demonstrations would only be greater if Johnson were present. Thus, even though he was still president, he had no real welcome even to make an appearance. As it was, the demonstrations that took place in Chicago during the convention seriously handicapped the Democrats in the November election.

At first the president determined that he would not take part in the election that fall, but when Hubert Humphrey came to him as the election approached and asked for help, Johnson had no trouble announcing his support.

Members of the press wondered whether Johnson really could slow down. Was he by nature such an aggressive, "take charge" personality that psychologically he would be incapable of moving at a slower pace? Most of the reporters felt that LBJ could not or would not relax and take life easy.[4] But once the decision was made, Johnson in his usual direct manner quickly began making plans for his retirement. He wanted to build a presidential library and the Lyndon Johnson School of Public Affairs at the University of Texas, and to write his memoirs as a defense of his administration. He had all of his public papers and many other records, some 31 million items,[5] sent to the University of Texas in Austin.

One of Johnson's chief interests in retirement was the Ranch, as LBJ called his home and the surrounding acres on the banks of the Pedernales River near Johnson City, Texas. Almost immediately after announcing that he was leaving office, the number of telephone calls to his ranch foreman, Dale Malechek, dramatically increased. The president wanted the Ranch in top condition when he left the White House and returned to Texas.

But there was no lessening of presidential activity as his term in the White House drew to a close. In spite of all the setbacks and rebuffs, LBJ still wanted to see peace come and to salvage as much of the Great Society as possible. Several of his advisors urged him to avoid the more controversial issues in his last State of the Union message to Congress. They regarded his last days in office as basically housekeeping in nature. But President Johnson would have none of it. He urged his own program to Congress as vigorously as if he had just taken office.

In December the president was briefly hospitalized at Bethesda for some sort of flu symptoms, but was not seriously ill. While in the hospital LBJ watched astronauts James Lovell, Frank Borman, and William Anders blast off for the moon. Though NASA and other governmental agencies were apprehensive about the launch, all went well and the president was able to send a congratulatory message to the space capsule. At about the same time, the crew of the *Pueblo,* a navy ship which the North Koreans had illegally detained, was set free. Christmas of 1968 was spent in the White House, the second time the Johnsons had remained in Washington for the holidays, and was a family affair.

Congress held a farewell reception for President Johnson at the Longworth Office Building. On January 14 he hosted his 118th Tuesday luncheon for top staff and administration leaders. Eggplant was served, and the president commented that it was the last time he was ever going to eat eggplant.[6]

On the same day he delivered his last State of the Union message to a packed house in the chamber of the House of Representatives. As he entered, enthusiastic cheers came from the audience. During the speech he was interrupted by applause 51 times. Johnson was still very much attached to the Congress, for it was there he began his public service. At the beginning of his career in Washington he had served as one of the doorkeepers. Later he became a member of the House and then the Senate, and finally, perhaps the greatest majority leader the Senate ever had. As he left the rostrum some began to sing "Auld Lang Syne."

At his final cabinet meeting he was presented with the chair in which he had sat while he presided. In this rather sentimental meeting, both the president and the cabinet members made expressions of high regard and affection for each other. LBJ's last press conference went rather well. No one, it seemed, was out to embarrass him. In the morning of his last Sunday in the White House, January 19, he attended the morning worship service at the National City Christian Church of Washington. Just four years and six days later, his funeral would be conducted in the same church.

Monday morning, January 20, was a busy one for the Johnson family. Aides had to hurry the retiring president, who was caring for a few last details in the Oval Office before receiving the new president. A few minutes after 11:00, the outgoing and the incoming presidents rode together to the Capitol for the inauguration of Richard Nixon. After the ceremony, Johnson was the guest of honor at a luncheon held in the home of Clark and Marnie Clifford. Clifford had been one of Johnson's close advisors in the last days of his administration. After the luncheon the Johnsons were driven to Andrews Air Force Base, where Air Force One took them home to Texas. It was the very same plane which, more than five years before had flown him to Washington moments after he had taken the oath of office. The same Boeing 707 would carry his body back to Washington to lie in state in the rotunda of the Capitol following his death on January 22, 1973.

Late in that same afternoon, Lyndon Johnson held his last press conference on the lawn of his Texas ranch. The man who had been president of the United States less than six hours earlier then helped to pick up the paper cups the reporters discarded after Lady Bird had served them refreshments.

No doubt it must have seemed a staggering prospect for the Johnsons as they arrived at the Ranch to see their considerable personal belongings in piles, and only a skeleton staff to begin the task of finding a place for the luggage. Since his election to the House upon the death of Representative James Paul Buchanan in 1937 — except for service in World War II as a naval officer — Johnson had been a part of the federal government as a representative, senator, vice president and president, until he came back to Texas as an ex-president, a private citizen, and a rancher. Not that their home at the Ranch wasn't luxurious, and their every need not met — for Johnson was a wealthy man with considerable influence and many friends — but the change must have been enormous. How could a man of Johnson's temperament adapt to the limits of his new life-style? To the superficial observer the adjustment came readily with no considerable trauma, but to intimates at the Ranch the change was dramatically difficult and often left Johnson deeply depressed.

There are those who regarded him as something of a hermit when he came back to the Ranch. A number of his Texas friends noted that after several months out of office they had not seen him even once. True, he attended to the construction of the library and went to his office in the federal building at least twice a week, but unlike his predecessors Hoover, Truman and Eisenhower, he basically kept to himself.

Marshall Frady, writing in *Harpers* in June of 1969, commented that it could not be imagined how a spirit such as Lyndon Johnson could ever give up power painlessly. The man who very much wanted to be remembered with admiration and respect found the loss of power quite devastating. Frady regarded Johnson as "a man of enormous dimensions, with a personality that would probably challenge Shakespeare."[7] Even in his crude moments, and he had them, there was an overpowering presence. Frady concludes that "he was, ironically, an awesome phenomenon simply as a human being, with an epic ego, exuberancies, glooms, ambitions, paranoias, generalities, will: a kind of ill-starred left-handed Prometheus."[8]

Is there any wonder that once he was on the Ranch any sort of time constraints irritated him? Johnson came to dinner when it suited him, even though invited guests were there: "Damn it. I'm not going to be pressured into keeping anyone's schedule but my own."[9] At other times he showed great consideration and could be very tender and compassionate. He was a complex personality exhibiting a wide range of emotions and reactions to those around him. *Life* magazine referred to him as "One of the most forceful, sulfureous . . . men ever to preside over the Republic."[10] His virtues as well as his faults were gargantuan. Within a few moments of time he could show love and petulance, tenderness and a violent temper.

To those who only knew Johnson by what they saw on television news, it was difficult to understand the dimensions of this man. Johnson simply froze before a television camera, a radio microphone, or a tape recorder. Johnson biographer Doris Kearns, who had only seen the president on television, was completely dumbfounded when she saw him in person. Johnson simply dominated the group of several hundred people she was with, and bore no resemblance to the pinched personality she expected.[11]

The last days of any administration are difficult for the staff of the president. Most of the Johnson appointees had no problem in finding employment, though several found it necessary to take jobs they did not want. Of the White House personnel, LBJ took W. Thomas (Tom) Johnson to Texas with him to act as the head of his staff. Tom Johnson had been LBJ's deputy press secretary and a special assistant to the president. Robert Hardesty and Harry Middleton moved to Texas to help in the writing of his memoirs. The trusted Walter Rostow went to be near his old boss, although he made the University of Texas his place of work. William J. Jorden joined LBJ in Texas as soon as he could leave the talks with the North Vietnamese in Paris.

Doris Kearns was one of those closest to President Johnson during the closing days of his administration. Early in 1967 she came to Washington from Harvard where she was completing the Ph.D. degree as a part of the White House Fellows program. In a matter of months she became a member of the White House staff and had an office two doors from the Oval Office. The president placed a high level of confidence in her and spent much time consulting with her as well as sharing his personal feelings. A month before leaving office, LBJ invited her to go back to the Ranch with him and work full time on his memoirs. "So for the next four years, while teaching at Harvard, I spent long weekends, parts of summer vacations, and winter holidays with the President and his wife at the ranch. The work . . . was fascinating but difficult."[12] She noted Johnson's reaction to the riots and protestors when he repeatedly asked, "How could these people be so ungrateful to me after I have given them so much?"[13]

Johnson was hurt by the fact that the Eastern intellectuals rejected him as a leader and as a thinker. His liberalism caused much of the South to turn against him, but ironically, the liberals in the North did not accept him as a true liberal. He never did believe the media understood him or accurately reported his motives. In his memoirs he tried to tell the story of his administration from his own point view, but he did not have the needed touch to communicate his feelings or thoughts. Once he remarked, "It's been determined ... I'm going to fail."[14]

Perhaps her most intimate glimpses of the tortured ex-president come when she tells of their early morning talks. When she was working on his memoirs she occupied one of the bedrooms at the Ranch. Johnson, who was an early riser like herself, frequently came to her room to talk. He often discussed his childhood, his mother and father, and the rather frequent nightmares that terrified him. A sort of early morning ritual developed. She would rise early, dress, and begin to read. Often he would knock on her door, and the former president, dressed in his pajamas and robe, would appear. "As I sat in a chair by the window, he climbed into the bed, looking like a cold and frightened child."[15] Perhaps the reason he talked so freely to her was the fact that at times she reminded him of his mother.

Lyndon Johnson was determined to make the Ranch a paying showplace of Texas. In Dale Malechek, LBJ had an excellent ranch foreman, but there were times when the ex-president took this responsibility on himself. Often he was up and at work by sunrise. No detail of management was too small for his personal attention. He was constantly trying to increase the productivity and lower the operating costs of the Ranch. He spent many hours helping to install a more modern irrigation system. He introduced new bloodlines into the herd, as well as new feeding schedules, and tried new types of food for the cattle and the most up-to-date methods of egg production. Johnson constantly drove about his lands, and those who did not do their jobs well improved or left the Ranch.

Johnson's main office was located in the new federal building in Austin. Most of one floor contained his suite of offices and a private apartment, including a kitchen, dining space, and fireplace. More often than not he would arrive as well as leave by helicopter, which landed on the roof. He would take the elevator to his floor, and only a few would know he had even been there. Once the Lyndon B. Johnson Library was completed, he spent most of his time while in Austin at his offices in the library.

There was little difficulty in raising the funds for the library building. Donations came quickly and in large amounts. Shortly after making up his mind to retire, he began planning for the library which he determined should be located on the campus of the University of Texas. It was here he also established the Lyndon B. Johnson School of Public Affairs. Even a casual observer could see his emotional attachment to the project and how deeply he was involved in every detail. He desperately wanted the library to speak to future generations about his administration, showing why the nation had no other choice but to engage the North Vietnamese in war, and how the Great Society could have changed America for the better. At the time of the dedication he said, "It's all here, the story of our time — with the bark off."[16]

May 22, 1971, the date set for the dedication of the library, was a blustery, Texas spring day. Among the three thousand who had been invited were such distinguished guests as President Nixon, Hubert Humphrey, Barry Goldwater, Edmund Muskie, C. Douglas Dillon, Philip Hart, most of the LBJ's official Washington family, and a host of celebrities. To LBJ it "was the greatest day in the world. He was in hog-heaven . . . he had them all there."[17] Johnson presided over most of the ceremony, and seemingly at ease, was very much in control of the celebration. President Nixon was magnanimous in his speech accepting the library for the nation.

The only discordant note was the more than 2,000 antiwar demonstrators who had found their way to Austin. The television cameras and the press recorded their protest, but the day was too significant and happy for Lyndon Baines Johnson to allow the occasion to be marred for him. The library remained one of the places the Johnsons frequently visited and received guests, for it seemed an extension of their lives, their aspirations and accomplishments.

As Johnson neared the end of his term he had become very much interested in history, and had begun to be concerned about what history would say about his administration. There is little doubt that he desperately wanted to be remembered as one of America's great presidents. But as problems mounted in his administration, he began to feel that the media did not accurately interpret his presidency. Hugh Sidey, writing in the November 5, 1971, issue of *Life* magazine, quotes LBJ as saying to the press, "I just want you to do your duty and don't put any damned lies in it, and no propaganda."[18] His distrust of the press was one of the great motivating forces behind his plans to write his memoirs.

He envisioned three or four volumes in his memoirs, but only completed one, which was entitled *The Vantage Point*. The work was not well received and did not sell in large numbers. Some called it the "sanitized" story of Lyndon Johnson. The simple fact is that he had considerable difficulty in marshalling his time and energy into the discipline of writing, for he only worked at the job spasmodically. Often he talked freely, and at times eloquently, about his past, but when the tape recorder was turned on, he immediately froze and the power of his personality was lost. When at times the writers would inject illustrative material or engaging anecdotes that he himself had told, he would delete them saying he wanted his memoirs to be "presidential."[19] In reading the volume he did write, one finds it stiff, devoid of emotion, and certainly not the Johnson that so many of those close to him described. Thus his considerable verbal skills were hidden from the public. The Johnson associates were keenly disappointed, as was Johnson himself who felt he would never be understood.

Johnson's influence on national politics was minimal once he was back at the Ranch. He kept in touch with a number of national figures, but policy was made with little regard to his feelings or opinions. Johnson was most disappointed when George McGovern was made the Democratic nominee for the presidency in 1972. He had hoped that Edmund Muskie would be the nominee. By contrast he considered McGovern an unfit candidate and an inept politician. LBJ did endorse McGovern, if only through a small local newspaper, though his endorsement later appeared in the national press. McGovern made a brief courtesy call on Johnson, but the meeting was short and rather cool.

Until Johnson's near fatal heart attack came without warning in 1955, he had been considered in good health. After his recovery he quit smoking and lost some weight, but continued his high-pressured, driving life-style. After the gall bladder surgery during his presidency he was pictured lifting his shirt and showing the incision to photographers. Though some criticized him for being crude, he confided to friends that he did not want anyone saying that he had cancer or another heart attack. Toward the end of 1967 he indicated that he felt something might be wrong with him. At times he was tired and occasionally suffered from a general malaise. He would comment that his father was only 60 when he died, and seemed to have a rather fatalistic attitude about an early death.

During his first year of retirement his health seemed satisfactory, though he had a few digestive problems and, on occasion, flu-like symptoms. He continued the medication begun after his heart attack, and probably did not drive himself as hard as he had in the White House, though he could work long hours if there was an emergency on the Ranch.

But in March of 1970 Johnson was hospitalized at Brooke Army Medical Center in San Antonio because of chest pains. The physicians discovered angina—a hardening of the arteries which was depriving the heart muscle of needed oxygen—but not another heart attack. Nitroglycerine tablets helped the condition, but he had recurring pain the rest of his life. Many viewers shared the tension when, in the middle of a speech at the Johnson Library, LBJ fumbled in his pocket for a "nitro" pill and put it under his tongue.

His doctors had assured him that he could lead a relatively normal life if he was careful. However, he had gained nearly 25 pounds since leaving the White House, and was advised to lose weight. A crash diet enabled him to lose 15 pounds, but he never was able to get his weight under control. In the middle of 1971 Johnson was hospitalized again at Brooke for a viral pneumonia which he overcame with no serious consequences.

To the utter dismay of his family and friends, shortly before Christmas of 1971 LBJ began to smoke again and soon became a chain smoker. He took the attitude that he was too old and sick for it to make that much difference. He refused to stay on the low-calorie, low-cholesterol diet the doctors prescribed.

In April 1972, Lyndon and Lady Bird Johnson traveled to Tennessee to attend a funeral, after which they went to Charlottesville to visit their daughter Lynda Bird Robb and her family. There, he suffered another massive heart attack. He was immediately hospitalized and listed in very critical condition. The ex-president reputedly said to his wife, "Bird, I'm going home to die—you can come with me if you want to."[20] How he arranged to be flown from Charlottesville to Brooke Medical Center is still not clearly understood, for the hospital administrator did not even know LBJ was considering such a move until his wheelchair was found in the parking lot. To the amazement of his doctors he survived the trip and later went home, but he never was the same. Pain was his constant companion for the few remaining months he had to live.

Shortly after this heart attack he developed severe abdominal pains which the doctors diagnosed as diverticulitis, little pockets in the intestine that trap food and become infected. As the condition did not improve, surgery was considered. The former president was flown to Houston to see Dr. Michael DeBakey, famed heart specialist and surgeon. After a thorough examination the doctor stated that the abdominal surgery would be too risky. He also decided against heart bypass surgery, although at least two of the coronary arteries were almost totally blocked.

Johnson knew and understood the serious nature of his physical condition, but he did not become maudlin nor allow himself to be overcome by the prospect of death. However, he did arrange his financial affairs, and considering the extent and diverse nature of his investments as well as the state of his health, he accomplished this skillfully. He had planned for some time to give certain rather personal holdings to the government for public use. These, among other things, included the home in which he was born, the Lyndon Johnson State Park, the vast resources of the presidential library, as well as the family home at the Ranch. His home was turned over to the national park service, but both the ex-president and Lady Bird would use it as long as they wished. By these valuable gifts he was able to obtain a tax benefit against the large profit he was making from his business ventures. It was estimated that he had doubled the value of his portfolio after he left the White House.

Johnson's assets included a large Austin television station (KTBC), businesses in Louisiana and Oklahoma, a photographic supply company, stock in nine Texas banks, and sizable land tracts in Texas, Alabama, Mexico and the Caribbean. As much as possible he turned these properties into fluid assets. When his dealings were complete, he was able to leave Lady Bird $4.7 million, and each of his daughters $1.3 million.

Johnson increasingly came to depend on his wife as his physical problems mounted. It seemed that he could never quite relax when she was not with him at the Ranch. His wife's presence had always been a stabilizing influence, though she did not attempt to shape his political decisions. When LBJ was most involved with politics, Lady Bird skillfully supervised their financial interests. Throughout their lives she remained the gracious hostess in Washington and at the Ranch.

When Richard Nixon was inaugurated president for the second time on January 20, 1973, Lyndon Johnson watched the happenings on television with little sense of satisfaction or pleasure. By now his step was slower, his speech at times hesitant. He moved about the Ranch less often and did not drive his own car as he supervised the work. The doctors were in constant contact with him. He frequently breathed from the oxygen tank by his bed, took daily naps, and continued to smoke.

On January 20 the *Washington Post* published the story of Nixon's inauguration for a second term. The January 21 *Post* reported the tentative peace with North Vietnam, and the account of the dismemberment of the Great Society by the Nixon administration. The next day the media carried the story of the passing of Lyndon Baines Johnson.

January 22 dawned as almost any other winter day might in the hill country of Texas. The ex-president had passed a fairly good night, though there were always the chest pains and shortness of breath. His doctor at Brooke Medical Center spoke briefly with him by phone. Neither the patient nor his doctor saw any particular reason for concern, but Lady Bird noticed he was unusually quiet. She needed to do some shopping and take care of a few matters in nearby Austin, so she left her husband who planned to putter around the Ranch. In the afternoon he went to his room for his usual nap. At 3:50 p.m. he called the switchboard and asked for Mike Howard, one of the Secret Service agents at the Ranch. Howard was not in his office at the moment, so two other agents responded immediately. They found Johnson on the floor of the bedroom, apparently dead.

However, the ex-president was rushed by air to the Brooke Medical Center where he was pronounced dead on arrival. Lady Bird was contacted in just ten minutes and took a helicopter from the library to Brooke, arriving at 4:49. She later returned to Austin where she spent the night in their apartment above the television station. In a few hours their two daughters arrived. The autopsy performed the next morning at Brooke found that death was caused by a large coronary blood clot.

At noon on January 23, 1973, the body of Lyndon Baines Johnson, 36th president of the United States, was brought to the Johnson Library on the campus of the University of Texas where it lay in state. An estimated 32,000 people passed by the casket. Lady Bird and the Johnson daughters stood for hours greeting many of those who came to pay their respects. President Nixon announced official mourning for the passing of President Johnson. At eight o'clock the next morning the body was flown by Air Force One to Andrews Air Force Base outside the city of Washington.

A motorcade took the body to the heart of the city, Constitution Avenue and 16th Street, where it was transferred to the horse-drawn caisson that took it to the rotunda of the Capitol. Again, the riderless horse, Black Jack, with the boots turned backwards in the saddle, was a part of the procession. After the body was placed on a catafalque in the rotunda, a brief ceremony was conducted at which Dean Rusk, Johnson's secretary of state, and Jake Pickle, who occupied Johnson's old Congressional seat, spoke briefly. Some 40,000 mourners stood in line, some for several hours, that cold and rainy day, to pay their last respects.

The next morning at nine-thirty, January 25, 1973, a motorcade took the body to the National City Christian Church. The Johnsons had known its pastor, Dr. George R. Davis, for more than 25 years. Dr. Davis conducted the simple service. Leontyne Price, the opera singer who had performed at the Johnson inauguration in 1965, sang "Precious Lord Take My Hand," and W. Melvin Watson, a former aide, gave a short eulogy. President and Mrs. Nixon, Thurgood Marshall of the Supreme Court, Mrs. Dwight D. Eisenhower, and many other Washington dignitaries attended the service.

A motorcade took the body to Andrews Air Base where it was placed aboard Air Force One and flown back to Texas for burial. The final graveside service was held at the small family cemetery under one of the enormous live oak trees on the north side of the Pedernales river on the LBJ Ranch. According to Johnson's wish, the service was brief and simple. Ex-Governor John Connally gave a personal tribute, and Anita Bryant sang "The Battle Hymn of the Republic"; a Roman Catholic priest, Fr. Wunibald Schneider, at whose church the Johnsons worshipped the last Sunday of his life, offered the prayer. The Rev. Dr. Billy Graham spoke of Johnson's humanitarian accomplishments, fulfilling Johnson's instructions to the letter, even those which told him where to stand. General William C. Westmoreland represented President Nixon and laid a wreath on the grave. Brigadier General James Cross gave the flag that had covered the casket to Lady Bird.

Many notables, including former Vice President Hubert Humphrey, came to the service but there were also those who came in pick-up trucks wearing broad-brimmed hats and blue jeans. Afterward, hundreds of people went to the Johnson residence to offer their personal sympathy to Mrs. Johnson and daughters, Lynda and Luci. Within 24 hours of the burial, more than 7,000 persons had visited the grave site.

In early December 1972, there had been two living ex-presidents in the United States, Truman and Johnson. Truman died less than a month before Johnson. Now for the fifth time in America's history there were no living ex-presidents.

Chapter Notes

The 1st, George Washington

1. James Thomas Flexner, *Washington: The Indispensable Man,* New York, New American Library, 1969, p. 370.
2. *Ibid.,* p. 376.
3. W.E. Woodward, *George Washington: The Image and the Man,* New York, Liveright Publishing Corp., 1946, p. 392.
4. John Alexander Carroll, and Mary Wells Ashworth, *George Washington,* Vol. 7, *First in Peace* (completing the biography by Douglas Southall Freeman), New York, Charles Scribner's Sons, 1957, p. 615.
5. Francis Rufus Bellamy, *The Private Life of George Washington,* New York, Thomas Y. Crowell Co., 1951, p. 383.
6. Flexner, p. 397.
7. *Ibid.,* p. 399.
8. Douglas Southall Freeman, *Washington,* New York, Charles Scribner's Sons, 1957, p. 751.
9. Bellamy, p. 384.
10. Flexner, p. 399.
11. *Ibid.,* p. 400.
12. Carroll, p. 623.
13. It is probable that Washington had a fear of being buried alive.
14. Freeman, p. 752.
15. Bellamy, p. 385.
16. Lee was a cavalryman in the Revolutionary War, and a neighbor and friend of Washington.
17. Bellamy, p. 385.

The 2nd, John Adams

1. W.E. Woodward, *A New American History,* New York, Literary Guild, 1937, p. 253.
2. Page Smith, *John Adams,* Vol. 2, Garden City, N.Y., Doubleday & Co., 1962, p. 1107.
3. *Ibid.*
4. Gilbert Chinard, *Honest John Adams,* Boston, Little, Brown & Co., 1933, p. 336.
5. *Ibid.*
6. Henry Steele Commager, and Alan Nevins, eds., *The Heritage of America,* Boston, Little, Brown & Co., 1951, p. 150.
7. John Adams, *The Adams-Jefferson Letters,* Edited by Lester J. Cappon, Vol. 2, Chapel Hill, University of North Carolina Press, 1959, p. 283.
8. Smith, p. 1103.
9. *Letters,* p. 291.
10. *Ibid.,* p. 296.
11. *Ibid.,* p. 610.
12. Lynne Withey, *Dearest Friend: A Life of Abigail Adams,* New York, Free Press, 1981, pp. 303–4.
13. *Letters,* p. 529.
14. *Ibid.*
15. *Ibid.*
16. Smith, p. 1133.
17. *Ibid.,* p. 1126.
18. John T. Morse, *John Adams,* New York, Houghton Mifflin & Co., 1896, p. 330.

The 3rd, Thomas Jefferson

1. William K. Bottorff, *Thomas Jefferson,* Boston, Twayne Publishers, 1979, p. 29.
2. Henry S. Randall, *The Life of Thomas Jefferson,* Vol. 3, Philadelphia, J.B. Lippincott Co., 1888, p. 515.

3. James Truslow Adams, *The Living Jefferson*, New York, Charles Scribner's Sons, 1949, p. 335.
4. Fawn M. Brodie, *Thomas Jefferson: An Intimate History*, New York, W.W. Norton & Co., 1974, p. 216.
5. Page Smith, *Jefferson: A Revealing Biography*, New York, American Heritage Publishing Co., 1976, p. 210.
6. *Ibid.*, p. 207.
7. Brodie, p. 353.
8. *Ibid.*, p. 16; Smith, p. 207.
9. Brodie, p. 474.
10. Virginius Dabney, *The Jefferson Scandals: A Rebuttal*, New York, Dodd, Mead & Co., 1981, p. 120.
11. Merrill D. Peterson, *The Jefferson Image in the American Mind*, New York, Oxford University Press, 1962, p. 184.
12. Smith, p. 147.
13. Dumas Malone, *The Sage of Monticello*, Jefferson and His Time, Vol. 6, Boston, Little, Brown & Co., 1981, p. 316.
14. Smith, p. 163.
15. Malone, p. 244.
16. Merrill D. Peterson, *Thomas Jefferson and the New Nation: A Biography*, New York, Oxford University Press, 1970, p. 1006.
17. Randall, p. 540.
18. Peterson, *Image*, p. 402.
19. Excellent records of the last hours of Jefferson's life are available from the accounts of Dr. Dunglison, and from family members which include Thomas Jefferson Randolph, his grandson; and Nicholas Trist, the husband of Jefferson's granddaughter, Virginia Randolph.
20. Randall, p. 549.
21. *Ibid.*
22. *Ibid.*, p. 544.
23. Smith, p. 303.
24. *Ibid.*

The 4th, James Madison

1. Ralph Ketcham, *James Madison: A Biography*, New York, Macmillan Co., 1971, p. 625.
2. Irving Brant, *The Fourth President: A Life of James Madison*, Indianapolis, Bobbs-Merrill Co., 1970, p. 617.
3. Ketcham, p. 616.
4. Gaillard Hunt, *The Life of James Madison*, New York, Doubleday, Page & Co., 1902, p. 369.
5. *Ibid.*, p. 367.
6. Ketcham, p. 667.
7. *Ibid.*, p. 660.

The 5th, James Monroe

1. W.P. Cresson, *James Monroe*, Chapel Hill, University of North Carolina Press, 1946, p. 492.
2. George Morgan, *The Life of James Monroe*, Boston, Small, Maynard & Co., 1921, p. 428.
3. Cresson, p. 458.
4. Morgan, p. 442.
5. Cresson, pp. 497–98.
6. Harry Ammon, *James Monroe: The Quest for National Identity*, New York, McGraw-Hill Book Co., 1971, p. 547.
7. Cresson, p. 494.
8. Morgan, p. 458.

The 6th, John Quincy Adams

1. John Quincy Adams, *The Diary of John Quincy Adams*, Edited by Allan Nevins, New York, Ungar Publishing Co., 1969, p. 406.
2. Marie B. Hecht, *John Quincy Adams*, New York, Macmillan Co., 1972, p. 490.
3. Leonard Falkner, *The President Who Wouldn't Retire*, New York, Coward-McCann, 1967, p. 299.
4. *Diary*, p. 519.
5. Falkner, p. 17.
6. *Ibid.*, p. 24.
7. *Ibid.*
8. *Ibid.*
9. *Diary*, p. 573.
10. Falkner, p. 255.
11. *Ibid.*, p. 131.
12. Hecht, p. 506.
13. *Ibid.*, p. 508.
14. *Ibid.*, p. 626.
15. *Ibid.*, p. 627.
16. *Ibid.*, p. 629.

The 7th, Andrew Jackson

1. Marquis James, *The Life of Andrew Jackson*, Indianapolis, Bobbs-Merrill Co., 1938, p. 785.
2. *Ibid.*
3. *Ibid.*, p. 786.

4. Gerald W. Johnson, *Andrew Jackson: An Epic in Homespun,* New York, Minton Balch & Co., p. 296.
5. Andrew Jackson, *Correspondence of Andrew Jackson,* Vol. 6, *1839–1845,* Washington, D.C., Carnegie Institution of Washington, 1933, p. 332.
6. *Ibid.,* p. 6.
7. William Graham Sumner, *Andrew Jackson,* Boston, Houghton Mifflin & Co., 1899, p. 453.
8. James C. Curtis, *Andrew Jackson and the Search for Vindication,* Edited by Oscar Handlin, Boston, Little, Brown & Co., 1976, p. 179.
9. Sumner, p. 453.
10. W.E. Woodward, *History, op. cit.,* p. 381.
11. James, p. 729.
12. *Correspondence,* p. 725.
13. *Ibid.*
14. *Ibid.,* p. 6.
15. James, p. 739.
16. *Correspondence,* p. 255.
17. *Ibid.,* p. 283.
18. *Ibid.,* p. 412.
19. *Ibid.,* p. 414.
20. James, p. 768.
21. *Ibid.,* p. 782.
22. Johnson, p. 296.
23. *Correspondence,* p. 41.
24. *Ibid.*
25. *Ibid.,* p. 40.
26. James, p. 737.
27. *Correspondence,* p. 147.
28. Herbert R. Collins and David B. Weaver. *Wills of the U.S. Presidents,* New York, Communication Channels, 1976, p. 67.
29. *Ibid.,* p. 79.
30. Curtis, p. 183.
31. Johnson, p. 301.
32. *Ibid.,* p. 302.
33. James, p. 732.
34. *Ibid.,* p. 733.
35. *Correspondence,* p. 380.
36. *Ibid.,* p. 330.
37. *Ibid.,* p. 407.
38. James, p. 780.
39. *Ibid.,* p. 783.

The 8th, Martin Van Buren

1. Holmes Alexander, *The American Talleyrand,* New York, Harper & Brothers, 1935, p. 298.

2. *Ibid.,* p. 405.
3. Edward M. Shepard, *Martin Van Buren,* Boston, Houghton Mifflin Co., 1972, p. 433.
4. Denis Tilden Lynch, *An Epoch and a Man,* New York, Horace Liveright, 1929, p. 522.
5. Alexander, p. 407.
6. Lynch, p. 542.
7. *Ibid.,* p. 543.
8. Page Smith, *The Nation Comes of Age: A People's History of the Ante-Bellum Years,* New York, McGraw-Hill Book Co., 1981, p. 99.

The 9th, William Henry Harrison

1. The nearest other occasion was when James A. Garfield was assassinated just 199 days after taking office and was succeeded by Chester A. Arthur, the vice-president.
2. Freeman Cleaves, *Old Tippecanoe,* New York, Charles Scribner's Sons, 1939, p. 321.
3. Page Smith, *Nation, op. cit.,* p. 183.
4. *Ibid.*
5. *Ibid.,* p. 182.
6. Stefan Lorant, *The Presidency from Washington to Truman,* New York, Macmillan Co., 1952, p. 187.
7. *Ibid.,* p. 160.
8. Joseph Nathan Kane, *Facts About the Presidents,* New York, Ace Books, 1976, p. 114.
9. Page Smith, *Nation, op. cit.,* p. 184.
10. Cleaves, p. 336.
11. Page Smith, *Nation, op. cit.,* p. 184.
12. *Niles National Register,* March 6, 1841.
13. *Ibid.,* April 10, 1841.
14. *Ibid.*
15. *Ibid.*
16. Page Smith, *Nation, op. cit.,* p. 185.
17. Collins and Weaver, *op cit.,* pp. 74–75.

The 10th, John Tyler

1. Oliver Perry Chitwood, *John Tyler: Champion of the Old South,* New York, Russell & Russell, 1964, p. 400.
2. Lyon Gardiner Tyler, *The Letters and Times of the Tylers,* Vol. 2, Richmond, Va., Whittet & Shepperson, 1885–96, p. 478.

310 Chapter Notes—Polk; Taylor; Fillmore; Pierce

3. Don Smith, *Peculiarities of the Presidents,* Van Wert, Ohio, Wilkinson Printing Co., 1938, p. 22.
4. *Letters,* Vols. 2 and 3.
5. *Letters,* Vol. 2, p. 533.
6. *Letters,* Vol. 3, p. 664.
7. Henry A. Wise, *Seven Decades of the Union,* Richmond, Va., J.W. Randolph & English, 1881, p. 278.
8. *Letters,* Vol. 3, p. 670.
9. *Ibid.,* p. 672.
10. *Ibid.*
11. *Ibid.*

The 11th, James K. Polk

1. Wayne C. Moore, of the Tennessee State Library Archives in Nashville, in a letter to the writer, recounts this story. It is also told by the official guides at the Capitol, and is recorded in at least three publications.
2. Collins and Weaver, *op. cit.,* p. 94.
3. Moore letter.
4. Bill Severn, *Frontier President: James K. Polk,* New York, Ives Washburn, 1965, p. 196.
5. James K. Polk, *Polk: The Diary of the President 1845-1849,* Edited by Allan Nevins, New York, Longmans, Green & Co., 1952, p. 380.
6. *Ibid.,* p. 386.
7. Severn, p. 200.
8. *Diary,* p. 389.
9. *Ibid.,* p. 388.
10. *Ibid.,* p. 386.
11. *Ibid.,* p. 387.
12. *Ibid.,* p. 388.
13. *Ibid.,* p. 392.
14. *Ibid.,* p. 393.
15. *Ibid.,* p. 395.
16. *Ibid.,* p. 396.
17. *Ibid.,* p. 398.
18. *Ibid.,* p. 403.
19. *Ibid.,* p. 404.
20. Severn, p. 217.

The 12th, Zachary Taylor

1. Page Smith, *Nation, op. cit.,* p. 1069.
2. Richard M. Ketchum, "Faces From the Past XII," *American Heritage Magazine,* New York, American Heritage Publishing Co., October 1963, p. 53.
3. Don Smith, *op. cit.,* p. 68.

4 .W.E. Woodward, *History, op. cit.,* p. 445.
5. Stefan Lorant, *Pictorial History, op. cit.,* p. 196.
6. Edwin P. Hoyt, *Zachary Taylor,* Chicago, Reilly & Co., 1966, p. 163.
7. *Ibid.*
8. Henry Steele Commager and Allan Nevins, eds., *op. cit.,* p. 628.
9. Holman Hamilton, *Zachary Taylor: Soldier in the White House,* Indianapolis, Bobbs-Merrill Co., 1951, p. 163.
10. *Ibid.*
11. The writer has consulted with Dr. Arch Logan of Spokane, Washington, a specialist in gastro-intestinal disorders, about Taylor's symptoms. He suggested that cholera could not be ruled out.
12. Hamilton, pp. 392-93.
13. *Ibid.,* p. 394.

The 13th, Millard Fillmore

1. Dorothea Dix, *The Lady and the President: The Letters of Dorothea Dix and Millard Fillmore,* Edited by Charles M. Snyder, Lexington, University Press of Kentucky, 1975, p. 215.
2. *Ibid.,* p. 252.
3. *Ibid.,* p. 244.
4. *Ibid.,* p. 252.
5. *Ibid.,* p. 258.
6. Robert J. Rayback, *Millard Fillmore,* Buffalo, N.Y., Henry Stewart, 1959, p. 422.
7. *Ibid.,* p. 420.
8. William Elliott Griffis, *Millard Fillmore,* Ithaca, N.Y., Andrus & Church, 1915, p. 143.

The 14th, Franklin Pierce

1. Page Smith, *Nation, op. cit.,* p. 1089.
2. *Ibid.*
3. Stuart Holbrook, *Lost Men of American History,* New York, Macmillan Co., 1946, p. 329.
4. Roy Franklin Nichols, *Franklin Pierce,* Philadelphia, University of Pennsylvania Press, 1931, p. 509.
5. *Ibid.*
6. *Ibid.,* p. 522.
7. *Ibid.,* p. 526.
8. Linda Ellerbee, *And So It Goes,* New York, Berkley Books, 1987, p. 142.

The 15th, James Buchanan

1. William Shakespeare, *Twelfth Night,* Act 2, Scene 5.
2. James Street, *The Civil War,* New York, Dial Press, 1953, p. 3.
3. Irving Sloan, ed., *James Buchanan, 1791–1868,* Dobbs Ferry, N.Y., Oceana Publications, 1968, p. 18.
4. Philip Shriver Klein, *President James Buchanan,* University Park, Pennsylvania State University Press, 1962, p. 402.
5. *Ibid.*
6. *Ibid.,* p. 409.
7. *Ibid.,* p. 410.
8. *Ibid.,* p. 414.
9. Philip Shriver Klein, *The Story of Wheatland,* Lancaster, Pa., Junior League of Lancaster, 1936, p. 52.
10. Elbert B. Smith, *The Presidency of James Buchanan,* Lawrence, University Press of Kansas, 1975, p. 30.
11. *Ibid.*
12. Klein, *President,* p. 427.
13. Klein, *Wheatland,* p. 55.

The 16th, Abraham Lincoln

1. Carl Sandburg, *Abraham Lincoln: The Prairie Years and the War Years,* New York, Harcourt, Brace & Co., 1954, p. 689.
2. Stephen B. Oates, *With Malice Toward None: The Life of Abraham Lincoln,* New York, Harper & Row, 1977, p. 426.
3. *Ibid.*
4. Stefan Lorant, *Lincoln: A Picture Story of His Life,* New York, W.W. Norton & Co., 1969, p. 264.
5. Sandburg, p. 704.
6. *Ibid.*
7. Jim Bishop, *The Day Lincoln Was Shot,* New York, Harper & Brothers, 1955, p. 145.
8. Sandburg, p. 710.
9. Bishop, p. 210.
10. *Ibid.,* p. 211.
11. *Ibid.,* p. 213.
12. Sandburg, p. 710.
13. Lorant, p. 229.
14. Oates, p. 434.
15. Stephen B. Oates, *Abraham Lincoln: The Man Behind the Myths,* New York, Harper & Row, 1984, pp. 170–77.
16. Guy W. Moore, *The Case of Mrs. Sur-
ratt,* Norman, University of Oklahoma Press, 1954, p. 93.
17. *Ibid.,* p. 118.
18. Bishop, p. 300.
19. *Ibid.,* p. 299.

The 17th, Andrew Johnson

1. James S. Jones, *Andrew Johnson: Seventeenth President of the United States,* Greeneville, Tenn., East Tennessee Publishing Co., 1901, p. 332.
2. Robert W. Winston, *Andrew Johnson: Plebeian and Patriot,* New York, Henry Holt & Co., 1928, p. 484.
3. *Ibid.,* p. 487.
4. *Ibid.,* p. 494.
5. Eric L. McKitrick, ed., *Andrew Johnson: A Profile,* New York, Hill & Wang, 1969, p. 199.
6. *Ibid.,* p. 207.
7. Lloyd Paul Stryker, *Andrew Johnson: A Study in Courage,* New York, Macmillan Co., 1929, p. 806.
8. Jones, p. 350.
9. McKitrick, p. 213.
10. Stryker, p. 811.
11. W.E. Woodward, *History, op. cit.,* p. 597.
12. McKitrick, p. 217.

The 18th, Ulysses S. Grant

1. W.E. Woodward, *Meet General Grant,* Literary Guild of America, 1928, p. 479.
2. *Ibid.,* p. 483.
3. William S. McFeely, *Grant,* New York, W.W. Norton & Co., 1981, p. 490.
4. Woodward, pp. 486–87.
5. William B. Hesseltine, *Ulysses S. Grant,* New York, Dodd, Mead & Co., 1935, p. 447.
6. Woodward, p. 450.
7. Richard Goldhurst, *Many Are the Hearts,* New York, Reader's Digest Press, 1975, p. 112.
8. Woodward, p. 450.
9. Goldhurst, p. 145.
10. McFeely, p. 496.
11. Goldhurst, p. 145.
12. McFeely, p. 496.
13. Goldhurst, p. 149.
14. McFeely, p. 505.
15. Edmund Wilson, *Patriotic Gore,* New York, Oxford University Press, 1962, p. 143.

16. Goldhurst, p. 199.
17. *Ibid.,* p. 190.
18. *New York Times,* March 3, 1885.
19. Harry Thurston Peck, *Twenty Years of the Republic: 1885-1905,* New York, Dodd, Mead & Co., 1907, p. 53.
20. Goldhurst, p. 230.
21. Hamlin Garland, *Ulysses S. Grant: His Life and Character,* New York, Doubleday & McClure Co., 1898, p. 524.

The 19th, Rutherford B. Hayes

1. Arthur Bishop, ed., *Rutherford B. Hayes, 1822-1893,* Dobbs Ferry, N.Y., Oceana Publications, 1969, p. 124.
2. Harry Barnard, *Rutherford B. Hayes and His Administration,* Indianapolis, Bobbs-Merrill Co., 1954, p. 496.
3. *Ibid.,* p. 498.
4. *Ibid.,* p. 514.
5. *Ibid.*
6. A third-party movement organized by farmers, westerners, workers, and small businessmen to bring greater financial benefits to a large segment of society.
7. Rutherford B. Hayes, *Diary and Letters of Rutherford Birchard Hayes,* Edited by Charles Richard Williams, Vol. 5, *1891-1892,* Columbus, Ohio State Archeological and Historical Society, 1926, p. 158.
8. Barnard, p. 522.

The 20th, James A. Garfield

1. John Clark Ridpath, *The Life and Work of James A. Garfield and the Tragic Story of His Death,* Cincinnati, Jones Brothers & Co., 1881, p. 517.
2. *Ibid.,* p. 607.
3. *Ibid.,* p. 625.
4. *Ibid.,* p. 627.
5. Allan Peskin, *Garfield,* Kent, Ohio, Kent State University Press, 1978, p. 604.
6. Justus D. Doenecke, *The Presidencies of James A. Garfield and Chester A. Arthur,* Lawrence, The Regents Press of Kansas, 1981, p. 53.
7. Peskin, p. 600.
8. Richard Shenkman, and Kurt Reiger, *One-Night Stands With American History,* New York, William Morrow & Co., 1980, p. 152.

9. Peskin, p. 601.
10. *Ibid.*
11. Ridpath, p. 625.
12. *Ibid.,* p. 631.
13. Don Smith, *op. cit.,* p. 121.

The 21st, Chester A. Arthur

1. Not all historians would agree with this view. Since Arthur's papers were destroyed, only conjecture can be made.
2. Thomas C. Reeves, *Gentleman Boss: The Life of Chester Alan Arthur,* New York, Alfred A. Knopf, 1975, p. 417.
3. Harry Thurston Peck, *op. cit.,* p. 6.
4. Don Smith, *op. cit.,* p. 80.
5. Reeves, p. 418.
6. *Ibid.*
7. W.E. Woodward, *History, op. cit.,* p. 655.

The 22nd and 24th, Grover Cleveland

1. Grover Cleveland, *Letters of Grover Cleveland, 1850-1908,* Edited by Allan Nevins, Boston, Houghton Mifflin Co., 1933, p. 728.
2. *Ibid.,* p. 727.
3. *Ibid.,* p. 515.
4. *Ibid.,* p. 495.
5. *Ibid.,* p. 741.
6. *Ibid.*
7. *Ibid.,* p. 579.
8. *Ibid.,* p. 737.
9. Denis Tilden Lynch, *Grover Cleveland,* New York, Horace Liveright, 1932, p. 761.
10. Robert McElroy, *Grover Cleveland: The Man and the Statesman,* New York, Harper & Brothers, 1923, p. 318.
11. *Ibid.*
12. Harry Thurston Peck, *op. cit.,* pp. 460-64.
13. *Letters,* p. 755.
14. *Ibid.,* p. 763.
15. *Ibid.*

The 23rd, Benjamin Harrison

1. The United States Constitution permits such to happen.

2. Leland Baldwin, *The Stream of American History,* Vol. 2, New York, American Book Co., 1952, p. 32.
3. Harry J. Sievers, *Benjamin Harrison: Hoosier Statesman,* New York, University Publishers, 1959, pp. 241–42.
4. Hayes accompanied the president on the trip back to Washington as far as Columbus, Ohio.
5. Sievers, p. 243.
6. Stefan Lorant, *Pictorial History, op. cit.,* p. 395.
7. *Ibid.,* p. 410.
8. No doubt referring to Edgar Allan Poe's poem, "The Raven."
9. Roger Butterfield, *The American Past,* New York, Simon & Schuster, 1947, p. 299.
10. Harry Thurston Peck, *op. cit.,* p. 171.
11. Sievers, p. 250.
12. *Ibid.,* p. 256.
13. Collins & Weaver, *op. cit.,* pp. 146–157.
14. Baldwin, p. 30.
15. *Ibid.*
16. David C. Whitney, *The Graphic Story of American Presidents,* Edited by Thomas C. Jones, Chicago, J.G. Ferguson Co., 1972, p. 257.

The 25th, William McKinley

1. *New York Times,* September 5, 1901.
2. *Ibid.,* September 7, 1901.
3. *Ibid.*
4. Selig Adler, "Operation on President McKinley," *Scientific American,* March 1963, p. 122.
5. *New York Times,* September 7, 1901.
6. *Ibid.,* September 8, 1901.
7. Adler, p. 126.
8. Because they must depend on the wire services, newspapers carried news of the previous day's events.
9. *New York Times,* September 11, 1901.
10. *Ibid.,* September 12, 1901.
11. *Ibid.,* September 13, 1901.
12. Margaret Leech, *In the Days of McKinley,* New York, Harper & Brothers, 1959, p. 601.
13. *Ibid.*
14. Adler, p. 128.
15. *New York Times,* September 14, 1901.
16. Adler, p. 128.
17. *Ibid.,* p. 118.
18. *Ibid.,* p. 129.
19. *Ibid.,* p. 127.
20. *New York Times,* October 27, 28, 29, 1901.

The 26th, Theodore Roosevelt

1. William Allen White, *Masks in a Pageant,* New York, Macmillan Co., 1929, p. 283.
2. Stefan Lorant, *The Life and Times of Theodore Roosevelt,* Garden City, N.Y., Doubleday & Co., 1959, p. 516.
3. Henry F. Pringle, *Theodore Roosevelt,* New York, Harcourt Brace Javanovich, 1931, p. 362.
4. *Ibid.*
5. Walter Johnson, *William Allen White's America,* New York, Henry Holt & Co., 1947, p. 202.
6. Lorant, p. 572.
7. *Ibid.*
8. *Ibid.,* p. 557.
9. Pringle, p. 402.
10. *Ibid.,* p. 403.
11. *Ibid.,* p. 415.
12. *Ibid.*
13. Hermann Hagedorn, *The Bugle That Woke America,* New York, John Day Co., 1940, p. 159.
14. Lorant, p. 503.
15. Pringle, p. 409.
16. Hermann Hagedorn, *The Roosevelt Family of Sagamore Hill,* New York, Macmillan Co., 1954, p. 412.
17. *Ibid.*
18. *Ibid.,* p. 416.
19. Lorant, p. 620.
20. *Ibid.*
21. *Ibid.,* p. 621.

The 27th, William Howard Taft

1. Henry R. Pringle, *The Life and Times of William Howard Taft,* Vol. 2, New York, Farrar & Rinehart, 1939, p. 847.
2. Frederick C. Hicks, *William Howard Taft: Yale Professor of Law & New Haven Citizen,* New Haven, Yale University Press, 1945, p. 2.
3. *Ibid.,* p. 7.
4. Pringle, p. 851.
5. Hicks, p. 21.

6. Don Smith, *op. cit.,* p. 80.
7. Hicks, p. 130.
8. Herbert S. Duffy, *William Howard Taft,* New York, Minton, Balch & Co., 1930, pp. 311–12.
9. Pringle, p. 1071.

The 28th, Woodrow Wilson

1. Gene Smith, *When the Cheering Stopped,* Alexandria, Va., Time-Life Books, 1964, p. 61.
2. Edith Bolling Wilson, *My Memoir,* 1939, Reprint, New York, Arno Press, 1980, p. 295.
3. Smith, p. 93.
4. *Memoir,* p. 286.
5. *Ibid.,* p. 289.
6. Smith, p. 92.
7. *Memoir,* p. 289.
8. *Ibid.,* p. 290.
9. *Ibid.,* p. 299.
10. Smith, p. 219.
11. Josephus Daniels, *Life of Woodrow Wilson,* New York, John C. Winston Co., 1924, p. 358.
12. Tom Schactman, *Edith and Woodrow,* Thorndike, Maine, Thorndike Press, 1981, p. 242.
13. William Allen White, *The Autobiography of William Allen White,* New York, Macmillan Co., 1946, pp. 590–91.
14. Smith, p. 160.
15. Schactman, p. 254.
16. *Ibid.*
17. Smith, p. 161.
18. *Ibid.,* p. 174.
19. *Ibid.,* p. 196.

The 29th, Warren G. Harding

1. Samuel Hopkins Adams, *The Incredible Era,* Boston, Houghton Mifflin Co., 1939 (title of book).
2. Isabel Leighton, *The Aspirin Age,* New York, Simon & Schuster, 1949, p. 84.
3. William Allen White, *Autobiography, op. cit.,* p. 616.
4. William Allen White, *Masks, op. cit.,* p. 422.
5. Walter Johnson, *op. cit.,* p. 370.

6. Robert K. Murray, *The Harding Era,* Minneapolis, University of Minnesota Press, 1969, p. 418.
7. White, *Autobiography, op. cit.,* p. 619.
8. Francis Russell, *The Shadow of Blooming Grove,* New York, McGraw-Hill Book Co., 1968, p. 80.
9. Murray, p. 458.
10. *Ibid.,* p. 438.
11. Adams, p. 334.
12. Russell, p. 466.
13. *Ibid.,* p. 566.
14. Herbert Hoover, *The Memoirs of Herbert Hoover: The Great Depression, 1929–1941,* New York, Macmillan Co., 1952, p. 49.
15. *Ibid.*
16. Murray, p. 447.
17. *New York Times,* July 27, 1923.
18. Hoover, p. 31.
19. Murray, p. 448.
20. *Ibid.,* p. 449.
21. Russell, p. 591.
22. *Ibid.*
23. *Ibid.,* p. 589.
24. *Ibid.,* p. 592.
25. *Ibid.,* p. 594.
26. Murray, p. 292.

The 30th, Calvin Coolidge

1. William Allen White, *Masks, op. cit.,* p. 437.
2. Claude M. Fuess, *Calvin Coolidge: The Man From Vermont,* Boston, Little, Brown & Co., 1940, p. 445.
3. *Ibid.*
4. *Ibid.,* p. 448.
5. Ishbel Ross, *Grace Coolidge and Her Era,* New York, Dodd, Mead & Co., 1962, p. 226.
6. Edward Connery Lathem, ed., *Meet Calvin Coolidge,* Brattleboro, Vt., Stephen Greene Press, 1960, p. 191.
7. Ross, p. 281.
8. William Allen White, *A Puritan in Babylon,* New York, Macmillan Co., 1958, p. 436.
9. *Ibid.,* p. 437.
10. *Ibid.,* p. 477.
11. *Ibid.,* p. 440.
12. Ross, p. 288.
13. Fuess, p. 464.

The 31st, Herbert Hoover

1. Richard Norton Smith, *An Uncommon Man: The Triumph of Herbert Hoover,* New York, Simon & Schuster, 1984, p. 120.
2. Leland Baldwin, *op. cit.,* p. 622.
3. Smith, p. 120.
4. Eugene Lyons, *Herbert Hoover: A Biography,* Garden City, N.Y., Doubleday & Co., 1964, p. 316.
5. *Ibid.,* p. 312.
6. *Ibid.,* p. 333.
7. *Ibid.,* p. 352.
8. *Ibid.,* p. 333.
9. *Ibid.,* p. 312.
10. Gary Dean Best, *Herbert Hoover: The Postpresidential Years,* Vol. 1, *1933–1945,* Stanford, Calif., Hoover Institution Press, 1983, p. 91.
11. Harold Wolfe, *Herbert Hoover,* New York, Exposition Press, 1956, p. 358.
12. Smith, p. 243.
13. Lyons, pp. 397–98.
14. The house later became the home of the president of Stanford.
15. Lyons, p. 372.
16. Anne Emery, *American Friend: Herbert Hoover,* New York, Rand McNally & Co., 1967, p. 198.
17. *Ibid.,* p. 209.
18. *Ibid.,* p. 416.
19. *Ibid.*
20. Smith, p. 425.
21. *Ibid.,* p. 409.

The 32nd, Franklin D. Roosevelt

1. Hugh Gregory Gallagher, *FDR's Splendid Deception,* New York, Dodd, Mead & Co., 1985, p. 186.
2. Jim Bishop, *FDR's Last Year,* New York, William Morrow & Co., 1974, p. 14.
3. *Ibid.,* p. 6.
4. *Ibid.,* p. 18.
5. *Ibid.,* p. 157.
6. Eleanor Roosevelt, *The Autobiography of Eleanor Roosevelt,* New York, Harper & Brothers, 1958, p. 273.
7. Finis Farr, *F.D.R.,* New Rochelle, N.Y., Arlington House, 1972, p. 418.
8. Bernard Asbell, *When F.D.R. Died,* New York, Holt, Rinehart & Winston, 1961, p. 19.
9. Eleanor Roosevelt, p. 275.
10. Bishop, p. 487.
11. *Ibid.,* p. 499.
12. William D. Hassett, *Off the Record With F.D.R., 1942–1945,* New Brunswick, N.J., Rutgers University Press, 1958, p. 327.
13. Bishop, p. 568.
14. *Ibid.,* p. 573.
15. *Ibid.*
16. Asbell, p. 38.

The 33rd, Harry S Truman

1. Harry S. Truman, *Off the Record: The Private Papers of Harry S. Truman,* Edited by Robert H. Ferrell, New York, Harper & Row, 1980, p. 224.
2. Margaret Truman, *Bess W. Truman,* New York, Macmillan Co., 1986, p. 390.
3. *Papers,* p. 287.
4. *Ibid.,* p. 288.
5. *Ibid.*
6. Charles Robbins, *Last of His Kind,* New York, William Morrow & Co., 1979, p. 147.
7. Sid Frank, and Arden Davis Melick, *The Presidents: Tidbits and Trivia,* New York, Greenwich House, 1984, p. 18.
8. Robbins, p. 133.
9. Margaret Truman, *Bess,* p. 397.
10. *Papers,* p. 239.
11. Margaret Truman, *Harry S. Truman,* New York, William Morrow & Co., 1973, p. 566.
12. *Papers,* p. 239.
13. Margaret Truman, *Bess,* p. 404.
14. *Papers,* p. 242.
15. *Ibid.,* pp. 266–67.
16. Margaret Truman, *Bess,* p. 390.
17. *Papers,* p. 268,
18. Margaret Truman, *Bess,* p. 405.
19. *Papers,* p. 375.
20. Margaret Truman, *Bess,* p. 416.
21. *Papers,* p. 247.
22. Margaret Truman, *Harry,* p. 564.

The 34th, Dwight D. Eisenhower

1. *New York Times,* January 8, 1961.
2. Stephen E. Ambrose, *Eisenhower,* Vol. 2, *The President,* New York, Simon & Schuster, 1984, p. 611.

3. *New York Times,* January 18, 1961.
4. Ambrose, p. 616.
5. Dwight D. Eisenhower, "Now That I Am a Private Citizen," *Saturday Evening Post,* May 13, 1961, p. 20.
6. Merlin Gustafson, "Religion of a President," *Christian Century,* April 30, 1969, p. 613.
7. Dr. Graham spoke at a Rotary Club meeting in Spokane, Washington.
8. Dwight D. Eisenhower, *The Eisenhower Diaries,* Edited by Robert H. Ferrell, New York, W.W. Norton & Co., 1981, p. 5.
9. Ambrose, p. 617.
10. *New York Times,* December 23, 1968.
11. *Ibid.,* October 14, 1965.
12. John Steele, "Coming Up All Roses for Ike," *Life,* September 24, 1965, p. 49.
13. *Ibid.,* p. 50.
14. Ambrose, p. 669.
15. "Ike's Gettysburg Farm: A Gift to the Nation," *U.S. News and World Report,* December 11, 1967, p. 17.
16. "General's Heart," *Newsweek,* September 2, 1968, p. 42.
17. Ambrose, p. 675.

The 35th, John F. Kennedy

1. William Manchester, *The Death of a President,* New York, Harper & Row, 1967, p. 87.
2. *Ibid.,* p. 113.
3. Jim Bishop, *The Day Kennedy Was Shot,* New York, Funk and Wagnalls, 1968, p. 61.
4. Manchester, p. 109.
5. Bishop, p. 32.
6. Ralph G. Martin, *A Hero for Our Time,* New York, Macmillan Co., 1983, p. 567.
7. Manchester, p. 121.
8. Bishop, p. 137.
9. Manchester, p. 160.
10. Bishop, p. 139.
11. Later L.B.J. was to honor Youngblood for this act of heroism.
12. Manchester, p. 160.
13. *Ibid.,* p. 162.
14. Jimmy Breslin, "A Death in Emergency Room No. One," *Saturday Evening Post,* December 14, 1963, p. 30.
15. Manchester, p. 186.
16. Breslin, p. 30.
17. *Ibid.*

18. Manchester, p. 217.
19. *Ibid.,* p. 348.
20. *Ibid.,* p. 218.
21. Bishop, p. 191.
22. Manchester, p. 283.
23. *Ibid.,* p. 289.
24. *Ibid.,* p. 297.
25. *Ibid.,* p. 298.
26. Bishop, p. 220.
27. *Ibid.*
28. *Ibid.,* p. 220.
29. Manchester, p. 305.
30. *Report of the President's Commission on the Assassination of President John F. Kennedy,* Washington, U.S. Government Printing Office, September 27, 1964, pp. 10–13.
31. *New York Times Index,* 1979, Vol. 67, p. 686.
32. *Ibid.*
33. *Ibid.*

The 36th, Lyndon B. Johnson

1. Merle Miller, *Lyndon,* New York, G.P. Putnam's Sons, 1980, p. 506.
2. Leo Janos, "The Last Days of the President—LBJ in Retirement," *Atlantic Monthly,* July 1973, p. 35.
3. Hugh Sidey, "The Presidency: Some Pages Not in L.B.J.'s Book," *Life,* November 5, 1971, p. 4.
4. George Christian, *The President Steps Down,* New York, Macmillan Co., 1970, p. 255.
5. Miller, p. 549.
6. Christian, p. 269.
7. Marshall Frady, "Cooling Off with LBJ," *Harper's Magazine,* June 1969, p. 66.
8. *Ibid.*
9. Janos, p. 37.
10. Sidey, p. 4.
11. Doris Kearns, *Lyndon Johnson and the American Dream,* New York, New American Library, 1976, p. 92.
12. *Ibid.,* p. 14.
13. *Ibid.,* p. 356.
14. *Ibid.,* p. 377.
15. *Ibid.,* p. 17.
16. Miller, p. 550.
17. *Ibid.*
18. Sidey, p. 4.
19. Kearns, p. 15.
20. Miller, p. 551.

Bibliography

Adams, Abigail. *The Book of Abigail and John: Selected Letters of the Adams Family, 1762–1784.* Edited by L.H. Butterfield, Marc Friedlaender and Mary Jo Kline. Cambridge, Mass.: Harvard University Press, 1975.

Adams, James Truslow. *The Living Jefferson.* New York: Charles Scribner's Sons, 1949.

Adams, John. *The Adams-Jefferson Letters.* Edited by Lester J. Cappon. 2 vols. Chapel Hill: University of North Carolina Press, 1959.

Adams, John Quincy. *The Diary of John Quincy Adams.* Edited by Allan Nevins. New York: Ungar Publishing Co., 1969.

Adams, Samuel Hopkins. *The Incredible Era.* Boston: Houghton Mifflin Co., 1939.

Adler, Selig. "Operation on President McKinley." *Scientific American,* March 1963, pp. 118–130.

Akers, Charles W. *Abigail Adams: An American Woman.* Edited by Oscar Handlin. Boston: Little, Brown & Co., 1980.

Alexander, Holmes. *The American Talleyrand.* New York: Harper & Brothers, 1935.

Ambrose, Stephen E. *Eisenhower: The President.* Vol. 2. New York: Simon & Schuster, 1984.

Ammon, Harry. *James Monroe: The Quest for National Identity.* New York: McGraw-Hill Book Co., 1971.

"As Eisenhower Looks to 1961." *U.S. News and World Report,* July 18, 1960, pp. 63–65.

Asbell, Bernard. *When F.D.R. Died.* New York: Holt, Rinehart & Winston, 1961.

Associated Press. *The Torch Is Passed: The Associated Press Story of the Death of a President.* New York, 1963.

Bailey, Thomas A. *A Diplomatic History of the American People.* New York: Appleton-Century-Crafts, 1955.

Baldwin, Leland. *The Stream of American History,* Vol. 2. New York: American Book Co., 1952.

Balsiger, David, and Charles E. Sellier, Jr. *The Lincoln Conspiracy.* Los Angeles: Schick Sunn Classic Books, 1977.

Bancroft, George. *Martin Van Buren to the End of His Public Career.* New York: Harper & Brothers, 1889.

Barnard, Harry. *Rutherford B. Hayes and His Administration.* Indianapolis: Bobbs-Merrill Co., 1954.

Barry, Richard H. *True Story of the Assassination of President McKinley at Buffalo.* Buffalo, N.Y.: Robert Allan Reid, 1901.

Bassett, John Spencer. *The Life of Andrew Jackson,* Vol. 2. Garden City, N.Y.: Doubleday, Page & Co., 1911.

Bellamy, Francis Rufus. *The Private Life of George Washington.* New York: Thomas Y. Crowell Co., 1951.

Belin, David W. *November 22, 1963: You Are the Jury.* New York: Quadrangle/ New York Times Book Co., 1973.

Best, Gary Dean. *Herbert Hoover: The Postpresidential Years.* Vol. 1, *1933-1945.* Stanford, Calif.: Hoover Institution Press, 1983.

Bishop, Arthur, ed. *Rutherford B. Hayes, 1822-1893.* Dobbs Ferry, N.Y.: Oceana Publications, 1969.

Bishop, Jim. *The Day Kennedy Was Shot.* New York: Funk & Wagnalls, 1968.

_____. *The Day Lincoln Was Shot.* New York: Harper & Brothers, 1955.

_____. *FDR's Last Year.* New York: William Morrow & Co., 1974.

Bishop, Joseph Bucklin. *Theodore Roosevelt and His Time.* Vol. 2. New York: Charles Scribner's Sons, 1920.

Bottorff, William K. *Thomas Jefferson.* Boston: Twayne Publishers, 1979.

Branch, Edward Douglas. *The Sentimental Years (1836-1860).* American Century Series. New York: Hill & Wang, 1934.

Brant, Irving. *The Fourth President: A Life of James Monroe.* Indianapolis, Bobbs-Merrill Co., 1970.

Breslin, Jimmy. "A Death in Emergency Room No. One." *Saturday Evening Post,* December 14, 1963, pp. 30-31.

Britton, Nan. *The President's Daughter.* New York: Elizabeth Ann Guild, 1927.

Brodie, Fawn M. *Thomas Jefferson: An Intimate History.* New York: W.W. Norton & Co., 1974.

Burner, David. *Herbert Hoover: A Public Life.* New York: Alfred A. Knopf, 1979.

Butterfield, Roger. *The American Past.* New York: Simon & Schuster, 1947.

Carroll, John Alexander, and Mary Wells Ashworth. *George Washington.* Vol. 7, *First in Peace.* (Completing the biography by Douglas Southall Freeman.) New York: Charles Scribner's Sons, 1957.

Chinard, Gilbert. *Honest John Adams.* Boston: Little, Brown & Co., 1933.

_____. *Thomas Jefferson: The Apostle of Americanism.* 2d ed., rev. 1939. Reprint. Ann Arbor: University of Michigan Press, 1957.

Chitwood, Oliver Perry. *John Tyler: Champion of the Old South.* New York: Russell & Russell, 1964.

Christian, George. *The President Steps Down.* New York: Macmillan Co., 1970.

Cleaves, Freeman. *Old Tippecanoe.* New York: Charles Scribner's Sons, 1939.

Cleveland, Grover. *Letters of Grover Cleveland, 1850-1908.* Edited by Allan Nevins. Boston: Houghton Mifflin Co., 1933.

Cole, Donald B. *Martin Van Buren and the American Political System.* Princeton, N.J.: Princeton University Press, 1984.

Coletta, Paolo E. *The Presidency of William Howard Taft.* Lawrence: University Press of Kansas, 1973.

Collins, Herbert R., and David B. Weaver. *Wills of the U.S. Presidents.* New York: Communication Channels, 1976.

Commager, Henry Steele, and Allan Nevins, eds. *The Heritage of America.* Boston: Little, Brown & Co., 1951.

Crawford, Kenneth. "A Reporter Remembers the Political Ike." *Newsweek,* April 7, 1969, pp. 22-27.

Cresson, W.P. *James Monroe.* Chapel Hill: University of North Carolina Press, 1946.

Curtis, James C. *Andrew Jackson and the Search for Vindication.* Edited by Oscar Handlin. Boston: Little, Brown & Co., 1976.

————. *The Fox at Bay.* Lexington: University Press of Kentucky, 1970.

Dabney, Virginius. *The Jefferson Scandals: A Rebuttal.* New York: Dodd, Mead & Co., 1981.

Daniels, Josephus. *Life of Woodrow Wilson.* New York: John C. Winston Co., 1924.

Daugherty, Harry, and Thomas Dixon. *The Inside Story of the Harding Tragedy.* New York: Churchill Co., 1932.

"The Day Kennedy Died." *Newsweek,* December 2, 1963, pp. 20–26.

Dix, Dorothea. *The Lady and the President: The Letters of Dorothea Dix and Millard Fillmore.* Edited by Charles M. Snyder. Lexington: University Press of Kentucky, 1975.

Doenecke, Justus D. *The Presidencies of James A. Garfield & Chester A. Arthur.* Lawrence: Regents Press of Kansas, 1981.

Duffy, Herbert S. *William Howard Taft.* New York: Minton, Balch & Co., 1930.

"Dwight D. Eisenhower, 1890–1969." *Newsweek,* April 7, 1969, pp. 18–21.

Eckenrode, H.J. *Rutherford B. Hayes: Statesman of Reunion.* Port Washington, N.Y.: Kennikat Press, 1963.

Eisenhower, Dwight D. *At Ease.* New York: Avon Books, 1967.

————. *The Eisenhower Diaries.* Edited by Robert H. Ferrell. New York: W.W. Norton & Co., 1981.

————. "Now That I Am a Private Citizen." *Saturday Evening Post,* May 13, 1961, p. 19.

Eisenschiml, Otto. *Why Was Lincoln Murdered?* New York: Grosset & Dunlap, 1937.

Ellerbee, Linda. *And So It Goes.* New York: Berkley Books, 1987.

Emery, Anne. *American Friend: Herbert Hoover.* New York: Rand McNally & Co., 1967.

"The Evolution of an Assassin." *Life,* February 21, 1964, pp. 68–80.

Falkner, Leonard. *The President Who Wouldn't Retire.* New York: Coward-McCann, 1967.

Farr, Finis. *F.D.R.* New Rochelle, N.Y.: Arlington House, 1972.

Ferrell, Robert H. *Truman: A Centenary Remembrance.* New York: Viking Press, 1984.

Flexner, James Thomas. *Washington: The Indispensable Man.* New York: New American Library, 1969.

Foote, Henry Stuart. *Eulogy upon the Life and Character of James K. Polk.* Washington: Thomas Ritchie, 1949.

Frady, Marshall. "Cooling Off with LBJ." *Harper's Magazine,* June 1969, pp. 65–67.

Frank, Sid, and Arden Davis Melick. *The Presidents: Tidbits and Trivia.* New York: Greenwich House, 1984.

Freeman, Douglas Southall. *Washington.* New York: Charles Scribner's Sons, 1957.

Fuess, Claude M. *Calvin Coolidge: The Man from Vermont.* Boston: Little, Brown & Co., 1940.

Gallagher, Hugh Gregory. *FDR's Splendid Deception.* New York: Dodd, Mead & Co., 1985.

Garland, Hamlin. *Ulysses S. Grant: His Life and Character.* New York: Doubleday & McClure Co., 1898.

320   Bibliography

Gay, Sidney Howard. *James Madison.* Boston: Houghton Mifflin Co., 1884.

"General's Heart." *Newsweek,* September 2, 1968, p. 42.

Gilman, Daniel C. *James Monroe.* Boston: Houghton Mifflin Co., 1883.

Goldhurst, Richard. *Many Are the Hearts.* New York: Reader's Digest Press, 1975.

Goldman, Eric F. "The White House and the Intellectuals." *Harper's Magazine,* January 1969, pp. 31–34.

Grant, U.S. *Personal Memoirs of U.S. Grant.* 2 vols. New York: Charles L. Webster & Co., 1885–86.

Griffis, William Elliot. *Millard Fillmore.* Ithaca, N.Y.: Andrus & Church, 1915.

Gunther, John. *Roosevelt in Retrospect.* New York: Harper & Brothers, 1950.

Gustafson, Merlin. "Religion of a President." *Christian Century,* April 30, 1969, p. 613.

Hagedorn, Hermann. *The Bugle that Woke America.* New York: John Day Co., 1940.

_____. *The Roosevelt Family of Sagamore Hill.* New York: Macmillan Co., 1954.

Halstead, Murat. *The Illustrious Life of William McKinley: Our Martyred President.* Chicago: Murat Halstead, 1901.

Hamilton, Holman. *Zachary Taylor: Soldier in the White House.* Indianapolis: Bobbs-Merrill Co., 1951.

Hassett, William D. *Off the Record with F.D.R., 1942–1945.* New Brunswick, N.J.: Rutgers University Press, 1958.

Hatch, Alden. *Franklin D. Roosevelt: An Informal Biography.* New York: Henry Holt & Co., 1947.

Hawthorne, Nathaniel. *The Life of Franklin Pierce.* New York: Garrett Press, 1970.

Hayes, Rutherford B. *Diary and Letters of Rutherford Birchard Hayes.* Edited by Charles Richard Williams. Vol. 5, *1891–1892.* Columbus: Ohio State Archeological and Historical Society, 1926.

Hecht, Marie B. *John Quincy Adams.* New York: Macmillan Co., 1972.

Helm, Katherine. *Mary: Wife of Lincoln.* New York: Harper & Brothers, 1928.

Hesseltine, William B. *Ulysses S. Grant.* New York: Dodd, Mead & Co., 1935.

Hicks, Frederick C. *William Howard Taft: Yale Professor of Law & New Haven Citizen.* New Haven: Yale University Press, 1945.

Holbrook, Stuart. *Lost Men of American History.* New York: Macmillan Co., 1946.

Holland, J.G. *The Life of Abraham Lincoln.* Springfield, Mass.: Gurdon Bill, 1866.

Hoover, Herbert. *The Memoirs of Herbert Hoover: The Great Depression, 1929–1941.* New York: Macmillan Co., 1952.

Hoyt, Edwin P. *Andrew Johnson.* Chicago: Reilly & Lee Co., 1965.

_____. *James A. Garfield.* Chicago: Reilly & Lee Co., 1964.

_____. *James Buchanan.* Chicago: Reilly & Lee Co., 1966.

_____. *James Knox Polk.* Chicago: Reilly & Lee Co., 1965.

_____. *Zachary Taylor.* Chicago: Reilly & Lee Co., 1966.

Hunt, Gaillard. *The Life of James Madison.* New York: Doubleday, Page & Co., 1902.

"Ike Returns to the Heart of America." *Newsweek,* April 14, 1969, pp. 38–43.

"Ike's Gettysburg Farm: A Gift to the Nation." *U.S. News and World Report,* December 11, 1967, p. 17.

"Ike's Health Secrets: Six Rules for Long Life." *U.S. News and World Report,* October 3, 1960, p. 77.

"Investigations." *Time,* February 14, 1964, pp. 16–20.

Jackson, Andrew. *Correspondence of Andrew Jackson.* Edited by John Spencer Bassett. Vol. 6, *1839–1845.* Washington, D.C.: Carnegie Institution of Washington, 1933.

James, Marquis. *The Life of Andrew Jackson.* Indianapolis: Bobbs-Merrill Co., 1938.

————. *They Had Their Hour.* Indianapolis: Bobbs-Merrill Co., 1934.

Janos, Leo. "The Last Days of the President—LBJ In Retirement." *Atlantic Monthly,* July 1973, pp. 35–40.

————. "'72 has not been kind to the ailing L.B.J." *U.S. News and World Report,* October 27, 1972, p. 75.

Jefferson, Thomas. *A Jefferson Profile as Revealed in His Letters.* Edited by Saul K. Padover. New York: John Day Co., 1956.

The JFK Memorial Issue. *Look,* Vol. 28, No. 23, November 17, 1964.

John F. Kennedy Memorial Edition. *Life,* 1963.

Johnson, Andrew. *Speeches of Andrew Johnson.* With a Biography and Introduction by Frank Moore. Boston: Little, Brown & Co., 1866.

Johnson, Gerald W. *Andrew Jackson: An Epic in Homespun.* New York: Minton Balch & Co., 1927.

Johnson, Walter. *William Allen White's America.* New York: Henry Holt & Co., 1947.

Jones, James S. *Andrew Johnson: Seventeenth President of the United States.* Greeneville, Tenn.: East Tennessee Publishing Co., 1901.

Kane, Joseph Nathan. *Facts About the Presidents.* New York: Ace Books, 1976.

Kearns, Doris. *Lyndon Johnson and the American Dream.* New York: New American Library, 1976.

"Kennedy's Last Journey." *Life,* December 6, 1963, pp. 38–49.

Ketcham, Ralph. *James Madison: A Biography.* New York: Macmillan Co., 1971.

Ketchum, Richard M. "Faces from the Past—XII." *American Heritage,* Vol. 14, No. 6, October 1963, pp. 52–53.

King, Larry L. "An Epitaph for LBJ." *Harper's Magazine,* March 1968, pp. 14–19.

Klein, Philip Shriver. *President James Buchanan.* University Park: Pennsylvania State University Press, 1962.

————. *The Story of Wheatland.* Lancaster, Pa.: Junior League of Lancaster, 1936.

Lane, Mark. *Rush to Judgment.* New York: Holt, Rinehart & Co., 1966.

Lash, Joseph P. *Eleanor and Franklin.* New York: W.W. Norton & Co., 1971.

Lathem, Edward Connery, ed. *Meet Calvin Coolidge.* Brattleboro, Vt.: Stephen Greene Press, 1960.

Leech, Margaret. *In the Days of McKinley.* New York: Harper & Brothers, 1959.

————. *Reveille in Washington, 1860–1865.* New York: Harper & Brothers, 1941.

Leighton, Isabel. *The Aspirin Age.* New York: Simon & Schuster, 1949.

Lifton, David S. *Best Evidence.* New York: Macmillan Co., 1980.

Logan, Arch, M.D. Spokane, Washington. Letter to writer concerning Zachary Taylor, dated November 7, 1986.

Lomask, Milton. *This Slender Reed: A Life of James K. Polk.* New York: Farrar, Straus & Giroux, 1966.

Lorant, Stefan. *The Life and Times of Theodore Roosevelt.* Garden City, N.Y.: Doubleday & Co., 1959.

————. *Lincoln: A Picture Story of His Life.* New York: W.W. Norton & Co., 1969.

322 Bibliography

_____. *The Presidency: A Pictorial History of Presidential Elections.* New York: Macmillan Co., 1952.

_____. *The Presidency from Washington to Truman.* New York: Macmillan Co., 1952.

Lynch, Denis Tilden. *An Epoch and a Man.* New York: Horace Liveright, 1929.

_____. *Grover Cleveland.* New York: Horace Liveright, 1932.

Lyons, Eugene. *Herbert Hoover: A Biography.* Garden City, N.Y.: Doubleday & Co., 1964.

McElroy, Robert. *Grover Cleveland: The Man and the Statesman.* New York: Harper & Brothers, 1923.

McFeely, William S. *Grant.* New York: W.W. Norton & Co., 1981.

McKitrick, Eric L., ed. *Andrew Johnson: A Profile.* New York: Hill & Wang, 1969.

Malone, Dumas. *The Sage of Monticello.* Jefferson and His Time, Vol. 6. Boston: Little, Brown & Co., 1981.

Manchester, William. *The Death of a President.* New York: Harper & Row, 1967.

Martin, Ralph G. *A Hero for Our Time.* New York: Macmillan Co., 1983.

Means, Gaston, and May Dixon Thacker. *The Strange Death of President Harding.* New York: Guild Publishing Corp., 1930.

Mee, Charles L., Jr. *The Ohio Gang.* New York: M. Evans & Co., 1981.

Miller, Merle. *Lyndon.* New York: G.P. Putnam's Sons, 1980.

Moore, Guy W. *The Case of Mrs. Surratt.* Norman: University of Oklahoma Press, 1954.

Moore, Wayne C. Archivist, Tennessee State Library and Archives. Letter to writer concerning James K. Polk, dated October 2, 1986.

Morgan, George. *The Life of James Monroe.* Boston: Small, Maynard & Co., 1921.

Morris, Richard B., and William Greenleaf. *U.S.A.: The History of a Nation.* 2 Vols. Chicago: Rand McNally & Co., 1969.

Morse, John T. *John Adams.* New York: Houghton Mifflin & Co., 1896.

Murray, Robert K. *The Harding Era.* Minneapolis: University of Minnesota Press, 1969.

Nevins, Allan. *Grover Cleveland: A Study in Courage.* New York: Dodd, Mead & Co., 1934.

New York Times, March 3, 1885 (Grant); September 5, 7, 8, 11, 12, 13, 14; October 27, 28, 29, 1901 (McKinley); July 27; August 7, 1923 (Harding); January 8, 18, 1961; October 14, 1965; December 23, 1968 (Eisenhower).

New York Times Index, 1979, Vol. 67. (Kennedy).

Nichols, Roy Franklin. *Franklin Pierce.* Philadelphia: University of Pennsylvania Press, 1931.

Niles, Blair. *Martha's Husband.* New York: McGraw-Hill Book Co., 1946.

Niles National Register, March 6; April 10, 1841 (William Henry Harrison).

Niven, John. *Martin Van Buren.* New York: Oxford University Press, 1983.

Northrop, Henry Davenport. *The Life and Public Services of Gen. Benj. Harrison.* Augusta, Maine: True & Co., 1888.

Oates, Stephen B. *Abraham Lincoln: The Man Behind the Myths.* New York: Harper & Row, 1984.

_____. *With Malice Toward None: The Life of Abraham Lincoln.* New York: Harper & Row, 1977.

O'Donnell, Kenneth P., and David F. Powers. *"Johnny, We Hardly Knew Ye."* Boston: Little, Brown & Co., 1970.

Peck, Harry Thurston. *Twenty Years of the Republic, 1885–1905.* New York: Dodd, Mead & Co., 1907.

Perkins, Dexter, and Glyndon G. Van Deusen. *The United States of America: A History,* Vol. 1. New York: Macmillan Co., 1968.

Peskin, Allan. *Garfield.* Kent, Ohio: Kent State University Press, 1978.

Peterson, Merrill D. *The Jefferson Image in the American Mind.* New York: Oxford University Press, 1962.

_____. *Thomas Jefferson and the New Nation: A Biography.* New York: Oxford University Press, 1970.

Polk, James K. *Polk: The Diary of a President, 1845-1849.* Edited by Allan Nevins. New York: Longmans, Green & Co., 1952.

Pringle, Henry F. *The Life and Times of William Howard Taft.* Vol. 2. New York: Farrar & Rinehart, 1939.

_____. *Theodore Roosevelt.* New York: Harcourt Brace Jovanovich, 1931.

Randall, Henry S. *The Life of Thomas Jefferson,* Vol. 3. Philadelphia: J.B. Lippincott Co., 1888.

Randolph, Sarah N. *The Domestic Life of Thomas Jefferson: Compiled from Family Letters and Reminiscences by His Great-Granddaughter.* New York: Frederick Ungar Publishing Co., 1958.

Rayback, Robert J. *Millard Fillmore.* Buffalo, N.Y.: Henry Stewart, 1959.

Reece, Brazillia Carroll. *The Courageous Commoner: A Biography of Andrew Johnson.* Charleston, W. Va.: Education Foundation, 1962.

Reeves, Thomas C. *Gentleman Boss: The Life of Chester Alan Arthur.* New York: Alfred A. Knopf, 1975.

Remini, Robert V. *Martin Van Buren and the Making of the Democratic Party.* New York: Columbia University Press, 1959.

Ridpath, John Clark. *The Life and Work of James A. Garfield and the Tragic Story of His Death.* Cincinnati: Jones Brothers & Co., 1881.

Robbins, Charles. *Last of His Kind.* New York: William Morrow & Co., 1979.

Roosevelt, Eleanor. *The Autobiography of Eleanor Roosevelt.* New York: Harper & Brothers, 1958.

Roosevelt, Theodore. *Autobiography.* New York: Charles Scribner's Sons, 1958.

Ross, Ishbel. *Grace Coolidge and Her Era.* New York: Dodd, Mead & Co., 1962.

Rozwenc, Edwin C., ed. *The Causes of the American Civil War.* Boston: D.C. Heath & Co., 1961.

Russell, Francis. *The Shadow of Blooming Grove.* New York: McGraw-Hill Book Co., 1968.

Sandburg, Carl. *Abraham Lincoln: The Prairie Years and the War Years.* New York: Harcourt, Brace & Co., 1954.

Sanford, Charles B. *The Religious Life of Thomas Jefferson.* Charlottesville: University Press of Virginia, 1984.

Schactman, Tom. *Edith and Woodrow.* Thorndike, Maine: Thorndike Press, 1981.

Seager, Robert. *And Tyler, Too: John and Julia Gardiner Tyler.* New York: McGraw-Hill Book Co., 1963.

Sellers, Charles *James K. Polk: Continentalist, 1843-1846.* Princeton, N.J.: Princeton University Press, 1966.

Severn, Bill. *Frontier President: James K. Polk.* New York: Ives Washburn, 1965.

Shakespeare, William. *Twelfth Night.* Act 2, Scene 5.

Shenkman, Richard, and Kurt Reiger. *One-Night Stands with American History.* New York: William Morrow & Co., 1980.

Shepard, Edward M. *Martin Van Buren.* Boston: Houghton Mifflin Co., 1972.

Sidey, Hugh. *John F. Kennedy, President.* New York: Atheneum, 1963.

_____. "The Presidency: Making History on the Pedernales." *Life,* February 20, 1970, p. 4.

_____. "The Presidency: Some Pages Not in L.B.J.'s Book." *Life,* November 5, 1971, p. 4.

Sievers, Harry J. *Benjamin Harrison: Hoosier Statesman, 1865–1888.* New York: University Publishers, 1959.

_____. *Benjamin Harrison: Hoosier Warrior, 1833–1865.* Chicago: Henry Regnery Co., 1952.

Simmons, Dawn Langley. *A Rose for Mrs. Lincoln.* Boston: Beacon Press, 1970.

Sinclair, Andrew. *The Available Man.* New York: Macmillan Co., 1965.

Sloan, Irving J., ed. *James Buchanan, 1791–1868.* Dobbs Ferry, N.Y.: Oceana Publications, 1968.

_____. *Martin Van Buren, 1782–1862: Chronology, Documents, Bibliographic Aids.* Dobbs Ferry, N.Y.: Oceana Publications, 1969.

Smith, Don. *Peculiarities of the Presidents.* Van Wert, Ohio: Wilkinson Printing Co., 1938.

Smith, Elbert B. *The Presidency of James Buchanan.* Lawrence: University Press of Kansas, 1975.

Smith, Gene. *When the Cheering Stopped.* Alexandria, Va.: Time-Life Books, 1964.

Smith, Page. *Jefferson: A Revealing Biography.* New York: American Heritage Publishing Co., 1976.

_____. *John Adams.* 2 vols. Garden City, N.Y.: Doubleday & Co., 1962.

_____. *The Nation Comes of Age: A People's History of the Ante-Bellum Years.* New York: McGraw-Hill Book Co., 1981.

Smith, Richard Norton. *An Uncommon Man: The Triumph of Herbert Hoover.* New York: Simon & Schuster, 1984.

Starling, Edmund W. *Starling of the White House.* New York: Simon & Schuster, 1946.

Steele, John. "Coming Up All Roses for Ike." *Life,* September 24, 1965, p. 49.

Stern, Philip Van Doren. *The Man Who Killed Lincoln.* New York: Dell Publishing Co., 1955.

Stoddard, William O. *Lives of Presidents Rutherford B. Hayes, James A. Garfield and Chester A. Arthur.* New York: F.A. Stokes & Brothers, 1889.

Street, James. *The Civil War.* New York: Dial Press, 1953.

Stryker, Lloyd Paul. *Andrew Johnson: A Study in Courage.* New York: Macmillan Co., 1929.

Sumner, William G. *Andrew Jackson.* Boston: Houghton Mifflin & Co., 1899.

Thayer, William M. *From Tannery to the White House.* New York: Hurst & Co., 1885.

Thomas, Benjamin P. *Abraham Lincoln.* New York: Alfred A. Knopf, 1952.

Thomas, Lately. *The First President Johnson.* New York: William Morrow & Co., 1968.

Train, Arthur. *The Strange Attacks on Herbert Hoover.* New York: John Day Co., 1932.

Truman, Harry S. *Off the Record: The Private Papers of Harry S. Truman.* Edited by Robert H. Ferrell. New York: Harper & Row, 1980.

Truman, Margaret. *Bess W. Truman.* New York: Macmillan Co., 1986.

_____. *Harry S. Truman.* New York: William Morrow & Co., 1973.

Tully, Grace. *F.D.R.: My Boss.* New York: Charles Scribner's Sons, 1949.

Turner, Justin G., and Linda Levitt Turner. *Mary Todd Lincoln: Her Life and Letters.* New York: Alfred A. Knopf, 1972.

Tyler, Lyon Gardiner. *The Letters and Times of the Tylers,* Vols. 2 & 3. Richmond, Va.: Whittet & Shepperson, 1885-96.

United States. 88th Congress, 2nd session, 1964. *Memorial Addresses in the Congress of the United States and Tributes in Eulogy of John Fitzgerald Kennedy.* Senate Document, No. 59. Washington: U.S. Government Printing Office, 1964.

_____. President's Commission on the Assassination of President Kennedy. *Report of the President's Commission on the Assassination of President John F. Kennedy.* Washington: U.S. Government Printing Office, 1964.

Wallace, Lew. *Gen. Ben Harrison.* Philadelphia: Hubbard Brothers, 1888.

Ward, John William. *Andrew Jackson: Symbol for an Age.* New York: Oxford University Press, 1955.

"The Warren Commission Report." *Newsweek,* October 5, 1964, pp. 32-64.

"The Warren Commission Report." *Time,* October 2, 1964, pp. 45-55.

"The Warren Report." *Life,* October 2, 1964, pp. 40-50.

White, William Allen. *The Autobiography of William Allen White.* New York: Macmillan Co., 1946.

_____. *Masks in a Pageant.* New York: Macmillan Co., 1929.

_____. *A Puritan in Babylon.* New York: Macmillan Co., 1958.

Whitney, David C. *The Graphic Story of the American Presidents.* Edited by Thomas C. Jones. Chicago: J.G. Ferguson Publishing Co., 1972.

Wilson, Edith Bolling. *My Memoir.* 1939. Reprint. New York: Arno Press, 1980.

Wilson, Edmund. *Patriotic Gore.* New York: Oxford University Press, 1962.

Wilson, Joan Huff. *Herbert Hoover: Forgotten Progressive.* Boston: Little, Brown & Co., 1975.

Winston, Robert W. *Andrew Johnson: Plebian and Patriot.* New York: Henry Holt & Co., 1928.

Wise, Henry A. *Seven Decades of the Union.* Richmond, Va.: J.W. Randolph & English, 1881.

Withey, Lynne. *Dearest Friend: A Life of Abigail Adams.* New York: Free Press, 1981.

Wolfe, Harold. *Herbert Hoover.* New York: Exposition Press, 1956.

Woodward, W.E. *George Washington: The Image and the Man.* New York: Liveright Publishing Corp., 1946.

_____. *Meet General Grant.* New York: Literary Guild of America, 1928.

_____. *A New American History.* New York: Literary Guild, 1937.

Index

60–65, 66, 67, 101, 264; Van Buren,
Abraham (son) 63; Van Buren,
John (son) 63; Van Buren, Martin,
II (son) 63; Van Buren, Smith
Thompson (son) 63
Vanderbilt, Cornelius 159
Vanderbilt, William H. 133, 134, 141

W

Waite, Morrison R. 159
Walker, Sen. Robert, Jr. 54
Wallace, Bess *see under* Truman,
Harry S
Wallace, Henry A. 231, 244
Wallace, Henry C. 214
Wallace, Margaret Gates 253
Wanbin, Dr. Eugene 175
Ward, Albert 56
Ward, Ferdinand 132, 133
Ward, Theron 289, 290
Warmoth, Henry 129
Warren, Mercy Otis 12
Washington, Booker T. 145
Washington, George 1–8, 18, 21, 37,
61, 296; Washington, Martha 2, 3,
6, 7, 8
Washington, Mrs. Warner 5
Watson, W. Melvin 305
Wayles, John 20
Webster, Sen. Daniel 33, 47, 66, 68,
70, 88, 89, 91
Webster-Hayne debates 33
Weed, Thurlow 108
Weld, Theodore 44
Wells, Gideon 112, 123
West, James 218
Westland (Grover Cleveland's estate)
161, 162
Westmoreland, Gen. William C. 305
Wheatland (James Buchanan's estate)
106, 108, 109

Wheeler, William 147
White, Edward 193
White, William Allen 204, 211, 212,
215
Wilbur, Ray 217, 218
Wilcox, Ansley 178
Wilkins, George C. 154
Willis, Nelly 35
Willkie, Wendell 234
Wilson, Edmund 138
Wilson, Henry 128, 129
Wilson, Woodrow 182, 183, 184, 186,
198–209, 229, 242, 256, 268;
Wilson, Edith Bolling 199, 200,
202, 203, 204, 206; Wilson,
Eleanor (Mrs. William G.
McAdoo, daughter) 201, 208;
Wilson, Jessie (Mrs. Frances Sayre,
daughter) 200, 208; Wilson,
Margaret (daughter) 201, 208;
Wilson, Joseph (brother) 201
Wise, Henry 48, 74
Wood, Charles 134
Wood, Gen. Leonard 162, 210
Wood, Dr. Robert C. 87, 88
Work, Hubert 214, 217
Worthington, Dr. N.W. 69
Wotherspoon, Dr. Alexander S. 87,
88

Y

Yarborough, Sen. Ralph 278, 279,
280, 283
Young, Owen D. 235
Youngblood, Rufus 283, 287

Z

Zapruder, Abe 282